Pilgrim Journey

Poetry by Naomi Long Madgett:

Songs to a Phantom Nightingale (1941)

One and the Many (1956)

Star by Star (1965, 1970)

Pink Ladies in the Afternoon (1972, 1990)

Exits and Entrances (1978)

Phantom Nightingale: Juvenilia (1981)

Octavia and Other Poems (1988)

Remembrances of Spring: Collected Early Poems (1993)

Octavia: Guthrie and Beyond (2002)

Connected Islands: New and Selected Poems (2004)

Pilgrim Journey

*To Rev. Rene Garcia
with all good wishes —
Naomi Long Madgett*

Autobiography
by

Naomi Long Madgett

Lotus Press
Detroit

Copyright 2006 by Naomi Long Madgett
First Edition
All rights reserved

International Standard Book Number: 0-916418-97-9

Manufactured in the United States of America

Gratefully acknowledgement is made for the helpful comments of Marvin Arnett and Paulette Childress.

Lotus Press, Inc.

Post Office Box 21607
Detroit, Michigan 48221

www.lotuspress.org

Contents

Prologue: A Time to Be Born   3

I. THE EAST ORANGE YEARS
     Beginning the Journey   13
     Rooms in a House   19
     Joys of a Thirties Childhood   25
     Emergence of a Poet   62
     The Southern North   70
     Two Worlds   81
     Discord in Paradise   87

II. THE ST. LOUIS YEARS
     Changing Course   97
     Continued Interlude   120

III. COLLEGE IN WARTIME
     On This Lofty Hill   145
     New Rochelle   164
     Sophomore Year   169
     Last Two Years   180
     After Graduation   194

IV. TURN IN THE ROAD
     A New City   203
     Second Chance   220
     A House Called Ugmo   226
     New Directions   237

V. BRINGING THE LIGHT

Preparation for Teaching   265

Northwestern High School   271

Eastern Michigan University   294

VI. FLOWER OF A NEW NILE

Stumbling into New Waters   313

Adam of Ife   337

VII. THE WRITTEN WORD

Integrating a Writers' Club   347

A Fellowship of Poets   349

The "Midway" Story   356

Irresponsible Scholarship   367

Recreating Octavia   373

VIII. FAMILY MATTERS

In Search of Grampa Long   397

Lineage   409

Lessons   416

Loss   428

IX. PROVIDENTIAL TIMING   439

X. A SENSE OF HOME   453

XI. REACH AND GRASP   473

Epilogue: In the Time of Age   479

Lotus Press Poets and Publications   489

Pilgrim Journey

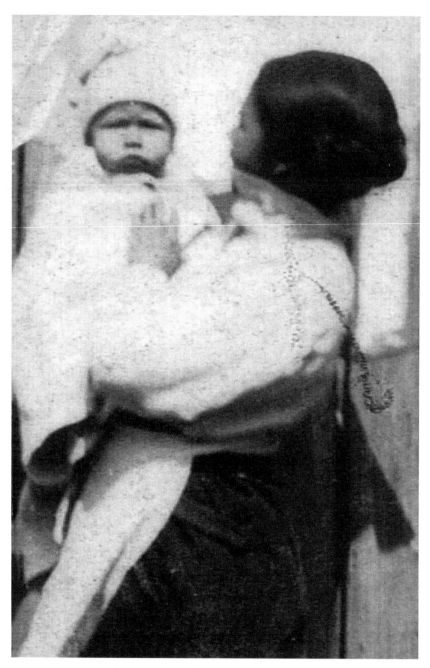
My first picture: Mama and me on washday

Prologue: A Time to Be Born

I was born into the Harlem Renaissance in the year of Jean Toomer's *Cane* and Robert Kerlin's anthology, *Negro Poets and Their Poems*. Ma Rainey made her recording debut in 1923, the year she composed "Moonshine Blues," and Bessie Smith signed with Columbia Records that year, recording the hit, "Gulf Coast Blues," which began her rise to fame as The Empress of the Blues. George Schuyler became editor of the radical black magazine, *The Messenger*, that year while the phenomenal success of tenor Roland Hayes in Europe won him recognition in the United States. In the same year Charles S. Johnson founded *Opportunity*, the official publication of the Urban League, which published creative writing and sponsored literary competitions, making the output of new black talent accessible to the public. And Carl van Vechten's second novel, *The Blind Bow-Boy*, was published that year. Young Langston Hughes made his first trip to Africa that summer, returning to the states in October and, shortly thereafter, taking a job as mess boy on the McKeesport. 1923 also witnessed the rampage by a white mob in the mostly black hamlet of Rosewood in Florida. Warren Harding had served two years as President of the United States but died of a heart attack a month after I was born and was succeeded by Calvin Coolidge. Abyssinia was admitted to the League of Nations. William Butler Yeats won the Nobel Prize for Literature. The first birth control clinic opened in New York. Marshal law was established in Oklahoma to protect people and property from attacks by the Ku Klux Klan, while a tri-state conclave of the Ku Klux Klan took place in Kokomo, Indiana with 200,000 members attending. Joseph "King" Oliver and "Jelly Roll" Morton recorded New Orleans jazz that year, and mainstream popular songs included "Yes, We Have No Bananas," "Barney Google," and "Tea for Two." The year before, Louis Armstrong arrived in Chicago from New Orleans and joined "King" Oliver's band. Countee Cullen's first book, *Color*, was still two years away from publication, as was Alain

Locke's *The New Negro*. Women had won the right to vote only three years earlier. Prohibition was still in effect.

I am the third child and only daughter of Texas-born Clarence Marcellus Long and Maude Selena (Hilton) Long from Richmond, Virginia. They met when he was a student in theology at Virginia Union University and married in 1913, a union that lasted for 63 years until my father's death.

My father was pastor first of a church in Hampton and then of First Baptist Church in Charlottesville, Virginia, where my two brothers, Clarence, Jr. and Wilbur Franklin, were born. He then became pastor of Bank Street Baptist Church in Norfolk. I was born July 5, 1923 in the parsonage at 6.?? Bank Street. The parsonage was so close to the church that my mother said members frequently dropped by to visit after Sunday services. She said she never wanted to live that close to a church again. Both the church and the parsonage were torn down many years ago, the church relocating close to the Virginia Beach border.

I was told that we had pet chickens in Norfolk, mine named Henny Penny. The back yard had a high wooden fence, and huge pans hung on the back of the house. I assume they were used for doing laundry, but I don't know. Mama once told me that she used to knock on the door of a room before entering to give an occasional visiting rat notice to vacate the premises.

The only picture I have ever seen of myself as an infant is a snapshot taken in the back yard on wash day. Mama, in a long skirt and apron, is holding me as I look over her shoulder. She has evidently stopped hanging wet clothes on the line to have the snapshot taken. The expression on my face is very solemn, almost a frown. I have two other snapshots of me at about a year old sitting in a wagon surrounded by my brothers and my visiting cousin Helen, her face shaded by a bonnet.

I remember nothing about Norfolk. Early in 1925 we moved to

East Orange, New Jersey where my father became pastor of Calvary Baptist Church. I was about seventeen months old.

The first home I remember was the parsonage at 55 North Clinton Street (later renumbered 75). It had evidently been built with gas jet burners which were later converted to electricity. The two rooms in the attic were still lit with gas jets. I vaguely recall a black stove in the kitchen, fed by either coal or wood. It didn't sit flush against a wall because it required a flue located near the large wooden table covered with oilcloth at the center of the room. This stove was soon replaced by a gas range that had to be lit by matches. It had a high back containing a warming shelf.

On the closed-in back porch was an icebox with a tray underneath for catching water from the melted ice. On the days the ice man was due, people would put a sign in their front window indicating what size block they needed. Then the ice man would use tongs to carry the block of ice to the icebox. We knew only one family that had an electric refrigerator.

If electric or gas washing machines and dryers existed then, we didn't know anybody who owned one. In one corner of our kitchen was a double washtub. When not in use it was topped by a wooden oilcloth-covered board that provided extra space for food preparation and dishes waiting to be washed. On washdays Mama removed the cover. Then she brought clothing and bed linens to the kitchen and sorted them. She boiled sheets on the stove in a huge black pot and scrubbed other items on a washboard with a commercial soap made for that purpose or a homemade bar made from grease and lye. I don't think detergents even existed then. Then came the rinsing, bluing added to white items, and the wringing by hand. The wet laundry would go into a large basket to be hung on the clothesline in the back yard to dry in the sun and wind. Then back it would come to be folded and ironed.

There were no convenient blends of cotton with manmade fabric to eliminate the need for ironing. Nothing came wrinkle-free. Rough-dried clothes were really rough. Ironing was an all-day affair, at the end of which my mother would be thoroughly exhausted, having also cooked and served three meals and turned over the task of washing the dishes to my brothers whose job it was to clean up the kitchen after dinner. At one time a church member, Mrs. Bates, came in to help Mama iron, but she died when I was still quite young. Every day Dad put on a clean white shirt with a detachable collar. These were laundered by a church member, Mrs. "Lizzie" Hicks, who earned her living by doing laundry in her basement.

I don't remember anyone's bathroom that was equipped with a shower, only a bathtub. Above our toilet was a brown wooden box containing water. To flush the toilet you pulled an attached chain. The sink was made of grayish-white marble.

The words *baby-sitter* and *teenager* had not yet been coined. I don't think any of the black people we knew had the money to pay someone to care for their children anyhow. Most women stayed at home, taking their children everywhere they went unless their husbands or an older child was home to care for the younger ones. I don't recall such an institution as a child care center.

The furnace in the cellar devoured coal that was poured from a truck through a chute into the coal bin. This fuel had to be shoveled by hand at certain intervals, shaken down, banked, and started up again in the morning. The man of the house or his sons had to get up in the cold and go through whatever actions it took to get the fire to the point where the rest of the family could get up in some degree of warmth.

Telephones were tall black objects with the ear piece cradled on the side. The telephone numbers consisted of a word relating to the location followed by three or four digits. Callers had to get the operator to ring the number for them.

Whenever it was necessary to call a taxi, a white man dressed in a chauffeur's uniform and boots arrived in a black sedan and rang the doorbell to let the passenger know he had arrived. It was not uncommon to see horse-drawn wagons, and one white woman often passed our house driving an electric car. Regular cars had to be cranked by hand to get the engine started, and the only heat came from the warmed-up engine. If you were going on a trip in the winter, there was always a lap blanket to throw over your knees. Some cars had rumble seats in the back; they opened like a modern trunk but in the opposite direction. Sedans were high and spacious with running boards. There was room enough for adults to stretch out their legs comfortably and still have room for a suitcase or two. Some luxury cars had two extra seats in front of the back seat that folded down into the floor when not in use.

Glass quart bottles of milk were delivered to the side door and deposited in a small enclosed area or left on the walk near the side door. It was not homogenized, so it had to be shaken before drinking for a good mix of milk and cream. In the winter the cream froze and pushed its way up out of the bottle, carrying the cardboard top with it. Bread, which cost five cents a loaf or less, was delivered, too. A child's dress could be purchased for about a dollar. My mother never bought a pair of Enna Jettick shoes because, at six dollars a pair, they were too expensive. There were no supermarkets, but a National Store, part of a chain of small grocery stores, was conveniently located around the corner from us on William Street. At the intersection of Clinton and William streets, a man stood in the middle of the street on a platform raising a sign to stop or motion traffic forward, serving the same purpose as an electric traffic light today.

People who were fortunate enough to travel did so by train, bus, or steamship. Only a few rich people flew overseas or anywhere else in an airplane. Sometimes on Sunday evenings we would drive to the Newark airport to see planes take off and land, always looking in vain for a movie star to appear en route to New York. A boy in my class whose family vacationed in Florida every winter traveled by train; another classmate whose family visited Belgium one year went by steamship.

Occasionally, the local train company would run a weekend excursion to other cities and, on several occasions, we took such excursions to Richmond. They were joyous affairs with plenty of food in boxes and baskets shared with family members and newly made acquaintances. Few colored people ventured into the dining car, but those who did were seated behind a black curtain so white passengers would not have to be offended by looking at them. Black people going farther south than Washington, DC. had to change in the nation's capital to the Jim Crow car directly behind the engine. Vehicles were not air-conditioned, so soot came through the open windows into the Jim Crow car. Most African Americans traveling south from New York or New Jersey took their seats in the first car behind the engine when they boarded to keep from having to change in Washington.

We had one Philco radio in the house. It was on the mantelpiece over the fireplace in the dining room. On certain nights we all gathered around it to listen to "Amos 'n' Andy" and later to the broadcasts of Joe Louis's fights. Eventually, Dad ordered a console radio with beautifully carved doors from Norfolk, and that was placed in the living room where I listened to "Little Orphan Annie" for a fifteen minute episode starting at 5:45; then my brothers listened to "Buck Rogers in the Twenty-fifth Century" or "Jack Armstrong, the All-American Boy." Frequently, we argued over what we would listen to when their choice and mine came on simultaneously.

Little white boys wore short pants long past the age that black boys did. Levis and blue jeans weren't heard of yet. From short pants the black boys graduated to knickerbockers, ("knickers," for short) and long heavy socks. At about sixteen, they asserted their approach to young manhood by being allowed to wear long trousers. What a rite of passage that was!

During my early years I wore high-top shoes that laced and cotton-rib stockings with long underwear tucked down inside during the winter. My mother braided my hair loosely into three braids, one on top that, for special occasions, was adorned with a large wide ribbon tied into a bow.

We occasionally received five dollar gold pieces from church members as Christmas gifts. They were not worth any more than five dollars in bills but made a more impressive gift. When my brothers ran errands for the lady across the street, she usually rewarded them with a nickel, but if the task was onerous, they might receive a whole dime and were glad to get it. They were never allowed to spend all of this fortune on candy. Dad always made them save some of it. He never let us put pennies in the offering at church because they weren't good enough for God. He always gave us nickels instead.

Textbooks were not attractive and did not contain many illustrations, and what illustrations there were were black and white. Publishers made no attempt to entice reluctant students into the learning process. Daily homework, especially in the higher grades, took several hours to complete.

And children learned. They learned basic arithmetic by rote and repetition. (Had anybody dreamed of a hand-held calculator then?) They were taught handwriting by the Palmer method, everyone writing uniformly and legibly with certain capital letters shaped like candy canes. They learned to read and spell phonetically, and while some students were better readers than others, there were no nonreaders or children who couldn't pronounce a word that was spelled the way it sounded. They learned grammar by diagramming sentences and wrote compositions that came back amply notated with red pencil marks to point out errors. They were openly corrected when they made grammatical errors in speaking. Those who failed to accomplish the goals for a particular grade were not promoted but had to repeat the entire year since our schools didn't have semesters. Black students, many of whose parents had migrated from the South and had only a third or fourth grade education, spoke and wrote standard English although they didn't always hear it at home.

Motion pictures were silent with printed captions at the bottom of the screen and they were always black and white. Technicolor was years away.

The year 1923 was not as bad a time to be born as it might have been, and I have never wished I had entered the world at any other time. I have been able to watch a lifetime of tremendous improvements in technology which have provided increased leisure time and ever more creative ways in which to use it. At the same time, I have seen elementary education decline to the point that many students reach adulthood without ever learning how to write legibly, and people holding college degrees, even people in very visible and highly respected positions, make numerous errors in speaking because they were never taught grammar and therefore have no way of determining the proper pronoun to use. They don't even know the parts of speech and their functions in a sentence.

I have also witnessed the loss of some of the cohesiveness of a more simple way of life and regret its passing. Every generation moves within its own particular circle of time and experiences. I'm glad this has been my time. I'd rather be on earth now than at any other time in history, and I consider myself fortunate to have lived long enough to experience not only the turn of another century but a new millennium, as well.

We are all pilgrims in the journey of life, and in 1923 mine had begun.

My birth place: 627 Bank Street, Norfolk

I.
The East Orange Years

55 North Clinton Street, East Orange

Beginning the Journey

Among my earliest memories is being held in my mother's arms in church and resting my sleepy head on her ample bosom. Her regular seat was on the end of the third row. Since we had an evening service every Sunday as well as one in the morning, I was often tired. If there was room on the pew next to her, she'd let me stretch out there to sleep.

I was about three years old when Mr. and Mrs. Luther Tate, members of our church, took us to Bear Mountain. My brother Wilbur told me there were bears there and I had better be careful. I believed him and couldn't enjoy the outing because I was so afraid.

Sometimes I took afternoon naps in my parents' bed. On one such occasion extreme fear kept me awake. My parents discussed everything freely in our presence at the dinner table, and I had heard them talking about "infantile paralysis" (poliomyelitis) which I understood could be caught from germs in the air. I thought that breathing would make me inhale one of the germs and I'd fall prey to the disease. I stayed awake as long as I could trying to hold my breath.

On another occasion Dad commented on a newspaper article about someone who had died from a blow to the temple. Soon after hearing that, I accidentally bumped into something, hitting my temple, and started crying uncontrollably. When asked why I was upset, I exclaimed, "I'm going to die!" It took my parents a long time to make the connection and assure me that my minor injury was not my doom.

Clarence and Wil were already in school, and I spent most of my days in the kitchen, where Mama worked all day at various tasks, playing in "my corner." It wasn't a corner at all but an indentation between the pantry and the cabinet that held the dishes. There I kept my dolls, my toys and picture books and whatever collection of items held my interest at a particular time, playing alone while Mama performed her numerous chores. Sometimes I made up stories and the first meaningless rhyme I can remember composing. "I am a statue; I stand so straight. When I look over I look in my plate." I frequently talked to myself. One of my subjects was people I saw at church. When Mama heard me talking about "Miss Lulie-Lulie," she asked me who that was. I answered, "You know. That lady that sits in the amen corner and says 'lulie-lulie' all the time." What she actually said was "hallelujah," but that's not what I heard. At church the next Sunday, Mama told the lady in my presence about the name I had given her. They both seemed to think it was cute, but I was tremendously embarrassed.

That space in the kitchen was my private world, and I felt secure in it. Whenever my brothers challenged the validity of something I had made up, my answer was always that it was true "in ours." Whatever I wished or pretended was possible in that "corner."

When I was about four, a young woman in our church, Isabel Anderson, took me to Newark for my first studio photograph. The high-top buttoned shoes and the cotton-rib stockings speak of the times. The length of the sleeves of my cotton dress, probably the best I had, indicate that I had already outgrown it. While we were waiting for the streetcar to take us back home, I had to go to the bathroom. Isabel took me between buildings where I relieved myself, wetting my underwear and stockings in the process.

Dad was seldom at home during the day. In addition to visiting the sick and performing other church duties, he was busy earning his Bachelor of Arts degree at Upsala College and then his Master of Arts at Drew University. When he was studying at night, he sat in the front bedroom in the rocking chair under the ceiling light with a pencil between his teeth, removing it frequently to underline passages or write in the margins of his book. Sometimes he let me sit in his lap while he read.

My first studio picture taken in Newark

When I was three years old, we had a visitor from my father's past. Rev. S.S. Jones had baptized my father in Oklahoma when he was nine years old and founded the family church in Guthrie. Throughout his lifetime he remained more of a father to Dad than his own father ever was. Then pastor of Antioch Baptist Church in Muskogee and secretary of the National Baptist Convention, he had traveled to the Holy Land and all over Europe in 1924-25, taking black and white motion pictures wherever he went. He had the vision to know that black life in Oklahoma, including the all-black towns, was important to record. Upon his return from overseas, he came to visit us in East Orange in 1926. I have a letter he wrote to my father from Jerusalem, a studio photograph of him with his wife and two young daughters, and a placard announcing his forthcoming trip abroad. During his visit with us, he took movies of the family on a rainy afternoon in the back yard and the next day as we sat on the front porch steps. I now have on video a picture of myself at three standing on a bench on the back porch and waving bye-bye.

In the mid-1930s I wrote a poem about my father which he sent to Rev. Jones who, in turn, wrote me a letter congratulating me on my work. His letter ends, "Goodbye to you. It looks like it's goodbye to me." He died shortly after that. Evidently his widow sent his film to Dad, and it eventually came into Clarence's possession. Laverne, Clarence's widow, had someone transfer some of the film to video. Some time later, I showed this video to a writer in Detroit who was planning to produce a short documentary film on the all-black towns of Oklahoma, and when she saw what I had, she asked me to send for the original reels of film. She received a grant to have the film cleaned up and used a portion of it in her short documentary film (Ann Eskridge, *Echoes Across the Prairie*). Later some seconds of it were used in a documentary film on Ralph Ellison. Other brief sections were used on the Oprah Winfrey Show to illustrate Toni Morrison's *Sula*, even though the novel takes place in a different state. But who has movies of little black boys taken in the 1920s? I have about seven hours of viewing that have been transferred to professional and regular video. I don't believe that any other archival film like it exists, and I plan to have it placed where it will be more accessible. Little did I know in 1926 what a storehouse of visual history this visitor was in the process of recording.

Dad was still a student at Upsala College when his father died in Hot Springs, Arkansas in 1928. Dad had recently been to visit him and couldn't leave for the funeral because of an examination. Aunt Ethel, who was raising three sons, couldn't attend either. It was left to Uncle Robert in St. Louis to represent the family. During the hour of the funeral, we all had to sit silently in the front bedroom. Soon a telegram from Uncle Robert arrived stating that he had not been able to attend. Dad broke down and cried because none of his father's three living children had been present at his funeral. As I got to know more about Grampa Long many years later, I considered their absence a kind of poetic justice.

When Dad was working on his master's degree at Drew University, he brought a minister from Philadelphia to speak at East Orange High School. Before the evening program, Dad brought the visitor to our house and introduced the Rev. Charles A. Tindley to us, saying that this was the man who wrote "Some Day," "Stand by Me," "Nothing Between," "Leave It There," "We'll Understand It Better Bye and Bye," and many other hymns that we sang in church. Meeting him, as young as I was, made a tremendous impression on me. He was tall, straight in bearing, and elderly. (He died several years later.) I remembered his color and height, and I knew that he was old, but I couldn't recall his face. I still treasure the booklet of his hymns, selected from about 150 for which he wrote the words and music, and his signed book of sermons.

Many years later I was passing through Philadelphia on a Saturday morning and decided to drive by Tindley Temple on Broad Street, the church he had served as pastor. I didn't expect to find the building open, but the organist was there rehearsing for a wedding and I was able to go inside. He showed me Rev. Tindley's portrait on a wall in the sanctuary and gave me a recording of the church choir singing some of his hymns. I feel deeply blessed to have met this pioneer in African American sacred music that preceded the traditional gospel music of Thomas A. Dorsey and others.

Eventually the time came for me to start school. How I had longed for that day! The kindergarten was a large, self-contained room in the front of the building next to the main entrance. There were two teachers, a heavyset lady named Miss King who shook the room when she walked, and kindly, crippled Miss Pierponte, who was my teacher. I knew two of the girls from church, Margaret Ross and Gladys Howard, but they were assigned to Miss King whose class was on the other side of the room, so we had no contact after the first day. (Had it already been decided that we would not be in the same division of the first grade? On what basis?)

My only memory of that year is being asked to pass something around to the children in my section of the class. Miss Pierponte commented on my good manners in serving myself last. I had not done it intentionally, but I learned from her compliment that that was the polite thing to do. Whatever we did in kindergarten I liked, and I looked forward to continuing my education.

Rooms in a House

The house at 55 North Clinton Street is still standing. Some years after we left, it was converted to a two-family house and is now a rooming house. The marble fireplaces in the living room, dining room, and front bedroom are probably still there. The marble sink in the house's one bathroom has probably been replaced, along with the wooden water tank above the toilet. The gas jets in the two rooms on the third floor no doubt have been replaced by electric lights. There is now a fire escape to the third floor.

When we lived there, the front door opened to a long hallway that ended in the kitchen. To the right of the kitchen door was the entrance to the cellar. (We didn't call it a basement.) A second door in the kitchen led to a small dining room with bay windows, and a third to a closed-in back porch that contained the ice box. The back porch door in the kitchen and the pantry door opened in opposite directions, making a safe space for me to crouch when there was a storm.

In the living room we had a piano and the suite of mahogany furniture upholstered in leather that my parents bought when they got married. It consisted of two rocking chairs, two straight chairs, and a settee.

The second floor had a long hallway leading to the front bedroom and my parents' adjoining bedroom with a closet between the two rooms. The hall had another door that opened to a stairway leading to two rooms on the third floor. Near the end of the hall was the bathroom on the left just before the hall ended at my father's study which, like the front room, extended across the width of the house. I was terrified of the dark hall at night and sometimes wet the bed rather than venturing into the threatening blackness even though Mama kept a chamber pot in the bedroom when I was small.

With only one bathroom we had no opportunity for modesty. If one person was taking a bath in the old-fashioned tub with ball and claw feet and another had to use the toilet, both did what needed to be done at the same time. Dad might be shaving when I had to use the toilet, or I might be in the tub when he had to urinate. He simply turned his back and did what he had to do. My brothers and I saw each other in the raw, so there was no mystery or curiosity about male and female differences. On one occasion, all five of us were in the bathroom at the same time and Dad laughed saying, "Call the cat."

It was a long time before I had my own bed. I don't remember where anyone except my parents slept originally, but for awhile Wil and I shared the same bed in the alcove of the front bedroom, arguing about who was usurping whose space and drawing an imaginary line down the center to keep each other off our designated side. I continued to sleep with Wil in the front bedroom through his measles, chicken pox, and every other children's disease he got. Mama wanted me to catch whatever he had and get it over with, but I never did. One year when Wil was sick in bed at Christmas time, Mama decided to put up the Christmas tree in front of the fireplace in the front bedroom so that he could enjoy it. It seemed a logical place anyhow since that was more of a family room than the living room. Every year after that, we put up the Christmas tree on Christmas Eve in that room.

It was there, when I still believed in Santa Claus, that I set my little table with an apple and a cookie for the gift-giver. In the morning the food was always gone and my presents were there instead. We never gave each other gifts and Santa's gifts were never wrapped. Eventually I knew that everything was provided by our parents and a few church members.

My parents' bedroom was so small that there was no room for their complete set of furniture, so Dad's chifferobe was in the front bedroom. In one of the drawers he kept a wallet that he referred to as "the pocketbook." It held a supply of cash that he replenished as necessary. We never got an allowance and had no money of our own. Whenever Mama went shopping or needed money for something else, she would tell him what she needed and he'd tell her to take it out of the pocketbook. He never asked her to account for what she spent. It was the same for things we wanted. We had to tell him how much we needed and what we would spend it for. I don't think he ever checked behind us to be sure we had taken the amount we asked for and no more. He always trusted us to be honest, a trust sometimes misplaced.

Eventually, when both boys slept in the attic, this front room became mine, but it never really belonged to me alone; it was everybody's room. Here Dad studied when he was a student. My mother filled up most of the dresser drawers with clothing and linens that weren't being used or that she didn't have space for in her room, leaving only one or two drawers that I could call mine.

As I approached puberty, she didn't know how to tell me what to expect. The Kotex company had published a pamphlet called *Marjorie May's Twelfth Birthday,* a copy of which Mama put in one of the drawers she used, assuming correctly that I would find it. I had already been told about menstruation by two girls I knew, but the way they described it and what I expected were quite different from my discovery of the first blood on my panties. When I called Mama, she gave me a clean cloth to use until she could buy some sanitary napkins. When she gave me the box of napkins she said she had never used them, which I took to mean that she had never menstruated. When I told that to a more knowledgeable friend, she explained that she had to have menstruated in order to have children. It was years before I figured out the relationship between "the curse" and pregnancy.

I spent a lot of time in the front room playing by myself. Hour after hour I inhabited a magic world, one day devising a tent from a pole and blanket, another time trying to create a walkie-talkie from two tin cans and a piece of string. There I read poems or pretended that I was a teacher, meticulously recording the attendance and progress of an imaginary class of children with made-up names like

Beason Merlin. At night after being told to turn off the light, I would duck under the cover with a flashlight to read one of the books I kept in the walnut bookcase with two glass doors in the alcove beside the bed. And in this room I wrote most of my early poems. I wrote in my diary, too, but my brothers always found it, no matter how well I thought I had hidden it, and taunted me about its contents.

Some nights when Dad came home late from a meeting, he brought us ice cream. Mama would wake me up to eat some; then I would snuggle under the covers to get warm again. Occasionally I saw the empty box in the kitchen the next morning and asked why I didn't get any, forgetting that I had indeed partaken of the treat.

Saturday was always a busy day in our home because we had to prepare for our long Sundays. Mama did all her cooking for Sunday's dinner so that it could just be warmed up after the next morning's church service. Her chicken dinners were fabulous, especially the stuffing which, try as I might in later years, I was never able to duplicate. Usually she made rolls and loaves of "light bread" and put them on the radiator in the dining room to rise. Keeping the Sabbath holy was important to Dad. We couldn't use scissors, and what play time we had was quiet. In the summer we could play hopscotch or hide-and-go-seek or catch lightning bugs in a bottle but nothing that involved game boards or toys. On Saturday we had to polish our shoes, study our Sunday school lesson, and take our weekly baths before going to bed.

While Mama was doing her chores in the kitchen she was regularly visited by one of two eccentric old church ladies who never seemed to run into each other. Both worked for white people as domestics, and both wore long dresses. Mrs. Caldwell also wore a very wiggy-looking wig, which was not the fashion then, and a hat—sometimes two hats, not realizing that she already had one on. Her clothing consisted of a lot of layering. Miss Rachael was thinner than Mrs. Caldwell and wore a lot of long strings of beads. She sometimes brought us extra loaves of Pennsylvania Dutch scrapple that the people she worked for had given her. She had a problem with her voice that she called "the bronichals"; it rose and fell to high and low notes with every syllable. Dad was usually rushing, and she would say to him, "Sweetheart, don't go so 'mazing fast." When he was preparing to go to Europe, she couldn't understand why he couldn't just drive across a bridge instead of taking a steamship. She had no concept of the size of an ocean.

After Mama was finished in the kitchen, she brought whichever visitor was there that night upstairs where she mended something, darned socks, or completed some other task forbidden on Sunday, her guest sitting on the couch at the foot of the bed. I lay in bed listening to their adult conversation and trying to stay awake so I wouldn't miss anything, but eventually I drifted off to sleep.

Dad stayed up late in the study preparing his sermon. He probably made notes or an outline since his sermons were always well organized, but I never saw him use a manuscript or notes when he preached.

I used to follow my brothers around all the time, especially Wil. He had a car that operated by pedals, and a ring of keys that he pretended went with the car. One day I followed him up to the front bedroom where he went to look for his keys. As we looked out the window at something in the street, we heard a loud noise behind us. When we turned, we saw that Mama's closet was on fire. Wil was always so nonchalant and unconcerned that I am still surprised that he took me by the hand and led me downstairs. Mama was drying silver, which she laid down on the steps, and took us next door to call the fire department. The fire was confined to the closet, but we lost bathrobes, blankets, and other clothing. Late in our adult years, I asked Wil about the fire, and he avoided discussing it with such a sheepish look that I knew he had something to do with it.

Moviegoing was rare in our house. One of our occasional

visitors, Miss Katie Wardlaw, had moved to New Jersey with her Wall Street broker employer and his family from Atlanta, where they had lived next door to the Mitchell family. She knew Margaret Mitchell, author of *Gone with the Wind*, as she was growing up. Except for the few times I was taken by an adult to see such films as *Trail of the Lonesome Pine, Imitation of Life,* films starring Shirley Temple, or *Green Pastures*, I wasn't allowed to go to the Ormont Theater on Main Street. By the time I was almost thirteen I could go to the movies alone on Saturday afternoons. It was then that I saw Dick Powell in naval uniform starring in *Shipmates Forever* and fell in love with him. By the time we were ready to move, the wall behind my bed was plastered with magazine pictures of him.

This everybody's-room that I considered mine was the most important of all the rooms in the first home that I remember.

Joys of a Thirties Childhood

While 1929 means the crash of the stock market and the beginning of the Great Depression to most people, it has a different significance for me. It was the year I started first grade and the beginning of my awareness of time. The Depression did not affect us as much as it did many people we knew. My father had a job, we lived in the parsonage rent-free, and our lives did not change in any memorable way. (Years later I learned that Dad had voluntarily reduced his salary, meager as it was, because he knew the members' ability to pay him had decreased.) We were aware that many of our church members lost their jobs and depended on welfare for their basic needs. Those who were more fortunate continued to work as domestics in the homes of white employers. Only a few of our members were well educated and self-employed.

For me, 1929 meant going with Dad to Drew University when he was turning in an assignment, playing on the campus, enjoying its spaciousness and beauty, watching squirrels and picking up horse chestnuts and acorns.

It also meant learning how to read. In first grade the teacher called students, one group at a time, to a large table in the front of the room. Each of us had a metal box of letter squares that were used to teach us to read and spell phonetically. I became an excellent reader, and a whole new world was opened up to me. Dad's study was lined with oak bookcases with glass doors. Most of his books were theological, but he also had a set of the *Harvard Classics*. When I had nothing else to do, he would give me Volume 17 which I wore thin from handling. It contained "Aesop's Fables" and other stories I could understand. There were also Bullfinch's *Mythology* and a large leather-bound book with gilt edges called *Pearls from Many Seas*. It contained short narratives and essays, poems, and illustrations. I automatically went to the poetry first. One illustration has stayed in my mind and I eventually used it in a poem. It was a pic-

25

ture of Jesus as a little boy walking toward his mother with his arms outstretched. The shadow cast behind him formed a cross. In Robert Kerlin's anthology, *Negro Poets and Their Poems*, I discovered the work of Paul Laurence Dunbar, a youthful Langston Hughes, Georgia Douglas Johnson, James Weldon Johnson, and many other African American poets. I teethed on their work at the same time I was reading poems by Tennyson and other English and American poets whose work was in my father's study. I was particularly fond of Tennyson's "The Brook" and the rhythm of Longfellow's "Song of Hiawatha."

Another of my favorites was my mother's elocution book that contained tongue-twisters and poems that I read over and over and sometimes memorized. I had some books for young children, one or two printed on cloth instead of paper. One of them was *Peter Pan*, but I didn't understand it and don't think I ever finished it. Later there were the "big little books," about four or five inches square and exactly the same number of inches thick. The only one I owned contained cartoons of Dick Tracy's adventures, but I read it over and over.

Three books rested, for some reason, on top of the kitchen cabinet. They were Shakespeare's complete works, *A Tale of Two Cities*, and *The Last Days of Pompeii*. Whenever Dad chided my brothers for their choice of reading material, mostly detective magazines, he would point to these books and urge them to read them instead. I don't think they ever took them down, but I stood on a chair to reach them and read the two novels and as much of Shakespeare as I could understand.

In the mid-Thirties I borrowed from a friend a teenage novel entitled *The Misty Flats* by Helen Woodbury. I enjoyed reading it, especially for the poem quoted at the beginning from which the title was taken and the fact that young Peter, one of the main characters, was an aspiring poet who quoted Keats. I checked out a copy of Keats's poems from the public library and struggled through many of the poems without understanding them. Yet something about them kept me reading. I also enjoyed reading the Nancy Drew mysteries.

Later Dad taught several adult education classes designed to provide employment during the Depression. It was sponsored by the government through the Works Progress Administration. One of these courses was Negro literature. The textbook was a mimeographed volume of poetry covered with thin blue paper. Several of the Harlem Renaissance poets had helped with the selection of material. Years later I had it bound to preserve this treasure which had been a part of my informal education. It is now part of the Naomi Long Madgett and Lotus Press Archive in the Special Collections Library at The University of Michigan in Ann Arbor.

We had the privilege of having both parents at home. Mama had entered normal school at the age of thirteen, graduating in 1902 at sixteen in the last class of Virginia Normal and Collegiate Institute (contrary to the statement in *Loyal Songs and Daughters: Virginia State University, 1882-1992* by Edgar Toppin) before the name was changed to Virginia Normal and Industrial Institute.) According to her records, she taught in one-room schools in rural Virginia from 1903 to 1912, but after her marriage in 1913, she never again worked outside the home. It was wonderful having a stay-at-home mom. And Dad had no office at church, so he was often at home after he completed his master's degree. All the students at Ashland School lived within walking distance and went home for lunch. Mama was always there with lunch prepared and welcomed us after school.

My parents' marriage was ideal. Dad respected my mother's opinions, which she never hesitated to offer. He didn't always agree with them, but sometimes he would reconsider what they had discussed and say, "Maude, I think you were right about [so-and-so]." I never heard them raise their voices to each other. They shared the same values, and my mother supported him totally in his work at church, the church being the source of almost all their social activity. We could never pit one parent against the other although we tried.

Whichever parent we thought was more likely to grant our request was the one approached. If it was Dad and he had no objection, he'd say, "Ask your mother." If we went to her first, it was "Ask your daddy." Her final answer was more likely "We'll see," which usually meant "Yes." They were undivided and totally supportive of and devoted to each other. Dad handled the payment of bills, but she was fully aware of the business side of operating a household and as capable of doing it as he was. He urged her to learn how to drive so that she could be more independent. She did take lessons and received her driver's license but never chose to drive. Every place we went was within walking distance or close to public transportation, which she preferred.

The square oak desk in Dad's study, which I still use, has a top that can be closed to make a flat surface. When it was open, a bolted-down typewriter was raised. (I removed the typewriter after he died.) The top was more often open than closed. I'd watch Dad type rapidly with his two index fingers, and when he wasn't at home, I sat there and followed his example, typing things I had written. He typed very fast losing time only when he had to look back and forth from the keys to something he had written by hand. I often read letters he had started. After his father's death he continued writing to his stepmother who had taken excellent care of Grampa Long during his years of illness. Dad's letters to her always began, "Dear Faithful and True."

The church paid a secretary, but she made so many mistakes in Dad's dictated letters that he sometimes asked me to type them over. I got so good at it that he later asked me to compose the letters, too. He would give me the name and address, tell me how to address the person, indicate what he wanted to say, and how to close. Then I composed and typed it and he signed and mailed it, satisfied that I had done a good job. He also taught me how to write checks, explaining that a line should follow the written amount so that no other figure could be added by another person.

The first cross street going from our house toward Ashland School was Carlton Street. Next was Melmore Gardens, which wasn't a street then but a hill the neighborhood kids used for belly-wopping on their sleds in the winter. Then there was Summit Street and then Park Avenue. East Orange didn't have alleys, and the back yards were long. Barrett's yard divided almost a block of North Clinton Street and Ashland Avenue, the street behind Clinton. The house was on Carlton Street, but the yard extended all the way to the lumber company next door at the end of Walter Purcell's yard and provided a perfect playground. I usually sat on the fence and watched the boys play ball. When they were not in Barrett's, they gathered in our yard to play baseball, using the clothesline posts for bases, or football, climbed the pear tree, or threw horseshoes. Sometimes Dad, working in his study and hearing the sound of boys playing, couldn't resist joining them. He was a boy again, thoroughly enjoying himself. One year he made a kite out of newspaper and strips of wood, a skill he had learned as a child. Then he helped us fly it high above the trees.

Dad sometimes played with me, too. One summer we played a game of tag that lasted all season. Whenever he thought about it, he would tag me and run or I would tag him and run around the house. Once we chased each other all around the block; the neighbors must have thought we were crazy, but we enjoyed the pursuit.

Every July 3 he packed us kids in the car and took us to Bloomfield to buy firecrackers—cherry bombs, caps, torpedoes, and other noisy devices for the boys and sparklers and quieter things for me. The concrete back of the commercial garages next door in Walter's yard were the perfect place to throw these devices and hear them explode.

Every year I got a doll for Christmas. Whatever else I received, I could count on a new doll. Only one year did I feel the effect of the Depression when Christmas morning came and I received nothing but a doll, some oranges, and new underwear. In response to my tears of disappointment, Dad explained that times were hard and we

29

were more fortunate than many people who had no money for Christmas at all.

We were taught a healthy respect for guns. When my family lived in Charlottesville before I was born, Dad used to hunt, but he evidently stopped after they moved. In the corner beside my parents' bed were always two loaded rifles or shotguns. (I still don't know the difference.) We knew better than to touch them. He had a 22 caliber and a 45 caliber handgun, too. He bought Clarence and Wil B.B. guns, giving them special instructions on where and how to use them. Periodically, we went to the cellar with Dad, lay on our stomachs on my old crib mattress, and shot at targets. When I outgrew dolls, we used them for target practice, all except the one with the bisque head and stuffed cloth body that Mama particularly favored because she said it looked like Wil when he was a baby. I kept that one for years and brought it to Detroit when I got married. My daughter played with it. Once Dad let me shoot his 45; I didn't expect its kick. I have never fired a gun since.

One of our winter joys was getting to the milk before Mama did and eating the frozen cream that pushed the cover up. Her reprimands and having to drink the rest of the bluish residue didn't deter us from stealing the cream again at the next opportunity. Another joyful theft was chips of ice. Whenever the ice man came, we waited for him to make a delivery and, while he was gone, we climbed onto the back of his truck and took all the chips we could cram into our mouths. We knew one family that had an electric refrigerator, and every time we visited them, I asked for ice cubes.

I don't know when we acquired our ordinary looking tabby cat, but Wil named him Wouzhey (pronounced like a French *J*). Everyone in the family loved him and he loved to ride in the car. If the car was parked in the driveway, he would sit there and wait for Dad to come out. As soon as the door opened he'd jump in and ride to Newark or wherever Dad might be headed. Four summers we took him with us to Richmond, and he was a perfect passenger, going from lap to lap to nap but never bothering the driver. When we stopped along the road to stretch our legs, he got out too and stayed close to the car. We never had to worry about his straying away. Once we got to Grandma's house, he went outside as he did at home and came in when called. When he got killed by a car, everybody cried, including Dad.

In between our own cats I played with Mufflejaw, the large gray Maltese cat owned by Lillian Matthews who moved into the house next door after Walter's family left. Once I paid a girl down the street eleven cents, my total wealth, for a black and white cat, but he ran away. I never really got attached to him the way I did to Wouzhey.

Later we acquired another cat that looked just like Wouzhey, and Wil named him Wouzhey, too. I think there was another Wouzhey after the second who detested cars. When we moved from East Orange, Clarence went back to the house shortly before time to catch the train to St. Louis, hoping to coax him into the basket he was carrying, but he refused to come out from under the house and we had to leave him. Lillian promised to feed him, but he just went wild after we left and disappeared.

While we had one of the Wouzheys, Wil had a high school English assignment to write a poem. He wrote it about Wouzhey. As far as I know, it was the only poem he ever wrote, but it was well written—in rhyme, of course, since all the poetry in the books we had rhymed. The poem was so good that the teacher didn't return it for a long time, convinced that it was plagiarized. When she failed to find it in any of her books, she reluctantly gave it back, still unconvinced. I don't know what grade she gave him.

In a way, radio was more interesting than television. During a prize fight, the announcer's rapid voice narrating the action made us see it more clearly than with our eyes. This was true, too, of the radio dramas with their sound effects. We listened to Gabriel Heater and the account of the execution of Bruno Hauptmann who was convicted of the kidnapping and killing of the Lindbergh baby.

Later my interest in popular music caught up with my brothers' and we often pleaded to stay up late enough to hear Lee Simms broadcast from Buffalo, New York. One of the songs she sang was "In the Dark" with words that were clearly articulated. Later another singer recorded the same song but she pronounced "fingertips on my lips" as "fingertips on my lil," and kids who heard her rendition snickered about the assumed part of the body that "lil" referred to.

Clarence aspired to be an actor. Somehow he managed to get a role as a voice in the crowd in two radio dramas, one of which starred Orson Welles before he became famous and the other, Burgess Meredith. We glued our ears to the radio trying futilely to distinguish Clarence's voice from all the others.

If we had an automobile before the Chandler, I don't remember it. I was about five when Dad brought the used car home and drove it on the grass in the backyard to take snapshots. Dressed in a lumberjacket, I took turns with Dad and my brothers sitting at the steering wheel, standing on the running board, or looking out the back window while Mama took snapshots with a box camera.

Later Dad bought a used green Packard that we kept for many years. Gas was only a few cents a gallon; still, whenever he went to the filling station, he ordered exactly five gallons. As long as he drove, I never knew him to fill up the tank. He bought only one new car in his life, a 1936 Pontiac in which my brothers learned to drive. Cars were not built for obsolescence then and we kept it for at least ten years.

Mr. Inge, an officer in Dad's former church in Charlottesville, owned a grocery store where he sold hams that he cured himself. The flavor doesn't compare with any other ham I've ever tasted. About once a year Dad sent back to Charlottesville for an Inge ham, and we feasted on it for many days. (Mama told us stories about official board meetings during which Dad and Mr. Inge had heated disagreements. The next day they'd go out hunting together.)

Dad also ordered salt herring from the South. A lifelong lover of salt, I always enjoyed this treat but didn't care for the many tiny bones that had to be removed. My aunts in Richmond sometimes sent us watercress. (They pronounced it "creeses.") It is not the variety of watercress used raw in sandwiches but a form of greens cooked to the perfection of Mama's combination of mustard and turnip greens but surpassing it in flavor. I have never liked bread, but Mama's freshly baked hot rolls and biscuits, dripping in melted butter, were always tasteful. I never wanted them the second day when they were just heated. A special treat was her spoon bread made with corn meal but more like custard than bread.

We all took piano and violin lessons from teachers who came to our house. Clarence was the most musical one of us and continued to play the violin in high school, as well as with a jazz orchestra. We could all read music, but he was the only one who could also play the piano by ear. I now confine my occasional piano playing to my home where no one can hear me struggling through the notes. My violin playing was terrible although I had the nerve to join the Ashland School orchestra. To this day I am grateful to the teacher, C. Paul Herfurth, for never saying anything about how unprepared I was. I finally realized for myself that I was the worst musician in the group and voluntarily left it.

Father Divine, who declared himself God, was more popular on the Eastern Seaboard than in other parts of the country. We knew of him from the radio and newspapers but also because several members of our church left to live in one of his "kingdoms." We knew of couples who separated because one was a believer and one was not. We heard that Father Divine was going to visit the home in our block of one of his followers. My brothers and several of their friends and I waited for him to arrive. When his car pulled into her driveway, two of the boys stood on the running board and tapped on the window with rolled-up newspapers. I knew he wasn't God and wondered how anyone so ordinary looking and who spoke with no particular wisdom or intelligence could be worshiped by anyone.

His followers had to give up all of their belongings (to him, of course) and live in one of his kingdoms where all their needs were supplied. As opposed to many such religious icons, he did some good by selling restaurant meals to anyone who wanted them for fifteen cents and providing haircuts for less than that. I give him credit for giving something back and making life easier for many who suffered severely during the Depression.

Sundays were always special in our home, the most important day of the week. Dad always got up happy, sometimes whistling as he got dressed. He turned on the radio to listen to a lady preacher who always opened the program with "Isn't this a glorious day!" Some man would sing, "If I have wounded any soul today / If I have caused one heart to go astray... Dear Lord, forgive."

When the season changed, Mama had to be absolutely certain there would be no more cold weather before she let us change from winter clothing. This ritual always took place on a warm Sunday morning. Dad would change from "union suits" to BVDs. He never wore undershirts or shorts. Clarence and Wil changed to lighter weight long socks and suits with "knickers," not graduating to long pants until they reached their teens. And I could remove the hated long underwear and cotton rib stockings for socks and patent leather shoes.

When everyone was dressed we went downstairs to breakfast where we usually sat at the kitchen table and waited for Dad to finish an especially lengthy prayer. He prayed for everybody he knew, it seemed, including our aunt and cousins in Wilberforce that we had never met, and always for "the Scottsboro boys." If he was in a particularly prayerful mood, we had to go to the living room and kneel in front of a chair. Sometimes when these prayers were interminable, Mama would get up, go to the kitchen and make a louder noise than necessary opening and closing the oven door where the biscuits were warming. He would stop, annoyed at this interruption, and wait until she got back to continue. After that we had to say a Bible verse before we could eat.

Then we went to Sunday school, we kids walking after we got old enough, Dad and Mama driving later in time for the eleven o'clock service. Dad always preceded his sermon with a "children's sermon," a very short narrative with a moral.

I always enjoyed his sermons and learned a great deal about the use of language from them. Even now I can think of very few preachers that I would consider his equal or who could surpass him in excellence. He didn't appeal to people's emotions; yet he was a spirited speaker, occasionally clapping his hands once to emphasize a point. Anyone who felt like responding was free to do so. Often in the middle of his sermon, sometimes just as he was reaching the climax, the Lackawanna train, whose tracks were recessed below street level in front of the church, chose that time to go by and he would have to wait for it to pass before continuing. He didn't wear a robe in those days but dressed in a dark suit and always in a white shirt. He was in his seventies before I ever saw him in a colored sport shirt. Occasionally, he wore one of two silk shirts that had been gifts of one of his members. Even less often in warm weather he wore a morning coat—or was it a Prince Albert?

After the service we were always the last ones to leave, Dad never trusting anyone else to lock up the church. On all Sundays except the first, we went home and ate dinner around one o'clock. Then Dad took a nap while we played quietly. Mama didn't have to tell us to keep quiet because we knew he needed to rest before the night service. Sometimes there was a special service in the afternoon or BYPU (Baptist Young People's Union) and later the night service, after which we sometimes went to visit Lloyd and Pinkie Davis who were members of our church. After they moved from East Orange, we drove to see them in Vaux Hall. We considered that a special treat. And if Mrs. Allen, a close family friend originally from Norfolk, was with us, we could expect ice cream when we got home.

The first Sunday of the month had its own unique features. That was the day when Communion was observed in the afternoon. Instead of going home after the morning service, we had a standing invitation to dinner at the Jeters' house. Mr. and Mrs. Jeter were both elderly, but Mr. Jeter seemed ancient. I didn't realize then how rare an example of old age he was. As kids we pretty much took him for granted. It was not until much later that I could fully appreciate his rugged durability although I knew that he had been a slave and fought in the Civil War. Probably in his nineties, he still worked for the city sweeping the streets with a broom. Small and wiry, he didn't wear glasses and sometimes boasted that he never drank water. As a deacon of the church, he rated a special chair in the left front, and most of the time he remained quietly seated during the sermon. Every now and then, though, he became so moved by the message that he suddenly exploded from his chair and strutted silently across the front of the sanctuary and up and down the aisle, lifting his knees high and throwing his arms out, then closing them in an emotional self-embrace.

The Jeters' house on North Oraton Parkway had a sun porch that held my favorite piece of furniture in all the world, a huge, comfortable chair that either rocked or reclined. Almost as soon as we entered the house, I clambered onto it and buried myself in its protective warmth. In the living room, which was crowded with furniture, knickknacks, and doilies, was an old-fashioned daybed that I also claimed as mine. I took naps on it sometimes when the long morning service had tired me, but it was the big friendly chair on the sun porch that I remember best.

Mrs. Jeter, white-aproned and bespectacled, was perhaps in her early or mid-eighties. Probably because she was younger than her husband, it didn't seem unusual to me then that a woman of her advanced years should still be cooking for company and doing all her own household chores. Everything she served was delicious, but her specialty—big yellow rolls lightly dusted with flour—always elicited comments. Although I detested bread in most forms, Mrs. Jeter's rolls delighted even me. They were so unusual that several times Dad implored her to share her recipe with some trusted friend or perhaps even sell it so that it would not be lost, but she resisted his advice. To the best of my knowledge, her secret died with her; I have never seen or tasted rolls like hers again.

After a sumptuous meal and adult conversation, to which we children listened quietly, we headed back up the hill to church at about three o'clock. When we arrived, there were already a few people engaged in singing and testifying. Others drifted in gradually even after the formal service had begun.

I don't recall an organist or choir at Communion, and there was no set agenda for this informal part of the service. Occasionally there were brief periods of silence. Then from somewhere in the pews would come a low moan, followed perhaps by humming. As soon as the tune was recognized, others joined in on some familiar old hymn or Negro spiritual, often with the lead singer "lining" the words before the congregation repeated them in song. (This practice of lining was a carryover from the poor churches of the South that

37

couldn't afford hymn books and had many members who would not have been able to read them anyhow.) Sometimes it was a good old traditional gospel song of the Thomas A. Dorsey variety, sung with the genuine emotion conjured up by the words, music, and foot-thumping rhythms alone and not accompanied by the more sophisticated theatrics of modern day gospel music. These songs moved me deeply and inexplicably; only later did I understand the sources of their fervor. The singers moaned, they intoned, they wailed, they pleaded, they praised, they exulted. Springing from the gut of bitter frustration, growing in trust, and blossoming into a fine, upward-spiraling supplication, these songs were the most honest, intimate, and splendid expression of the oppressed but triumphant human spirit that I have ever witnessed. I am sure that my love of choral music—and of black folk music, in particular—was born in the informality of those afternoon Communion services at Calvary and not in later classroom instructions and choir rehearsals that concentrated on printed sheet music and some composer's degreed expertise. It was all I needed to learn of the cruelty and treacheries of slavery and Reconstruction, segregation, injustice, weary backs bending in a brutal southern sun, migration, and the hunger and want of the current Great Depression.

Interspersed between the songs were spontaneous prayers and testimonies of personal experiences, happy and sad; gratitude for various blessings, ordinary and spectacular; and assurances that the speaker "loved everybody" although, even as children overhearing adult conversations, we knew that relationships among some members were not always as harmonious and benevolent as the speaker would have everyone believe.

Eventually my father emerged from the back room, knelt at his chair, then took his position at the lectern, a sign that the formal service was about to begin. I remember little about the details of that part of the service. I'm sure we sang a hymn or two, still without instrumental accompaniment. Dad probably preached a short sermon. Perhaps he called on one of the deacons to pray.

Every time a particular deacon prayed, my mother was certain to have to chastise us kids because we anticipated phrases and whole passages that that person always repeated. We would recite them under our breath, then giggle when the deacon repeated them a second later. We knew at what point he would begin his emotional intoning, rocking back and forth on the same two notes and rising in volume, and on what phrase he would reach the climax. Immediately would follow the tempered and quiet closing that invariably began, "And now, oh Lord, reach down with thy lily-white hand . . . . " I later came to understand what conditioning had caused him to pray to a Caucasian God, but I still have trouble singing hymns that implore Him to "wash me whiter than snow." At other times, an elderly "jackleg" minister, who had no official position in the church but often sat on the pulpit with Dad, was called on to pray, and again we would crack up with laughter when he got to the word *unctions*, which, although a legitimate word, was unfamiliar to our ears and therefore excruciatingly funny.

After preliminaries, the observation of Communion began. At various churches I have seen other kinds of bread or wafers used, but at Calvary we had a special small loaf with no crust that had been purchased at a religious supply store. It was as white as angel food cake and as finely textured. I craved a taste of this loaf because I expected it to be as sweet as the confection it resembled. When, after my baptism, I was allowed to partake of it, I was disappointed to find that, with all its whiteness and fine texture, it tasted like ordinary bread. Its ceremonial symbolism was temporarily lost to me then. Dad would hold this loaf in both hands and break it in half as he recited the this-is-My-body-broken-for-you scripture, placing each half on a silver plate held by a deacon who then moved with it from row to row until everyone was served. Each member would pinch off a small piece. During this time someone would strike up another chorus and everyone would join in, singing a familiar hymn such as "I want Jesus to walk with me. I want Jesus to walk with me. All along my pilgrim journey, Lord, I want Jesus to walk with me."

When the deacons returned to the front, Dad served each of them; then one of them would take back the plate and hold it for him to be served. After that he would repeat the do-this-in-remembrance-of-Me passage, and the small wads of bread would be consumed. The same routine followed with the grape juice, symbolic of Christ's shed blood, with more impromptu singing.

At the end of this ritual, Dad would quote: "And they all sang a song and went out to the Mount of Olives," bringing the service to a close. The members again joined their voices in a hymn, most often "What a Fellowship," as they turned to shake hands with one another, moving as they sang out into the afternoon sun.

As the years passed, the Communion ritual changed in subtle ways in the several other churches I attended, and I sublimated the conscious memory of my earliest impressions. It was not until my father retired that it all came back to me with shattering force. It was at Bethesda Baptist Church in New Rochelle, New York, and Dad had asked his best friend and protégé, the Rev. Dr. J. Raymond Henderson, pastor of Second Baptist Church in Los Angeles, to be the guest speaker at his last service as a pastor. I had grown up, married, and moved away to Detroit but on this occasion I was home on vacation. I was always happy to see "Joe," whose "little sugar plum" I had always been, but if I had been able to anticipate my emotional state, I think I would have skipped church that day.

At Bethesda the Communion was observed directly after morning worship, so after Joe concluded his sermon, Dad took charge of the last Lord's Supper at which he would ever officiate. It was the end of a major part of his life and, in a way, my own as well. I don't know at what point I began to cry, but my tears, which started as a catch in the throat, first trickled, then gushed in an uncontrollable flood.

At first I thought my reaction was due solely to the end of Dad's long service as a pastor, but later I realized that it was just as much the Communion service itself as I had first known it and never would experience again. It was like suddenly discovering that a valued old keepsake is forever lost. As if you haven't seen this treasure for a long time but haven't really missed it because you've always known it was there. But then when you stumble upon the empty space where it ought to be, you suddenly know how lost you feel without it. Surely it was that memory of lost innocence and truth that devastated my spirit that morning—that spirituality that had been awakened long ago by the saints at Calvary on first Sunday as they went out singing, praying, and testifying their brave and wondrous lives into the garden of my years.

Dad and Joe Henderson taken that day

When I was in third grade, my cousin, Helen Sampson, and her mother Sadie came from Chicago to live with us. She was in fifth grade. That was a very happy time for me because, for the first time, I had a girl to play with. Sadie was my mother's youngest sister, cute and petite and very stylish. I liked to listen to her play the piano and sing. My brothers would play with her, tussling with her, sometimes wrestling her to the floor. It was all in good fun. Sadie, Helen and I slept on the third floor. Sadie, an excellent seamstress, made identical clothes for Helen and me, including winter coats and matching hats.

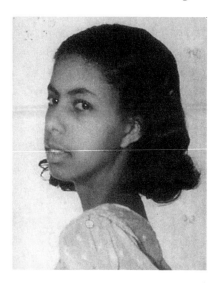

Cousin Helen
a few years later

At some time during their two-year stay, Sadie looked out the window and saw an old beat-up car pulling into the driveway. "Oh, my God!" she said. "It's Bowen." Sadie and Milton, her estranged husband, had known him in Chicago. He had the nerve of the proverbial brass monkey. We had never met him before but he proceeded to move into our basement anyhow. He banged out a mean piano, and we loved to listen to him. His trade was making dentures, but he had evidently lost his license. That didn't stop him from setting up shop in our basement and soliciting business from some of our church members. Even after Sadie and Helen left to live in Richmond, he continued to stay on awhile. The last we saw of him was on Roosevelt Boulevard nearing Philadelphia as he trailed us southward to Richmond. We saw his car stopped and smoking but couldn't stop.

Another of our live-ins at a different time was my mother's brother, Wilbur Hilton. (All her life Mama referred to him by his full name to distinguish him from my brother who was named after him.) He worked in New York as a confidential messenger for the Standard Oil Company. He was jolly and fun to be around and always brought back so much news about what was going on in the city that we nicknamed him Billboard. He frequently sang his favorite songs. I don't recall how long he lived with us, but he eventually moved to Manhattan and visited us periodically. We were always glad to see him, and when he left, we'd ask, "Billboard, when

Uncle Wilbur "Billboard"

are you coming back?" His answer was invariably, "A week from some Tuesday."

Occasionally we had a house guest who had known Dad in his youth in the Southwest. Listening to their after-dinner conversations and laughter about the past was a real joy. We would sit there with them after the table had been cleared, fascinated with their stories and learning things about Dad's early life.

I also enjoyed the meetings of the Junior Missionaries, whom my mother had organized—church members who were in high school or graduates of East Orange High. The meetings were at our house, and I liked to listen to what was going on.

On two occasions when my grandmother was ill, Mama went to Richmond alone to relieve her sister Minnie who was an elementary school teacher. One of those times we stayed in the home of a church member, Mrs. Foster, and her grown daughter Pocahontas, whose sister Aurelia had married and moved away from home. The next time Mama had to leave, she had Jimmy Stewart stay with us. He was evidently not working at the time and took complete charge of things. We had known the Stewart family for as long as I can remember, but Jimmy, the eldest of five children, was most familiar as he often visited and spent hours talking to Mama. He could cook, clean, and run a household as well as the best of women. I never had a birthday party as a child, but I did have cakes, birthday or not; Jimmy saw to that. They were always chocolate, my favorite, and their dramatic presentation was usually preceded with much pleading on my part, for nobody could make a cake as well as he.

Jimmy comes to mind every time I see on other people's plates in fast food restaurants those pale and limpid imitations that pass for french fries. Jimmy always cut potatoes into cubes and deep-fried them to crisp, deep golden perfection. When I cook them his way, I still refer to them as Jimmy potatoes.

He kept things running smoothly in our household and provided for my particular needs and wishes without spoiling me. He had an uncanny way of reading people, and it was futile to try to put anything over on him because he could see straight through the most subtle deception and guile. Whatever wasn't genuine and real, Jimmy could sense in a minute, and he would have none of it.

Whenever as an adult I become frustrated over the lack of progress in interracial understanding, I remember Jimmy's frequent kitchen conversations with Mama when he related how he had "gotten his white folks told" and in various ways outwitted whatever family he happened to be working for at the time. I learned from him a great deal about small victories and racial pride in those Depression days when there was not much to feel proud and triumphant about. In that complex world of which I was not yet a full part, I was nevertheless already experienced in prejudice and shame. Jimmy was the conqueror who taught me about covert and imaginative ways to win personal victories.

Jimmy Stewart

During World War II Jimmy served in the Navy, and during one of the summers when I lived with his family, he came home on furlough. Requested to sing a solo in church, he stood in the front in uniform and mesmerized the congregation with his rendition of the hymn, "I trust in God wherever I may be/Upon the land or on the stormy sea. . . ." I'm sure the congregation associated his choice of song with life-threatening combat situations. But the truth was that he had never sailed anywhere and spent his whole tour of duty safely landlocked on the shores of Bainbridge, Maryland.

When I graduated from high school in St. Louis, Jimmy came for the occasion and sang a solo at the baccalaureate service that my class had voted to have at our church.

Clarence, who was younger than Jimmy, had made him promise that, if he should die first, Jimmy would sing at his funeral. Jimmy kept that promise although by that time he was ailing and his memory was beginning to fade. When he forgot some of the words, his youngest brother Billy picked up and helped him carry on.

The last time I saw Jimmy on a visit to East Orange, the onset of dementia had robbed him of the laughter and enthusiasm that were so much a part of him. He nevertheless surprised me by showing me a scrapbook he had kept on my career—photographs and clippings covering many years, meticulously affixed to the pages. Memory of his love and pride in me still has the power to sustain me many times when my efforts seem futile.

We never had godparents, Dad believing that, as a pastor, he and Mama could not show favoritism. I've always felt that if I had had a godmother, it would have been Elizabeth Allen. She had known me since birth and called me Chiss. At some time after we left Norfolk, she and her husband David moved to Philadelphia where we occasionally visited them. They were a handsome couple, both of large build. They had a lovely home with beautiful china and furnishings. When the marriage ended for reasons unknown, she moved to New Jersey and worked as a live-in domestic. She spent her days off with us, Thursdays and every other Sunday, staying overnight and leaving early the next morning for work in Summit. Dad affectionately called her Lizzie and she called my mother Longie.

We especially enjoyed her visits because she always bought ice cream in blocks. Each of us would plead to be the one to cut it into servings, but she understood why. "You cut," she would say to one of us, "and you pick," pointing to another. If the cut was uneven, the person to choose would take the larger portion. In that way she could be sure that the portions were reasonably even. During her visits she, Mama and I sometimes went to the movies. We also went to Radio City Music Hall to see the Rockettes and other shows.

Mrs. Allen was accustomed to nice things and, although she worked as a domestic, she made her own rules. When one family gave her special dishes for herself, she put them on the floor for the dog and ate from the same dishes the family did. On one occasion when her employers were out of town, she had me spend several days with her as her guest. Like Jimmy Stewart, she didn't take any "stuff" from the white people she worked for. She was often more in charge than they were.

Rev. Dr. J. Raymond Henderson in his youth

I always thought of "Joe" Henderson as my unofficial godfather. He was Dad's protégé and lifelong best friend. Dad had known him as a boy in Charlottesville and inspired him to enter the ministry. I remember him first as a single seminary student who visited us in East Orange. We all called him "Joe" but he became the distinguished Rev. Dr. J. Raymond Henderson, once pastor of Wheat Street Baptist Church in Atlanta, later pastor of Bethesda Baptist Church in New Rochelle, NY (preceding Dad), and eventually pastor of Second Baptist Church in Los Angeles. When he married his beautiful wife, whom he called "Bunny," she insisted that we call her by that nickname since we called her husband by his. They had four sons, one of whom was given the middle name Long after my father. We stayed in touch with him after his first wife's death and became friends with his second wife, Velva. I still have a letter he once wrote to Dad promising that, if anything happened to Dad, he would help in the responsibility of our care. It was he, of course, who officiated at my father's funeral in 1976.

Dad invited various ministers to Calvary to conduct week-long revivals, but one who returned frequently was Rev. Samuel Wilson. He had a beautiful singing voice, and I enjoyed his sermons. Once when we were singing, "Blessed Assurance," he stopped in the middle of the hymn to describe his mother as she made a cake. She would give him the bowl of leftover batter. He went through the motion of running his finger around the bowl and licking the batter off his finger to indicate a foretaste of the baked cake. Every time we got to the line, "Oh, what a foretaste of glory divine," he repeated this gesture.

Dad was always going somewhere. He recognized the educational value of travel. Sometimes he went to visit relatives and old friends; other times he simply wanted to see places he had never been. I don't recall his ever going to just one place on a trip. He always had several nearby destinations. He sent us many cards and letters, advising my brothers to take good care of Mother and Sister and cautioning them not to tease me. He always brought us souvenirs, several of which I still have. His travel by train put no strain on family finances. He knew ministers all over the country and, wherever he planned to go, he was granted an invitation to preach. The special collection taken up for the visiting minister paid his travel expenses.

Dr. Tilden and his wife lived across the street from us. He was a kindly, fatherly man. The first time I made a telephone call by myself it was to him. He was more than our doctor; he was our friend. Whenever Dad traveled to other states he always informed Dr. Tilden of his plans. If Dr. Tilden noticed lights on at our house after a certain time, he called to find out if everything was all right. Once when he was examining Clarence, my mother, who thought spinach was essential to our diet, told the doctor that Clarence wouldn't eat it, thinking that he would advise him to comply. His answer was: "I don't blame you, son. I don't like it myself."

Mrs. Tilden often crossed the street and sat on our front porch in the summer while she sent one of the boys to the store. She taught classes in handcrafts at her home, and Mama attended them. Her students learned how to make beaded lampshades and trace patterns of flowers on silk, filling them in with oil paint. They traced other art as well. (It had to be traced because Mama was by no means an artist.) I still value her picture done in pastel of the Appian Way outside Rome. They also painted frameable pictures on glass.

Once a year Mrs. Tilden rented the high school auditorium and put on a pageant. Her students made all the costumes out of crepe paper which they learned to crimp with their fingers. I have a picture of myself in a crepe paper dress with a doll carriage decorated to look like a swan. During the performance I wheeled my crepe paper swan down the aisle.

The Tildens' house sat on a small hill that got higher as it went farther back in their yard. Next door to his house was an auto repair shop. The boys and I delighted in going to the Tildens' back yard and climbing onto the roof of the garage which was at ground level. We would run across the roof until we got tired of that and then come back down into the doctor's back yard.

Dad firmly believed in family vacations. Never in my life have I lived in a state where I had cousins, aunts, or uncles, nieces or nephews living nearby. So it was that every summer, and once or

49

twice in the winter, we drove to Richmond to visit my mother's family. My grandparents' house at 747 North Fifth Street became the most stable home in my life even though I never lived there. After they died my mother's sister Minnie remained there and, when they left our house, Helen and Sadie lived there, too. It was always a joy

747 North Fifth Street after it was remodeled

to be in Richmond. The summer smells, the games on the brick sidewalk, the swing in the backyard under the grape arbor, and the friends we made were wonderful. My older cousins, Eleanor and Ruth Jackson, and their younger brother "Bubba" (Giles Beecher Jackson, II, named after his famous grandfather for whom Jackson Ward in Richmond was named) lived on North Sixth Street. Bubba was a year or so younger than I; his sisters were in a split generation between the younger cousins and my mother's youngest sibling. Aunt Bessie, their mother, had rheumatoid arthritis. I never saw her without her crutches, but she did her own cooking and spent a lot of time at the front window observing and making comical remarks about the people walking past in the street. She had a tremendous sense of humor. Eleanor and Ruth frequently cut through the alley past Navy Hill School behind Grandma's house and came through the back door on Fifth Street. Often they wanted to borrow stockings or a piece of clothing from Minnie or Sadie since they were all about the same size.

Grandma's house was built on a brick foundation and had no basement. It was a frame house with no central heating. Between the kitchen and the front parlor stood a piano and a console Victrola that had to be wound up. I don't recall many records, but the one I played over and over was "Tiptoe Through the Tulips," rewinding when the sound began to slow down. In that room was also a heater that provided warmth in the winter for the first floor. Upstairs were the front room and the "middle room" where there was another heater. The unheated bathroom had been added on, along with the cold back bedroom. When we were there in the winter, we spent as little time in the bathroom as possible, rushing to get under the cover for warmth. In the summer the dark green blinds in the bathroom shut out the sun, but I vividly remember the smell of flowers and fruit sold by vendors in horse-drawn wagons. There had also been added an outdoor stairway to the first floor. The windows in the parlor went from the ceiling to the floor. It was in the parlor that Grampa's and Grandma's bodies lay in state and where their funerals were held. At one time Edgar Allan Poe lived about five blocks away.

Behind the frame house, just a few feet from the back steps, was a small two-story brick building. Grampa, who was self-employed as a roof tinner, stored his tools there. I have always wondered why that extra house was there. Perhaps the original owners had slaves who lived in the building behind the house. Many years later, Minnie rented out the house in back and had the main house remodeled, shortening the windows in the process.

51

We were usually in Richmond during the last two weeks of August, so I never got a chance to taste the Concord grapes because they were not yet ripe. If we went in the winter, it was in our spacious green Packard. We covered ourselves with lap blankets, warmed by the heat of our own bodies, until the engine got warm. On one occasion when Sadie was visiting us in East Orange, she took me back to Richmond with her to spend some time with Helen. That year she cut my hair, and I no longer wore braids. That was the beginning of getting my hair straightened and curled.

During the early years Dad did all the driving himself. It seemed a much longer trip then than it is now, and there were no motels or places where black people could stay. We did make several stops along the way, though. We sometimes stayed overnight in Philadelphia with the Thomases, who owned a bakery in the front of the house, or with the Allens. We usually stopped in Baltimore for an hour or two with a family there, and after reaching Virginia we paused for a short visit with a family my parents knew in Ashland.

Dad carried a gun with him, and when he got tired of driving, he pulled over into a field to catch a quick nap while Mama stayed awake to keep watch. He later took someone with him to help him drive before Clarence and Wil were old enough. Several times it was Mr. Peterson, a member of Calvary who had grown up in a city in New Jersey where there were very few African Americans. He was obviously of mixed race. In Richmond he was fascinated to see so many black people. Every morning he got up early to walk to Second and Leigh streets, a corner where there were a number of black businesses and people just standing around.

As we traveled to and from Richmond, we looked forward to the Burma Shave signs. There were about four of them, the first one displaying the first part of a rhyme, the next one, a short distance away, showing the next part, until we got to the last one that completed the rhyme.

Every summer we spent a few days at the beach in Long Branch. Sometimes the church went there for a day's picnic in the section of the beach reserved for African Americans, but when we stayed longer it was at a rooming house owned by another black church. I always wanted to see the beach before we went to the house. Blocks before we reached it, we could smell the salt from the ocean. A black couple had a concession on the beach where they sold hot dogs with sauerkraut and other refreshments. Hot dogs never tasted so good as those we ate there, even with a few grains of sand on them. Dad was a good swimmer and swam beyond the safety ropes, but the rest of us just held on to the rope and rose and fell with the waves. Sometimes Dad doused me in the water; I really didn't like that because the salt water went up my nose, but I didn't know how to tell him.

Every May 30 a number of black Baptist churches throughout the state went to Bordentown School for an outing. (I recently heard that Bordentown School is now white, but it was all black then.) It was a boarding school whose principal was a Dr. Valentine. It was a spacious, beautiful campus, and the students dressed in military uniforms. I was so impressed with the campus and uniforms that I set my heart on attending. One of my earliest poems was about Bordentown School. I pleaded with my parents to let me attend, but Jimmy Stewart explained that many of the students had no family to care for them or had difficulties at home. He tried to convince me that I didn't belong there, but his explanation only partly dulled my disappointment.

Every year the various church choirs participated in a contest, each singing the same anthem. Calvary won so many times that they finally discontinued the competition, but every time my present church choir sings, "God So Loved the World," fond memories of Bordentown return.

In 1934, in spite of the Depression, Calvary sent Dad to Berlin as a delegate to the World Baptist Alliance. He had never used any kind of camera, but John Simmons, a member of Calvary, owned a black and white 16 mm. movie camera (silent, of course) that he let Dad borrow, instructing him on how to move the camera slowly and pan a building. The night the S.S. Europa, then the largest ship in the world, sailed, we went on board. I couldn't understand how such a vehicle could stay afloat and was amazed to see automobiles being raised onto the ship. For the first time I saw Dad wearing a white cap. After we walked back down the gangplank and the ship finally sailed, we continued to wave as the white cap receded farther and farther into the darkness.

It was an interesting time to be in Germany. Dad took movies of the brown-shirted soldiers goose-stepping down the streets, the swastika prominently displayed in the background. After the convention was over, he spent the rest of the summer touring the Holy Land, Europe, and Egypt. It was not until I read the Pulitzer Prize-winning book, *Parting the Waters: America in the King Years* by Taylor Branch, that I learned how Dad and Dr. Martin Luther King, Sr. had become friends; they were on the same itinerary. Dad took movies everywhere he went. He and the minister who was his roommate baptized each other in the Jordan River. I still treasure some of the cards he sent back, one showing him with a group of other tourists in an open tour bus in Berlin. He wrote frequent letters home, advising Clarence and Wil to take care of Mother and Sister and signing himself, "Devotedly, Dad."

When he returned, the film had to be sent to Kodak for processing. The reels came back at different times. Sometimes when I came home from school, Mr. Simmons's borrowed projector was already showing the developed film that had arrived that day. There were days when no one thought about eating dinner because the film was so fascinating that we couldn't tear ourselves away. Dad on a camel in front of the Great Pyramid. Dad being baptized in the Jordan River with a cat walking along the shore in the background. Dad standing at the edge of the crater on Mt. Vesuvius, closer than his guide would venture, lava bubbling all around his feet. Dad standing in St. Mark's Square in Venice. Dad's dark-skinned roommate being pursued by European women who wanted his autograph, none of them paying attention to my light-skinned father. To Italians, in particular, the familiar saying,"The blacker the berry, the sweeter the juice" applied. This was before the English and Americans transferred their notion of racial inferiority to Europeans.

When all the film was back, Dad asked Irving, my brothers' high school friend, to draw a large map of the places he had photographed. Dad mounted it on an easel and used a pointer when he showed his film and lectured at churches and other organizations.

He brought me back a silver bracelet made in Jerusalem and my mother perfume extract from Paris and a string of beads from Venice. I'm sure he brought souvenirs for my brothers, too, but I don't remember them. He also brought a piece of stone from the Garden Tomb in Jerusalem, pieces of lava from Mt. Vesuvius, mustard seed from the Garden of Gethsemane, and other items that Mama put in separate jars and labeled. There were also two soft drink bottles, one filled with water from the Jordan River and the other from the Dead Sea. They had to be sealed with wax in order to be brought out of the country. In spite of that, most of the water has evaporated over the years, but some from the Dead Sea is still in the bottle. I eventually gave the remaining water from the Jordan River to the assistant minister of our church in Detroit to use for his infant daughter's christening.

After Dad's return from Europe John Simmons took movies one Sunday of everyone coming out of church after the service. He stood on the bridge over the Lackawanna train tracks filming all the members filing out and the old cars, one with a rumble seat, passing by as people left the premises. When our family came out, I was feeling very self-conscious and showing it. Just in case the photographer had missed us, we went back inside and filed out again, Dad stopping to talk to someone, then walking to our trusty green Packard parked across the street.

Thanks to my sister-in-law Laverne, I now have on video these pictures of myself at twelve years old with my family and all the church members who were in attendance that day. How different a still photo is from one in motion! When I viewed this video for the first time as an adult, I recognized many of the old members, not only from their faces and their clothing, but from the way they moved. I had forgotten all that in the intervening years and was surprised to rediscover the body language of many of the members.

I had learned how to operate the projector, but the Christmas after Dad's return from Europe, I wanted only one thing, a toy movie projector of my own. Until the last minute, Mr. Simmons had me convinced that there was no such thing available. But then, on Christmas morning, there it was, complete with a short silent film starring Laurel and Hardy. The projector was run by turning a handle. I was so happy to own it, even though I never got another film for it, that I showed the same one over and over for my own amusement. After I had outgrown it, I was still reluctant to let it go. Only when I went away to college did I bid it farewell.

Since we had never met my father's sister Ethel and her family, Dad decided to visit them on the campus at Wilberforce University where Uncle William worked as the custodian of buildings and grounds, "church side."

Along the way, armed with the movie camera that Dad eventually purchased from Mr. Simmons, we stopped for a spectacular view of the Monongahela River. We arrived at the house late in the day and didn't have dinner until about eleven o'clock that night. Aunt Ethel didn't seem to be able to work and talk at the same time, so it took her hours to prepare dinner. While we were there Dad took movies of buildings on the campus that were later destroyed by a tornado. He also had someone photograph the whole family outside the house: Uncle William, who looked like a little Jew; Aunt Ethel, wearing a long dress; Harold, the eldest, who became a career Army officer, dressed in military uniform; Kenneth, the middle one; and William, the youngest, who was shorter than I although several years older. People on campus nicknamed him "Cotton Top," later shortened to "Cotton," because of his naturally blond hair. Then there was my family, I looking very self-conscious and wearing unnecessary glasses that I had insisted on having since Clarence wore them. I thought Harold was so handsome that I immediately fell in love with him.

It was in the living room at Wilberforce that I first saw the Long family piano built in 1895, now in my possession. Dad told us it had been in floods in Oklahoma. I don't remember how long our visit lasted, but it was like a perfect day. When we got back to New Jersey, I wrote Harold a letter that I was embarrassed to learn he shared with the rest of the family. Aunt Ethel found it amusing.

John Simmons was always promoting prizefighters, quartets, or whatever. He took us to Pompton Lakes to watch Joe Louis train. On one occasion when Dad and I went back, a large man wearing a tam walked toward us and passed us on the sidewalk. Dad told me it was Jack Johnson, the legendary prizefighter.

Mr. Simmons must have given us an 8-by-10-inch full-length photograph, apparently professionally taken, in 1936. It showed Joe Louis standing next to another man who was looking up at him as if in admiration. It stayed in the family. After Clarence died and Laverne was going through some of his things, she showed me the picture. Clarence had written the year on it and labeled it, "Joe Louis and unknown companion." I asked my sister-in-law if I could borrow it because I knew someone who was a very close friend of Joe Louis and thought he would be able to identify the other man. I never got around to asking him because, the more I looked at the picture, the more familiar this person seemed. It eventually occurred to me that it was Richard Wright. I went through my biographies of Wright in search of pictures of him taken about the same time and was convinced. I also learned that Wright's first journalism, published that year, was about Joe Louis. I have never seen this picture anywhere else.

One year Mama bought some root beer extract, along with corked bottles to be filled until the liquid matured and fermented. She scrubbed the double washtubs in the kitchen thoroughly and made the root beer there before putting it in bottles. Anxiously we waited and waited for the liquid to ferment but eventually drank it all before any of the fizz developed. It tasted just as good to us that way.

When I became old enough to cross Carlton Street alone, I played with the Banks sisters whose mother and my mother had known each other as girls in Richmond although "Miss Bea's" sister was closer to Mama's age. The Banks girls were younger than I but that didn't seem to matter; they were girls and they welcomed me. Later one of Billboard's friends moved his recently divorced sister and her three daughters to his home on Ashland Avenue, the street behind us, and we became friends.

Eventually I could take the bus or trolley across Central Avenue to visit two sisters, Pearl and Eva, who had joined Calvary only a few years before we left. At first I despised them because I envied their good looks and Pearl's long curls and sophistication, but we later became friends.

As I was growing up I had few chores. I had to make up my bed, set the table, dust the living room furniture, and sometimes iron my father's handkerchiefs, but other than that, the boys did most of the work. They took care of the furnace when they were old enough and washed and dried the dishes. Dad thought Mama should be teaching me how to cook and do more house work, but her duties were so all-consuming that I think she felt I had a lifetime of such labor ahead of me and she wanted to spare me as long as possible. I never had to wash the dishes until my brothers went away to college.

During his years at Virginia Union University, Dad had worked as a waiter in Cape May during the summer. He instructed Clarence and Wil on the proper way to wipe the oilcloth-covered table after a meal. For some reason, the only way he found acceptable was in a counterclockwise direction. If he came home from an evening meeting and the table was not cleaned to his satisfaction, he got my brothers out of bed and made them do it right. I didn't at all mind being spared the responsibility of this job.

I was forever falling in love with some boy or another and writing poems and diary entries about him. For the four years my brothers attended East Orange High School, I envied them, for now they had moved beyond me. When we were all at Ashland I could occasionally catch a glimpse of one of them in the hall and know that I was not alone in that sea of whiteness. At home they discussed teachers whose faces were familiar to me and occasionally students about whom even those on my lowly level were aware. But their graduation in June, 1933, separated us in a way I wasn't ready for.

Since there was only one high school to serve all the students in the city, my brothers were now in daily contact with some of the boys from church, and their after-school talk about Bob and Waverly Stewart, among others, suddenly cast them in a new light for me. They met a lot of new people, too, both students and teachers, whose names became only legend for me.

Besides, being in high school gave them certain privileges denied me. They assumed a real spirit of school loyalty through intramural football games played at the stadium behind Ashland School. They could belong to exciting clubs and occasionally go on field trips as Clarence once did when the Railroad Club visited Scranton, Pennsylvania. And they were free to move through the halls from class to class independently instead of with their class. They even had lockers in the halls instead of the cloak rooms contained in each classroom in grammar school. Then there were the huge study halls, 121 and 221, where all kinds of antics evidently took place. High school sounded like pure heaven and I yearned to enter this challenging new realm.

When I finally graduated from grammar school in June, 1937, a day before or after my brothers' graduation from high school, I was eager for September to arrive so that I could begin. In addition, I was now eligible to join the choir at church.

Like my brothers, I signed up for the "classical" curriculum intended for the college-bound, running into no resistance. I think Dad's reputation for a good fight was well enough established that the counselors did not even suggest the "general" or other watered down programs they recommended for other black students. The classical curriculum included four years of Latin, at least two years of French, algebra, and geometry—the whole works. I loved the challenge. My gray-haired Latin teacher, obviously enamored of one of my pretty blond classmates from Ashland, seated her on the front row and directed many of his comments to her, but he managed to teach the basics we needed notwithstanding. And I was thrilled to finally witness the openness of Study Hall 121.

My earlier experience with school music had been confined to the "brown book" and the "green book" and hymns we sang in chapel. So when I got to high school, I chose voice as an elective and joined the Spirituals Choir, composed of all black students. "Jonesie," the vocal music teacher, had a habit of putting one foot on a chair while he occasionally scratched his rear end. But this white man kept alive the value of these "sorrow songs," as W.E.B. DuBois called them, and did what he could to instill in his black students pride in their heritage.

Dad had recently accepted a position as pastor of historic Central Baptist Church in St. Louis. When he announced his resignation at Calvary, it seems that everybody cried. His former enemy, Deacon Moses, now totally blind, stood up and said, "Rev. Long wasn't what we wanted, but he was what we needed." I anticipated this move with excitement. Dad told me about the all-black high school I would attend and the parsonage where we would live. Because the new house was larger than our present one, he bought some used furniture, including a desk for me with book shelves on the side.

I attended East Orange High just long enough to get my first report card. My parents had set a date when we would leave for St. Louis and, based on that, I stopped attending classes. But the date kept getting changed and I was out of school for several weeks earlier than I needed to be. Eventually the furniture was shipped to St. Louis and we spent the last night or two with church members before leaving East Orange by train for our new home. It was late December in 1937, and one phase of my life had come to an end.

Emergence of a Poet

In spite of a fortunate childhood, those years seem happier in retrospect than when I was living them. I was a lonely and introverted child who felt alienated. For decades I carried with me the memory of myself on a brisk fall day, probably before I started school, wearing a navy blue straw hat with a streamer down the back, alone on the front porch. I had probably annoyed my mother past her endurance, and sending me outside to play was her only relief. To play? With whom? To do what, alone and cold? In spite of my imploring, she didn't let me back inside for a long time. That memory symbolized my loneliness and sense of exclusion.

Family in Charlottesville before my birth

On my mother's dresser was a studio photograph taken of my parents and brothers. I could never understand why I wasn't included. When Mama told me I wasn't born yet, I didn't understand what that meant, and for several years I thought it was because they didn't want me in the picture. I later learned that the picture was taken because my father was going to the hospital for surgery and didn't know if he would survive.

My loneliness and sense of alienation were reinforced at school where I was the only black child in my class through the eighth grade. While I got along well with most of the girls in my class, the prejudice I experienced from other students, mainly several boys, as well as some of the teachers, took its toll. One teacher gave the class an assignment to write as many aphorisms as we could think of. I made up one of my own. I wrote: "Where you're not wanted, don't stay."

I liked to use adhesive tape just because it was available. One day when it was my turn to see the visiting school nurse, I had a piece of tape wrapped around my wrist. Since nothing was wrong with it, she removed it, tsk-tsking at the difference in color between the clean skin where the tape had been and the rest of my dirty arm. I was so embarrassed that, to this day, when I do a quickie between daily showers, I always wash up to my elbows.

I didn't dress like my classmates. They wore bobby sox and snowsuits. I wore my brother's outgrown coats and cotton rib stockings with long underwear that Mama folded as neatly as possible inside. When I had to change clothes for gym, I was embarrassed by what I was wearing and, when I got dressed again, I could never fold the legs of the underwear as smoothly as Mama did. I wore dresses that children of church members had outgrown or that had been given to them by the white people they worked for. The style didn't matter; if they fit, I wore them. My "good" clothes were reserved for church. The first new school coat that I can remember was purchased when I was in seventh grade.

I was an outsider at play. My brothers and their friends didn't want me tagging along after them, and, except for the two years that my cousin Helen was there, I felt rejected until I became old enough to cross Carlton Street and visit the Banks sisters in the next block. My schoolmates exchanged playing cards for the pictures on the back. We were not allowed to play cards or even bring a collection into the house. Dad associated cards with gambling, which he called "getting something for nothing." As teenagers we were not allowed to dance although we sneaked and did it anyhow, but I've never learned to do anything but the waltz and the two-step, even when everybody else was jitterbugging.

New Jersey was serious about the quarantine of people with children's diseases. The Board of Health posted a sign on the door of a house where a stricken child lived. When I was eight years old, I had a sore throat which Dr. Tilden diagnosed as scarlet fever. My skin never peeled as my brothers' had done, and I never had any other symptoms. But for some reason, even though Clarence and Wil had already had scarlet fever, they would have had to stay at home if I did, so it was decided that I would go to Soho, an isolation hospital in a nearby city.

Except for the last month of my pregnancy years later, that month in Soho was the longest month of my life. After the first day I felt perfectly fine but was nevertheless confined to bed. Radio programs were piped into the room, and I looked forward to hearing "Singin' Sam" every day. Other than than the music, there was nothing on the radio that interested me. The wall facing the hall was glass, and the entrance to the room was through a private bathroom. No one but doctors and nurses could enter. Visitors had to stand outside the glass wall and try to communicate with raised voices or motions. Church members sent me toys, but the days were interminable.

My first roommate—black, of course—was a young married woman named Gertrude. We got along fine, and our conversations were my salvation. She was probably impressed with her precocious roommate and later came to visit me at home. After Gertrude left, my new roommate was a younger child with whom conversation was impossible. When our meals came, I took it on myself to teach her proper table manners and in other ways boss her around. When the month finally ended, I had to leave all the toys behind because they were contaminated. I left the room by way of the bathroom where I was given a special decontaminating bath and freshly washed clothing from home.

I have no childhood snapshots of myself smiling. I'd like to blame that on the sun, my eyes having always been extremely sensitive to bright light. But I seldom felt like smiling. I was very withdrawn and didn't speak to people as enthusiastically as Mama thought I should. "These people are your bread and butter," she reminded me. "Speak to them as if you mean it." As if to counteract my somber expression, as a teenager I began one poem, "I smile because I can smile."

Almost all of my early poems were melancholy. I felt as if I had the weight of the world on my shoulders. Sometimes I got blamed for something I didn't do. Clarence, whom my mother sometimes called Mouth Almighty, could always outtalk me, making me appear guilty for something he had done, and I was the one who got punished. I still have a penciled note I once wrote. One side reads: "Beware the running away of Naomi Long sometimes [*sic*] in the latter part of July." Everything except my name was printed, my name written in cursive. The other side of this small piece of paper, written in cursive, reads: "Beware! A person that treats one child as a dog and the others as angels from heaven!" My mother saved it, probably thinking it was cute. I can laugh at it now, but it wasn't funny then. At another time I wrote Dad a note trying to explain to him how misunderstood and excluded I felt. He didn't understand what I was trying to say and told me I should have been more grate-

65

ful since I was so much better off during those hard times than most of the other black people we knew. I began to think of my parents as repressive and suppressive. My frustration spilled out into a poem I wrote in my middle teens that begins, "I have learned to be silent."

My brothers teased me mercilessly. One summer day Wil told me he would give me a dime if I walked to the corner to Kolb's filling station and brought back a pint of pigeon's milk. Taking the bait, I walked the few doors toward William Street and told the owner what I wanted. He informed me there was no such thing. I went back home demanding the promised dime. Wil wouldn't pay me since I hadn't brought back what he sent me for. When I cried, Dad made him pay me the dime anyhow. Then Wil cried and Dad gave him another dime to comfort him.

When Helen, Sadie and I shared the front bedroom on the third floor, my brothers padlocked the door to the back room, used mainly for storage but now claimed as their "club house," making sure Helen and I couldn't gain access to it. Once they crept through the crawl space from the back room to the front, making strange noises and frightening us. When we followed them to Walter Purcell's house next door, they tied us both to a bed post in his bedroom to keep us from tagging along.

At the far end of Walter's yard was a lumber company where Barrett's yard ended. A lot of scrap lumber ended up behind our garage or was easily accessible near the building entrance. One year Walter and my brothers gathered enough of this wood to build a small house in our back yard. It had three tiny rooms with ceilings high enough for a grown man to stand comfortably. It also had three doors, including a trap door on top. The boys put locks on all of them to keep me out. It was their second club house, and I was not a member. On one or two occasions when Dad's friend from Long Island, the Rev. A.A. Graham, came to visit, he played cops and robbers with the boys, running across the top of the house in the process. It was well enough built to bear his weight. Eventually they got tired of it and tore it down.

Mama was so tired after a long day's work that she usually went upstairs shortly after dinner. Left alone in the kitchen with my brothers while they washed and dried the dishes, I was constantly teased. If I tried to call my mother, they would drown out my voice with "Mama's in the sugar bowl." I doubt that she ever heard me but if she did, she was too tired to respond. Sometimes the boys tussled with me and grabbed me by my wrists. I eventually learned how to protect myself by letting my fingernails grow long. When one of them grabbed me, I managed to turn my wrists and scratch him on his forearm, sometimes drawing blood. When I learned how to retaliate, Wil left me alone, but Clarence continued for a while. Once when he was washing dishes, he turned around and threw a glassful of water all over my dress. I took all the clean spoons from their container on the table and threw them at him, one by one. In time he realized that I wasn't going to take the teasing anymore and stopped.

While Helen was there, she took as much of the teasing as I did, so I wasn't alone. When she and Sadie left and moved to Richmond, I was devastated. It was then that I wrote, "The Reason Why I'm Lonely." When Dad was preparing to go to Europe, I wrote another poem that expressed my fear for his safety. The Atlantic Ocean seemed so wide, and I couldn't bear the thought that the ship might sink. I kept on writing more and more poems, counting as I wrote. By the time I was twelve, I had written one hundred. Then I stopped counting. Among the first hundred, "Welfare Days" reflected my concern about the Depression although my knowledge was related more to dinner table discussions and church members who brought their problems to the parsonage than to personal inconvenience. I was aware of strange men coming to the back door begging for food or money, but I had no personal sense of being poor ourselves.

Several times Dad took me to Newark with him to watch the Negro League play baseball, but I wasn't interested in sitting through the game and he left me in the park to play on the swings and slides by myself. There were other children there, but I didn't know them. It was a safer time then when children could be left alone.

A number of my poems appeared in the mimeographed Ashland School paper. When my brothers were in high school, one of Clarence's classmates selected poems for the "Poet's Corner" in the *Orange Daily Courier*. Clarence showed him one of mine, "My Choice," which he included in 1936. This was my first published poem except for those in the school paper.

I was so fond of books that I made my own out of folded sheets of paper held together with safety pins. If staplers existed then, I didn't know anything about them. My short life of crime began with a stolen notebook. East Orange schools provided all the books and supplies for their students. They were kept in a closet in each classroom. I liked the lined notebooks because they had no printing on the covers, unlike those available at the five and ten cents store. Since it was important for me to put my own title on the cover, I stole a school notebook for my own writing. I got caught and punished, but I was allowed to keep the notebook in which I had already written. Another of my crimes was stealing walnuts out of an open barrel at the National Store where Mama shopped. When we returned home, I gave myself away by keeping my hands behind me. She asked me what I was hiding and I said, "Nothing." When she insisted that I open my hands, she saw the stolen nuts and marched me right back to the store where I had to return them and tell the clerk what I had done. Dad often used Luden's cough drops which he shared with me. If I wanted to buy candy from the confectionery on Park Avenue, I would tell him I wanted money for cough drops. Once, though, I didn't eat all the candy and brought some of it home. Caught again! I finally decided crime didn't pay.

In addition to poems, I typed my own newspaper. It was after the kidnapping of Charles Lindbergh's infant son. I didn't know how to spell his last name, so I avoided it by referring to "the poor Lindy baby," saying that the "kops" and "nerses" were doing all they could to find the missing child. Clarence never let me forget that article and my misspellings.

I was fully aware of the prejudice in East Orange and often experienced it first hand. Dad subscribed to the Norfolk *Journal and Guide* and discussed articles in it at the dinner table, and since he always included "the Scottsboro boys" in his prayer, I learned about racial injustice on a national level. I became a fourth grade rebel. I stopped saluting the flag and refused to repeat the Pledge of Allegiance. Eventually I began to realize that the rage I felt was more destructive to me than to those responsible for it and that "building in salt is no better than building in sand." I learned that I couldn't change attitudes through hatred and found more productive ways of dealing with racial problems. While some of my mature poems are more overtly racial in content, few of the early ones are as direct as "On Democracy," written when I was a high school freshman.

Irving Washington, a high school friend of my brothers, taught me how to scan a poem, that is, determine the pattern of the rhyme and rhythm. I was doing a pretty good job of writing traditional poetry following the pattern of other poems I had read, but he taught me how to write it better. By the time I reached high school, I had become a prolific poet and knew that I would spend the rest of my life writing.

The Southern North

Anyone who has moved to East Orange since World War II or who visits today would never recognize it as the hometown I knew. The population has grown considerably to make it the second largest city in New Jersey, which at that time had less than 70,000 residents, a minority of them black. As the city has grown, the ethnicity of its citizens has changed. The large majority of the population is now black, with a sizable representation from Haiti and other areas of the Caribbean. Mayor Bowser and his family belonged to our church when we lived there.

Sandwiched between Newark and Orange, it was undoubtedly one of the most racist cities of the North. While a few African Americans were hired as teachers in Newark and Orange, there were none in East Orange. In fact, there were no black employees in any capacity in the entire school system. Newspaper clippings that my father saved indicate that he and several other influential black men tried to persuade the Board of Education to hire at least one black teacher, but the only condition under which the board would consider it was if she or he taught an all black class at Ashland School. That was not acceptable. It was not until 1944 after we had left that East Orange hired its first black teacher. I was not aware at the time but have since learned that completely separate schools for black and white students were legal in the southern part of the state, but East Orange was not in that region.

My brothers and I attended Ashland Grammar School at 450 Park Avenue, four blocks from where we lived. In recent years it was destroyed by fire and has not been rebuilt. East Orange schools went from kindergarten through eighth grade; there were no junior high or middle schools, and East Orange High School was the only senior high school in the city. At Ashland, each grade was divided into an *A, B*, and *C* division. The *A* division of each grade had one or no

70

black students, the *B* had perhaps six or seven, and the rest of the black and Italian students were relegated to the *C* division. Clarence had started school before we moved to New Jersey and was placed in the *C* division of the second grade. Wil was probably in first grade and was placed in *1B*. After a year in kindergarten I was promoted to *1A* where I would remain the only black student in my class through the eighth grade. It has always been a mystery to me what criteria were used to place us in different categories. It certainly wasn't based on intelligence or our ability to learn.

When I was in fifth grade, the girls in all three divisions met together for health class. The *5B* teacher who taught the class seated all the black girls in the same row next to the windows. When I mentioned this arrangement at home, Dad visited the class and protested. The teacher refused to make a change, and for the rest of the year I was excused from attendance and sat in my homeroom alone.

Clarence missed a significant part of one year due to illness. Since we didn't have semesters, he was held back a year, so Wil caught up with him, and they graduated from Ashland in 1933 and entered high school in the same class. When they came home and reported that the high school swimming classes were segregated, my father and several other community leaders protested. Instead of making a change, the administrators closed the pool, preventing any swimming at all. The pool has never reopened. Some years after we left, an addition was built onto the original building, still without a pool. I was interested to read a reference to the closing of the pool at East Orange High in Stephen Roth's novel, *The Human Stain*, but he placed it at a later date than the actual year, 1933. But then, he wasn't born until 1933. East Orange High has now been scheduled for demolition and two elementary schools will be built on the site. A new high school will be erected on the campus of Upsala College, now closed.

Many of the black high school students that we knew from church worked for white families after school as mothers' helpers or part-time maids. They graduated from high school but only a few attended college. Higher education was not a tradition in their families, and after all, it was the middle of the Depression. Those few who did graduate from college were unable to find employment at home because of their race. People who had earned degrees in education were forced to move to other cities and states to practice their profession. The problem was particularly acute for young black male college graduates who, if they were able to find jobs at all, were forced to work as waiters or porters on the railroad or do whatever menial work was available at home.

But I must say that, in spite of the racism apparent throughout the city, the educational system was excellent. All the grammar I have ever known I learned by the time I graduated from grammar school, and the black students in the *C* division had a better command of the language than many of their parents, spoke well, and wrote beautiful letters in standard English. Reading one of their letters or hearing them speak, one would assume that they had college degrees. How I wish that the so-called educated television anchors and college English majors today were as well grounded in the written and spoken word as the products of East Orange schools were!

Irving Washington's father was a "Mohammedan" and wore a long beard. I never met him but I sometimes saw him passing our house; Irving looked just like him. After Irving's mother's death, his father had remarried and had other children. Irving and his stepmother didn't get along, and he felt like an outsider in the family, so he came to our house after school and spent all his afternoons there. Irving was a good-looking brownskin young man who was very personable and multitalented. He had a wonderful tenor voice and exceptional stage presence; he won most of the Saturday amateur contests at the Ormont Theater in East Orange. He was also a very good artist, and he wrote impressive poetry, too. We enjoyed sharing each other's work. Irving was so well liked by all the students, black and white, that many of them wanted him to run for Student Council. The authorities would not even permit his name to be entered on the ballot.

The Ormont was located on Main Street. When black patrons attended movies there, they were ushered upstairs to the balcony. This kind of segregation was illegal, but it was practiced in East Orange anyhow. If an adult insisted on speaking to the manager and demanding his rights, he would be permitted to sit on the main floor, but most adults, arriving shortly before the movie was to begin, didn't take the time or trouble to protest, and children's pleas would have been ignored. On one occasion, my class went to the Ormont on a field trip to see a particular movie, and all the way there I wondered if I was going to be separated from my classmates and sent to the balcony alone. I wasn't. That was the only time I ever sat on the main floor.

Next door to the theater was an ice cream parlor with several tables and chairs. An African American could order ice cream at the counter and take it out but was not allowed to sit at a table to eat. Knowing that, our family friend, Elizabeth Allen, with me in tow, once ordered several quarts or gallons of hand-dipped ice cream with widely mixed flavors in each container. After the boxes had been filled, she said, "Now we'll have a dish of chocolate to eat here." Of course, they would not allow that, so we walked out, leaving the unpaid for containers of mixed flavors on the counter, knowing they could not be resold.

My father had earned a Bachelor of Theology degree at Virginia Union University, but he was eager to continue his education. One of the major reasons he left the large and impressive Bank Street Baptist Church in Norfolk for little Calvary in East Orange was that he knew the educational opportunities were much better in the North.

The same year that we moved, 1925, he enrolled in Upsala College, a private Swedish college in East Orange, to pursue a Bachelor of Arts degree. Working full time and supporting a wife and three children, he was nevertheless a diligent student. When he completed his degree requirements, he was the highest ranking student and the first Negro to graduate. The president of the college, Dr. Carl G. Erickson, called him into his office and informed him that he would not be permitted to make the valedictory address, and if he insisted, the college would never admit another Negro student. My father was willing to let another person make the address and didn't want to be responsible for denying other black students an opportunity to attend college locally, but he insisted that he be given credit on the commencement program for his achievement. That was done. I can't imagine why any of his classmates would have objected to his making the speech, for their comments in his yearbook were full of praise. One classmate who signed himself "Joe" wrote: "You have helped me to command a deeper and more lasting respect toward your race, Reverend. Good luck to you!" Another wrote, "To one who deserves all credit of genius." Still another: "To the Socrates of history class." And another: "If I succeed as well as you have, I will be satisfied. Much success for the future." And there were indications that some had shared good times with him outside of class. So many complimentary remarks from his classmates! How did they feel about the injustice done to him? Were they aware of it before the ceremony took place? Possibly not. But if they were, where were the protests?

Coincidentally, Philip Roth's protagonist in *The Human Stain*, Coleman Silk, was light-skinned like my father and went through a similar experience although at a later time and on another educational level. He was the first black valedictorian at East Orange High School and was offered a bribe to do poorly on his two weakest subjects so that someone else could be given the honor. Stubbornly he refused the bribe, making fictional history as my father had done in real life in 1928 at Upsala College. In spite of this incident, Dad sent contributions to the college all of his life, and when he died, his obituary appeared in the Upsala newspaper—without mention, of course, of the incident concerning the valedictory address.

Ashland School had a stable student body. Many who began first grade with me also remained in the same class to graduate. There were some newcomers, of course, and a few of the students moved away. Somewhere along the way, the family of one of my classmates, Nate Cartmell, moved to an estate in another city. His mother sent an invitation to visit their home to all the students who had been in his class when he left. When this announcement was made in class, I wondered if I would be included. When the teacher read off the names, mine was one. Different parents agreed to drive several children in their cars. I was assigned to ride with Mae Jean Ehrman's mother, who would not let me come inside their apartment although I could play with Mae outside on the sidewalk. I can only guess what her thoughts were when I climbed in. When we arrived at the estate with its great rolling hills and I emerged from the car, Nate's mother hugged me and told me she was glad I had come. I felt really welcome and felt even better when I caught a fly ball playing baseball with my classmates.

When I was in fifth grade a contest was held to determine who did the best job reciting a poem. My mother helped me select a poem to memorize from her normal school elocution book. Public recitation was fairly common to me because of my experiences at church. I memorized the poem, but that wasn't enough. Mama drilled me and drilled me in speaking clearly and putting expression into my presentation. When the big day came, I was thoroughly prepared. As I listened to each of the other fifth graders recite, my confidence grew. I didn't feel that any of their performances measured up to mine. But when the judges announced the first, second, third, and fourth place winners, I was not one of them. My fifth grade teacher, a Quaker, told my mother afterwards, "Everybody knows Naomi won first prize."

I was always excellent in reading and English without even trying. I hated math, never could understand long division, and always got low marks in it, but I evidently did well enough otherwise to remain in the *A* division. Still I was aware that I didn't always receive the credit I had earned in other endeavors. One of my teachers told my mother that I could do better but didn't try hard enough. What was the point in trying harder when I was so often denied credit for my achievements?

Some of the teachers permitted racial jokes in class, and one did her best to ignore me. When we studied American history and got to the issue of slavery, I wanted to go through the floor. The often repeated lie that slavery was benign, that Negroes were lazy and incompetent and that they were lucky to have been saved from savagery by kindly masters made me cringe. My fourth grade teacher, who seated me in the back row next to the least capable boy in the class, contributed to my rebellion. Although I didn't particularly like the study of current events, I got a heavy dose of them at home at the dinner table. I knew about the lynchings and racial injustices practiced in this country and around the world. I also knew about Haile Selassie in Ethiopia and the achievements of African Americans and their contributions to the building of this country and its culture. I knew that I was being shortchanged in my formal education.

In sixth grade we studied ancient history. My father had spent the summer before touring Europe, Egypt, and the Holy Land, taking moving pictures everywhere he went. When we were studying Egypt, how proud I was when my teacher said I could show his film in class! To know that all my classmates were watching my father riding on a camel in front of the Great Pyramid was a tremendous delight. I also gained great pleasure whenever Joe Louis won a fight and everybody at school was talking about it. These victories somewhat soothed the sting of the negative aspects of school life.

On the positive side, we took field trips to the planetarium and the museums in New York, as well as the Edison laboratory where the father of one of my classmates was employed.

I got along well with the girls in my class. I shared my poems with one named Helen who made helpful comments. I was invited to a birthday party at Virginia Petersen's house and talked to Carmen Boom whose mother and my mother had attended some of the same meetings at the Lincoln Settlement. Some of the boys were all right, too. I fell secretly in love with John Brohm and liked Leonard Dunlap who lived across the street from the school. Ramsey Forbush, whose father was a minister, was nice, too. But some of the others were not. When we were in the early grades and the boys and girls had gym classes together, the girls were once instructed to choose boys for their folk dancing partners. I chose John. Two boys who were cousins chided him and tried to discourage him from dancing with me. I don't remember if he did or not.

In spite of getting along well, I knew I was different. I stood out like a sore thumb. I don't think there was a single teacher in the school who didn't know me by name. Once in a while the difference was nice. For special occasions my mother sometimes let me wear my hair "loose" (unbraided). One of the girls felt it and asked me how I got it so soft. But usually the awareness of difference had a negative effect on me. Some of my classmates were from well-to-do families. Patricia Whelan, for one, was sometimes driven to school by the family's chauffeur. Richard Hamilton's family spent every winter in Florida, and I assume he had a tutor during the months he was gone. Another boy and his family visited Belgium during the school year at a time when only the rich, with few exceptions, went overseas.

I felt particularly comfortable with Margaret Knabe, a newcomer. We talked a great deal but never visited each other's homes. She told me that her parents were prejudiced against Negroes, but she apparently didn't share their views. Another newcomer was Leah Cohen. I didn't realize until much later how many of my classmates were Jewish; I didn't recognize them by their names, even when it was announced that Evelyn Levine's last name had been changed to Lavin and a similar announcement was made regarding another classmate's name change. But Leah's ethnicity was unmistakable. Her parents, who spoke with a thick Eastern European accent, bought and operated a confectionery between my house and the school and built an addition in the back for living quarters. Leah was a round-faced girl with long blond curls. She drew fashions and wanted to be a designer. On my way to school I often stopped by the store to pick her up. Her parents were always nice to me. We usually walked home together. I think we became best friends because we both felt like outsiders. After a year or so, they moved to California. I missed her.

The music teacher, Mrs. Meredith, a widow with a young daughter named Ruthie, came to our classroom about twice a week. We sang songs from "the brown book" and "the green book" mostly, but we sang songs from sheet music, too, accompanied on the piano by the 5C teacher whom Clarence particularly liked. I didn't realize that some of the selections were Confederate songs about the joy of being "way down South in Dixie" We also sang a popular song called "Lazy Bones." The cover of the sheet music showed a picture of a Negro with his hat pulled over his face slumped against a tree dozing. When the school was planning to put on an operetta, Mrs. Murdock asked for volunteers to sing in it. Leah and I were among those who raised their hands. She selected all of the volunteers except Leah and me. Later, evidently not having gotten enough volunteers, she asked again, and this time we were chosen. When my mother attended the performance, she said she couldn't at first find me among the white students, I had been made up so well to look white.

With all the protest today to words, "under God" in the Pledge of Allegiance, it is difficult to understand how the principal got away with having chapel services two or three days a week in the auditorium, but Dr. Hollingshead read the Scripture at these services and we sang hymns along with secular songs. I don't know if all the Scripture was from the Old Testament, but I have since wondered how the Jewish students must have felt when the hymns were sung. Apparently their feelings were ignored as much as those of African Americans in other situations.

One year several of my classmates invited me to attend their Girl Scout meeting which was held at the troop leader's home. They wanted me to join their troop and I was eager to oblige. The troop leader was concentrating that day on how to make up a bed with hospital corners. She looked at me and said, "But you already know how to do this, don't you." I answered yes since one of my few chores at home was to make up my bed. I didn't realize at the time the implication of her comment. She assumed that my mother was a domestic servant for some white family and that I was being groomed for the same future. When the time came to discuss my joining the troop, she told me I would have to join the colored one that met across town. Since I was not yet riding public transportation alone and didn't know anyone in that neighborhood, I never became a Girl Scout.

When it was time for my class to graduate, the teacher asked for the names of all the students in my class whose fathers were ministers. Teachers in the other divisions asked their students, too. Altogether there were four, three in *8A*, including my father. The principal knew my father very well because I was the third child in my family to attend Ashland. Dad had spoken to Dr. Hollingshead on numerous occasions, sometimes selling him tickets to concerts at our church. He knew that Dad was an intelligent, well-spoken, educated man who now held an M.A. from Drew University and an honorary degree from Virginia Union University. Nevertheless, the other three ministers, all white, participated in the graduation ceremony, but my father was excluded.

By the time we graduated, I could see the climate changing. We had reached the age of interest in the opposite sex, and friendships across racial boundaries had begun to decrease. Walter Purcell, our former white next door neighbor who had once been inseparable from my brothers, now walked past our house without speaking and looking the other way.

The curriculum in East Orange has probably gone through many changes since we were there, as it has nationally. While education has advanced in science and technology, instruction in liberal arts has sharply declined. With all its faults, the schools of this northern southern city offered a better education in my time than I would have received in many other places.

Two Worlds

I grew up in two worlds, week days and Sundays. Week days meant white teachers and classmates and the people in our neighborhood. Our neighborhood was stable and racially mixed. When we first moved to East Orange, two elderly white sisters lived next door. Between the houses was a back gate that was freely used for brief visits. When these ladies moved, they gave my mother two lovely antique vases (which they pronounced "vahses") that Mama always treasured. The new occupants were also white, the Purcell family whose son Walter was inseparable from my brothers. Mrs. Purcell sometimes had Easter egg hunts in her back yard and, since I was small, she'd hint to me where some of the eggs were hidden. Two doors down in the other direction lived a white lady we often saw but didn't know. We nicknamed her "Pink Hat." Diagonally across the street was an elderly white lady who remained in her house until her son finally had to move her. There were pockets of white and black families scattered throughout the neighborhood. Across Park Avenue was a black neighborhood that included streets like Edgerton Terrace where Margaret Ross lived. We were the same age, but I never saw her at school after kindergarten because she was in the *C* division. Many of our church members lived on the other side of town on Sussex Avenue, Steuben and Halsted streets. My brothers' playmates included black boys named "Stinky" Davis, Larry Allen, and St. Clair and Raphael Delaney ("Saint" and "Ray"), twins from the South who lived in the corner house with the aunt who was raising them. There were other people in the neighborhood with nicknames like "Bo Peep" and "Chicken Bones." In addition to Walter, my brothers' white playmates included two brothers who lived in Barrett's house, nicknamed "Red" and "Whitey" because of their hair color. I was the only girl in the block so I was always tagging along after my brothers, often sitting on the fence to watch them play in Barrett's yard. I was a good enough tomboy to play tackle with them in our own yard when they would let me, and I could climb the pear tree as well as they did, putting my foot in the knothole where I could get a good grip. Sometimes I roller skated alone. I knew every seam in the slate sidewalk and where the roots of a tree buckled it. All the boys called me "Prete." Wil said that when I was little I used to raise my hand as Dad did in church when he pronounced the benediction, so he nicknamed me "Preacher," which was later shortened.

On Sundays I moved in the world of church. It was my opportunity to enjoy being an African American among my own kind without the baggage of being "the only one" in a sea of white faces. It was at church that I met my black friends whom I didn't see during the week. Some lived across town and attended other schools, so the only time I saw them was Sunday. It was at church that I felt most at home

Being the preacher's kid, I enjoyed special attention that I didn't get at school. Some of the children I knew admired my soft hair worn in three braids that were longer than their straightened uncurled hair that was too short to braid. They made me feel like a little princess. Adults, too, favored me as the minister's only little girl. I grew accustomed to their adoration and being set apart as someone special. But sometimes when we were invited to dinner at a member's home, we sat at the dining room table with the adults while the children in the host's family ate in the kitchen. I didn't feel comfortable with this arrangement. I preferred to be with the other children.

For a while my brothers and I sat in church with Mama. During the singing of hymns we sometimes changed the words under our breath. "It was there by faith I received my sight, / And now I am happy all the day" became "It was there by chance that I tore my Sunday pants / And now I wear my old ones every day." We would crack up and cause Mama to nudge us in the ribs. We found a lot of things funny and got frequent nudges or severe disapproving looks.

Eventually Clarence and Wil deserted their seats to sit with friends.

The deacons sat in special swivel chairs in front, and the same few people sat in "the amen corner," several rows to the left that ran perpendicular to the other seats. To the right was the choir stand with the organ in front of it. The first organist and choir director I remember was Albert Tillery. He was replaced by Henry Smith who came to our house once a week to give us piano lessons. We had only one choir which I thought was excellent. I learned my love of language from the words of familiar hymns, anthems, and spirituals they sang and from the composition of my father's sermons.

Sunday school was held before the eleven o'clock service. All the classes were held in various areas of the one large room in the basement. My first teacher, Mrs. Rosa Clark, whose husband sang bass in the choir, always brought raisins to pass out to the children. I didn't know what to do with them since I never liked raisins. I tried to conceal them in my hand until I could find some place to throw them away. At the end of the lessons, Mr. John Early, the superintendent, who always pronounced my name "NAY-oh-MY," would make some announcements and comments and then dismiss us to go upstairs for the regular service. Mrs. Clark sat in the row in front of us and slept through much of the sermon, but even in sleep, she continued to nod her head as if in agreement.

My father occasionally called the young people who hadn't been baptized to the front row where he tried to coerce them into accepting Christ. Several times I was one of those who continued to sit unmoved. Eventually, when I was eight years old, I reasoned that I might as well stand and get it over with since he was going to pester me until I did. My "conversion" was a matter of expedience rather than a change of heart. In fact, there was nothing to change. I don't remember any time in my life when I became "converted." I had been born into a Christian family and had never known anything different. My parents lived their Christianity with moral behavior and integrity, and I simply accepted their beliefs and values without question. I was a child "trained up" in Christian doctrine, and have never departed from it.

When it was time for baptism, a ceremony that took place during the Sunday service after the sermon, the pulpit furniture was removed and the floor that covered the pool was taken off. Dad wore waist-high boots and a robe as he entered the pool from the left side. (He didn't begin wearing a robe in the pulpit until years later.) There were about four steps down into the water, and those who were to be baptized, dressed in white robes, entered the pool from the front and, after being baptized, exited through the door at the right, wet material clinging to their bodies.

There were several children to be baptized with me. We were supposed to be arranged by height, the shortest one going first. But because I was the preacher's kid, Mrs. Clark put me at the head of the line even though there were others shorter than I. In baptizing, Dad clasped the person's hands together in his left hand and put his right hand on the person's back. Then he would say, "In the name of the Father, the Son, and the Holy Ghost" and on the "Amen" he doused him in the water and raised him back up. We always giggled when we saw women emerging from the pool, especially the ones with ample behinds. When he baptized children, he whispered to them to hold their noses between their clenched hands, but he either forgot to tell me that or assumed that I already knew I should do it, but I didn't, so a lot of water went up my nose and I came up coughing. I didn't feel any more saved then than I did before, but at least the dreaded ritual was over and now I could take Communion.

I liked the way the adults at church talked, often not in standard English but with picturesque expressions and the soft accents of their native South. Many of their week day jobs, if they were lucky enough to have them, required subservience, but in the black church everybody had the same opportunity to be important. They could dress in their best clothes and participate in any activities they chose as equals. They could don white uniforms and serve as ushers, teach

Sunday school, sing in the choir, be called on to pray, be deacons or other officers, and cast an equal vote in church meetings. They were free to express themselves, let off the steam of frustration from the week before, comment during Dad's sermons in the call and response tradition of the southern black church, and speak freely about their problems and blessings during the informal beginning of the Communion service or at any other time they chose.

Except for the family, the black church has always been and still is the most powerful and significant institution in African American society. It was no accident that the Civil Rights Movement evolved from the black church and was led by its ministers.

I consider it a tremendous loss that many of today's black church choirs have lost interest in preserving our musical history, ignoring the Negro spirituals that W.E.B. DuBois called "the sorrow songs" and the traditional gospel music by composers like Thomas A. Dorsey and Lucie Campbell. I am not moved by the hollering of much of the contemporary gospel music with barely discernible, repetitious, often meaningless words and with the swaying and clapping carefully choreographed rather than spiritually felt. I regret, too, that in some black churches, the elders are no longer honored but are largely ignored and put out to pasture. That is indeed a cultural loss. I am aware that the future of the church depends upon the young who need to be encouraged and trained early to participate, but not to the exclusion of the elderly from whom they could learn so much. There needs to be more interaction between the generations; otherwise, the blind are merely leading the blind.

As a result, children run through the church whooping and hollering as if they were on a playground. At one time older members felt free to advise them that such behavior was not acceptable in the house of the Lord, but that time has sadly passed. The church building has become as common as a park, and young parents who see nothing wrong with this behavior would be offended if an older person tried to advise their children. The loss of continuity and tradition in the black church has weakened its importance in our culture at a time when we are more in need of "a solid rock" than ever before in our history.

Discord in Paradise

When the woman I will call Mrs. Rowell died just before reaching the age of 102, someone in East Orange sent me her funeral program. When I read her obituary it was hard to believe that this saintly old mother of the church was the same woman I remembered. She was extolled for her example and good works as deaconess, trustee, and participant in many other church activities. The obituary did not mention her last name when she first came to East Orange from Norfolk, Virginia or her being a soloist in the choir. I still associate the hymn, "I'm Going Through," with her. Nor did it mention the forced interruption in her membership at Calvary Baptist Church in the Thirties. But most of the people who knew her then are dead, and those still living have probably forgotten the long-ago past, overshadowed by more recent acts. Several years ago when she was already 100 and living in a nursing home, one of the old-timers did tell me that she was really a character in her old age, suggesting that some of the old mischief I remember was still there.

Dad had known her family in Norfolk, so when he read in the *Journal and Guide* that Mrs. Rowell had killed her husband, he clipped the article. I don't know the circumstances, and, as far as I know, Dad never revealed this information except to the family. I assume that the killing was considered justified and that she never was convicted of a crime, but I don't know.

It was after that that she moved to East Orange in 1927, two years after we did. Mrs. Rowell became close friends with another member of the church, whom I'll call Mrs. Taylor. Both of them were particularly friendly with our family, often giving us gifts together with cards signed, "from Rowell and Taylor." Mrs. Rowell was especially fond of me. When I returned to Calvary many years later as the Women's Day speaker, she reminded me that my first night spent away from home was in her apartment. During my childhood she gave me many toys, some of which must have been quite expensive, considering the times. She was considered such a close family friend that one summer we took her with us for a few days to Long Branch. Since there were no hotels available for African Americans, we stayed in a rooming house owned by another black church. Mrs. Rowell and I shared a bed. In order to get to the bathroom, we had to go through my parents' room. My mother slept on the inside next to the wall with Dad on the outside. Mrs. Rowell had gotten up at some time during the night to use the bathroom. When Dad got up the next morning, he found a twenty dollar bill on the floor. He mentioned it to my mother, chiding her for her carelessness. Her response was, "Where would I get twenty dollars?" He later returned the money to Mrs. Rowell cautioning her, "Sister Rowell, you need to be more careful with your money; these are hard times."

I wasn't aware of this incident but was told about it when I was an adolescent. I don't know at what point Mama became suspicious, but the friendship between Rowell and Taylor cooled, and Mama started supervising my play with the toys Mrs. Rowell had given me, making sure they didn't get broken, and putting them away when I lost interest in them. When her suspicion became awareness of Mrs. Rowell's intentions, she packed up the toys and had them returned to her. That act signified a declaration of war. Years later, when I mentioned these events to an older woman, she told me that everybody knew Mrs. Rowell was seeking my father's attentions and was trying to get to him through me.

There were several other church members who became enemies. One was an officer who handled money. Dad had caught him with his hand in the till and exposed him. When Dad received an anonymous letter in the mail, typed on a torn half sheet of paper, he suspected that it was from this disgruntled officer whom I will call Mr. Slate. Mr. Slate and his brother, who was not a member of Calvary, owned a thriving business. One day when Dad knew that Mr. Slate was not on the premises, he went to his place of business and asked his brother if he could use the office typewriter. On the desk he found the other half of the sheet of paper on which the anonymous letter had been written. He typed a copy of it and found the same filled-in *e* and slightly turned *t* that were in the original. I don't know what he did with this information, but it proved the identity of the writer.

Another friend-turned-enemy was Mr. Moses, the chairman of the deacon board, who lived in a rooming house about three blocks down the street from us. In the past Dad had encouraged the church to pay him a little something to take care of our furnace before my brothers were old enough to do it. When Deacon Moses started going blind, Dad drove the three blocks out of his way to pick him up and drive him to church, returning him home after the service. The only reason I can think of for his change was that Mrs. Rowell, whom he called his "honeydew," had turned him against us, but there may be more to the story that I don't know.

One Saturday night when Dad was preparing his sermon for the next day, Deacon Moses' landlady called Dad to tell him that the deacon and his guest, who turned out to be Mr. Slate, were carrying on a loud conversation that she could hear from the hall and that he should come and listen to it. Dad went and stood silently outside the door listening as they talked negatively about him. When they started talking about my mother, he knocked on the door and said, "You can talk about me all you want, but if you say another word about my wife, I'll sue you."

There were two other men in the church who were marginal. We children were fully aware of what was going on, and we knew how to speak to the enemies politely and smile when we encountered them. My brothers nicknamed one of them "the weasel." The other man disliked Dad for reasons I don't know and, years later, when the church celebrated a major anniversary, his written report of my father's contributions purposely neglected most of what he had done for the church during our thirteen years there.

These negative forces converged when we started receiving more anonymous letters written by hand. At least one of them threatened our lives and warned us to leave town by a certain date or suffer the consequences. Mama recognized the handwriting as Mrs. Rowell's from signed notes and cards she had sent during friendlier times. My brothers and I were forbidden to eat candy or any other food outside our home, and we were never left alone in the house. Even fruit with the skin on it was not exempt. When one of my mother's Saturday night visitors cautioned, "Look for pinholes," we laughed at her, but we later realized that an apple or orange could be poisoned by injection without being detected. When the family went out at night, we always left lights on.

This hostility originated with only a handful of members. Following the threat on our lives and the ultimatum that we leave town, some action became necessary. A special church meeting was called. In the midst of the Depression, Dad paid a handwriting expert fifty dollars to compare Mrs. Rowell's signed and unsigned letters and testify that they were written by the same person. I didn't know it then, but things had reached the point that either Dad or Mrs. Rowell would be dismissed from the church.

The majority of the church members were good people, the salt of the earth, and they adored my parents. Dad had baptized their children, gotten some of them out of jail on his word, advised them, encouraged them, taught them, and provided the incentive for the church to send several of them to college. He was always stressing the need for education, and he was friendly and approachable to everyone. These people knew him to be an honest man whom they respected and supported wholeheartedly. And my mother was the perfect preacher's wife, supportive of his work, friendly to everyone, confidante to some, and involved in the lives of many.

There was one member in particular, Lee Myrick, a gigantic, jet-black, double-jointed man with bloodshot eyes, who had been a sinner all his life. He and his wife lived on Jones Street, which was only one block long. Although Stephen Roth in his novel, *The*

Human Stain, described it as the center of black activity in East Orange, it was actually the only disreputable street in town containing at least one speakeasy. Mrs. Myrick, a church member, came to the parsonage periodically to report to Dad that her husband had beaten her, appealing for his help. Dad would go and talk to the abusive husband and get him to promise not to be violent again. But eventually she would come back saying, "Reverend, Lee beat me again last night," and again Dad would speak to the offender, no doubt trying to convert him to Christianity. Somewhere in the process Mr. Myrick gained so much respect for Dad that he became converted and joined the church. Dad had difficulty baptizing him because of his size. At church meetings he always sat on the first row, and if anyone raised his voice at Dad or spoke to him in what he considered a disrespectful manner, he would rise to his feet in a threatening manner and stay on his feet until Dad said, "Sit down, Brother Myrick; it's all right." He could have asked for no more faithful a protector. Every now and then he would backslide and abuse his wife again, but the occurrences were much fewer than before, and he was always repentant when Dad talked to him.

Most of the mature members of our church had migrated from the South and didn't have the benefit of a formal education. They didn't know parliamentary procedure, so as the decisive church meeting approached, Dad selected individuals to instruct. He told one person to make a motion to dismiss Mrs. Rowell from membership after the handwriting expert's testimony. He instructed another to immediately second the motion, and so on. He walked them through the whole process. Without this preparation, the enemies, who were better educated, and their supporters might have succeeded in getting my father voted out.

We children were not allowed to attend the meeting. Mama arranged for one of the male members of the church to stay at home with us with all the lights on. We were told that police were present outside the church, just in case. Everything went as planned, and the motion to dismiss Mrs. Rowell was passed with a vast majority supporting it.

After that, things in the church moved smoothly for several years. Dad received several offers to become the pastor of churches in other cities, and I became excited about the prospect of moving to Philadelphia, Columbus, or Richmond, but he was determined not to leave East Orange under a cloud. He eventually accepted an appointment as pastor of historic Central Baptist Church in St. Louis, established in 1847. On the Sunday that he announced his resignation, there were many tears and pleas for him to reconsider, but it was time to move on. The deacon whose "honeydew" had been dismissed stood up in front of the church and said, "Rev. Long wasn't what we wanted, but he was what we needed."

It was some time after we left East Orange that Mrs. Rowell returned to Calvary but evidently not to the choir. She later married a man who preceded her in death; it was only by his name that she is mentioned in her obituary which lists, among other contributions, her membership on the Trustee Board and the Building Fund Committee and her presidency of the Willing Workers Club and the Silver Leaf Club, one of the organizations Dad had organized years before.

Years later, reading the letter my grandfather had written to my father in 1909 when Dad was preparing to preach, I realized that he had taken his father's advice. "You must educate the people and not get down to their level." He discovered that much of what he had been taught about administering a church did not apply to black churches. The splits in black churches, which are still common today, are apparent in the names of the new spin-off churches—New, Second, Greater. Running a black church requires knowledge which a minister has to learn from experience. Churches may be considered a form of paradise on earth, but most of them are fraught with various kinds of discord at one time or another. When those times come, a black Baptist minister is on his own.

There was another member of Calvary who had her eyes on Dad after the Rowell incident. In 1936 Dad taught adult education classes sponsored by the WPA (Works Progress Administration), and this spinster lady, who lived in the next block, attended the classes, along with my mother. By now we were old enough to be left in the house alone. This lady would walk to our house and ride in the car with my parents to the building where the classes were held. She frequently requested Dad's advice on business matters, and when she came to the house to discuss such matters with him, she required privacy. Mama caught on to her intentions and began calling her "Madam X" behind her back.

Unwilling to give up, she moved to St. Louis shortly after we did and continued her visits to our house for a while. Suddenly the visits ended. I suspect that my mother discouraged her from coming back. I don't know if she returned to East Orange or not, but we never saw her again.

A man in the public eye who has a personal relationship with others—doctors, lawyers, ministers—is extremely susceptible to the attentions of women even though he doesn't encourage them. It takes a strong man not to be flattered by this admiration, and many succumb. But in many ways, Dad was an innocent man who didn't suspect people of ulterior motives. He loved my mother devotedly, and no one could ever convince me that he was ever unfaithful to her. I once heard him say that if he were ever to become interested in another woman, she would have to be more attractive, more intelligent, more loyal, and more caring and have more common sense than his wife, and he had never met such a woman. In spite of my two failed marriages, my strong belief in the institution is based on the successful relationship between my mother and father.

My parents at their fiftieth wedding anniversary

II.
The St. Louis Years

Changing Course

The train chugged into Union Station in St. Louis on a dismal, gray morning late in December, 1937. It was during the Christmas holidays, but I don't remember Christmas that year at all. Someone from the church met us and drove us to our new home, the parsonage at 4219W Finney Avenue. I had no idea what a brief interlude the coming years would be or that the change at that particular time of my life would be so significant.

The St. Louis parsonage in recent years

Our new home was a sturdy brick house with a few steps leading up to a small front porch. We entered the foyer through an extremely wide front door with heavy beveled glass in the upper portion. I was immediately impressed with what I saw—a much larger house than the one we had left. The spacious living room had parquet floors and a fireplace. The dining room looked out into the back yard and had a small utility room beside it. A butler's pantry connected the dining room to the kitchen. The wide staircase split at the landing, one section leading up to the second floor and the other to the kitchen. On the landing were two colorful stained glass windows.

Members of the church had already arranged the furniture before our arrival. The front bedroom belonged to my parents. A second smaller room on the front was Dad's study. The large middle room, which also had a fireplace, was intended for my brothers and their twin beds, but my double bed had been placed there instead, along with the secondhand desk Dad had bought, so this became my room. Clarence and Wil's room behind mine was smaller and narrower than mine. Each bedroom could be entered from the room or rooms connecting them, as well as from the hall where the one bathroom in the house was located.

From my bedroom I could look out both side windows, but there was nothing to see but the house next door. The back yard and garage were visible from the window in the back. There was no driveway and the only way to approach the garage was from the alley.

A door in the hall led to an unfinished attic. This was where Dad's first cousin, James Arthur from Victoria, Texas, slept for the two or three years he lived with us.

Soon after our arrival, a reporter and photographer of one of the two black weekly newspapers arrived to take a family picture, Mama and I sitting on the partially upholstered mahogany settee that was a part of my parents' original living room suite, Dad and my brothers standing behind us.

The granddaughters of the retired minister who had preceded my father, Rev. George Stevens, paid us an early visit. Felicia Rhetta took me to see Forest Park—its museum at the top of Art Hill, with a statue of the saint king on a horse outside; the lagoon at the bottom of the hill; the Municipal Opera, with seats built on a natural slope and a tree growing on the stage; the flower conservatory, and many other wonders that make it the most spacious and impressive urban park I have ever seen. Josephine Rhetta, her younger sister, was still a student at Sumner High School and a member of the Twelve Tops, a club of light-skinned girls, the darkest one of whom had naturally straight hair and was the daughter of one of the leading black undertakers. Jo invited my brothers and me to the Twelve Tops' annual ball held at the Carioca Ballroom with a real orchestra playing. The ball was by invitation only and was chaperoned by the girls' parents. The dress was formal.

I was totally unfamiliar with this kind of sophistication. I wore the best street-length dress I owned, reasoning that I could be forgiven since we had hardly had time to unpack. The idea of owning a formal gown was completely foreign to me, and I didn't know how to dance and wouldn't have been allowed to, even if I did. My brothers' only experience with dances was their high school senior prom which the black graduating seniors at East Orange High had held separately at the black YMCA in Orange. For this event they wore their best Sunday suits. I suppose the only reason we were allowed to go was that Dad might have felt that our refusal to accept the invitation from the former minister's granddaughter would have seemed an insult. Already I knew that even here, among my own people, I was still an outsider.

The dismal day of our arrival in the city turned out to be typical of St. Louis winters. I remember more gray days than sunny ones. And the camel's hair coat Mama had bought me in New York turned out to be a mistake. It was always at the cleaner's. There were no driveways where a coal truck could pull up and channel coal through a chute to the coal bin. And the coal itself was different from what we burned in East Orange. It was soft coal dumped on the side of the house. I don't recall how it reached the basement, but it produced an enormous amount of soot. Specks of it floated in the air, dotting everyone's face and clothing. A perpetual haze hung over the city. And the trees back east that turned yellow or red in the fall couldn't be found in St. Louis. Here they simply changed from green to brown.

After the Christmas holidays, on January 3, 1938, I enrolled at historic Charles Sumner High School, founded in 1874, located in "the Ville" on Cottage Avenue ten long blocks away from our house. The school was on the semester system, and the first semester of my freshman year would end in three or four weeks. Sumner was one of two all-black high schools in St. Louis, the other being Vashon. It was a much smaller school than East Orange High. As the only student entering at that odd time of the year, I found that all the students were aware of the new girl. By then I was wearing silk stockings and nicer clothing than I had worn in grammar school and was feeling less self-conscious about my appearance, even though the other girls wore bobby sox.

One day in the hall a nice-looking, well-dressed student introduced himself to me as Julian Witherspoon. I don't remember seeing him again except perhaps in passing in the hall as he was graduating in the January class. There was no way of predicting that our paths would cross again and he would change my life forever.

I had never seen so many young black people together in one place before. The students were friendly, introducing themselves and welcoming me. I appreciated their warmth, but I didn't feel quite at ease with some of them. Many of the students were from well-educated, professional, middle-class families, and I was not accustomed to black people like them.

At the end of one class period shortly after I entered, the bell rang and we gathered our books, impatiently waiting for the teacher to dismiss us. Then, leaving the room in controlled disorder, we went to the third floor auditorium to attend a National Honor Society induction ceremony. I sat in one of the two facing balconies that ran the length of the auditorium and waited for the other students to come in and take their seats.

As soon as everyone was settled, the house lights dimmed, and without any call for silence, the murmur of voices ceased. The band, that had already taken its place, began to play in subdued harmony, and I held my breath with anticipation.

First, one student came into view at the back of the auditorium and proceeded down the aisle toward the stage. Close behind followed about twelve or fifteen others, all carrying unlit torches. The boys were dressed in white shirts and trousers and maroon sweaters and the girls in identical maroon dresses with white collars and cuffs. As they ascended to the stage, the curtain opened to reveal the flame of a large torch in the center. The students arranged themselves in a semicircle around the torch. One student then recited a speech on scholarship. She was followed by others who spoke on character, service, and leadership. These attributes, I soon learned, were the basis on which students were selected every semester, in a very keen competition, for membership in Chapter 81 of the National Honor Society.

At some point, one of the inductees lit his torch from the large flame and passed on the fire to the student next to him and then to the next until all the torches were lit. The candles cast a warm glow over the darkened auditorium. The audience was absolutely silent, and I, who had never witnessed such a solemn and inspirational ceremony, was certainly one of the most affected observers.

After the students left the stage, the principal made some remarks. Following them, an unimpressive looking 16-year-old boy went to the stage and an accompanist to the piano. What followed was a baritone solo, "Through the Years" by Vincent Youmans, sung in a baritone voice such as I had never heard before. The singer's name was Robert McFerrin. Years later, during the 1950s, when I noticed a small item in the *Detroit Free Press* headed "Negro Makes Met," I knew even before I read it that it was Robert McFerrin.

Witnessing these two events in the same day was the turning

101

point of my life. Remembering what I had earned that I didn't receive credit for in East Orange, I looked down from that old balcony and said to myself, "Here's a place where you can be anything you're good enough to be," and from that point on, I took off running. My first goal was to be inducted into the National Honor Society.

Earning this honor required a great deal. One had to establish a record of leadership as an officer in one or more school organizations; serve the school by doing volunteer work such as helping in the office during free periods, accompanying one of the vocal groups, or working for a teacher; establish a record of good character; and maintain a high grade point average.

Several references made in biographical entries and articles make the assumption that, because Sumner was an all-black school, its curriculum was somewhat Afrocentric, but this was not true. I was assigned the same courses I had taken in East Orange, and the content was very much the same. When I arrived, the students in my English class were reciting memorized speeches from Shakespeare. Since I had already memorized two of them in East Orange, I was prepared to take my turn.

One day my English teacher, Mr. F. Luther Merry, asked me if I had read Homer's *Iliad* and *Odyssey*. I lied and answered that I had. I had indeed read the *Iliad*, but I had stopped attending classes at East Orange High just before my class was assigned the *Odyssey*. The teacher informed me that he would give me an oral examination on both books the next day. Since I was familiar with Dad's copy of Bullfinch's *Mythology*, I found it in one of the boxes he hadn't yet unpacked and read the summary of the *Odyssey*. The next day I passed the test with flying colors. I later learned from one of the secretaries in the office, both of whom were members of our church, that Mr. Merry had asked the principal, Mr. Charles D. Brantley, how he should grade me at the end of the semester since I had just

102

entered his class but was doing better than most of my classmates. He replied, "Give her what she deserves." So at the end of the semester I received an *A* in English. I also received an *A* or *B* in Latin but a *C* in history.

At the beginning of the second semester of my freshman year, I joined the A Cappella Choir under the exceptional leadership of Wirt D. Walton, Robert McFerrin's first voice teacher. All the choir members were assigned to choir the first period of every day after homeroom. In addition, during a large part of the school year, Mr. Walton insisted that we come to school 45 minutes early for "early morning rehearsal," so we actually rehearsed the equivalent of two periods every day. Anyone who missed the early rehearsal or came late got the evil eye and a strong reprimand. Most of us were there every day on time. My brothers couldn't understand the hold Mr. Walton had on us, but we had an exceptional choir and were well disciplined. We dared not let our eyes roam from the director's skilled hands while we were singing. There were other excellent soloists in our choir, but Robert was the most outstanding.

We gave occasional concerts, once at a large white church downtown, and twice we toured the state by bus. It was on one of these tours, which included Lincoln University in Jefferson City, that I encountered Julian Witherspoon again, and we spoke as he walked across the campus. (He and my brother Clarence were roommates.) Every year all the high school choirs in the city joined to participate in a program called "Musica Americana." It took place in what was then called simply the Municipal Auditorium, but it was later named the Kiel Auditorium. Each school had its separate act and its own dressing rooms.

It was early in my membership in the choir that Robert McFerrin and I became friends. One day he asked me if he could come to see me. This question had never come up before because in East Orange my brothers and I knew all the same boys, and if any of them were interested in me, their visits could be interpreted as visits with my brothers. I was fourteen and knew that I would not be allowed to date until I became sixteen. But how could I pass up Robert's special attention? That night I lay in bed for what seemed hours trying to get up the courage to ask my father. When I did, he said that Robert could visit me at home, but I couldn't go out with him. When he walked me home from school, we would sit on the living room floor and play Pick-up Sticks. But sometimes he came in the evening and we would sit at the kitchen table. I would say, "Robert, sing . . . ." followed by every popular song I liked and some that we sang in choir, and he was always happy to oblige. I never got enough of listening, and he loved to sing. I wrote poems about him, especially after he extended his interest to other girls, but we have remained lifelong friends.

At some point in our friendship, I discovered that he didn't have a middle name. "Why don't you give me one," he suggested. My favorite male name at the time was Keith, so he became Robert Keith McFerrin, a name which he later made legal. In a recent phone conversation with his famous son, Bobby McFerrin, I learned that he was unaware of the story behind his being named Robert Keith McFerrin, Jr.

Because women teachers had to be single, it was rumored that a considerable number of them secretly lived with the men they normally would have married. At least one member of our church was legally married, but if that had become known, she would have been fired and required to pay back the money she had earned since her marriage. In his sermons Dad often talked about the immorality involved in these unofficial arrangements, stepping on a lot of people's toes.

The timing of one of these sermons in which he had been particularly critical had its effect on me. The Sumner choir, with Robert as its star, had just given a concert at a white church downtown, after which a large number of us crowded into Lee's Chinese restaurant on Sarah Street—the more crowded because there were already other customers there. About six of us squeezed into a booth intended for four. I was one of a number of students who were smoking. Robert had brought a bottle of wine with him, and he generously went around to several of the booths sharing it. He poured some into a glass for me. Returning home, I told my mother excitedly about the success of the concert and our visit to Lee's afterwards. I mentioned that I was with two of the girls in the choir whom my mother had met.

About two days later, Dad cleared his throat and ordered me into his study, closing the door. I knew I was in for something but didn't know what. He asked, "Where did you go after Robert's concert?" "Lee's," I answered. "Who were you with?" By that time Mama had opened the study door and joined us. "June and Jewel," I told him. My mother quickly verified that this was the information I had given her that night. "Did you see anyone smoking?" "Yes, a lot of people were." "Were you smoking?" The first lie was a denial. "Was anybody drinking?" My answer: "They don't serve alcohol at Lee's." Then the reason for his questions was revealed. A woman who had identified herself as "Mrs. Smith" had called Dad to tell him that I was the only girl in a booth with boys, that I was smoking, and that I drank alcohol from a bottle." This was part lie but with enough truth to make me uncomfortable. It seems that Dad had asked "Mrs. Smith" for her phone number and she had said she was calling from a pay phone. Enough suspicion to save me. Dad reasoned that the whole story was a lie and that the mysterious caller was reacting to his last sermon about sexual impropriety, trying to get back at him through me. I was off the hook. Nevertheless, I was forbidden to ever go back to Lee's again, even though it was the most popular hangout for the black high school and college students.

The seats in the music room at Sumner faced the main entrance of the school, and the wall between the room and the corridor was glass. We could see everyone who entered the building and went into the office. Occasionally we saw celebrities such as Henry Armstrong, the prizefighter, who were former Sumnerites, visiting the school on their trips back home. Sometimes Mr. Brantley would call a special assembly to have a distinguished former student speak. So many Sumner students later became famous that the school now has a Hall of Fame. E. Simms Campbell, who was famous for his cartoons in *Esquire* magazine, Arthur Ashe, Grace Bumbry, Margaret Bush Wilson, whose sister Ermine was in my class, Robert McFerrin, of course, Dick Gregory, and numerous others are among those who once walked the halls I was walking now. I am honored to have my picture included on the wall of the Hall of Fame.

Sometimes after school we had a dance in the gymnasium. Dr. Herman Dreer, the assistant principal, was always present to chaperone. He was also a minister and member of our church. He occasionally preached an intellectual sermon which I always enjoyed, especially when he quoted Robert Browning, my favorite poet. Because I was not allowed to dance, I stood around at the after-school dances and watched the other students, afraid that if Dr. Dreer saw me dancing, he would tell my father. But then I realized that his two grown daughters probably danced, and St. Louis was more liberal than East Orange and less likely to impose on a minister's children restrictions that didn't apply to their own. So I eventually took the chance and participated in the dancing as best I could.

Shortly after we moved to St. Louis, the doorbell rang and Mama went to see what the white lady at the door wanted. We never saw any white people in our neighborhoods except employees at the Kroger store near our corner and clerks at small white-owned shops on Easton Avenue. For blocks and blocks, the neighborhoods were solidly black and self-contained with black-owned businesses and largely black-owned entertainment. Our trips downtown to the two department stores, Styx, Baer and Fuller and Famous Barr, were infrequent. So seeing a white lady at the door was a rarity.

We soon learned that the visitor, Mrs. Ross, was a neighbor who had come to welcome us. One of her parents had been German, but she considered herself black. She had several grown children, beautiful golden daughters and handsome sons. Myron, The youngest child, and I became close friends. He was not yet in high school, but we became buddies nonetheless. I often walked down the block to his house where we had more freedom than at my house. Sometimes we went up to his roof and drank beer, which was not prohibited in his home. I don't know how my parents failed to detect the odor on my breath but they never did. Often on a summer Sunday morning, Myron and I got up early and walked to Forest Park, hung around awhile, then walked back home to get dressed for church.

While sports was an important part of high school life, it was academic excellence that was emphasized. Making honor roll meant earning As in all four or five of your academic classes. Gym didn't count. Honorable mention was granted those who made all As with one B. After each card marking, the principal sent a letter to the parents of each student who had made honor roll, and a special recognition program was held in the auditorium, the honor roll students being called to the stage and the honorable mention students standing at their seats as their names were called. It was popular to be smart. The faculty was highly qualified, most of them holding master's degrees in their subject areas. The majority of the teachers were excellent. And almost everybody was college-bound. St. Louis had two teachers' colleges, Harris, for white students and Stowe, for blacks. Stowe Teachers College, I was told, had one of the highest percentages of Ph.D.s on its faculty in the country. Both colleges were a part of the public school system. Black students who were graduated from high school in the top third of their class could attend Stowe Teachers College free. They did not even have to pay for their books. Those graduating in the upper two-thirds could attend Stowe Junior College for two years under the same arrangement. Stowe graduates had no problem finding employment in the black public schools. My brothers attended Stowe for two years before transferring to Lincoln University in Jefferson City.

Stowe had only one building which was located across the street perpendicular to Sumner and facing, across Sumner's sports field, the Homer G. Phillips Hospital where a large number of black medical doctors from across the country did their residencies. Stowe and Sumner students mingled freely, often meeting after classes at Billie Burk's, a place that sold hamburgers and soft drinks. I seldom spent the 25 cents I was given for lunch in the school cafeteria, eating cookies instead or a doughnut I had bought on the way to school. Instead I went after school to Billie Burk's where I spent my lunch money on a hamburger and Pepsi Cola. Another place sold barbecued rib tip sandwiches for five cents. The decision of where to eat my after school snack depended on who I was with.

Almost all of the classrooms at Sumner were on the first and second floors with a few teachers' offices and the auditorium on the third floor. The cafeteria was in the basement. All the students who had classes on the first floor went to lunch at the same time. When it was time for them to return, all the students with classes on the second floor went to lunch. During lunch hour, we were free to go to our lockers, mill around in the hall, or visit a teacher in his or her classroom—or just sit with friends in an empty classroom and talk. It was amazing how quiet we were; we never heard any complaints from the floor still in class about lunchtime noise. Teachers didn't have hall duty. An organization of male students had seats in the hall to keep order, but I don't recall that they served any real purpose. Their presence was all the reminder we needed.

One history teacher, Horace Payne, whose son was a student, always had a group of girls congregating in his classroom during lunch hour on the second floor. I was one of them. We talked to him about our problems, our boyfriends, or whatever we had on our minds. I showed him my poems and he often made favorable comments about them. He also asked me why I couldn't keep a boyfriend. The truth was that I fell in and out of love so quickly that after a few weeks I'd dump the one I had for someone I thought was cuter or that I liked better at the moment.

In spite of the positive aspects of Sumner, my arrival there was something of a culture shock. It was a complete contrast to what I had been accustomed to in East Orange. I had never before encountered so many good-looking, well dressed, sophisticated black youngsters, many of whose parents were middle-class professionals. If any of their families had suffered hardship during the Depression, it certainly wasn't apparent. Suddenly I felt small and insignificant. Even though I soon became admired as a poet and an excellent student and my father was pastor of a major church (but without the high salary that many of my schoolmates' parents enjoyed), I developed a terrible inferiority complex. Our street wasn't Enright Avenue, the most prestigious street on which to live in our all-black neighborhood, but it was within the realm of good addresses. Still I felt insecure.

Shortly after entering Sumner I met "Tid" (Margaret) Bowles whose sister Jane was a year ahead of us. The whole family looked Caucasian. Tid and her sister, both members of the Twelve Tops, lived with friends of their parents while their mother worked as principal of a delinquent girls' school in Tipton, Missouri and their father practiced law. Tid and I quickly became friends and I felt very comfortable with her. She admired my poetry and wrote an article about me in the school yearbook. But I didn't feel comfortable with her friends. She and Jane lived on the next block from me, and we walked home from school in the same direction, I often alone. If I saw Tid walking slowly with some of her friends as they laughed and talked, I crossed the street to avoid them. I didn't want to pass Tid with just a simple greeting , but I was so uncomfortable with the others that I didn't feel welcome to join them. I considered one male friend of hers the handsomest boy I had ever seen, and I hated him with a passion, unable to admit to myself that the reason for this feeling was that I knew he would never be interested in me. Sometimes I didn't speak to people because I didn't think they knew or saw me. I felt invisible.

Margaret Bowles ("Tid") in recent years

I never belonged to a group. I knew some of the students from church and became friends with other schoolmates on an individual basis. Some came from lower socioeconomic backgrounds than mine; more often, I had no knowledge of their backgrounds and didn't care. They came in all colors, and their appearance didn't matter either. What mattered was that I felt comfortable with them. One of the mostly light-skinned Twelve Tops once told me one day,

"You're a cute girl, Naomi, but you go around with the wrong people." Such snobbery had never been a part of my life. My mother would not have allowed it. There were occasional rumors about one or another of the elite girls and her sexual activity, even an abortion. Their lifestyle was certainly more liberal than mine.

One year the mother of an honor student who was an accomplished pianist approached my mother about having me join a social club she planned to organize in contrast to the Twelve Tops. It was intended to be just as selective in its membership and just as prestigious but with emphasis on propriety. The club was to be called The Victorians. My mother, knowing that I was not allowed to dance, questioned the lady about its proposed activities. Satisfied with the answer that it did not include giving dances, she gave her permission. Contrary to what Mama had been told, one of its first activities was the sponsorship of a formal dance. I belonged to the club for a very short time, realizing that I would not be permitted to participate in its activities.

In my quest for good grades, I found algebra almost my undoing. I was never good at math. My first report card that semester bore three *A*s and a *D* minus. Mama went to school to talk to my teacher, Mr. Richard Fox, two of whose children were Sumner students. He was a very soft-spoken, gentle man who gave my mother his phone number, inviting me to call him at home whenever I encountered a problem while doing my homework. I took advantage of his offer only twice, once on a Sunday night when he paused a moment to say goodbye to visitors. On each occasion, he walked me through the problem and helped me understand it. As low key as he was, he was a superb and patient teacher. Gradually I began to understand what he was talking about, and on the second card marking I received three *A*s and a *C* plus. The third card marking showed continued improvement, and at the end of the semester I was equaling the smartest student in the class, both of us receiving *A*s.

The last grade was the only one that counted. Any teacher who could make me understand and even like math had to be a genius.

I evidently learned enough chemistry to get at least a *B* but I'm not sure I remember how. I was distracted by a cartoon book expertly drawn by one of the students, James Gordon, depicting sexual encounters. It was surreptitiously passed around the room during class. Such pornography was completely new to me, and I was both embarrassed and fascinated by what I saw. There were other distractions as well, and I didn't really like the subject.

Latin was one of my favorite but most challenging subjects. All the girls in Mr. Carter's class must have had a crush on him. He was young and single and had a sister Annette who was a Sumner student. Many of my homework hours were spent translating *Julius Caesar*. I think every Latin student's textbook bore the handwritten inscription: "Latin is a dead, dead language, as dead as dead can be. / It slowly killed the Romans, and now it's killing me." But studying it was good discipline, and a physically appealing teacher made it interesting. The next Latin teacher didn't elicit the same dedication. I think he had suffered a stroke and walked slowly and with some difficulty. During an examination he made it a practice of walking around the room, but the students sitting in the back rows had ample time to close their books before he got back that far.

Mr. Beatty, who taught American history, was one of the best teachers I can recall. He had an unusual sense of humor but never smiled or laughed even though he often made the class laugh at his anecdotes, his sarcasm, and his insulting responses to wrong answers to his questions. Some students remember only the unimportant details or examples, missing the main point. If Mr. Beatty asked the class a question and got the wrong answer or an I-don't-know from more than two or three students, he would begin opening his desk drawers, supposedly looking for an imaginary gun with which to shoot them. He described historical events with such humorous and dramatic details that even I, who have always had difficulty remembering dates and other numbers, found it easy. He

112

told one story about the first battle of Bull Run, saying that the Union soldiers retreated so fast that a Negro standing by the road played cards on their coattails. When I got to college several years later and met a student from Manassas, Virginia, I blurted out with no hesitation, "First Battle of Bull Run, 1861."

Another of his illustrations concerned a detail of someone beating a drum. The unlucky student he called on had not grasped the point he was making. To his question she answered, "They were playing drums." He answered, *"That's* right. *That's* right. They weren't playing havoc with their rifles; they were beating those drums." I don't know if the ridiculed student ever did get it straight.

It was easy to study for his exams because we knew exactly what he expected us to know, which included candidates for presidency, their party, election years, the issues, and the winner. Robert McFerrin found Mr. Beatty's class so entertaining that he failed it on purpose, not needing the credit, so that he could take it over the next semester. Sometimes the teacher was so funny that Robert had to leave the class in hilarious laughter. On exam days Mr. Beatty assigned us to different seats to make it harder for us to cheat by writing something on the surface of our assigned desk. He evidently wasn't aware of how easy it was to write something in the palm of your hand in indelible ink. But many of those inclined to cheat might have learned something my brother discovered when he was in high school, that writing something repeatedly helps to fix it in your mind. Once when Wil was preparing to take a high school test, he made a "pony" (later called a "cheat sheet") containing the facts he hadn't memorized. Realizing that the pony was too large a sheet of paper, he made a smaller one that was still too large to go undetected. By the time he wrote the third even smaller one, he discovered he didn't need it because, in copying the information several times, he had fixed it in his mind. I, too, found that copying lecture notes is much more effective than simply reading them.

James Gordon and I had worked together on the *Challenger*, a mimeographed school magazine, he contributing illustrations, and I serving as editor and including poems and badly written short stories. Mr. Joseph Carpenter was the faculty advisor. On one or two occasions he had to call me at home. I was impressed by the way he introduced himself: "Miss Long, this is Joseph Carpenter." (The teachers always called female students by their last names, preceded by "Miss" and the male students simply by their last names.) I learned from Mr. Carpenter that it was good manners to identify yourself by your first and last name, leaving it to others to confer a title upon you.

Sumner did not have special rooms for study hall. During our study periods we were assigned to classrooms where instruction was in progress. We were expected to be quiet, but a certain amount of whispered conversation was inevitable.

All during my first full semester, Tid and I sat together and talked about Camp River Cliff, a rustic camp located in the foothills of the Ozark Mountains. The camp was owned by the Pine Street (black) YMCA, but for ten days every summer the YWCA was allowed to use it. Tid told me how much fun she had had there in the years she attended and described it in every detail. I knew I just had to go there that summer and was full of delight and anticipation when my parents gave their permission.

We met at the Y where we were loaded into cattle trucks, some girls sitting on benches and others on the floor, and getting to know one another. Many of us were Sumner students but didn't share any classes or extracurricular activities.

When we finally arrived several hours later and climbed out of the truck in front of the dining cabin, we were greeted by Mr. Cook from the Pine Street YMCA. Each girl was assigned to one of ten cabins that stood in a row, each housing eight girls, four sleeping on upper bunks. The lower part was made of wood, but the upper part, extending to the roof, had only screen for protection again inclement weather. There was no electricity anywhere on the site, and the only running water, which had to be pumped, was outside the dining cabin. The common bathroom was an outhouse across from the campers' cabins. It was scrupulously clean and had no odor. Tid had told me that this outhouse was nicknamed KYBO for "keep your bowels open."

Mr. Cook and the lifeguards, male college students, lived in another section of the grounds in a building called The Nunnery which I never saw.

We had a counselor, the mother of one of my male classmates, who walked past the cabins every morning calling, "Uppie, uppie, uppie, girls; uppie uppie uppie!" Reluctantly we rose and walked barefoot, towels and toothbrushes in hand, along a path whose small stones bruised our feet to a creek where we brushed our teeth and washed up as well as we could, sharing the water with tadpoles. After getting dressed in our shorts, we heard Mr. Cook ringing a large bell suspended outside the dining cabin letting us know that breakfast was ready. Our plates were delivered to us already served, so I, who had never tasted syrup and knew I didn't like it, was forced to eat my pancakes with syrup already applied—and was glad to get it.

We took hikes, did handcrafty things, I think, and went to the river to swim or play around in the water. "Jelly" Turner, one of the lifeguards, took a chair into a shallow part of the river where he sat and watched over us. There was a raft that swimmers perched on or dived from. I have never learned how to swim although I can move short distances by floating and moving my arms, and I can float on my back, but Mr. Cook was determined to make me try. Somehow he got me on the raft, then unceremoniously pushed me off. I made it the short distance to shore, but I'm not sure how.

At dusk we all sat on long benches in front of the dining cabin and sang camp songs. As it grew dark, we lit our oil lamps and walked, still singing, back to our cabins. The lamps had to be extinguished by nine o'clock, and it was assumed that we would then go to sleep. But we stayed awake talking for hours, and a few of us at a time sneaked out to KYBO, sat on the floor and smoked forbidden cigarettes.

At camp I made friends with Doris Cloud, who was two years ahead of me at Sumner. I already knew June Elliott and Jewel Busch from the choir, but after that summer we became closer friends.

By the time our ten days ended, we were all suntanned, and those whose hair was normally straightened were forced to braid it in no particular style because exposure to the river had made it "go back." Our camp clothing was comfortable but not particularly fashionable. Nobody seemed concerned about our appearance. Our feet, at first tender and sore from the small stones, had now hardened. We all hated to see the time end and cried as we climbed into the cattle trucks that would take us back to St. Louis. Just before we started moving, Mr. Cook rang the bell, and our tears flowed even more copiously. Those ten days were some of the happiest in my life.

By the next year the YWCA had purchased its own camp at another location. I attended Camp Derricotte only once, extremely disappointed at its modern conveniences. We had latrines with running water, showers, real beds, and a swimming pool. And my cabin mates from the year before weren't there. There was no reason to want to go to camp again.

It was after attending Camp River Cliff and meeting Doris Cloud that her half-brother, John Parker, and Wil became friends. He was older than Wil and most of the other students at Stowe and nine and a half years older than I. He was a perennial student who probably didn't have the money to go to Lincoln but took every course offered at Stowe. He came to our house frequently and sat with us at the dining room table doing our homework. I fell madly in love with him. Often when I went to visit Doris it was in the hope that he would be there, too. When he rang the doorbell at our house, I rushed to answer; we sometimes exchanged notes as both of our

116

hands touched on the doorknob. At other times we held hands or touched knees under the table. Under the landing on the steps leading to the second floor was an indented area where Mama kept a trunk. It made a perfect seat for talking on the downstairs extension phone placed on a ledge there. John and I talked on the phone whenever we could, but there was always a chance that someone was listening in upstairs. Now and then we met in the afternoon at the Douglass Theater where we sat in the back row, held hands, and kissed. That's as far as our romance ever went, but it was enough.

The problem was that John, as I describe him redundantly in one of the many poems I wrote about him, was "fickle, inconstant, and irresolute." Occasionally he lost interest in me and talked to my brothers in my presence about other girls. His interest in me came and went, and I was either very happy or miserable.

I was miserable a lot of the time during my adolescence. In spite of my love of St. Louis and the positive aspects of my life there, my melancholy grew and my poems expressed my continued feeling of alienation. I took to walking at night, alone with my sadness, finding some relief in going nowhere in particular except a few blocks down Finney and back. Many adults have forgotten how much anguish many adolescents experience, but I am vividly aware that emotionally that was the most difficult period of my life. It wasn't just John; it was my whole life converging.

During the summer the Municipal Opera in Forest Park presented performances—not operas but plays that were sometimes musicals—performed by nationally known actors. On Sunday evenings, the last several rows in the audience were free. Many of the young people made it a point to get there early enough to occupy one of the free seats. I met Vincent Price during the week that he was starring there. Sumner's choir sang on a radio program in which he participated. He was very friendly, taking several girls' hands and looking into their eyes intently as he spoke to them.

The African Americans in St. Louis were extremely supportive of the arts and actively encouraged the young people who were talented. Robert was always being asked to sing somewhere, and I was beginning to read my own poetry. I was about fifteen when I read for the first time on the radio. I also entered my poems in various contests and usually won.

The judges of one of the competitions, a poet in her own right, was a first cousin of Sara Teasdale. She became interested in my work and visited me at home. She was responsible for the publication of one of my poems in the *Missouri School Journal.*

It was in 1940 that I first met Langston Hughes. An organization of African American women had invited him to read, and Mama took me to the meeting at one of the member's homes. When I told him that I was writing poetry, he gave me a signed copy of *A New Song* and advised me to never pay to have my poems published. He also said some words of encouragement to me.

My brothers and I learned that if we referred to dances as parties, we stood a better chance of getting permission to attend. Dad possibly thought that they consisted of conversation and refreshments and did not include dancing. Still, this permission was granted sporadically; I could never account for Dad's permission to attend one party and not another. One special dance was coming up that I particularly wanted to attend but wasn't allowed to. It was such an important occasion that Tid's mother came from Tipton to St. Louis to make her daughters' formal gowns. I was at their house on Cook Avenue during the process and found myself in tears because I couldn't go. I wanted to join the Girl Reserves but was not voted in because, as I was told later, someone said, "She can't do anything anyhow."

When I turned sixteen, I went to a party on my first date, arranged by my mother and Wesley East's aunt who was raising him. I had no particular interest in him, but that was the only way I could go. Mama made me a long dress that looked like it was intended for a little girl. Still, it was a significant occasion, indicating that I was growing up.

Before my brothers left Stowe for Lincoln, they were given permission to attend a prom at Stowe, but they had to be home by one o'clock. It was Dad's belief that any decent activity should take place early. The prom was scheduled from ten to two, and after that, couples usually went somewhere to get something to eat. I felt sorry for my brothers for having to take their dates home even before the dance ended.

A girl I will call Merle Scott, a student at Stowe whom I had first met at church, and I were also invited to the prom. We thought we would be smart; if I spent the night at her house, we wouldn't have to leave early. But her mother found out what time my brothers had to be in and said we would have to abide by the same rules. Our dates were Reuben Fraser, a student at Lincoln, and Robert McFerrin. We left the prom on time but stayed up all night at Merle's house, dancing to records and eating barbecue that Reuben and Robert sent out for. We had a much better time than we would have had if we had stayed at the dance.

My first two years in St. Louis were coming to an end. Robert and some other upperclassmen that I knew were graduating. My brothers would soon be transferring to Lincoln University, leaving me as the only child at home.

Continued Interlude

Central Baptist Church was a huge stone building that stood on the corner of Washington and Ewing. It had two entrances and a balcony that extended around three sides of the sanctuary and lowered in the front to form the choir loft. Mama sat in the front row on the right facing the pulpit. Many of the teenagers went to Vashon, and I never saw them except on Sundays. After Sunday school a lot of us would go to a place that had a juke box and play our favorite songs until well after the service had started. Then we would come in late and sit together in the center of the balcony. When everybody read together the statement of faith printed in the Baptist hymnal, we all kept silent when we got to the part about abstaining from alcohol. There was no age limit on drinking in St. Louis, and all of us had been to bars and sampled beer, rum and coke, or some other alcoholic beverage.

Central Baptist Church

Next to the church was a two-story brick parish house where many of the children's Sunday school classes were taught. I taught one of them for a while.

Dad still didn't wear a robe in the pulpit. He waited until the preliminary part of the service was over; then he came in, knelt at his seat to pray, and then sat down. I had gotten my driver's license but had never driven alone. Shortly after Dad entered the pulpit one Sunday, an usher came to the balcony and told me my mother wanted to see me. When Dad knelt at his chair, she had noticed a rip in the seam of his pants. She sent a note to him by an usher, then sent for me to drive home and get him another pair of trousers. I was nervous about driving alone and was very cautious, but I concluded my task and congratulated myself on my first solo experience.

It was at church that I first met Miss Julia Davis, an elementary school master teacher. On one of Dad's visits to St. Louis prior to our moving, Miss Davis's brother had asked Dad to have me write a poem about "an old man who would be young." I don't know how serious his request was, but I obliged, and Dad sent him the poem. Miss Davis had once been married to Mr. John Buckner, who later married my friend Sarah Hudley's aunt. I knew Sarah from church and school. She dubbed Mr. Buckner "Buzzin' Buck." He had a son from a previous marriage who was an invalid. When Julia Davis was married to Mr. Buckner, they had a son together who, strangely, was also named John Buckner. This John was one of my schoolmates at Sumner and later became its principal and national president of Alpha Phi Alpha Fraternity. When the couple divorced, Julia took back her maiden name.

In recent years, Sarah mentioned to me that, when she was doing her student teaching, She was Sarah's critic teacher. She told me how helpful and exacting she had been. Miss Davis had inspired and demanded excellence from hundreds of black students who had sat in her classroom. Miss Davis had a thorough grasp of African

American history. In her old age, she bemoaned the ignorance of young people then in school, many of whom graduated without any interest in or knowledge of the rich legacy of achievement of African Americans. A branch library was named for her during her lifetime.

When my husband and I went back to St. Louis for my 45-year Sumner class reunion, I phoned Miss Davis. Learning that Leonard was, like her son now dead, a member of Alpha Phi Alpha Fraternity, she insisted that I put him on the phone, and together they sang the Alpha hymn. I told her that we intended to worship at Central that Sunday, which would have been my father's 103rd birthday. The stately stone building had burned down some years before, and a smaller, more modern building erected in its place. Few of the people who knew my family were still members. Miss Davis got on the phone and made sure that our presence was announced in the bulletin and that one of the ushers who was there when we were would see to it that others I knew greeted me. About 99 years old then, walking with difficulty but with as sharp a mind as ever, she made it a point to be at church that day and show me my father's picture in the vestibule as part of the history of the church. Our presence was announced not only in the printed bulletin but from the pulpit as well, including the fact that Leonard was an Alpha. There was a minute of silence in remembrance of Dad. Since the service was overlong and I wanted to get back to the hotel before all those attending the reunion went back to their various cities, we left before the service ended, only to be followed by about four Alphas who wanted to give Leonard a special greeting as brothers.

By the time Miss Davis reached one hundred, a new Julia Davis Branch Library had been erected. I wrote a poem for her birthday and sent it to the library to be read at the celebration being given there in her honor. When she turned 101, I called her to wish her a happy birthday. "Are you going to send me something?" she asked. I hurried to write something in her honor and faxed it to the library so that it would get there in time to be read. There was only one Julia Davis, but she was an outstanding example of the excellent preparation of most of the black teachers who taught in the black schools in St. Louis.

When I first knew Merle, her family lived in South St. Louis, and she and her sister Dolores were students at Vashon. In personality I was much more like her sister than Merle, but it was Merle and I who became best friends. On weekends I often rode the streetcar to her house. Sometimes we walked to a nearby park, smoking forbidden cigarettes and talking about things we were both interested in. She was writing poetry, too, and we were happy to share our compositions.

After her graduation from Vashon, her family moved to the Ville to be closer to Stowe Teachers College where she and her sister would be attending. Merle and I often met at Billie Burk's after school and took turns risking getting caught with the one pack of cigarettes we owned together. Mama smelled the smoke in my sweater and asked me about it. I lied and said it was other people's smoke. I know she knew better. Merle and I often visited Forest Park together and sat on Art Hill overlooking the lagoon reading poetry aloud, sometimes ours and sometimes other poetry that we liked.

My dates usually consisted of going to see a movie at the Douglass Theater located a block or so from my house and then to Lee's, the popular Chinese restaurant on Sarah Street which was the gathering place for all the Stowe and Sumner students. There was one older young man that I was allowed to date, a student at Lincoln. My mother was so impressed with his good manners that she let me go out with him even though he was older than I. She trusted him completely. What she didn't know was that, in the back seat of a car, he was like an octopus who had to be forcefully restrained in his physical advances.

One summer our family friend, Elizabeth Allen, from Norfolk,

123

Philadelphia, and New Jersey, came to St. Louis for a visit. Sarah's aunt and "Buzzin' Buck" invited my parents and Mrs. Allen to a night out at the Municipal Opera in Forest Park, leaving me to spend the time with Sarah. We could think of nothing better to do than order a bottle of gin from the drugstore and have it delivered. I don't know why we chose gin; I didn't know a thing about it and in what proportions it should be mixed with soda or juice. We might have even mixed water with it for all I know. I must have consumed a whole glass before feeling its effect. Sarah suggested that we go for a walk. I remember that I walked very straight, and talked a great deal about John. By the time we got back to Sarah's house, I felt nauseated, but neither of us knew how to induce vomiting, so she sat with me in the bathroom for what seemed like hours, my head over the bathtub. Sarah was relieved when I finally threw up; if I had waited until I got home, she reasoned, my mother would have smelled the gin. Then she suggested that I lie down. When the adults returned, Sarah told them that I had had an upset stomach. Mama and Mrs. Allen wracked their brains to discover what I had eaten to make me sick. The next morning everything smelled like gin to me, especially Dad's after-shave lotion.

At some point, our cousin, James Arthur from Victoria, Texas, came to live with us. Dark-skinned with keen features, he was the son of Dad's mother's half-sister. Because of his amiable disposition, John and Wil called him "Smiling James," a nickname suggested by a comic strip character. John had gotten Wil and James interested in flying. I often accompanied them to an aviation school in East St. Louis for their flight lessons. Wil had not yet soloed and couldn't take up passengers, but for a dollar anyone could take a 15-minute plane ride with a licensed pilot. One day I decided I would take advantage of this opportunity. Mama must have read my mind. Before we left she said to me, "Now don't *you* go up in an airplane." I didn't know what to do. Wil said, "She always tells me that," so I decided to go up anyhow. John's twin cousins were also present that day. It was an open plane and had room for only the pilot and two passengers. One of John's cousins and I went up together and took the short ride over the Mississippi River and over a part of St. Louis. I hadn't anticipated what the wind would do to my unprotected hair. When we landed it felt like straw. But I was happy about my first flight.

Wil and I went a lot of places together. Some Sunday afternoons he borrowed the car and he, John Parker, John Moten, a girl Wil was dating whose name I have forgotten, and I would drive across the bridge to East St. Louis to a place that was little more than a water hole. Dad always cautioned Wil about getting back in time for him to go to the night service at church. We had to change into our bathing suits in the car before playing around in the water. I liked being with Wil because he didn't pay any attention to me—not like Clarence who, at a dance, stood on the sidelines and watched me like a hawk to make sure the boy I was dancing with didn't hold me too close. He had seemingly appointed himself as a third parent. When Wil and Merle started dating, I often accompanied him on his visits to her South St. Louis home.

After the Clarence and Wil went to Lincoln, I sometimes slept in one of their twin beds. They had a table radio in their room, and I enjoyed listening to the blues being broadcast from Kansas City. When I was tired of their room, I'd go back and sleep in my own bed. Once when we had a visiting minister, he slept in my brothers' room. Since the bedrooms had connecting doors, Mama placed the back of a chair under the doorknob on my side, just in case, minister or not, he might be tempted to take advantage of my proximity.

One year Dad took me with him to a BYPU convention in Columbus, Ohio. He had once been called to a church in Columbus and wanted to visit a woman there who had taught with his sister

Octavia in Guthrie, Oklahoma. From there we went to Wilberforce to pay a short visit to Aunt Ethel and her family. She asked him to let me come back for a longer visit. I was about fifteen.

Later that summer I took my first train trip alone to spend some time on the campus at Wilberforce. My cousin "Cotton" was still at home, but Harold and Kenneth were not. I think it was on that occasion, though, that I did see Kenneth once and was introduced to his fiancée Evelyn. Cotton, like other youngsters on campus, had been driving since he was ten years old. Their driving, however, was confined to the campus and, being ineligible for a license, they never ventured into nearby Xenia. Cotton and I frequented a student hang-out on campus that had a juke box on which I played over and over the young Frank Sinatra's rendition of "I'll Never Smile Again," accompanied by the Tommy Dorsey orchestra. I couldn't get enough of it. I also met some of the other young people who had been raised on campus, including Jean Lane, daughter of the dean, who was a national champion in track, and the two Spivey sisters whose father was also on the faculty.

Aunt Ethel's house was the second one after the main entrance that led to Galloway Hall. She had raised three fine sons with the polish and good manners that were a part of her personality and upbringing. Evidently she must have absorbed her mother's tradition to a greater extent than any of her siblings. She had a sweet disposition but was very exacting. I still had a lot of rough edges.

Only a few students were still on campus, possibly working. I think I remember a tennis tournament there. One of the students known as Bill was a tall, good-looking basketball player from White Plains, New York, with beautiful, wavy hair. I had just discovered eyebrow pencil to fill in the sparse hairs above my birdlike eyes, as well as brilliant lipstick. On one occasion Bill told me that I had on too much lipstick, not realizing that it was not the amount but the shade that was wrong. I heeded his comment and bought a different shade as soon as I could. I enjoyed talking to him whenever we met on campus, and he evidently saw something in me that he found interesting.

In order to get to the campus post office, I had to walk up Galloway Hill and then downhill. One day I wrote some postcards and went to mail them. On the way back I ran into Bill and we started talking, first standing and then sitting on a park bench. Eventually, he slid off the bench to the ground and, while we talked, threw his arm, open hand up, across my knees. I began running my fingers through his hair. I didn't realize how long I had been gone. Suddenly I looked up and saw Aunt Ethel in her long dress marching up the hill in our direction. I realized that our position, though perfectly innocent, looked compromising, but she had already seen us and it was too late to change. When she reached us, she said, "Young man, you are too familiar!" Being tall, he was accustomed to looking down at people. He made no response but simply tilted his head back and looked down his nose at her. She then marched me back to the house in deep humiliation. Did I remind her of her sister Octavia?

I met another student who appeared older than most college students. He actually looked ageless and somewhat mysterious. His name was Don T. Wyatt, and he was a poet. We had so much in common to talk about! Since I had brought some of my poems with me, he asked me if he could visit me one evening to share and discuss our work. When he arrived we sat in the living room, and Aunt Ethel took her position at the dining room table with a newspaper. I don't think she ever turned a page. We were certainly not going to talk about anything that was improper, but we did want to discuss the source of some of the poems, and her presence was a hindrance. I kept wondering when she was going to go upstairs and leave us to our free discussion. Of course, she never did. It took me years to understand that, according to her upbringing, a young girl was never left alone with a young man without a chaperone.

Since Aunt Ethel and Dad were the only two of the children in their family who had offspring and I was the only girl, she gave me a yellow gold ring with two tiny pearls that had belonged to Aunt Octavia.

127

After I left Wilberforce, Don and I wrote each other often—long, long letters in which I talked about my parents' cruelty and my love for John, he crying the blues over a girl named Gertrude who had broken up with him. We sent each other poems we had just written. He was my sounding board, the person to whom I bared my soul as he did his to me. The letters came with such frequency and were so long that I'm sure my mother made it a point to find and read some of them. Ageless, intense, and seemingly wise, he was a man who fell in love hard and suffered deeply until he fell in love with someone else with the same intensity. He was a drifter who left Wilberforce not too long after my visit. He moved from place to place. When he felt it was time to move on, he'd give away most of his books, go to the bus depot, and take the first bus that came along, not caring where it was going. His letters came from Detroit, Cleveland, Philadelphia, and other cities. He said he had tried to commit suicide several times. He was really weird, but I appreciated his receptive ear.

Having met my first school goal of induction into the National Honor Society, I had set a second goal of graduating from Sumner with an average above ninety percent. An *A* could be anything from 90% to 100%, but I had to overcome the *C* I had earned in history several weeks after my arrival and the one I had been given in plane geometry, so I continued to study hard. But once I took an incredible chance of blowing it all. One of my history teachers was an excellent instructor and an amiable person. The semester I was in his class he gave a long-term assignment, a handwritten notebook summarizing all the chapters in the textbook. Instead of working on the assignment gradually, I was one of the many students who waited until the last minute. Shortly before the deadline, I mentioned to Tid the predicament I was in. It turned out that her parents and the teacher's family were friends, and she had occasionally accompanied them to his home. She had been there when he was grading notebooks. She told me, "He doesn't read them all the way through. I've seen him in the process." Looking for an easy way out, I foolishly jeopardized the high grade I had earned so far. I began and ended each chapter appropriately, covering the required material for about the first two pages, but in the middle I interspersed the words of popular songs or any nonsense that came to mind, ending the chapter with something related to the textbook. In the middle of one of the last chapters I really got bold, ending a sentence with: ". . . and if you read this far you're crazier than I think you are." When I got my notebook back, it had a large red *A* on the cover.

Wil continued his training as a pilot at Lincoln, the first of his group to solo. After his junior year he left Lincoln to work toward his pilot's license at a black-owned flight school in Chicago. Clarence remained at Lincoln. John was preparing to move from St. Louis, later joining the Army. While the thought of his absence was devastating, I gained a sense of release. I wrote more poems about him, beginning one: "My last night in bondage, / Your last night in town."

The next day in school, when it was time for his train to leave, I cried uncontrollably. Years later Tid told me she was certain we had been having sex because I was so emotionally involved with him. Sex was the farthest thing from my mind.

In those days the annual contest for high school students in art and literature sponsored by *Scholastic Magazine* was judged nationally. The *St. Louis Globe-Democrat* carried an article on Sunday, May 11, 1941 that reads:

> James M. Gordon, 18-year-old Negro High School student from Sumner High School, received two first prizes, one for a design for shoes and one for a design for costume in competition entered by 40,000 students in American High Schools and sponsored by Scholastic, a high school weekly, according to an announcement from Carnegie Institute where his work was exhibited yesterday in the National High School

Art Exhibition.

Three other students from the St. Louis area won honorable mention in literary competitions held in conjunction. They are Bernice Long, 17, of Soldan High School; Mary Lee Cox, 16, of Normandy High School, and Naomi C. Long, 17, of Sumner High School.

Soldan and Normandy high schools were all white, while Sumner was all black. It's amazing that, of all the white high schools in St. Louis, two of the five students whose work was recognized attended Sumner. Another article, which appeared in the weekly *St. Louis Call* or *St. Louis Argus*, on May 16 included a photograph of James and me under the heading, "Win In National Contest."

In 1939 Dad signed a contract with the Pegasus Publishing Company in New York to have a small collection of my poems published. The undated flier reads:

With the publication of SONGS TO A PHANTOM NIGHTINGALE, a new poetic voice is heard, a voice that speaks with lyric beauty and dramatic clarity of those things near to the hearts of men and women.

Naomi C. Long's poetry is not bounded by traditions or poetic "schools." In some of her work are seen evidences of the romanticist, in others the modernist. By turns she employs a tender sentimentalism, a frank and refreshing realism, and a gentle irony.

But no matter how she employs her facile pen, the stamp of her genius is unmistakable in the vibrant beauty of the lines, in the zest and vigor with which she writes. Even when her verse is inspired by a gray mood, there is no bitterness here, but rather a profound understanding of life . . . .

No reference is made to my age, and these words, obviously intended to sell books rather than tell the whole truth, are attributed to "June West, (Book Reviewer)." At the bottom of the order form is a note: "The publication of this book depends upon obtaining a sufficient number of advance orders."

During the next two years, while the accepted manuscript languished, the company went through a change of ownership. It was not until June, 1941 that, the required number of prepaid orders having been received, *Songs to a Phantom Nightingale* was published by Fortuny's Publishers, Inc. With about three exceptions, this volume did not include any of the poems written during the two-year delay. The small cloth-covered collection was finally published several days after my high school graduation and a few weeks before my eighteenth birthday. I was then the same age as Phillis Wheatley when her first poem was published in 1770. Margaret Walker's first book, *For My People,* was published in 1942 and Gwendolyn Brooks's first collection, *A Street in Bronzeville*, appeared in 1945. My book did not possess the maturity or excellence of the others, and it attracted little attention, but the very fact of its existence is important. Dexter Fisher, in her introduction to *The Third Woman: Minority Women Writers in the United States* (1980), cited my book as the beginning of a 31-year period of contemporary poetry by African American women, so there is some historical significance in its publication.

A number of local people bought my book, which cost only one dollar, and a schoolmate, Sarah Hudley, wrote a review that was published in one of the two black weekly papers. Dad wrote letters to ministers and other friends he knew all over the country, enclosing a copy of the book to be purchased on approval. I think everybody sent him the dollar. I was surprised years later to learn that Jay Levine, a Detroit collector of books by African Americans, had found a used copy of this book in Ohio and purchased it. He didn't recognize that I was the author, since the book was published under the name Naomi Cornelia Long and the photograph on the frontispiece was my high school graduation picture.

One year we had hopes of becoming rich. Having spent much of his life in the Southwest, especially the oil-rich state of Oklahoma,

Dad was acquainted with oil wells and, when given an opportunity of joining the Black Panther Oil Company which was drilling for oil, he took it. I remember vividly the day that we drove to an area of Illinois not far from St. Louis to witness the final probe of the oil wells. Clarence and I went with Dad. The work was being done by Indians who were living on the grounds in trailers. One of my schoolmates was present, I recall, with her aunt who was going with one of the men in the corporation. I stood in awe of the casual way of life in a trailer when a woman freshening up did not bother to hide the details of her toiletry from male bystanders.

The moment when the oil "came in" was exciting. The gush of black gold from the earth was an unforgettable joy. Clarence had read somewhere about verifying the oil by the taste, and he didn't hesitate to try it. We were all ecstatic, and I was certain that I would never again have to ration my 25 cents lunch allowance. Next year, I was sure, I would have whatever I wanted.

But nothing happened—no change in my lifestyle occurred, no sudden wealth. My visions of sugar plums quickly vanished. It seemed that some of the men in the corporation belonged to another corporation that prohibited dual membership, and a lawsuit was necessary to settle the matter. In the meantime, the uninvolved members would have to put up more money to protect their interest. Dad didn't feel that he could risk any more money, so he withdrew with nothing but a worthless cylinder of rock pulled up from the earth by the drill as a memento.

Years later I met one of the other corporation members, a Chicago physician, in Idlewild, Michigan. I learned from him that they had won the lawsuit and that the corporation to which Dad had belonged was still drawing income from the same oil wells. Rather than feeling regret that Dad hadn't had more nerve and more money to invest, I accepted that some fate had decreed that wealth was not to be my reward in life. I have never since planted my hope in any strike-it-rich venture. My earned income has been too hard to come by for me to take a chance on losing any of it. A paycheck's certainty to me has always been preferable to a gamble.

I have rarely benefited materially from chance. Once when I was a teenager I did win a clock at a grocery store raffle, but since I have always tried to be on time, I already owned a clock and had long ago appointed myself the official waker-upper at my house. While I hear others' reports of the thousands of dollars they have won at this or that casino, I am convinced that I'll never have much if I have to depend on chance. But then, I have never believed that real wealth has anything to do with money anyhow.

If making as much money as possible became everyone's goal, there would be few university professors, symphony orchestras, or operas, little visual art, poetry, or serious drama because there wouldn't be enough people to create or perform them. Hospitals would have difficulty operating because potential nurses would be working more profitably as scientific technicians or specialists instead of easing pain and suffering, regardless of whether or not their career choice made them happy. Service professions would have few practitioners because everybody would rather make large salaries than contribute to society in ways that make a positive difference in people's lives. One could easily anticipate vast changes in civilized life as we know it, none for the better, if college students were foolish enough to select majors for the sole reason that they could earn more money in related careers than they would if they prepared themselves for what they really wanted to do.

There used to be a time when people considered among the primary purposes of education an understanding of other peoples and their cultures, the values and insights to be derived from philosophy and literature, an appreciation and enjoyment of music, dance, and visual art, the personal satisfaction of being able to think creatively and critically and to carry on interesting discourse about serious matters with others. They took pleasure and pride in doing their chosen work well, receiving satisfaction from knowing that they were contributing something to society. Haven't we had enough of overpaid athletes, too often with no moral values? Of business

133

executives who exploit those who do the actual work on which their fortunes are built? Of greedy government officials who cheat and steal without any regard for their taxpaying victims? Of money-hungry, power-hungry people in all professions who create nothing in society but havoc?

No wonder so many students think it's perfectly all right to cheat on research papers, experiments, and exams. Too many have come to believe that any means is acceptable to attain the goal of a degree that can be immediately redeemed for cash and status.

I vaguely remember Uncle Robert and Aunt Shirley's visit to East Orange when I was very small. Wil, who remembered their visit better, told me that they had not been in the house an hour when Dad had some harsh words with Shirley about the way she had treated his sister Octavia during her illness with tuberculosis. Shirley resented Robert's family anyhow because of their light skin color, and Dad's sharp words helped to turn her totally against him. So it was that, shortly before we moved to St. Louis, Dad's brother and his wife moved to Hannibal, not returning to St. Louis until after we left. We visited them once in Hannibal, but on Dad's return visits to St. Louis after we had moved back east, he never stayed at his brother's house and was told of phone calls that Shirley made to church members saying every negative thing she could think of about him.

At some point during my anguished adolescent years in St. Louis, I came to realize that the father whom I had always idolized was not perfect. I can't pinpoint any particular incident, but I began to think of him as my god dethroned. He couldn't stand to see us idle; we always had to be busy doing something. In the summertime, if he was out somewhere and we were sitting in the living room listening to the radio, as soon as we saw his car pull up in front of the house, we all scattered to other rooms to avoid his criticism. He granted or denied permission for me to go somewhere or do something capriciously. I felt repressed in not being allowed to do many of the things my friends did, and I began to feel rebellious toward both parents. But I couldn't get away with acting out my rebellion. I could only write it. Our cousin James had left and I was alone in the house with my parents. I began sleeping in the unfinished attic, listening to the whistle and wheels of trains and longing for the day when I could leave home.

By the time I reached my senior year, many of Tid's friends, by whom I felt intimidated, had graduated, leaving only two of the girls in her inner circle behind. I desperately wanted to be the fourth girl in that circle, but I never managed to feel an accepted part of it. In the meantime, Merle and I had drifted apart. Her sense of what was proper and my rough edges seemed to have separated us, or it might have been that we just had less in common than before and embraced different values.

I didn't know what college I wanted to attend. I knew it wouldn't be Stowe, and Dad didn't think much of Wilberforce, which I wouldn't have considered anyhow because I would have been expected to live with Aunt Ethel. I knew I wanted to experience dormitory life, but I didn't consider Lincoln because Clarence was still there.

One of the church officers, Ellis Outlaw, brought his visiting cousin to our house. He was Dr. John M. Gandy, president of Virginia State College, the institution from which my mother had been graduated in 1902 when it was still a normal school. I was so impressed with Dr. Gandy that I immediately decided that that was where I wanted to go. For two years, anyhow; then I planned to transfer to the University of Kansas (because of Octavia?) and major in journalism. It never occurred to me that I would do anything but write. It may have been during this visit that he invited Dad to preach the baccalaureate sermon in May, 1942. My cousin Giles was already there, and Ettrick was only 23 miles from Richmond where

Helen now lived, along with all my other maternal cousins and aunts. I had never seen the campus, but I knew with all certainty that Virginia State was the place for me.

I managed to achieve my goal of graduating with an average above ninety percent, the fifth ranking student in my class, on June 11, 1941. There were 140 graduates in the June class. My class had voted to have the baccalaureate service at Central Baptist Church. Jimmy Stewart had come from East Orange for my commencement and sang a solo at the service. At graduation I made the welcome address. Tid told me later that, as I spoke, a plane passed overhead, symbolic, she felt, of a high and bright future. Mr. Brantley announced that my book would be published within the next few days.

I had worked so hard and done so well in high school that I announced to my parents that I was going to stay out all night after graduation. A group of us visited several bars and restaurants and managed to spend time doing nothing in particular, determined to have a good time. We passed the time somehow, and daylight was breaking when I finally got home. Neither of my parents reprimanded me; I saw my mother's hand in their silence.

In spite of the fact that many students attended bars and had an occasional drink, alcohol was not a problem. I recall no instances in which students drank excessively. I never heard of anyone, young or old, who used illegal drugs; it just wasn't a problem then.

I had taken an examination with other high-ranking seniors in black schools in St. Louis and Kansas City for a scholarship to Howard University. I came in second, but the person who received the highest grade declined to accept, and the scholarship was offered to me. I had already decided on Virginia State, but even if I hadn't, Dad made it clear that he was not going to send me to Howard. I received another scholarship to Drake University, as well as one to an all-girls' college in Elmira, New York. I had no desire to go to either of these institutions, especially one where there were no boys. It was just as well. When the college in Elmira found out that Sumner was an all-black school, they rescinded their offer.

I wanted a summer job, but Dad wasn't particular about my working. The job I found, though, met with his approval. A student at Lincoln, Kenneth Billups, directed a choir sponsored by the government during the Depression to provide jobs for young people. The NYA (The National Youth Administration) choir paid $18 a month for our rehearsals in the Poro Building for four hours every afternoon; by the end of the summer the pay was increased to $21 a month. Once in a while we gave a free concert, but most of the time we just rehearsed.

I often walked to work with the older sister of a girl I had met at Camp River Cliff who lived in the next block. When I talked about my current boyfriend and she discovered that I was a virgin, she asked me, "Why do you have a boyfriend if you aren't having sex?" (She put it more bluntly than that.) She said that she always had sex with married men because they had more to lose if they didn't protect her against pregnancy. I found her admission shocking.

The Poro Building was not air-conditioned. We rehearsed on the second floor which, during a typical St. Louis summer, was unbearably hot. Mr. Billups, perspiration running down his face, forbade us to fan. He said it was bad psychology. The personnel frequently changed as members left to go away to college or take better jobs. On a member's last day, he or she had the privilege of selecting a favorite song in our repertoire to be sung as a parting gift.

Mr. Billups let us take sheet music home, but we were not permitted to use it during rehearsals. On my first day, not knowing the music, I just sat there and listened, but only for a moment. He looked at me and asked, "What are you doing here?" I said, "I don't know the music." His quick demand was, "Sing." "But I don't know—" "Sing!" he repeated more forcefully, I learned that

I could listen to the alto next to me and pick up the first syllable of a word and the note, following her lead a split-second later without even knowing what the next syllable would be. His method of directing was so different from Mr. Walton's at Sumner that it took me a while to get used to it. There were a number of solo voices in the choir, but they seemed to stand out instead of blending in. Mr. Billups made us memorize a quotation that began, "Zeal for fine music . . . ." and repeat it back to him.

When he wanted to rehearse the men alone, the girls went outside and stood on the sidewalk talking, some smoking. When he was ready for us to return, he would come down and summon us back with a broad sweep of his arm and a command, "Let's *go*-oh!" When he wanted to rehearse the women, the men got a break.

Occasionally he started a rehearsal with something he had composed the night before with two possible endings and asked us which one we liked better. His arrangement of spirituals was unique, having the feeling and interpretation that I imagine must have been closer to the way slaves sang the songs as they worked in the fields than the more sophisticated arrangements of well known composers.

One of his compositions had only the one word, *Missouri,* in it. The basses started off with the emphasis on the second syllable, singing, "MisSOUri MisSOU- MisSOUri," repeating the phrase on a different note. Then the baritones came in, followed by the tenors, altos and sopranos. When all voices were in, the basses shifted the emphasis to the first syllable, singing, "MISsouri MISsou- MISsouri," until all the voices were in. Then the emphasis changed to the last syllable: "Missou-RI Missou- MissouRI" until the song ended with the sopranos' entrance. The rendition was quite effective.

Another of his arrangements was from a Biblical passage: "The axe shall be laid to the root of the trees, and every tree that bringeth not forth good fruit shall be hewn down and cast into the fire" (Matt. 3:10). After *laid,* he added parenthetically "Hew, hew!" It was this song that remained, spinning around in the recesses of my memory and coming forth when I needed it as though I had sung it only yesterday. The quotation and the parenthetical addition is repeated as we sang it in my poem, "Grand Circus Park."

When my last day came, my request was for "Thy Song" that contained the words, "More sweet than the perfume of snow-white jasmine." I have never heard it sung again, but I recently ordered a jasmine plant over the internet because I wanted to experience for myself the fragrance of this flower.

My freshman roommate in college was one of the few students I knew who owned a radio. She turned it on on Sunday mornings to listen to "Wings Over Jordan." When that choir was overseas, others sang in its place. One morning when I heard the first strains of "Free grace, free-ee grace. . . ." I said, "That's Ken Billups." I recognized at once his style in his chorale's rendition. I'm glad I had the experience of singing with two directors as different as Wirt D. Walton and Kenneth Billups.

During my senior year I started writing what I thought was going to be the great American novel. The title, *Naught of Injury*, was taken from the National Honor Society speech on character. It was my own story, but in an effort to try to disguise the autobiographical aspects, I placed the action in Pittsburgh. I knew nothing about Pittsburgh, having passed through there only once, except that, like St. Louis, it was dirty. It never occurred to me that no two cities are interchangeable and that dirt in the air was not enough of a similarity to justify such a radical change in setting. The St. Louis dirt was soot from soft coal. Pittsburgh's dirt came from an entirely different source and was apparent in the folds of clean bed linens and a gummy substance on the front porch that couldn't be eliminated by sweeping. The terrain of the cities was vastly different, as were other aspects. Nevertheless, every evening during the summer after choir rehearsal I continued to write.

As if my parents weren't strict enough, Clarence took it upon himself to assist them, searching for me and reprimanding me if I didn't come straight home after rehearsal. But whenever I got home and made myself something to eat, I went to the desk in my bedroom, resisting my mother's plea to come and sit on the front porch with her to catch what there was of a breeze.

The severe heat of a St. Louis summer could not deter me from my task. Only Dad's rushing outside to buy treats from a man who went through the neighborhood calling, "Hot tamales, *red* hot!" or another who sold bags of fried pork skins with hot sauce would get me away from my room to share Dad's purchases. I almost finished the first draft of the novel in longhand before leaving St. Louis, but in college I found more interesting things to do. I finally destroyed the manuscript when I realized how terrible it was.

Cyrena Doxey, one of my high school classmates, and I shopped for clothes on Easton Avenue, buying suits that were identical except for color, sweaters and skirts, saddle oxfords and socks. I wanted the independence of buying my own clothes for college, which I succeeded in doing except for the winter coat that my meager earnings from the choir didn't cover. Aunt Ethel came from Wilberforce to visit us and hemmed one of my skirts for me.

During the summer I was frequently visited by one of our church members who had been two years ahead of me at Sumner and was now attending college in Iowa. Sammy Canaan was his parents' only child and the only nephew of his two aunts, both unmarried school teachers. He was the apple of their eyes and they wanted only the best for him. His aunts disliked the girl he was dating, considering her a bit too worldly. I was the innocent-faced girl whom boys' mothers wanted them to marry. I don't know if his aunts' suggestions had anything to do with it, but Sammy and I spent a lot of time together. When Dad learned that his friend, the Rev. J. Raymond Henderson, was leaving New Rochelle, New York to become pastor of Second Baptist Church in Los Angeles, he was granted an opportunity to preach at Bethesda Baptist Church. After Dad accepted the call, we were not supposed to tell anyone until he was ready to announce his resignation. Even though all of Sammy's family belonged to Central, I told him anyhow. He was the only person that I confided in, and I trusted him to keep the secret.

A very significant era in my life was ending. Some of my classmates would be going out of town to other colleges, and when they said, "See you at Christmas," I knew it wasn't going to happen, but I couldn't tell them. Even if I did come back, I knew it wouldn't be the same. I was ambivalent about moving from St. Louis. I didn't really want to go, but at the same time, I was eager to get away from home and its parental restraints. Living in another city would present a change, but New Rochelle didn't sound particularly exciting. I wanted to leave home, but I wasn't ready to make the move permanent.

No one else in my family loved that city as much as I did. Mama described it as a sprawling country town. She missed the kinds of salt water fish that had always been available on the Eastern Seaboard. Clarence and Wil spent less time in the city than I did, attending Lincoln and working on the boats in the summer. Dad had grown up in the Southwest and preferred life in the East. Under his able leadership, Central had paid off a large mortgage, and he had made many other significant contributions to the progress of the church. But unlike the members of Calvary in East Orange, many at Central were doctors, lawyers, principals, teachers, and other professionals. They were not as likely to agree with him on how the church should be run as his former members, and he was not accustomed to their occasional opposition. He felt unappreciated.

My longing to get away was stronger than my desire to remain. Many nights I slept on the cot in the attic alone with my thoughts and my longing. The distant train wheels beckoned me toward a new life.

141

I decided to leave two weeks before the beginning of the semester in order to visit with my cousin Helen and other Richmond relatives before starting college. It was understood that I would also spend the Christmas holidays in Richmond as my parents would be in the process of packing for the move to New Rochelle. I wrote to Don Wyatt, my constant correspondent, and gave him my aunt's address in Richmond and the date I would arrive there so that he would know where to write me.

Then I bade farewell to the city that had meant so much to me and boarded the train at Union Station. Although I didn't have access to the journal where I recorded most of my thoughts and feelings, I know that somewhere between St. Louis and Richmond I wrote on a sheet of paper how happy I was to get away from home and how free I felt as the distance increased. That piece of writing would come back to haunt me later that year. The St. Louis interlude had ended, and I looked forward to the next phase of my life.

Me in front of Sumner fifty years later wearing a school tee shirt

III.
College in Wartime

On This Lofty Hill

When my cousins met me at the train station in Richmond, one of them asked me if I knew someone named Wyatt. Don had arrived in Richmond ahead of me, this time not taking the first bus to anywhere but intending to spend time with me. By the time I got to State two weeks later, he had decided that he was in love with me and had already become a nuisance. What did he do but follow me to the campus. For something like a week, he stayed in the room with my cousin Giles and then with Reuben Smith from East Orange. When they could put up with him no longer, Reuben asked me if it was all right with me if they put him out. By that time I was thoroughly sick of his attention and made it clear to him. He tore up my picture, which I had sent him long before, mailed it to me, and left for Washington where he got a job with the telephone company. Still he insisted on trying to reach me by phone, which wasn't easy because students didn't have telephones in their rooms, and several people were always waiting to use the one pay phone down the hall. He managed to get through a couple of times, but he eventually got the point that I was not interested, and I never heard from him again.

In Richmond Helen's boyfriend, Clem Givings, whom I already knew from other summer visits, was working as a photographer for the Norfolk *Journal and Guide*. He introduced me to Alvin Morris, an upperclassman at Virginia State, and the four of us double-dated. So when the semester began, Alvin dumped his former girlfriend and we became a twosome. We were so restricted that we could only "socialize" at the appropriate times for freshman, meet secretly in Petersburg to attend the only movie theater available to African Americans, and drink a soda at the only drugstore that would serve us. We were very congenial and I liked him very much as he did me.

The average student going away to college today requires a van to transport all the equipment considered necessary for survival. This usually includes a television set, a sophisticated music system, and a computer with all the peripherals. Our luggage was likely to include nothing but clothing. A few students had radios, but I didn't. Television and computers were still years away, and the size and arrangement of the dormitory rooms would not have accommodated these luxuries even if they had been available. 241 Byrd Hall, typical of the other rooms, contained two single beds, two chairs, two tables, and two closets. That was it. Many of the girls made colorful skirts to go around their tables, and a few bought small cardboard chests of drawers covered in attractive fabric. My roommate, Ernestine Davis from Durham, was prosperous enough to bring along a radio over which we often listened to big bands broadcasting late at night from Glen Island Casino in New Rochelle. Since few students purchased newspapers, we were only minimally aware of what was going on in the country and the world. We were truly isolated on our lofty hill. Tiny Ettrick a short distance away had a post office and not much else. Petersburg was within walking distance.

When my aunt took me to the campus and met Ernestine, who I didn't know at the time was only fourteen, her comment was, "She's a wide-awake little girl." "Steen" had spent her high school years at an exclusive black boarding school in the South and was indeed "wide awake." She told me that all the boys knew how to gain entrance into the girls' dormitory and there probably wasn't a virgin on campus. I was fascinated by her knowledge of sex and asked a lot of questions which she answered with no hesitation. She and I got along very well, and when we went home for the summer I looked forward to sharing a room with her in the fall, but she had chosen to attend summer school and was expelled for some major misbehavior. It was decades before I saw her again.

Many of the professors helped with students' schedules. One of them was Marguerite Worthington, originally from Rhode Island. Her first words to me, in her New England accent were: "Are you sma't?" I didn't know how to answer, not wanting to brag by saying I had a good academic record. Everybody called her "Madame," and she was the professor I got to know best.

She lived on campus in a building inhabited by single faculty members and staff. She was a widow and had a young daughter, Pat, who stayed in Petersburg with a friend except on weekends. Sometimes I baby-sat with her. In Madame's apartment I felt free to raid the refrigerator when I was hungry. She was the faculty advisor of the undergraduate chapter of Alpha Kappa Alpha Sorority, and I soon got to know her better in that capacity. She was also my first French professor in college, a class in which we read the novel, *Eugenie Grandét*. Foreign languages were taught then with emphasis on grammar and the written word, not on speaking.

When all the new students took the required freshman entrance exam, I made the highest score, and Clem came to the campus to take my picture sitting on the ledge of Virginia Hall; it was published in the *Journal and Guide* under the caption, "Smart Freshman."

In the freshman dining hall we chose our permanent tables where the same eight students sat for lunch and dinner, served by student waiters. At breakfast we could sit anywhere, but everyone tried to anticipate where the student waiter would place the platter of bacon and eggs and sit as close to that end as possible. There was hardly enough bacon to go around, and when seconds were brought, there was usually no bacon at all, only eggs. I swore that if I ever got a chance I was going to eat a whole pound of bacon in one sitting. Sunday dinners, served at lunchtime, consisted invariably of chicken, and supper was always applesauce and a rubbery cheese processed by the Agriculture Department. If we even bothered to look into the dining room hoping for something different, we were never surprised and immediately headed for the Grille. That's where most of my meager resources went.

Among my table mates were my roommate Ernestine and a boy named Oliver Taylor who had attended the same private boarding school she did where he had been nicknamed "Squirt." He happened to be a member of the church in New Rochelle where my father would soon become pastor. All year long I asked him ques-

147

tions about the city, the parsonage, the church, and the people there. He answered all my questions, but I still didn't know what to expect in the new city I had yet to see.

Twice a week we were required to go to chapel for worship services. Evidently someone took attendance, for absence called for a reprimand. Sleeping as late as we could on Sundays, we sometimes rolled up our pajama legs, threw on a coat, put a pair of socks over our hands for gloves, and headed to Virginia Hall to snooze through the droning sermons by Dr. Davis, delivered with an accent from the West Indies or Africa.

Because for a while all three of us were in college at the same time and Dad's salary was never high, I was conscious of the financial strain on family resources. I was determined to be as independent as possible. I didn't make telephone calls home and never asked for money or items of clothing. My mother occasionally sent me a box containing cookies and chicken, which I had no way of refrigerating, but I don't recall that it ever spoiled before my roommate and I consumed it. I have no idea what amount Dad was required to pay at the beginning of the school year, but every month he mailed me a check for thirty dollars which I was to take to the cashier's office. There I paid $26 and received four dollars in change. That was my allowance for the month, and I managed to get by on it. After all, there wasn't much to spend it on.

If I had any illusions that college would represent freedom, they were soon dispelled. True, we were out of the glare of parental eyes, but the college did a perfect job of operating *in loco parentis*. Freshman girls were allowed to "socialize" for one hour on Sunday afternoons, the definition of that term being carrying on an extensive conversation with a member of the opposite sex. The visit could be in the dormitory lounge or on the front campus where there were lights under every shrub to prevent any possibility of hanky-panky. One earned new privileges with time, but a female student had to reach the last month or so of her senior year before she was allowed to go into town to the movies with a young man. Of course, we got around that

148

by meeting boys at the movies and returning to campus separately. The eventual advent of weekly campus movies in Virginia Hall did permit a limited amount of social contact, and fraternity and sorority dances, of course, allowed the mingling of the genders. But these exceptions were all too rare.

Because many of the upperclass men had deserted their former girlfriends in favor of freshman, there was always a great deal of activity after meals when the men left the upperclass dining hall with its separate entrance to talk to their new girlfriends. The practice of just hanging around and talking was so widespread that nobody considered it a source of trouble, but the Guidance Committee had other ideas. There were too many offenders to punish everyone, so they chose four girls on whom to wreak their wrath. (The men, of course, were equally involved, but not one of them was ever disciplined.)

Three of the girls called before the Guidance Committee were considered the prettiest or most popular freshmen. I was the fourth, singled out because of my academic record. Elwood Boone, dean of men and a member of the Guidance Committee, later admitted feeling that Alvin was not good enough for me, and this was his way of trying to break us up. Naturally, Alvin was eager to know what had transpired during the meeting. Dean Boone watched me from the window when I left and reportedly commented, "There she goes, right back to him." I don't know why his disapproval was so strong, but he made it very apparent. Whenever there was a dance in the gymnasium, Billy Taylor, now famous, and the college orchestra always played a 17-minute rendition of "Stardust." With the first strain, a young man would leave the person he was dancing with to get back to his girlfriend. They would slow-dance in the darkest corners of the gym. On one such occasion, Dean Boone made it a point to get to me before Alvin did, held me at arm's length, and as fast as the music allowed, made the rounds of all the corners. The action of the Guidance Committee may have caused some of the students to be more cautious, but as far as I could tell, little was

149

changed; the practice of socializing after meals continued.

Fifty years after graduation, sitting next to Dean Boone, then retired from another position at the college, I laughingly related his earlier stated opinion that Alvin wasn't good enough for me. "Well, he wasn't," he asserted.

Along with the official reprimand during the Guidance Committee encounter and a temporary loss of social privileges, went official letters to the offenders' parents written by the dean of women, informing them of the violation of rules. I don't recall seeing the letter, but in its wake, Dad wrote me a four-page, typed, single-spaced letter divided into two parts. The first was a lengthy statement about his disappointment in my behavior. According to the impression he had received from the dean's letter, I had completely disgraced myself in the most public and shameful way imaginable. Having been invited by President John M. Gandy to deliver the baccalaureate sermon for the class of 1942, Dad said he felt so disgraced by my behavior that he had thoughts of canceling his commitment.

Part 2 of his letter concerned what I had written on the train after leaving St. Louis. Mind you, I hadn't seen him since, and there was no way that he could have read my written expression. But he was certain that, somewhere between St. Louis and Richmond, I had written words "to this effect." He practically quoted what I had written about being happy to be away from home and free, coming so close to my original words that it was frightening. I had the feeling that he could read every thought I had. This was the first of three instances in which he dreamed something that he could not have known. He didn't see significance in everything he dreamed, but he once said that his part-Cherokee mother had a gift of revelation in dreams and he felt that he had inherited it.

My response to his letter was also in two parts, the first explaining that my reason for being called before the Guidance Committee had been blown way out of proportion and that I had been guilty of doing nothing but carrying on a normal conversation with Alvin for about fifteen minutes after lunch or dinner in plain

150

view of all the other students who were doing the same thing. Part 2 was an expression of my feelings of repression and alienation at home, something I had tried without success to explain to him as a child.

When my parents came in May, guests in the president's home, they were pleasantly surprised to learn from Dr. Gandy and many faculty members how well thought of I was. Everything they heard about me was positive. The dean of women's letter had been a cruel, misleading, and unnecessary missive, but such was the protective nature of many black colleges of the South.

In spite of incidents like this, the strict rules really weren't as bad as they must seem to today's liberated youth. All the students were subject to the same requirements, so no one felt any more repressed than others. Furthermore, there was really no place to go on a date. Isolated as we were, we were satisfied to make our own fun on campus. "The Grille" at the foot of the hill on the front campus was a lively meeting place, and it was there that we found our greatest joy outside of informal gatherings in each other's rooms and all-night pinochle games for those who, unlike me, knew how to play. Those bolder students seeking more intimate pleasures could always find a way, for rules and regulations have never prevented anyone determined to break them from succeeding.

Everyone seemed to be on the same economic level. There was no way to tell whose parents were well-off and whose were not. Only one girl that I knew had a fur coat. There were certainly others who could afford one, but nobody flaunted wealth. The following year I would learn by accident that one girl was the daughter of a Texan who owned a ranch and oil fields. I was closer to her roommate than to her and was present when "Tex" was preparing to go to bed. She was the only girl I knew who read the Bible her grandmother had given her and got down on her knees to say her prayers in the presence of company. Some students had campus jobs, but it made no difference to anyone who worked and who didn't. There were just no social divisions.

151

The campus population was so small that all the students knew each other by face if not by name. No matter how many times a day you saw the same person, he or she was always greeted with "Hey." Everybody's roommate, whether male or female, was called "Ol' Gal."

On March 11, 1942, Langston Hughes came to Virginia State for an evening reading of his poetry. I belonged to a small literary group that met with him the afternoon before his reading. I took a neatly typed collection of my unpublished poems entitled *Drops of Water* to this meeting and timidly asked him to look over several of them if he had the time. He took the notebook and said he would return it after the program.

That evening during the reading of his own poems, he read several of mine, saying some words of praise that left me dizzy. After he returned the collection to me, I discovered that he had read the entire manuscript and penciled in several comments which I immediately covered with scotch tape.

The calm and normalcy with which my freshman year began was soon shattered one Sunday afternoon during that first winter. I was among a group of girls who had been selected to go by bus to nearby Camp Lee to entertain black soldiers stationed there. (The military service was not yet integrated.) When we reached the entrance gate, we were stopped by an officer and, after a brief conversation with our driver, we returned to the campus. We had no inkling of why we were sent back.

It was by word of mouth that we learned that Pearl Harbor had been attacked. We had no idea where that was or what the implications were, but since my roommate had a radio, we probably turned it on that evening, December 7, 1941.

The next day the students in my early European history class took up most of the period asking our professor, Nat Sims, questions about what we could expect as a result of the declaration of war and trying to interpret his answers in terms of changes in our daily living.

The effects of war did not manifest themselves immediately, but gradually they came. The young men started getting drafted into military service with increasing frequency so that two of the three men's dormitories were eventually assigned to women, sometimes with certain rooms reserved for unmarried staff members or graduate students. When it became impossible to maintain an cappella choir because of the shortage of men, a Women's Symphonic Choir was organized and, when Dr. J. Harold Montague, the director, was drafted, not to return until after the war, Professor Undine Moore became director. Under her more expert leadership, I joined the choir.

Those who were accustomed to purchasing clothing during the year found it more difficult to buy shoes, for which ration coupons were required. Nat Sims, who had a reputation among students for wearing the same clothes *ad infinitum*, was happy to give his shoe coupons to Laura Mann, who later became my roommate, the only one of us who had nerve enough to ask. As for me, I didn't have the money for new shoes anyhow, so there was no point in having the coupons. One or the other of my aunts in Richmond occasionally sent me a piece of new clothing. If Sadie bought Helen a sweater and skirt set, she often bought me the same in a different color. I was indebted to her for a navy blue linen suit which I loved and a summer dress she made. In addition, a woman in New Rochelle worked for a white couple whose daughter was my size. My best clothing through college and several years after came from her. Many of the items had never been worn and still had the original tags on them.

Silk stockings were not rationed but next to impossible to find. They stopped appearing in the stores and the only way to get a pair was through some generous soldier who seemed to have access to hard-to-find items. Only a few people I knew had begun to wear the new nylon stockings—not pantyhose, which hadn't yet been invented—but they, too, seemed unattainable. We were reduced to misshapen rayon stockings which looked and felt just awful and wrinkled on our legs. To give them a better sheen and fit, some of the girls had learned the trick of rubbing Vaseline over them after putting them on.

Another scarcity was the rubber necessary for the elastic in ladies' underwear. As a substitute, drawstrings were used in panties to hold them up around the waist. Among some of my closest friends in the dormitory, I earned the nickname of "Droopy Drawers"; evidently I was able to cope with the change less efficiently than they. My mother occasionally mentioned in her letters the stockpile of sugar, also rationed, that she had begun to hoard, purchased unnecessarily with coupons that church members sometimes gave her. By the end of the war, she had accumulated enough sugar, now turned into hard lumps, to sweeten the Atlantic Ocean.

By the time Christmas came in 1941, the songs had already taken on a tinge of gloom. Many were about war and separation, of bluebirds eventually returning to the white cliffs of Dover and spring coming late. The season couldn't be tinsel and home going as usual because the shadow of war hung like a pall over the landscape. Many of those called into military service were already far from loved ones, while others knew that their departure from familiar surroundings was imminent. But as threatening as the wartime sky seemed for all of us, there was for me an additional sadness.

I didn't mind spending my first Christmas in Richmond. I didn't want to return to the house in St. Louis already beginning to miss me as I would forever miss it. I enjoyed being with Helen and looked forward to double-dating with Clem and Alvin again, away from the accusing eyes of the Guidance Committee.

Still, there was a pain that year that I had felt during no other holiday season I could remember. For the first time, I had no home to go to. Home wasn't that house piled high with boxes and disarray, the furniture that would be left behind, including the desk I had studied on for four years, because the parsonage in New Rochelle was already furnished. Even now, hearing "I'll Be Home for Christmas" on the radio tugs at my emotions almost unbearably. Who would have ever thought then that that old song would still be around after more than sixty years and that the memory of my first Christmas away from home would still be sad?

New Rochelle wasn't home, but St. Louis wasn't either. I had been there too short a time, and that dramatic period of growth and revelation had ended with high school. It was time to move on. Destinations change; so does the traveler. Even though the concept of home bore the image of my parents' faces and welcoming smiles, still that picture dangled in meaningless space and left me no place to settle into.

Next December I would join the crowd of students heading North who would huddle together in the little "colored" waiting room at the railroad station in Petersburg, but that would have to wait.

This year I would ride the bus to Richmond instead, singing softly to myself the nostalgic plea for "snow and mistletoe," dangling in space between a home I could never return to and one that was yet to be, but vowing still to "be home for Christmas—if only in my dreams."

No member of a sorority or fraternity who was not initiated as an undergraduate on a black college campus during my time can fully appreciate its significance. The process of joining has since changed drastically, and hazing, intended to be good clean fun, has been outlawed by most if not all fraternal organizations because the practice was frequently abused, sometimes leading to physical injury or even death. But Madame, the faculty advisor of Alpha Kappa Alpha, made sure that no such physical abuse took place at Virginia State. Even with the good-natured hazing, I can think of nothing to equal my experience of joining the sorority. During my freshman year the various sororities courted likely students, inviting them to teas in an attempt to get them committed to pledge. Before I left St. Louis, Tid had said, "Don't come back to St. Louis as anything but an AKA." As I observed members of both Alpha Kappa Alpha and Delta Sigma Theta sororities, I knew for myself which way I wanted to go.

One of the things I liked about Virginia State was that there was no enmity among the various fraternal organizations, only a friendly rivalry. One identical twin that I knew was an AKA and the other a Delta, and one of my best friends, who later became basileus of our chapter, had a roommate who became basileus of the Delta chapter. They remained lifelong friends.

Every grading period, the combined grade point averages for each fraternal organization were published in *The Virginia Statesman,* and invariably Alpha Kappa Alpha and Alpha Phi Alpha, sister and brother organizations, were in the lead. A disproportionate number of Alphas made up the male section of the a cappella choir when we had one. And it was the AKAs whom I most admired. Their bearing and general demeanor exemplified dignity. These were the young women that I wanted to be like. I wanted desperately to become a part of them. Some members "dressed" for dinner, meaning only that they changed their saddle oxfords and socks to stockings and high-heeled shoes. These young women came in all sizes and skin colors, the basileus being a very dark-skinned student from Buffalo, New York. There were other dark-skinned members, as was also true of the Deltas, a denial of the accusation that certain sororities pledged only light-skinned girls.

At that time the college had only one main street, the three women's dormitories at one end and the three men's at the other end near Faculty Row, homes of some of the faculty members and their families. One day you would go to breakfast and see a line of men dressed in dark suits standing in front of the dining hall and bowing in unison when a "big brother" passed in front of them. These were the "dogs" who had begun some days of probation. At every meal they stood in line paying tribute to their "superiors." Later it would be rumored that the Alphas were going "off pro" that night. We went to bed as usual, but some time during the night we were wakened by male voices singing. Peering from a window, we saw their lighted emblem between two dormitories and heard them harmonize on their fraternity hymn. At another time it would be the AKAs standing on the steps of Trinkle Hall next door with their emblem lit, singing their hymn. Then the Alphas sang their hymn, followed by the Kappas who sang their Sweetheart Song. What an experience to aspire to!

Like Sumner High School in St. Louis, Virginia State College was all black. The entire administration, faculty, and student body were African American. My advisor and first composition professor was a young gray-eyed bachelor named Bernadin F. Dabney. His poor sight caused him to turn up his nose in a peculiar fashion, which made him more attractive to me. I wrote a couple of poems about him and showed them to him. He must have known that the gray eyes I referred to were his, but he didn't let on. In later years, after he married and we got to know his wife Margaret, Laura and I sometimes baby-sat with their two little girls. Laura did most of the work since I didn't know anything about caring for babies. All I knew how to do was write, and I did write a poem dedicated to Peggy when she was an infant.

One of Mr. Dabney's assignments was a narrative composition that could be in the form of prose or poetry. I chose to tell the story in a poem, "Pyramus and Thisbe." When I got the paper back, I saw a *B* on it. The only comment he made was that *ventured* was not the right word to use, having a different connotation than I intended. Marking my poem down for one word might have seemed harsh, but I realized that he knew I was capable of doing better and was holding me to a higher standard. I am still appreciative of his confidence in my ability.

Virginia State was well ahead of its time by almost thirty years, and students had not had to resort to pleas and demonstrations to have those courses included. But black schools in the South, even with their inadequate textbooks and unequally paid teachers, had always been ahead of their northern neighbors in telling the truth about our contributions. One of the courses offered was Negro history. I was not able to fit this class into my schedule, but I did take an American history class taught by the same eminent scholar, Dr. Luther Porter Jackson, Sr. He was the foremost authority of the free Negro in Virginia. I don't think I missed much since he included the African American experience in the general course. He was single-minded in his support of Negro History Week, the NAACP, and insistence that students reaching the age of 21 pay their poll tax and vote. He even accompanied them to the tiny polling place in Ettrick. I still have a snapshot of several other students and me taken with Dr. Jackson the first time we voted.

As the majority of students at Virginia State lived in Virginia or had Virginia family connections, Dr. Jackson began the first class session in American history by having all of us introduce ourselves and tell where we were from. There were two cousins in the class who looked like white girls. When they announced their names and where they were from, he told them more of their family's history than they knew themselves. There was another student from Akron, Ohio whose family name he knew. Excitedly he said: "Oh, yes, yes, yes! Your great-grandfather had the finest carriages in the county and owned [so many and so many] slaves." That was the first I had ever heard of black people as slave owners. He also told us the locations of slave marts on streets in Petersburg with which we were familiar and nearby fields where Civil War battles had been fought.

For a short time during my freshman year I worked for him part time, underlining the names of black legislators during Reconstruction. Naturally, I read what they had to say, learning firsthand how the history books had lied in depicting them as ignoramuses. I soon quit because the job interfered with my social life.

A course in Negro literature was also offered. It was taught by Zatella R. Turner. The textbook was *The Negro Caravan*, but it was fairly expensive and I couldn't afford to buy my own copy. I borrowed someone else's. Years later I had to pay many times the cost of the original volume for a reprint, but I didn't mind at all, considering myself fortunate to finally be able to have my very own copy of this marvelous anthology.

Miss Turner also taught a course in Robert Browning, a poet whose work still rates among my all-time favorites. She had us memorize touchstone lines and once assigned the recitation from memory of a Browning poem of at least a certain number of lines. When I recited the entire much longer poem, "Evelyn Hope," I could feel the angry stares of my classmates, but I had not chosen it for a higher grade; I just liked the poem.

Long before I took Miss Turner's class in English literature, I learned about two requirements for which she was best known on campus. Some years earlier, she had won a competitive fellowship sponsored by Alpha Kappa Alpha Sorority which provided for a year of study in England. She later self-published a slim red volume entitled, *My Wonderful Year*. Nobody, it was said, got out of her class successfully without making some pretense at reading it.

The one historical oddity that I recall from this book was that, during that one year, 1936, she had seen three kings of England. She viewed the body of King George V, who died January 20, lying in state. Later she caught a glimpse of his successor, King Edward VIII, who served only eleven months before abdicating the throne on December 10 to marry an American divorcée, Wallis Warfield Simpson. She also saw King George VI who ascended to the throne on December 12 of the same year. He was the father of the present Queen Elizabeth.

Miss Turner liked poetry, and her other requirement was that each of her students would learn to appreciate the intricacies of a sonnet by writing one. Since some of my poems had been published in *The Virginia Statesman*, several students in her English literature class appealed to me in desperation. I had written a few fairly decent sonnets in high school and was willing to oblige—for a price. I reasoned that, since my monthly spending allowance was only four dollars, I could increase my wealth considerably by charging a quarter for each fourteen line stanza, written to order for that particular customer. That would provide me with a few extra hamburgers or a trip to the movies. Not wanting to cause any suspicion and thereby ruin a good thing, I used what information I had or what I surmised concerning the customer's interests as a basis for the subject of each poem and its slant. I was also careful not to make the poem too good, letting the rhythm limp here and there and including a false rhyme or two for authenticity. The plan evidently worked, and the following semester the number of students requesting my services increased. Miss Turner never suspected that there was a ghost writer lurking in the shadows whose sonnets were for sale.

By the time I took her class, business was really flourishing. All but one of the classmates who requested my services were careful to see me before the due date and settle their debt in time to copy their poems in their own handwriting before turning them in. The one memorable exception was Luther Porter Jackson, Jr., son of the history professor. That day he came to class late, nonchalantly taking a seat across the room from me. He seemed not at all concerned about whether he turned in his assignment or not, but I had put a considerable amount of effort into the writing and didn't want to see it go to waste. As unobtrusively as possible, I passed it through several secret hands to his location in time for it to be turned in with the others. After class he disappeared into thin air, and I never did get my hard-earned 25 cents.

It was not until recent years that time caught up with him. His son, Luther, III, a reporter for the *Detroit Free Press* for a while, somehow located me, along with other local alumni, and wrote to ask if I had known his grandfather on whom he was doing research. I quickly responded that I had, and we arranged a taped interview. I showed him the picture taken at the polling place in Ettrick.

It was after that interview that my debtor came to town to visit his son. Retired or about to retire as a professor of journalism at Columbia University, he had enjoyed a successful and productive career. One of his former students, Chuck Stokes, editorial director of a local television channel, brought him to my home. It was wonderful to see him again and share our common interests. They invited me to go to lunch with them.

As we sat reminiscing at a table in a noisy popular restaurant, I told his protégé the story of the ghostwritten sonnet and reminded Luther that he still owed me for it. With a good-natured laugh, he shoved a quarter across the table. I wasn't really serious about collecting, but since he insisted on paying, I didn't have the nerve to mention almost a half-century's interest on the overdue debt.

When I became a teacher I didn't ask students to write poems except in a creative writing class. Such assignments, I feel, encourage plagiarism. I would hate to be judged as a singer alongside someone who was born musically gifted or enter a dance contest knowing that my stiff and self-conscious movements wouldn't hold a chance against someone more lithe and fluid. Not all people have a sense of rhythm. Not all people can carry a tune. To demand that everyone in a class complete a task that requires qualities they do not have seems unfair. That doesn't mean that an attempt at writing a sonnet should be avoided completely. If it is done in a spirit of experimentation and fun—with no letter grade given and no penalties for not doing it well—it can be a useful exercise.

Miss Felicia D. Anderson, who taught literature and drama and directed the Theatre Guild, made a tremendous and lasting impression on me. When I sat in her literature class, it was as if no

Professor Felicia D. Anderson

one existed but the two of us. Her deep appreciation of literature and her vast knowledge kept me entranced, and I drank in her every word. "Felicia D.," as we called her behind her back, wore clothing that was unique, some dresses having pockets in the back. She was in every way her own person. If the class was inclined to get noisy, she would raise one hand and quote from Shakespeare in her inimitable voice, "'Absent thee from felicity awhile.'" I sometimes had discussions with her outside class and asked her once: "Miss Anderson, don't you get discouraged that so few of your students really appreciate the wealth of knowledge you are trying to communicate to them?" Her answer was: "No. No. If in one college generation one student catches the vision, that is enough." I thought, "How terrible! How can she be satisfied with such a low percentage?" But years later when I became a teacher, it was her words that came back to me and sustained me. Her words and the eventual realization that a teacher never really knows whom he or she may be reaching or in what ways. Sometimes it might be the unlikeliest students.

When my parents came to the campus for the baccalaureate sermon at the end of my freshman year, I stayed on campus longer than I normally would have. Most of the students left as soon as their last final examinations were over. Being one of the few still there was somewhat lonely. When we left the campus we spent a few days in Richmond with relatives. Helen decided to leave with us to spend part of the summer in New Rochelle. Alvin accompanied us to the station and kissed me goodbye.

New Rochelle

Dad, Mama, Helen and I rode the train from Richmond into Pennsylvania Station in New York City, then transferred to Grand Central Station where we caught the New York, New Haven and Hartford commuter train to New Rochelle.

The parsonage, 22 Clinton Avenue, was halfway up a hill as "Squirt" had told me. Stucco, like many houses in that area, it was tiny compared to the house in St. Louis and smaller than the one in East Orange. It had a sun room on the front and only three bedrooms, one of which was used for Dad's study. My room, which I shared with Helen, was down a short hall from the study, and my parents' bedroom was around the corner from it. It was several days before Clarence arrived from Lincoln for the first time. He must have slept in the basement. I wondered how Joe Henderson and Bunny were able to accommodate four little boys in that house. They must have shared one room with two bunk beds.

Bethesda Baptist Church, too, was tiny compared to the stately stone building in St. Louis, but the people were warm and friendly. Westchester County, I was told, was the wealthiest county in the nation, and many of the white families hired staffs of servants who lived on the premises. A number of the church members held such jobs and rented rooms or small apartments in large homes where they spent their Thursdays and every other Sunday. Most of the black people we knew lived in the same neighborhood where we did, and Lincoln School, across the street from the church, had a mostly, if not totally, black student body. It was this elementary school that was to play a major role later in a Supreme Court ruling on *de facto* segregation.

Helen and I met two boys with whom we double-dated. Helen was better looking than I and had a more outgoing personality, so the more personable of the young men dated her. I liked him better than the one I was left with, but he was all right. Sometimes we went out with several other young people, including two of the many children of the now deceased founder of the church, Rev. Boddie, and another girl from church named Rosetta Brown. A couple of times when a group of us went to New York City, we missed the last train back and spent the rest of the night sleeping on the benches at Grand Central Station. Sometimes we went to Harlem to watch the dancers at the Savoy Ballroom doing some serious jitterbugging or took in a performance at the Apollo Theater. Harlem was fun during the Forties and not at all a dangerous place to be.

On one occasion Helen and I visited a fellow student from State who lived in an apartment in Harlem. As we sat in his living room and talked, I was surprised that he didn't introduce us to a man who passed through the living room on his way out. In fact, he didn't even speak to him. It took me a while to realize that no available space in a Harlem apartment went unrented, no matter if that space accommodated little more than a twin bed. It was unthinkable to me that a family would share its living quarters with someone they hardly knew.

We met some of the other young people in the church, including Katie Butler, whom my brother Wilbur later married, Ora Brown, and Virginia Brown (now Toone). I already knew "Squirt" and saw him often at church.

After Helen went back to Richmond, I got a job in Mt. Vernon at what was originally a powder puff factory, but it had been taken over by the government to make military insignia. It was a very boring assembly line job in which I sat and placed metal USs or silver wings in little holes in a long wooden board that then went to the next person for polishing. It was very hard on my hands, which became rough and difficult to get clean. But I was earning money for whatever new clothing I would take back to college in the fall. Mama and I sometimes took the bus but more often walked to "the Village," the city's small commercial area, and attended a movie or shopped at Bloomingdale's. Occasionally we looked at clothing at Arnold Constable, but it was too expensive for our purses.

165

Ever since my arrival in New Rochelle, Dad had been insisting that I meet a young woman named Constance Grayson who lived across the street. He said that she was an invalid and talked about what a remarkable person she was. What was I to say to her? Dreading the visit, I put it off as long as I could. When I could no longer find an excuse for not going, I was amazed. She was a very intelligent, personable, articulate woman who defied any pity I had expected to feel. We talked about literature, and I read her some of my favorite poems, eagerly sharing with her many of my own. I visited Connie as often as I could because we had so much to talk about and share.

She was confined to her bed, located in the sun room in the front of the house so that she could look out the window. She belonged to the Seventh Day Adventist church on the street behind Clinton Avenue and taught a Sabbath school class, the children coming to her house for instruction. She also had a radio hookup so that she could hear the services and sometimes speak. Her brother and his Jewish wife were frequent Sunday visitors, along with other members of her church, including a man from Argentina. The sun room was often occupied with what looked like representatives from the United Nations. But nobody came to comfort Connie. It was we who were comforted by her presence, her cheerfulness, and her interesting conversation. The telephone company arranged for her to have a phone that didn't have to be dialed. She was unable to sit up without being propped or to feed herself. Lying on her pillow she made calls selling greeting cards and hosiery to supplement the family income. She was such a good sales person that people made purchases on the strength of her appeal.

I learned that Connie had been an undergraduate at Hunter College when she was stricken with what I assume was rheumatoid arthritis. During one of my evening visits, she asked her mother to bring out a painting to show me. It was the picture of a young woman. She asked me what I saw in it. I found it interesting and thought it was well done and said as much. "But what do you see in

166

it?" she insisted. I looked closer. The woman didn't look familiar, but her posture and the expression on her face elicited the impression that she was facing something dreadful but was determined not to be afraid. She assured me that my interpretation was correct. "That's a self-portrait I painted when I first realized that I was going to be an invalid for life," she said.

One year she was taken to the Seventh Day Adventist hospital in Alabama for therapy. When I saw her again, she was able to feed herself and attend services at her church in a wheelchair. On one of my visits I saw her still in bed but sitting up. She asked her mother to help her out of bed and then, to my amazement, she took two steps. What a miraculous improvement!

After I moved to Detroit I stayed in touch with her by mail and visited her whenever I went back to see my parents, but we were never as close again as when we lived in the parsonage across the street. I was saddened to learn some time later that she had died of pneumonia. She remains in my memory as the most remarkable person I have ever met.

New Rochelle is not a great distance from East Orange, and one day, John Simmons, the man who had loaned Dad his movie camera and projector and took us to Pompton Lakes in the Thirties, the man who was always promoting someone, was now interested in a newly formed quartet that sang religious music. Such quartets were very popular then. I don't know if it was for the purpose of requesting an engagement for them to sing at Bethesda or not, but for whatever reason, he brought them to our house. I came downstairs wearing a long red housecoat with white polka dots and saw the interested smile of one of the singers. If ever there was love at first sight, this was it. Originally from Baltimore, he (I will call him Burt.) was now rooming in East Orange with a family friend who belonged to Calvary. I later learned that he was the brother of the lead singer of a popular and successful quartet that I will refer to as "The Rovers." (If there is or ever was an actual group by this name, it is not to them that I am referring.)

Burt seemed to be working as a shipping clerk or doing other odd jobs, and at times he might not have been working at all. He came to visit me on one occasion looking somewhat shabby in mismatched clothes, having probably pawned his best clothes to have money for the train. The parsonage didn't have a guest closet, and Clarence took his coat to the basement, going through his pockets searching in vain for condoms. I don't recall where we went or what we did in particular, but I must have made a few trips to East Orange where we engaged in a torrid romance. We were totally, completely in love, and I started a series of poems to him called "Unfinished Song." When it was time to go back to Virginia State, we vowed to write each other frequently.

Sophomore Year

Back at State in September, 1942, I debated what to do about Alvin. As sophomores we were now allowed to sit in the dining hall reserved for upperclassmen. Alvin and three other men immediately secured a table for themselves and their girlfriends. Although I thought I was in love with him the year before, my feelings had now changed. Not being sexually involved with him, I would have been smart to keep Burt a secret and enjoy Alvin's company on campus, but I found it impossible to feign a feeling that no longer existed. So, although the four couples still shared a table, I told him I had fallen in love with someone else. It wasn't long before he started going with another girl, and I had no male companion on campus.

My dormitory room this year was over the main entrance to Byrd Hall. Hiding doughnuts in my closet to keep them from being completely devoured by other students who came to my room, I discovered that I was getting help anyhow. Now and then, if my roommate or I was taking an afternoon nap, a mouse would come out of the closet and boldly run across the room. When I complained to the house mother, she said, "Oh, he lives in that room." So we named him Elmer and learned to coexist with him, but I stopped leaving anything edible in the closet.

Two of my classmates, Emilyn Syphax, Margaret Spencer, and I made friends with three girls in the freshman class, Marguerite Mills, Lois Brown and Lillian "Baby Doll" Fisher, who had a beautiful lyric soprano voice, and we took them under our wings.

At some point during that year or the next, a male music major whom I will call Dan transferred, we were told, from Northwestern University. He played the piano and organ expertly, and I wondered why he had left a university like Northwestern to attend little Virginia State. He and Baby Doll became a pair, and he would let no one else accompany her when she sang. Sometimes after chapel several of us

169

would gather around the organ and ask him to play our favorite songs. I had recently seen a movie whose theme song I liked so much that I purchased the sheet music. After Dan played it at my request, he said, "You know, I composed that." With considerable doubt, I went back to my room and checked the name of the composer on the sheet music. It wasn't his. When I asked him about it, he replied, "That's the name I use in Hollywood." Still doubting, I went to the library and looked up the composer. The book showed his picture, a Russian considerably older than Dan, with a long list of credits. Dan was a quiet young man with an unassuming demeanor, not the kind of person anyone would expect to lie about something that could be so easily checked. He later made another claim that I found to be untrue.

Suddenly he disappeared from campus, and Madame confided in me the reason for his departure. He had never completed high school and had forged his transcript from Northwestern. He was given the option of attending the laboratory high school on campus or leaving. He left. Years later I had occasion to talk to Baby Doll's sister who had kept in touch with him for several years. She told me that, after he left State, he played the organ for a large white church in Boston.

Only a few years after that, he came to Detroit but would not permit an interview with the black-owned *Michigan Chronicle* whose editor was a former professor at Virginia State. During his appearance on television he was asked, "I understand you have two PhDs, one in music and one in psychology." Still very low-key and scholarly looking, he replied, "Yes, that's right." He was also written up in *Life* magazine in an article that claimed the same accomplishments. Not enough time had elapsed for him to earn a GED and receive even a bachelor's degree, let alone one Ph.D. How he got away with this, his most colossal lie, remains a mystery to me. Obviously, nobody bothered to check the institutions' records. He had become famous for his unique style and his performances with a small group of other musicians. I still enjoy listening to the recording I have of his trio but wonder why, with his remarkable talent, he felt it necessary to invent an educational background that was not needed for his success.

Before going home after our freshman year, the AKA pledgees had been informed of exactly what materials we would need to bring back for fall initiation. Among the things we needed was a formal dress for the banquet that would follow our initiation. I couldn't afford to buy such a dress out of my summer earnings. Dad agreed to pay the necessary fees involved with membership and the money needed for special supplies for probation, but for some reason he thought the formal dress was unnecessary. Mama, who had no money except what Dad gave her, went shopping with me and bought the dress without telling Dad, knowing that he never asked her to account for the money she spent. Even if she wasn't acquainted with the song, "God Bless the Child Who's Got His Own," she was wise enough not to depend entirely on his usual generosity and had probably saved some of the grocery money for her own use.

Before we went on probation, each pledgee was assigned a "big sister" for whom she had to perform minor daily chores such as emptying her wastebasket or ironing a blouse. When we actually went "on pro," we met in the sorority room for our nightly hazing with Madame always present. Whenever we were told to "assume the angle," the sorority member doing the paddling had to put one hand on the tailbone of the pledgee and use the paddle with the other. Madame saw to it that the paddling was light. We had to learn the Greek alphabet and memorize the names of the founders and national presidents. All of us were given "worm" names; I became "Worm Oops" because that was the way I pronounced the first syllable of *upsilon*. Before being dismissed at about 10:30 or 11:00 o'clock each night, we were told what we had to wear the next day.

There were only five of us being "made" in the fall of 1942. Two of us lived in Byrd Hall, two in Trinkle, and one in Eggleston. Since the phone down the hall would be shut off by the time we got back to our rooms, we had to be in absolute agreement before we separated. Every day's costume was different and had to be made from scratch the night before. One day we had to wear crepe paper pantaloons and top hats whose cardboard crowns and brims had to have identical measurements. Students on pro were not allowed to miss any classes, so our friends in the dormitory stayed up with us all night making the costume for the next day.

Miriam Gould, Margaret Spencer, Theresa Green, me, and Theresita Norris

Before breakfast and other meals, we had to meet in front of Byrd Hall, march down the street in line and stand in front of the upperclassmen's dining hall until all the students had gone in. Each time a big sister passed in front of us, we had to make a deep bow and say in unison, "Good morning, Superior [So-and-So]." When an Alpha passed, we had to nod our heads in silent greeting. During the day, we were given such duties as scrubbing the dining hall steps with toothbrushes and thimbles of water. We were also required to count the blades of grass between certain buildings. No matter what number we agreed on, it was wrong, of course. In the sorority room we had to make sure we stayed off the tail of an imaginary creature named Bismarck. We were also forbidden to partake of any sweets. A lot of silliness, but no one was hurt and the difficulties we had to endure made our final acceptance as members more meaningful.

Before we went off pro, we were instructed to collect worms in a jar, which a boy from New Jersey did for me, and to dress warmly. When the night came, we were blindfolded and taken across the Eastern Seaboard railroad tracks that divided the main campus from the Agricultural Department. We had to eat what we were expected to believe were the worms we had caught and literally "cross the burning sands." Someone instructed me to call Alvin. This command was followed by the voice of the big sister who was now going with him. "You better not call Alvin." As a train approached, we were supposed to believe that we were standing on the tracks, led away just a second before the train reached that point.

After the blindfolds were removed and the formal ceremony took place, we gathered between dormitories in the middle of the night with our emblem lit, the twenty pearls glowing in the dark, to sing our national hymn. The Alphas and Kappas followed with their songs, a ritual that had so inspired me the first time I saw it. The banquet followed a day or so later. I was now a member of Alpha Epsilon Chapter of the first African American sorority, founded in 1908 at Howard University. I felt fully accepted into this sisterhood that stands for character, merit, service, and friendship. Wherever I would go for the rest of my life, my identification as a soror would bind me immediately to other members I might meet.

When Christmas vacation came, all the students going north met in the tiny "colored" railroad station waiting room, huddling around the potbellied stove trying to keep warm and singing as we waited for the late train that would take me to my first Christmas in New Rochelle. When the train finally arrived, the Jim Crow car was already completely occupied and, although the car behind it was almost empty, we were not allowed to sit there. The best we could do was stand for short periods and sit on our suitcases in the aisle until we got to Washington where we could then sit anywhere there was an empty seat.

173

Alpha Epsilon Chapter, 1943 or 1944. I am third from the left, second row. Madame Worthington is top row center.

Burt's mother was visiting his brother Bob in Long Island for the holidays, and I was invited there for Christmas dinner. I was impressed with the spacious house, the piano inscribed with Bob's name and that of his Puerto Rican wife, and the elaborate train set that occupied the entire third floor. Burt's mother was evidently very favorably impressed with me. It was clear that she hoped we would marry. The last time I saw her was 1954 when she was in Detroit for a convention and I was preparing to remarry. Even though Burt and I had broken up years before, she had never given up hope that we would eventually get back together and begged me to postpone my marriage and give Burt another chance. After our Christmas dinner we went to visit another member of the Rovers who was married to a plump Italian woman and had a house full of beautiful golden children.

After the holidays, Burt began to travel with the quartet he sang with and wrote me short letters about his activities. Madame demanded to see his letters to make sure there was nothing improper in them. I had no objection since he made few references to anything personal except to say he loved me.

Tid was in her sophomore year at Howard University and invited me to visit her there for a weekend. I received the necessary permission letter from home. Burt decided to visit his mother in Baltimore at the same time and meet me in Washington. My weekend, which turned out to be five days, was enlightening. On Howard's campus we spent many evening hours in the *Hilltop* newspaper office, talking and consuming the ale and barbecued ribs that Tid and some of her friends sent out for. I learned that she and her sister received an allowance of about fifty dollars a week, and at Howard a fur coat seemed to be a requirement. There was also a great deal of color prejudice and enmity between the various Greek letter organizations. I was glad I was a student at Virginia State instead of Howard. The climate was completely different. My four-dollar-a-month allowance would not have gotten me through one day on this campus located in a city where there were so many off-campus places one could go and so much more to do. Burt and I found some time to spend together. Burt's photograph was on my table at State and visible to any student who visited the room I shared with Zelda Lassiter. Some of the students knew I had met him in Washington. One of our visitors told a Baltimore friend of hers about our meeting; she in turn informed a girl named Marian with whom Burt had had a relationship when he was still living in Baltimore. I was not aware that information about our meeting in Washington had been passed on.

On Easter Sunday morning, Marian appeared at the parsonage in New Rochelle before the morning service, armed with letters that Burt had written to her during an earlier period. She had to wait until the service was over before telling my parents her story. She claimed that Burt had asked her to marry him. It was apparent from his letters that she had been sending him money, but there was no evidence that he had proposed marriage. Determined that, if she couldn't have him, I wouldn't either, she left the letters with my parents. Dad called Burt and had him come to the parsonage where he forbade him to ever see me again.

I don't remember which letter I received first, the one from Dad or the one from Burt who lamely tried to explain himself. He admitted taking money from her, supplied by two well-to-do uncles, but denied that he had ever proposed marriage. He also mentioned that she had a health problem. In the process he asked for my forgiveness. I felt deceived and was heartbroken. I must have answered his letter, but I don't know what I said.

At the end of the school year I spent a few days in Richmond during which time the Rovers had a singing engagement there. There was no place to go in Richmond for entertainment except Bob Long's Market Inn in the country outside Richmond and no place for black visitors to stay except one black-owned hotel on Second and Leigh near the black Hippodrome movie theater. I was very hurt but still very much in love. Deciding to get some advice from Burt's brother Bob, I went to Eggleston's Hotel and sent a message to his room that I wanted to see him. He came downstairs and talked to me.

176

It was clear that the two didn't get along, and Bob was disgusted with his brother's lack of success or even a decent job. "Do you know how much older I am than he?" he asked me. Of course, I didn't. Burt would never tell me his age. "Five minutes," he said. I have never seen in print any mention of the fact that these brothers were fraternal twins, but I had it straight from the horse's mouth. Bob said nothing to convince me that Burt was deserving of my further attention, but I think I had already made up my mind to forgive him. My "Unfinished Song" was still unfinished.

That summer Evelyn Stewart from East Orange was working at the Office of Dependency Benefits, a branch of the War Department, in Newark and suggested that I apply for a temporary job there. I was hired, and Mrs. Stewart let me live at their family home, a third floor flat in East Orange. Burt was still rooming in a house nearby, making the continuation of our relationship convenient. It was soon after that that I learned Marian, his former girlfriend, had died. I spent every week at the Stewarts' house, going to New Rochelle for the weekend. I was earning $25 a week, and Mrs. Stewart charged me three dollars for room and board. She didn't want me to feel like a freeloader and felt that this small amount would make me feel that I was contributing. She laundered my clothes and prepared my favorite meals. During some part of the summer Jimmy came home from the Navy on furlough and Bob from the Army.

The ODB had taken over a newly constructed building owned by an insurance company that did not insure African Americans, but it could not prevent our working there. Our job was to read letters from the dependents of military personnel and search the records on three different floors to obtain enough information to draft a reply. For some reason the structure had been built without air conditioning. Because we were at war, no lights were supposed to be visible from the sky, and the rooms in which we worked were heavily curtained. During the night shift, which I sometimes worked, the curtains had to be opened periodically for an influx of fresh air during which time the lights had to be turned off. This occurred on different floors at different times. When the people in my unit discovered the time when each of the floors on which we searched records was due for a blackout, we managed to be on that floor, catching as many as three blackouts every evening during which time we couldn't work.

Mrs. Stewart was a very wise woman. She didn't feel that Burt was the kind of man my family would want me to marry and said as much, but she wasn't persistent. Burt was free to come to her house to pick me up or meet me at the bus stop and walk me home after work. On one occasion I was waiting for him to come when Dad suddenly appeared at their open door at the top of the stairs. I had no idea that he was in East Orange and certainly didn't want him to run into Burt. Mrs. Stewart, in spite of her disapproval of Burt, managed to hurry Dad out before the appointed time of my date.

My usual attire was dirty saddle oxfords and bobby sox. On only one occasion that summer do I recall dressing up. This was for a date with Burt to hear the Rovers and a famous female singer at the Apollo Theater. For this special occasion I put on high-heeled shoes and stockings (still the cursed rayon ones). We had our picture taken, and he took me backstage to meet the female singer. It was perhaps the same night that we went into a bar in Harlem and he pointed out Billie Holiday surrounded by a group of white men who were no doubt thrilled to be granted a minute of her attention.

The following summer I again lived with the Stewarts and worked with Evelyn at the ODB. By this time Burt had moved to a room in an apartment in Harlem. Although I was beginning to disapprove of some of his errant ways and swore, over and over again, that I wouldn't see him again, I kept coming back. By the time I went back to State for my senior year, I had come to realize how rotten he was, and this time I knew it was over for good.

One of the Rovers died, and the personnel went through several changes. In 1945 Burt became a member of the famous group. Although I have never regretted the end of our relationship, I still listen to his recorded speaking voice and understand why, in my youth, I had been so vulnerable.

Last Two Years

I think it was during my junior year that my cousin Helen came to Virginia State to earn her master's degree. As a graduate student, she lived at the other end of the campus, and I didn't see much of her, but she had a lot more clothes than I did, and I asked her if I could borrow her red Macintosh. I think I wore it the whole winter.

At one point, Sammy Canaan, my friend from St. Louis, who was now stationed at Camp Lee, came to the campus several times to see me. One evening we took a long walk in the rain heading toward Petersburg. When Wil joined the Army Air Corps, he left his civilian leather flying helmet in New Rochelle, and I had taken it back to campus. I often wore it to protect my hair from the rain, and when I walked with Sammy, I was wearing blue jeans, Helen's Macintosh, and Wil's helmet. That became my uniform whenever it rained.

About this time, I joined the Women's Symphonic Choir under the excellent direction of Professor Undine Moore. Today many of the streets and buildings on campus bear the names of professors whom I knew; the fact that nothing bears Professor Moore's name completely baffles me, for she was without doubt one of its most accomplished faculty members. I am delighted whenever the church choir to which I now belong sings one of her compositions or arrangements. Some years ago Billy Taylor was responsible for her receiving an honorary doctorate from another institution. No one was more deserving.

I was already familiar with Countee Cullen's poetry, but I discovered two of his juvenile books in the library and fell in love with them. *The Lost Zoo,* with its fictional extinct animals that missed getting on Noah's Ark, fascinated me. I have always loved cats, and *My Lives and How I Lost Them by Christopher Cat as Told to Countee Cullen* fascinated me even more, especially with the feline author's derogatory remarks about Mr. Cullen. I also found a copy of *The Negro Yearbook* which listed Countee Cullen's address. I had never been to Tuckahoe, New York but knew that it was in Westchester County and couldn't be too far from New Rochelle, so I wrote him a letter commending his work and asking if I might visit him when I left State for the summer. He graciously responded with his phone number, suggesting that I call him when I returned to New Rochelle.

On my return in the summer of 1944, I called him and he gave me the directions to his house. Dad drove me, but we had trouble finding the house as many of the streets took numerous curves through wooded areas. We stopped someone on the street for directions. "Oh, the poet," he responded. He gave us the guidance we needed.

We were met at the door by Mr. Cullen's second wife Ida, a kitten at her ankles. His father, also a minister, was sitting in the living room. Then Mr. Cullen appeared and invited me into his study while our fathers conversed. He told me that the kitten at the door was Christopher's grandson.

Mr. Cullen was a short, rotund man with eyes that twinkled as he talked. He read some of the poems I had brought and said, "Well, you're a poet!" Those encouraging words from him could not have been more reassuring. He told me not to be discouraged by rejection slips, to plan to paper my walls with them, but to keep sending out my work to magazines and journals. He showed me a short poem of his own which he said he had never been able to get published. I have always regretted that I didn't make a note of the title. He had been famous for many years, his major work behind him. That one of his poems had been continually rejected drove home his point. When he died less than two years later, his wife sent me an announcement.

It was my intention when I first went to State to transfer in my junior year to the University of Kansas and major in journalism, but living in a dormitory on a southern black campus meant so much to me that no one could have pried me away. When Bill Sims, faculty advisor of *The Virginia Statesman*, warned me that journalism would have a negative effect on my creativity as a poet, I was quick to believe him. Furthermore, I enjoyed my courses in literature so much that I knew there should be no other major for me but English.

I took every English course that was offered, except two that I couldn't fit into my schedule and one intended for business majors. Most of my electives were in English. No other English major in my class had as many credits in that subject as I did.

While liberal arts students majored in specific fields, most of them took advantage of the laboratory elementary and high schools on campus. They used some of their electives for the education courses required for a teaching certificate in Virginia and did their student teaching at one of these schools. But not I. Determined as I was never to teach, I was one of only two students in my class who didn't take advantage of this opportunity. What I thought I was going to do with my degree in English I had no idea. Editorial positions were usually not available to African Americans, but I'd worry about that later. I knew that I couldn't make a living as a poet, but perhaps I would write other things. When Dad found out after graduation that I was not prepared for any available position, he was really annoyed with me. Even after I started work on an M.A. in English at New York University, I still had no idea what kind of employment I would be able to get.

While I was writing for *The Virginia Statesman*, James A. Eaton and I became very good friends. He had not been drafted and remained at State to graduate. He was editor and I was assistant editor for awhile. He also wrote poetry, and we enjoyed sharing each other's work. One year we had a severe ice storm that coated the branches of trees, severely damaging many of them. One of us wrote a column about the destruction; the other wrote about the beauty of the scene. The two columns were published side by side. I spent a great deal of time with James and enjoyed his company. We had a great deal in common. Many years after graduation, we made contact again, and I am happy to say that we still correspond on a regular basis.

By now I was rooming with Laura B. Mann from New Jersey. When she was on pro, I participated in the hazing in the sorority room. Back in our room, I offered her candy. After she had innocently accepted and consumed it, I threatened to expose and punish her at the next meeting, but I had no intention of doing it. It was all in the fun of the procedure. We laughed about it later.

That year we lived in Langston Hall, named after Langston Hughes's great-uncle, a Congressman during Reconstruction. This was one of the former men's dormitories. Our room was across the hall from a science professor and his wife and baby. We often left our doors open to listen to the music on their record player. Nat "King" Cole's "Sweet Loraine" was my favorite at the time, and I pleaded to listen to it over and over. Nat Sims often visited this family. Sometimes if he was driving to Richmond for something, he invited Laura or me, whichever one of us happened to be in the room, to go along with him for the ride. We got the impression that he was interested in one of us but we could never figure out which one. He probably only wanted company and thought it would be a break for us to get off campus for awhile. It was several years after we graduated that he got married for the first time and fathered a child. His view was that marriage was simply a legal contract and had no purpose except to produce children. He was an excellent photographer and for many years he sent us Christmas cards showing campus scenes. When we graduated, he took 16mm movies of our procession into Virginia Hall, showing Laura's mother and my parents on the sidelines. He also took movies of the sorority members singing in a circle around the sun dial on the front campus.

When I went to my class's fifty year reunion, I had these films transferred to videotape and showed them at a party one of my classmates had at her home. Everyone was fascinated to see this record of our youthful days on campus.

Mrs. Otelia Howard, who had once taught me composition, was impressed with my ability to write creatively. She told me that she could write a perfect composition but it lacked the imaginative quality that my work possessed. Somewhere in my papers I still have one of my in-class assignments, an example of description, that began, "Gardener, let the leaves lie."

When I was finishing up my junior year, she called me into her office one day and indicated that she had checked my records. She said that, if I took twenty hours the next semester, I could graduate in three and a half years. Otherwise, I would need to spend my last semester on campus for only one three-hour course. She suggested that I talk to Dean James Hugo Johnston and ask for his permission. I followed her advice, but he quickly responded, "No, that's not possible." A day or so later, he sent for me and asked, "Do you think you can handle it?" I said I could. "Then go ahead," he told me. So the first semester of my senior year, I took the twenty hours and earned a 4.0 average for the first time. (I had worked so hard in high school that, when I entered Virginia State, I made a conscious decision to do well but not excel. I wanted to enjoy the social experience of college along with the educational. I did graduate with high honors, but my grade point average could have been higher if I had applied myself more.)

The chairman of the English Department, Mr. Thomas Pawley, Sr., was, on the surface, a sweet-tempered man who had written a freshman composition book useful only to students whose high school education had been deficient. Shelby Rooks, who was from

Norfolk and had a good educational background, and I were bored with his class because we had learned all he had to teach and more many years earlier.

I learned the hard way that, in spite of Mr. Pawley's deceptively sweet disposition, he was really a vindictive man. In one class in English poetry, he invited us to question and even disagree with him whenever we felt so inclined. Ostensibly that was a way to get a good discussion going. I took him at his word and sometimes questioned his interpretations of poems. His interpretations were what he would have meant if he had written the poems but had nothing to do with what the author wrote. Sometimes it was just the opposite. When I asked him where in a certain poem he saw this or that, he could never answer it to my satisfaction. Stupid me! I didn't realize until too late that he resented being questioned. After taking the final examination, I left the room, satisfied that I had written an excellent paper that deserved an *A*. When it was returned I was shocked to see instead a big red *C* minus, the lowest grade I had ever received in a literature or composition class in my life. My final grade was *C*. He had written no comments on my paper. When I went to his office to inquire, his only response was that some of the students had written more than I had. I asked him if he was interested in quantity or quality and what information I had failed to provide. He refused to discuss the matter further.

The following semester I was required to take The Growth and Structure of the English Language. Mr. Pawley was the only person teaching it, and I was stuck with him in a course that, by comparison to other English courses, was dull and uninteresting. I made up my mind what I was going to do.

Margaret Spencer, also an English major, sat next to me on the front row. Students at Virginia State normally called their professors Mr., Dr., Mrs. or Miss, but together we decided to "butter him up" in order to receive good grades. When he pursed his lips and make some statement that he evidently thought exemplified wisdom, one of us would say, "Oh, Professor Pawley, that is so philosophical! Why don't you write a book on it?" He was likely to answer, "I would, but I just don't have the time." This dialogue was repeated so often, our remarks always addressed to "Professor" Pawley, that the students in the back of the room snickered, but he never caught on. Neither Margaret nor I read many of the textbook assignments, simply taking notes on his class lectures and never, never questioning anything he said. On the final exam we simply gave him back the information he had provided, quoting him amply. Both of us received *A*s as our final grade.

One of the English professors offered an annual award to the English major with the highest average in that subject. Because of Mr. Pawley's *C*, the award went to Margaret who had used many of her electives to earn a teaching certificate and had taken nowhere near the number of English courses that I had. When I saw Mr. Pawley again, he said, "Miss Long, I'm surprised you didn't win the English award." I answered, "I would have if you hadn't given me a *C*." "When did I ever give you a *C*?" he asked, my earlier questioning now erased by the later flattery.

When I spoke to "Felicia D" about this matter, she confided in me that, because she had once disagreed with him, he assigned her to freshman composition classes only, but the president of the college overruled his effort to punish her. What a disservice that would have been to the students to whom she gave so much of her rich knowledge and appreciation of literature!

One semester several of us had two Saturday morning classes with Mr. Pawley running back to back. He kept some of the most interesting classes for himself. For the short period between classes, he usually visited with Dr. Harry Roberts in the hall, leaving his pocket watch on the desk. One Saturday after the first class was over, Syphax decided to set his watch ahead by fifteen minutes so that we could leave early. When he came back for the second class, he glanced at his watch and said, "Oh, have I been gone that long?" Syphax replied, "You *were* gone for quite a while." When, according to his watch, it was time for the second class to end, he said, "It must be time to go, but I didn't hear the bell ring." Someone said, "The bell isn't working today." "Go, go, go," he urged, "or you'll be late for lunch." We all scampered for the stairs. When I looked back, he was standing under the clock in the hall looking up at it and then down at his watch, obviously puzzled.

Again I spent most of the summer in New Jersey living with the Stewart family and working for the Office of Dependency Benefits in Newark. Wil had earned his wings at Tuskegee Institute and was preparing to go into battle overseas. Mama called me to let me know that he would be in Richmond for a weekend before leaving the country. She and I took a train to Richmond, and Helen and I spent the weekend palling around with Wil, Richard Macon, and an officer named Patton, all members of the same class. (Patton was killed overseas, and Macon and I met again some years later at Northern High School in Detroit where both of us were teaching.)

Alexander Jefferson, Wil, and Richard Macon, all fighter pilots and prisoners of war, when they met again in Detroit in 1996

187

Although Merle and I had drifted apart before I left St. Louis, her engagement to Wil had caused us to renew our friendship. She invited me to visit her in St. Louis before going back to State for my senior year. She entertained me royally, planning every minute of my time. I saw a number of friends again, including Robert McFerrin who was home on furlough; he showed me official papers that indicated that he had legalized the middle name I once gave him.

Wil wrote to Merle regularly. I should have sensed that something was wrong when she threw one of his letters on the floor after reading it. When she gave it to me to read, I couldn't understand why it displeased her. He had said all the things one might have expected in a letter to his fiancée. There were other signs of dissatisfaction, as well. And her ridiculous insistence upon propriety annoyed me as it had done before I moved from St. Louis. One Saturday we were invited to an afternoon card party at someone's house and instructed to dress very casually. The other guests complied; at Merle's insistence, we were the only guests decked out in hat, pocketbook, and gloves. Nevertheless, I thoroughly enjoyed my visit with her and deeply appreciated the tremendous effort she went to to assure that I was well entertained. After I returned to State we corresponded regularly and looked forward to being sisters-in-law when the war was over.

Sometime in September I received an urgent call from "Madame" to come to her apartment. Mama knew how fond of Madame I was and had somehow gotten in contact with her to break the bad news to me. My parents had received a telegram that Wil was missing in action. Suddenly war became very personal, and I became more painfully involved in it than had ever happened through news reports, even the one in the Norfolk *Journal and Guide* about Clem's death as a fighter pilot. Dad vacillated between a certainty that Wil was dead and a gut feeling that he was still alive, the latter bolstered by one of his mysterious dreams that turned out to be amazingly accurate in every detail. Mama managed to sustain some sense of sanity by rereading Psalm 91, which I am sure she believed was written especially for her. Perhaps the remoteness of the campus from the real world and the routine of our everyday lives kept me going to classes and somewhat focused on homework assignments. Although Wil, missing in action, and Clem (Helen's boyfriend), killed in action, merged in my mind and in my poem, "White Cross," there was still room for hope.

Helen warned me not to go to see a movie about a dead Army pilot whose ghost returned because of its devastating effect on her. But like a fool, I went to see it anyhow when it came to campus, probably because everyone else was going and there was nothing else to do. Our weekly campus movie included a black newsreel. After all, I had withstood the news reports of the battles, victories, and deaths of members of the 99th Pursuit Squadron and the 332nd Fighter Group without caving in, constantly fearing that my old schoolmate from Sumner High, handsome Wendell Pruitt, would be one of the casualties reported. But each week, it seemed, he was shown in a steady continuation of heroic victories, and he seemed invincible. I had even endured somehow the pictures of mass graves containing the emaciated bodies of prisoners of war, so I was sure I could handle this movie. But I was wrong. I left the auditorium in Virginia Hall in hysterics before it was over.

It was many weeks later that we learned Wil was a prisoner of war in Germany. He was allowed to write one censored penciled letter and a card at specified intervals. Whoever received this communication sent it to Merle and the other members of the family. Merle continued to write hopeful letters to Mama and me. Then during the winter, her letters stopped. I assumed she was still writing to Mama, and Mama made the same assumption about letters to me. It was about this time that allied troops were moving across the continent liberating prisoners. Was this timing significant? Had she expected him not to return? I later learned that, during my summer visit with her, she was already seeing a doctor in residency at Homer Phillips Hospital, whom she later married.

With most of the male students in military service, nearby Camp Lee and Camp Pickett were our salvation. A unit of engineers was stationed on campus, and military athletes practiced on our field. At different times I went out with two officers from Camp Lee, one from Detroit and the other from Philadelphia. It was the Philadelphian who gave me the second birthday party in my life. It was at the bar of the black officers' club, which they nicknamed "Uncle Tom's Cabin," and consisted of a sponge cake with a dinner candle in the middle. The other officers who happened to be there participated in the celebration, and the waiter sang my favorite song, which I requested as often as I could. It wasn't really much of a party, but his thoughtfulness moved me deeply.

Then one day I received a surprise visit from Julian Witherspoon, whom I had met just before his graduation from Sumner High School. Someone had told him that Long's sister was on campus, and he looked me up. We saw each other on a regular basis for a few weeks before he was shipped out, first to Texas and then to Oahu, Hawaii. Our courtship from then on was by frequent letters. And it was by mail that we eventually became engaged and I received a ring.

When I turned 21, Dr. Luther Porter Jackson, having seen to it earlier that we paid our poll tax, which was intended in Virginia to discourage black people from voting, escorted Syphax, Laura, another student and me to the little polling place in Ettrick where we cast our first vote. I had read somewhere that at regular intervals a president died in office, and I hesitated to vote for Franklin Delano Roosevelt because, if this pattern continued, he would die and the vice-president, Harry S. Truman, would become president. I wasn't sure I would want Truman as president since he was from Missouri, but I voted for FDR anyhow; he did die in office. During Truman's administration I came to have great respect and admiration for him and was happy that I had voted as I did.

The college didn't have a midyear commencement ceremony, and there seemed no purpose in leaving campus after completing my degree requirements. Now engaged to Julian, I had no idea what I was going to do with my life after college except get married. I saw no point in going back to New Rochelle only to return in May to "march." I had fallen in love with State and didn't want to leave. So I stayed on as one of a handful of graduate students, got a part-time job and took three courses in education, correctly assuming they would be easy. The job paid for my tuition, so I wrote home and asked Dad if he could send me twelve dollars a month as an allowance instead of the usual four. I don't know what I spent it for, but suddenly I felt rich.

Alice Hawks and I roomed together in a dormitory reserved for graduate and married students and single faculty and staff members. We had more privileges than undergraduates had. We both worked in the morning for "Ma" Hunter, head of the Home Economics Department. After she left for class, we often put our heads down on the desk and went to sleep, having stayed up late the night before, sometimes at Camp Lee.

Evidently Dr. Hunter was involved in some kind of survey, and occasionally she took Alice and me out into the country with her. I had heard of one-room school houses, but I didn't know they still existed. With Ma Hunter I saw them for myself, small rooms with not enough storage space or supplies, rugged seats, and a potbelly stove in the middle of the room providing the only heat. Black teachers in Virginia schools were paid lower salaries than whites and were given the used, outdated textbooks discarded by white schools. It's a wonder to me how so many black students, coming out of these inferior circumstances, still managed to gain a good basic early education in reading, writing, and mathematics. Perhaps the answer is that, in their isolation, the teachers retained the tried and true methods of teaching that worked, and did not, like the more "progressive" schools of the North, change the curriculum and teaching methods with every new educational theory that came along.

191

Before my parents left New Rochelle for my graduation, they received word that Wil had been liberated and would soon be on his way back to the States. They left word with a friend how to reach them if any more news came during their absence. After the graduation ceremony, my parents and I were in my room when the phone down the hall rang. The message was that Wil was on his way back to America. We were dealing with our jubilation when the second phone call came saying that he was already in the States! When the AKA's had finished singing our hymn around the sun dial on the front campus, one of my classmates showed some of us the watch her parents had given her for graduation. When she showed it to me, she asked, "What did you get?" I replied, "I got my brother back."

Since I still didn't want to leave the campus, even after graduation, I made plans to continue to work until August. My parents returned to New Rochelle to wait for Wil to go through the usual examination and other procedure before getting time off. I think he had been to New Rochelle only once before. As soon as I learned that he was free to return, I took a few days off and rode the train to see him and talk about his experiences. He answered questions but didn't volunteer much other information about prison camp.

Only allied officers were in his camp, and they were not physically mistreated, but the barracks was always cold and he was constantly hungry. The officers received some supplies from the Red Cross, but he never got any mail that we sent him, nor did he get any of the packages, with the contents specified, that my mother was allowed to send periodically.

Other than a loss of weight and a scar where his nose had hit the instruments when his P-51 fighter plane was shot down over Hungary and he crash-landed in Poland, he seemed little less the worse for wear. When he was liberated, he had lice and was wearing the same clothes he had been wearing nine months before when he was captured, including the scarf, still stained with blood, that Merle had given him. It was the first time we had all been together in years, and we went to a photo studio and had a family picture taken with Wil still in uniform.

Every day Wil called Merle in St. Louis, eager to see her and get married. It was not until about the third day that she told him there was no point in his coming because she wasn't going to marry him. He didn't show his feelings, but I sensed his tremendous disappointment and loneliness in a city where he knew nobody but his immediate family. I'm sure his thoughts of her and the promise that came with the engagement ring had sustained him through his roughest moments in prison camp. And I felt helpless to ease his pain. In response to her long-delayed letter of explanation to me, I wrote an accusatory letter that I have always regretted mailing. If I had simply never answered her letter, she would have felt guilty, but because I harshly retaliated, the guilt was shifted to me and she was let off the hook. From this experience I learned that it is often better to keep silent than to respond in anger and suffer years of regret. The only solace I have is the certainty that, if they had gotten married, it would have been a mistake and the marriage would not have lasted long. Their personalities and values were much too different, and after the novelty of having married "Dr. Long's son," soon to be out of uniform, had worn off, her social ambitions and insistence on always being proper would not have been able to coexist with his unpretentiousness and "old shoe" personality.

I returned to State to finish my job. When August came and I could find no reason for staying any longer, I said my reluctant goodbye to the buildings "high above the Appomatox on this lofty hill" and went back to New Rochelle.

After Graduation

Encouraged by Dad to begin work on a master's degree in English, I enrolled at New York University for the fall semester. I still had no idea what I would do with another degree in English. I was simply biding my time before Julian was discharged from the Army.

Clarence had changed his major at Lincoln University, delaying his graduation. Because black students were not allowed to attend the University of Missouri, Lincoln had hastily established a school of journalism and he became its first graduate. During my senior year at State he lived in Baltimore and wrote for a black weekly newspaper there.

At some time during that summer, back in New Rochelle, Clarence brought home the woman he planned to marry, Laverne Stansbury. I liked her immediately and looked forward to having a congenial sister-in-law. For years I told him that marrying her was the wisest thing he had ever done. If I had ever had a sister, I would have wanted her to be just like Laverne. She was more a sister to me than an in-law. Her death in November, 2005, following a long illness left me feeling lonely indeed.

For the rest of the summer of 1945 I worked in a nursery school where all the children were white, later transferring to Lincoln School where all the students were black. Once Clarence and I had settled in New Rochelle, it was obvious that the parsonage was too small. Dad decided to buy his own house and have the church rent out the parsonage, paying him the equivalent of the rent as a housing allowance. The large white stucco house to which we would soon move is on a hill and was visible from the playground of Lincoln School where I spent a great deal of time during the working day. I was extremely dissatisfied at home and eager to leave. The house became a symbol of my dissatisfaction, and I wrote a poem about it.

194

Dad still wanted to treat me like a little girl, and we locked horns on several occasions. I felt that I had outgrown his dictatorial policies. And I didn't enjoy being in New Rochelle. It wasn't St. Louis, and many of the young people I met seemed not to have the ambitions of those in St. Louis. I had few friends. The people in general were quite provincial. If a neighbor saw me "dressed up" going somewhere, before I reached the corner, phones would be ringing in speculation of where I was headed. The best thing New Rochelle had going for it, in spite of being a beautiful city, was its proximity to Manhattan.

I became friendly with a young woman who rented a third floor apartment a few doors down on Lathers Park. She worked for a white family as the domestic staff supervisor. When she was at home I often visited her, and I still treasure the demitasse set she gave me as a wedding present. Katie Butler had entered NYU as a freshman, and we sometimes rode the train together to the campus.

During that summer Oscar Micheaux, the black film maker and novelist, came to our door in New Rochelle peddling his books. I wasn't there at the time, but he evidently stayed for a long time, telling Dad the plots of his novels. Dad bought two of them and asked him to come back before he left the area so that I could meet him. He did return when I was at home and fascinated me with his stories. After reading the books, though, which were self-published, I was not impressed with the quality of his writing. He wrote exactly the way he told the stories orally, and I didn't keep the books. I have always regretted that I didn't value them more and recognize his importance as a pioneer in black film.

One of the two officers I had dated at Camp Lee called me one day to say that he was in New York City and asked me to meet him there. We attended a movie in Times Square. As we watched, the film was interrupted with words flashed across the screen that Japan had surrendered. Almost all the people in the theater threw their hats up in the air and left the theater. We were going to play it cool and stay to the end. When we finally got outside, it was pure bedlam. Times

Square was more crowded than on New Year's Eve, and no traffic could get through the streets. Strangers were hugging and kissing, and everyone was celebrating V-J Day, the end of World War II. Somehow we managed to make our way to Grand Central Station and catch the crowded and noisy train to New Rochelle. Everyone on the train was wild, people carrying their shoes in their hands and otherwise giving some indication that the celebration had just begun.

55 Lathers Park, New Rochelle

Lathers Park is a T-shaped street with two dead ends. Our house faced Lincoln Avenue at the end of the entrance portion. It had a lovely wide veranda with a swing connected to the ceiling, a foyer, a living room, dining room, butler's pantry, and large kitchen. Like the house in St. Louis, the stairway divided at the landing, several of the steps leading to the kitchen and the others going to the second floor. The second floor had four ample bedrooms and a bathroom at the end of the hall. Dad used one of the bedrooms for his study. The third floor also had four slightly smaller bedrooms with another bathroom at the end of the hall. My bedroom was on the front, as was my parents', with Clarence's room halfway down the hall. When Dad bought the house, it came with longtime tenants who continued to occupy their rooms on the third floor. Mr. and Mrs. Littlejohn rented two of the rooms, and Anne Thompkins occupied another. After I left, Anne moved to the second floor into what had been my room. Later a Mr. Bostic moved in. These were good people who seemed more like members of the family than tenants. The front door key admitted them to the entire house. Sometimes they would sit down for a few minutes and visit with my parents, but they spent most of their time on the third floor. The basement had a kitchen which the tenants, except Anne, used. Anne always shared our kitchen and usually cooked her own meals but ate with us in the dining room. She was indeed "Miss Anne" with a lovely place setting of her own china, rubber gloves for washing her dishes, and always manicured nails. When my niece Patricia was born, Anne became her godmother.

The day we moved to Lathers Park, I began classes at NYU. I made myself sick with gas pains because I had neglected to eat all day during the move and had to see a doctor before going to the campus.

New York University was a far cry from Virginia State College where all the students knew each other by face, if not by name, and the faculty members lived on campus and were easily accessible. My professors were certainly knowledgeable but not good teachers. I made it a practice of sitting on the front row. The seats in all the classrooms were the hardest and most uncomfortable ones I had ever had to sit on. One of my professors sat on his platform and mumbled into the cuff of his sleeve for three hours, seldom looking up and never entertaining discussion or class participation. Another who taught drama was more interesting, identifying places in the city where certain plays had been performed. The most interesting class was on three American poets of the same period and included an assignment which required us to go to the rare books room of the main public library and compare editions of certain poems in every detail. That was the most enjoyable experience I had as a graduate student at NYU. There were only two other students that I became acquainted with, one an African American girl whom I visited in the brownstone where she lived, and a Jewish boy who sometimes walked me to the subway.

For a while I worked part-time for the family doctor, helping his receptionist, Ora Brown, with the records. His office was on the first floor and his living quarters upstairs. He occasionally invited us to stay for dinner, which his housekeeper prepared. Ora and I became friends and her daughter, Valarie, not yet born, eventually became best friends with my daughter during our summer visits from Detroit.

By now Dad had been appointed to the Board of Education, the first African American in the state of New York to be appointed to this position. He served for ten years, gaining the respect of the entire community and causing his colleagues to consider moral aspects of various issues under consideration.

I did not enroll for the second semester at NYU. My dissatisfaction at home became so acute that I considered moving out. A young married woman I knew was planning to leave her husband and rent an apartment. We discussed the possibility of my moving in with her and sharing the expenses, but I didn't have a job. What I finally decided to do was go to Richmond and seek employment there. The day before I left, I received a telegram from Julian informing me that he was back in the states and would soon be discharged. I said nothing to my parents, but sent him my aunt's address and phone number.

So it was that, after spending some days in Richmond and

revisiting the campus in Petersburg, I met Julian in Washington, DC. After several days there we left for New Rochelle where he was a guest in my parents' home. They were meeting him for the first time. That Sunday Dad announced in church that we would be married the following Sunday, March 31, 1946, following the morning service, and everyone was welcome to stay for the ceremony.

Mama took me to the Village and helped me select a street-length light blue dress. Since Clarence was the only person Julian knew, he served as best man, and Laura Mann, my college roommate, was my maid of honor. Dad, of course, performed the ceremony. Several members of the Stewart family and a few other friends came from East Orange. Billboard was there, too. A photographer took some pictures. Since I had never wanted a large wedding, I was happy with the arrangements, especially since nobody felt obligated to give us a gift. I still treasure some that we did receive and recall the people who gave them.

Mama had arranged for a small reception at home several hours after the wedding but didn't take into account that we would not be able to wait for the guests to arrive before catching the train for Detroit. So the only people we saw were the New Jersey guests who went to our house directly from church. My picture later appeared in the New Rochelle *Standard Star,* and Mama sent announcements to out-of-town friends after we left.

So my residence in New Rochelle ended. I had never spent a full year there, the middle of August, 1945 through March, 1946 being the longest period I had lived there. I was not unhappy to leave.

Julian and me after the marriage ceremony

IV.
Turn in the Road

A New City

The train pulled into Michigan Central Station on the morning of April 1, 1946, the bride and groom having slept in our seats all night as best we could. We had between us $300 that I had saved from summer jobs and the first of three segments of his mustering out pay, or what was left of it after Washington. In his letters from Oahu, Julian had estimated how much we would need to furnish a four or five-room apartment, indicating that he had not saved that much. What he didn't tell me was that he hadn't saved anything. In Washington he had pawned his expensive pocket watch and a small diamond ring that Aunt Minnie had given me. Of course, we never saw them again. All the signs were there. I should have anticipated the problems that were to come, but I reasoned with myself that my parents had started their marriage with very little and, with work and careful spending, we, too, could make it. I assumed that, once we got to Detroit, we would both get jobs. The truth was that I didn't really know him well enough to make any assumptions, and I was so eager to leave home permanently that I didn't listen to the cautions whispering in my ear. Besides, he had such an outgoing personality, was so convincing, and had such charisma that it was easy to believe he was the man with whom I wanted to spend the rest of my life.

The buses and streetcars were on strike, so we took a taxi to the Gotham Hotel where we rented a room for several days. I was impressed with this large, first class, black-owned hotel on John R., across from a hospital with its back facing the Paradise Theater on Woodward. Julian had told my parents that we would be living with his aunt and had given them her address. We did go by to see her, but it was immediately apparent that he had made no such arrangement with her.

Due to the huge influx of people who had come to Detroit to work in the war plants, apartments were impossible to find. After a few days at the Gotham, we rented a room in a private home far out on the east side of Detroit where not many black people lived. The owner made it clear, though, that rent did not include kitchen privileges. I didn't know much about cooking anyhow, so I was satisfied to eat out.

One of the places we went was the black Lucy Thurman YWCA, across the street from the black St. Antoine YMCA where Julian had lived before entering military service. It was after having dinner and returning to the St. Antoine Y during the race riot of 1943 that he had been shot in the back by state troopers as he stood on the steps; they had left him lying on the floor while they lined up some of the other residents. It turned out to be a flesh wound, and the state paid his hospital expenses, but people who were in Detroit then remembered him because of this incident.

It was at the YWCA that I met Alfred Williams and Irene Hunter who were planning to be married. Julian had known them before the war. I liked them right away and we were destined to become lifelong friends.

Julian reasoned that, because he was going to begin law school at the University of Detroit on the G.I. Bill, there was no point in applying for a job. Instead, he enrolled in a correspondence course in law and spent most of his time studying. When my meager savings were gone and it became apparent that his mustering out pay would soon end, I decided to look for work. *The Michigan Chronicle*, a black weekly newspaper, had as its city editor Charles "Duke" Wartman who had grown up on the campus of Virginia State and, like his father, had taught there. He hired me for weekends as a staff writer and copy reader, paying me fifteen dollars. I wrote feature stories, along with other news stories, and began to learn my way around Detroit on public transportation as I visited people for interviews. I also published some of my poems in the paper under the name Naomi L. Witherspoon. I found working as a journalist interesting and challenging. Shortly after I was hired, the paper printed a picture of me on the front page at the polls, supposedly voting, encouraging others to exercise their rights as citizens. But I was only going through the motions as I hadn't been in Detroit long enough to be a registered voter.

The *Chronicle* was then located in a house at 268 Eliot Street, a long distance from our east side rented room. In addition to my own stories, I had to read and edit everything that went into the paper before it was taken to Chicago, where it was printed.

Grace Saddler, a coworker, seemed to know everybody in town and took me under her wing. I went with her once to the golf course where Joe Louis was playing, and she introduced me to him. He made some complimentary remark about the *Chronicle* hiring some "glamour." Grace and I spent long "lunch" hours at dinner time in the dining room of the Gotham Hotel, seeing all the black celebrities who stayed there because they were not allowed in the white hotels. She knew a lot of them and had lengthy conversations with some.

When we eventually got back to the office, Grace was full of stories about her encounters at the Gotham. Russ Cowans, the sports editor, kept urging her, "Write it down, Gracie, write it down!" as she kept talking. On Sunday nights, I had to stay until all the writing was finished and proofread. Duke Wartman would be standing near the door with his hat on, anxious to fly the material to Chicago. By the time Julian came from the east side to pick me up and we finally got back to our room, it was after one o'clock in the morning.

Louis Martin, the publisher, was seldom in town. On one of the rare occasions when he was in his second floor office, he sent for me. He had been reading my poems in the paper and was evidently impressed with them. I think he was aware that my first little volume of poems had been published in 1941. He gave me a copy of Robert Hayden's *Heart-Shape in the Dust*, his first collection, which had been published by the *Chronicle* under the name Falcon Press, and Gwendolyn Brooks's first collection, *A Street in Bronzeville*. I had never heard of either of these black poets and was very happy to read their early work.

Through Julian I met Raymond Nero, who had attended Lincoln with him and my brothers, and his wife Dorothy. They lived in a building just off Woodward at 82 Watson. Their second floor apartment consisted of a large living-bedroom and a kitchen. They shared with other tenants a bathroom down the hall. Through them we were able to rent a small bedroom and bath on the first floor near the front door. It was within close walking distance of the *Chronicle* office where I was now working full time, eliminating the need for hours of transportation to and from work. We had no kitchen facilities, however, and, to save money, I cooked on a hotplate on the granite bathroom floor, consuming all the food at one sitting because there was no place for storage, and if even a morsel of food was left out, caravans of little red ants invaded the bathroom. I soon discovered I was pregnant, and bending over to cook on the floor became increasingly uncomfortable.

When my parents announced that they were going to visit Detroit for a few days and stay with friends, we cleaned up the room and made it look as presentable as possible in case they wanted to see where we lived. I had not yet begun to show, and we didn't tell them that I was pregnant. Although they didn't visit our room, Dad said he couldn't enjoy his home knowing that we were living in a rented room. He advised us to look for a small house for sale, offering to make the down payment. I worked as long as I could, my last beat being the Wayne County Circuit Court. When I became so uncomfortable that I had to sit down on the marble steps, I knew it was time to quit.

We closed the deal on a little house at 9381 Richter Street, a quiet street one block long in a racially mixed, blue collar neighborhood, and moved in in February, 1947. At Julian's insistence, Al and Irene came to live with us when they got married. They occupied the added-on back room on the first floor, sharing the kitchen and upstairs bathroom with us. However, they notified us when they came that their tenancy would be temporary as they planned to buy their own house.

206

9381 Richter Street

By this time, Julian was attending law school and had gotten a job at one of the automobile plants. Al drove a bus, and every day I waited for him to come home on the swing shift so that I would have someone to eat with. It was a real joy having them live with us.

The baby was due in March. I had never been around anyone who had had a baby, but the doctor evidently assumed that I knew more than I did and failed to give me some of the advice I should have had. He never advised me about moderate exercise. If the weather was bad, I didn't take a chance of falling by going for a walk alone and spent a lot of time in bed, getting no exercise at all. I had weighed about 103 pounds for years, and during my pregnancy I gained fifty. The doctor assumed that my normal weight should have been about 125 pounds and that I could afford to gain an additional 25 pounds. This was a mistake, but I didn't know any better than to take him at his word. Mama came two weeks before the baby was due, but Jill didn't arrive until April 18, 1947. I was in labor two days and two nights, suffering a great deal of pain and discomfort. I begged for a Caesarian section. At one time ten doctors stood around the bed, each one poking painfully, but the decision was that I could deliver normally, so I waited and suffered. When she finally did arrive, I didn't even see my doctor and wouldn't have believed that he was there except that Julian was present and could verify it.

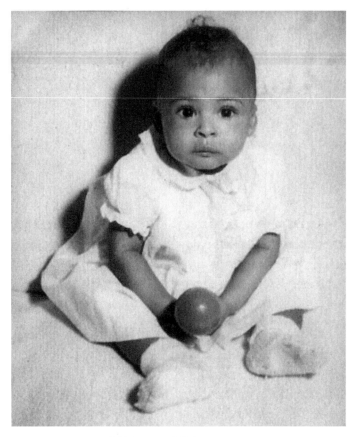

Jill Annette Witherspoon

The day we took Jill home, both Al and Irene stayed home from work. I had suffered a painful tear that kept me in bed for several days. I didn't realize how nervous Mama was when she bathed Jill, the first baby she had cared for since my own infancy. The doctor had given me a formula, but I was determined to nurse her. She would nurse and go to sleep and then wake up crying a short time later. I didn't realize that she wasn't getting enough nourishment. We had her in a bassinet in our room, but after a couple of nights of her frequent crying, Julian moved into the guest room and Mama moved in with me. Jill woke up crying so often that, even when she wasn't crying, I'd dream that she was. A few nights later, I moved into the guest room with Julian and left Mama in the room with Jill. For years afterward, Al loved to relate my mother's morning routine. She was always standing in front of the stove tying on her apron as she prepared to sterilize water, and shaking her head, she would say, "That child sure led me down a dusty road last night." Eventually I realized the problem; once I started giving her the formula and gave up trying to nurse her, she quieted down, slept through the night, and rarely cried.

I will speak no further of my marriage except to say that it was fraught with deception, extreme unnecessary debt, and infidelity. I certainly didn't look forward to raising a child alone, and I provided every reasonable opportunity to keep the marriage intact while trying to preserve my sanity, but after three years I had absolutely no choice but to seek a divorce.

It was obvious that I had to get a job. My neighbor two doors down had a daughter two or three years older than Jill. She told me about a job opening at the segregated public office of Michigan Bell Telephone Company at 1413 Gratiot. One of the five African American girls employed there under the direction of a black manager, trailblazer Ramon S. Scruggs, was going on maternity leave. My neighbor, who put me in touch with one of her friends who worked there, warned me that they would not hire me if they knew I had a small child, assuming that I would be absent every time she had the sniffles. She also advised me not to let them know that I had a college degree because they would feel that I was overqualified and would soon find something more commensurate with my education.

I would be paid more for two years of college than for a high school diploma, but I must not admit to more than that.

I made the appointment for an interview with Mr. Scruggs but was afraid that he would remember me. When Julian and I first moved into the house, telephone service in that area was delayed by a number of weeks. Julian had gone to this same office and insisted on immediate service because of my invented medical complications. Mr. Scruggs knew him from the days when both of them had lived at the Y. He came to our house to verify that I was indeed pregnant, and we received the telephone service right away. Even though a year and a half had passed, I was afraid he would remember me. I introduced myself as Naomi Long, admitted to the two years of college, and received no indication that he recognized me. The interview went well, and he sent me to the main building at 1365 Cass Avenue to complete the application process. After the paper work was done, I was given an appointment for a physical examination.

All that weekend I worried about the physical. I knew that my stretch marks would give me away if the examination was at all thorough. I finally reasoned that the medical department and the commercial department were completely separate, and whatever nurse examined me was not interested in my morals. Sure enough, when the white nurse looked at my stomach, she gasped and asked, "Have you had a pregnancy?" I tried to sound as aloof as possible, answering, "Yeah." After a pause, she asked, "How long ago?" I said, "Oh, about two or three years, I guess." I expected the vagueness of time to assure her that I had put the child up for adoption. It worked, and I was hired.

But what was I going to do about Jill's care? I knew of no child care centers anywhere in the city except for one settlement that was so far from my east side home that it would have been impossible for me to take her there, go to work, and pick her up after work using public transportation. Rev. and Mrs. Rogers, who had been members of our church in St. Louis and now lived in Detroit, came to my rescue. They loved children but had none of their own. They agreed

210

to keep her during the week and let me pick her up on weekends.

I borrowed five dollars from a visiting friend for carfare to work on my first day. I had bought no new clothes except two maternity dresses since coming to Detroit, and hemlines had changed so drastically that I couldn't go to work in my old clothes. With the $45 Dad sent me, I bought a pair of shoes, two blouses and two cheap skirts in a basement store. The other girls earned more than I did because they had been there longer, had no children, and could afford to spend much more money on clothing. I had to try to look as presentable as they did, stretching my few dollars as far as I could. My beginning salary was $37.00 a week.

As I went through two months of training at the main building and then began work as a service representative at 1413 Gratiot, things were working out well. Eventually, though, the Rogerses' landlord objected to the patter of little feet in their second floor flat, and I had to make other arrangements.

I was put in touch with a Mr. and Mrs. Fields who had won awards as licensed foster parents. They lived some distance away, but they were my salvation. They cared for one other little girl and a biracial baby whose parents had deserted him. They also had a 13-year-old adopted daughter whom they had cared for since infancy. She was so mannerly and well brought up that I felt confident her parents were doing a good job. On several occasions I dropped in during the week unannounced, but things were in such good order that I felt assured of Jill's good care. When I went to pick her up on weekends, all her clothing was neatly arranged. All the children seemed to love Mrs. Fields and "Uncle-o."

For the first year of my employment, there was no provision for paid absence for illness. If an employee went home sick, she would be paid for that day, but no full-day absences were covered. Since I could not afford to lose a day's pay, when Jill came down with what was at first thought to be a children's disease, I didn't go near her, never having had measles or chicken pox.

Lucille Davenport and I immediately became close friends and remained so for the rest of her life. I confided my secret to her. When I felt that I had been working long enough to establish a good record of attendance, I asked her to let the secret of my child and married name slip out. It happened not a minute too soon. While I was waiting for my new name plate to be made, a man who knew Julian and had met me when I first came to Detroit looked at the "Miss Long" on my desk and said, "I thought her name was Witherspoon."

On one occasion I told Mr. Scruggs how fearful I had been when I first went to see him for my interview. He answered, "I knew who you were. All I cared about was how you would do your job." That's the kind of man he was. He was the most wonderful person to work for that anyone could ever want. I never heard him raise his voice. When one girl was at lunch and the office got busy with customers, he would come out from his office in the back and work in her place. He welcomed suggestions from the girls about better ways of doing things and, on one occasion when he faced a difficult problem, asked one of them what she had found out when she looked up the same problem in one of the books of practice, knowing that he could trust her to give him the right answer. Some Fridays, after the report had been balanced and the office closed, he would take us all to the Alpha Phi Alpha house where the housekeeper had prepared dinner for us. We would stand around and joke and call him by his first name, but on Monday morning he was "Mr. Scruggs" again (or "the boss" behind his back), not because we couldn't call him Ramon but because we respected him too much. If he had not been hired away by AT&T to be a trailblazer again, it is possible that I would have remained with the telephone company until retirement.

I learned so much from him about how to treat other people and show the same respect for everyone who came into the office! Since we took care of any and all business that people had with the company, he reminded us that many customers would be angry because of something like a long distance call or other charge on their bill that they didn't recognize and would take that anger out on us because, to them, we *were* the telephone company. But he reminded us that if we remained calm, the customer would soon calm down. On one occasion he proved that this method works. When, he heard a woman's loud voice, he came out front where she had refused the take the seat the service representative offered her. He greeted her and asked, "Madam, may I help you?" She replied, "Don't you say nothin' to me. I'll take this chair and knock you down," to which he replied very calmly, "I wouldn't do that if I were you, Madam." She immediately became flustered and apologetic, sat down quietly, and permitted the service representative to deal with her problem.

After spending my two-week vacation with Jill in New Rochelle at my parents' home, I returned to Detroit on a Sunday, expecting to take Jill back to the Fieldses and go back to work the next day. When I called to tell them I was back, Mrs. Fields informed me that she just couldn't keep Jill anymore because of her father's attitude and frequent disruptions of her schedule. On the spur of the moment, I had to make some calls, one of which put me in touch with Mr. and Mrs. Sidney Spurlock who lived on my side of town and had a son several years older than Jill. I had never met them before, but they were from St. Louis and knew Julian. They agreed to keep Jill during the week as long as they didn't have to come in contact with him. That meant that, on the alternate weekends when she visited her father, I had to pick her up from the Spurlocks' house and bring her home. Julian would then pick her up from my house and return her to me Sunday night. Then I had to depend on a friend who had a car or ride public transportation back to the Spurlocks' house, often returning home after midnight.

The Spurlocks were very good people, like the others who had cared for Jill, and Jill and their son got along like sister and brother. At one time they had an emergency in their family and had to go to

St. Louis for a few days. What was I to do with Jill during their absence? They said that, if I didn't mind, they would take her with them. Since I trusted them, I agreed, asking them to call Uncle Robert, my father's brother, when they got there so that he could see my daughter for the first time. They did call his home, but his wife Shirley never gave him the message. A week or so after their return, he wrote me saying that he never heard from the Spurlocks and assumed they had changed their plans.

Later a friend told me about a Mrs. Garfield, a woman in her sixties, who was raising her grandchild. She needed a place to stay because the house where she was living was scheduled to be torn down. Her granddaughter Sylvia was about a year younger than Jill. After talking to Mrs. Garfield, I thought her presence would be a good opportunity to bring Jill home, and Jill would have a little girl close to her own age to play with. Mrs. Garfield was willing to care for Jill in exchange for meals and a place to stay. This arrangement proved to be unsatisfactory. Mrs. Garfield would sit in the kitchen and go to sleep while Jill and Sylvia tore up the house, pulling the rubber treads off the stairs and getting into whatever trouble they could think of. On weekends she and Sylvia went to visit her sister. Opening the door to the back porch pantry, I always found garbage scattered on the floor. I concluded that, instead of putting it in the container provided for it, she simply tossed it and left it wherever it fell. In addition, she washed dishes in cold water, and it was common to see old food still stuck to the supposedly clean forks. I tried to think of a nice way of telling her without seeming to accuse her of carelessness. I made up a magazine article entitled, "Lady, You're Killing Yourself," which reportedly discussed the health hazards involved with improper dishwashing. She didn't take the hint and didn't change her habits. I knew I had to make a change.

Someone told me about a couple with a small son who were looking for a place to stay. After Mrs. Garfield and Sylvia left, Sam and Geneva moved in with little Sam. Again the arrangement was that Geneva would take care of Jill in return for a place for their family to stay. The couple had come to Detroit from Mississippi. While not formally educated, Geneva was very smart and creative in many ways. She was a very beautiful young woman whose hair was so straight it would not hold a curl; she looked as if she could have been Mexican. But when she opened her mouth, her voice was so harsh and raspy that it didn't seem possible it could be coming from her. The couple's relationship was very uneven, sometimes extremely loving, while at other times they argued and fought with a real passion. Later I learned that, on occasion, she would leave little Sam and Jill with a friend of hers while she met the same friend's husband with whom she was having an affair.

One day when I came home from work, my next door neighbor told me that the police had been at my house that day. Geneva had attempted to commit suicide by drinking a concoction containing Drano. However, she probably didn't really intend to die because she knew what the antidote was and had it on hand. When she was taken to the hospital, she was told, "You aren't going to die, but you'll wish to hell you had." Tubes were inserted down her throat and she could consume only liquids and baby food for several weeks.

While they were living with me, they had a second child. Her labor was extremely easy. Almost before Sam could get her to the hospital, pausing, then driving through red lights, she was on the phone announcing that it was another boy. This new baby slept in the spare bedroom and suffered from frequent rashes. It was only after they broke up and moved that I discovered why. The dust under their bed was voluminous, and their bed was full of bedbugs. I suppose these creatures were so well satisfied with baby flesh that they never crossed the hall to my bedroom. I sealed off their rooms, fumigated them, and got rid of the beds.

215

The final arrangement was with a 19-year-old girl who had had a baby for whom her mother was caring. It was time for Jill to start school and therefore important that she be at home. Jill's father had bought her our first television set, and Jill and Judy would watch it together in the back room on the first floor that I now used for a den. I thought it was unfortunate that a girl that young didn't have any marketable skills. I planned to teach her how to type so that she would be prepared to get a paying job. But I soon learned that her mentality was about on the same level as Jill's. When Jill started Pingree School and her first report card came, I was shocked at the number of times she was reported tardy and absent. Judy was not getting her dressed for school on time, and if she was too late, she let her come back home.

The white woman next door, a southerner, wouldn't speak to me for a long time although her husband and Julian used to talk over the back fence. Eventually she changed and was glad to get Jill's outgrown clothes for her little girl. I worked out an arrangement with this couple for Jill to stay with them until time for school, returning after school until I got home from work several hours later. I also found a girl in the neighborhood who occasionally baby-sat on the occasions when I wanted to go out in the evening.

Our raises at the telephone company were automatic. Mr. Scruggs didn't even discuss them with us. As soon as we were eligible, he approved. I got through those difficult years by staying out of debt and buying only what I could afford. My first purchase after Julian left was a vacuum cleaner, which I paid for in installments. When Jill was about four years old and Sam and Geneva were living with us, I bought my first car. I didn't trust a used car, and the cheapest car I could find was a tiny English Ford, a Prefect, which cost $995.00. I think I was one of the first persons in Detroit to buy a foreign car. It didn't go above 55 miles an hour and was so light that two little boys could lift the back end. The first time I drove it to work I was terrified to be sandwiched between two trucks. When the first snow fell, one of my coworkers asked the boss to let me go home early. I put the car in the garage—or rather, two little boys pushed it into the garage which was entered from the street behind Richter and left it there until the snow melted, taking a bus and streetcar to work as I had done before. Children laughed when I turned the corner. I kept the car for five years, never taking it out of town. When I decided to begin driving to New Rochelle instead of taking the train, I bought my second car.

Through all the changes Jill had to go through, I was not much help to her because of my own stress and unhappiness. I felt burdened by my responsibility for her care and didn't enjoy her childhood as I wish I could have done. That she turned out to be the whole, well-adjusted, thoughtful person that she is seems like a miracle.

After the dissolution of my marriage I met and eventually fell in love with "Buddy," who was a friend of neighbors. I depended on him heavily for the year or so that we dated. He was about two years younger than I, but the age difference didn't matter. He was very thoughtful and helpful and wrote me letters declaring his love for me. We talked about getting married, but I had no intention of marrying again so soon. He was my Golden Boy, but I felt that my marriage to Julian had occurred too soon. My life before that had been too sheltered; I should have taken more time to work, decide what I wanted to do with my life, date other men, and gain a sense of independence before making such a commitment. Buddy worked for the post office and didn't seem inclined to enroll in college and earn a degree. That didn't bother me since government jobs offered security. But we argued so much and disagreed on so many things that I couldn't see being with him constantly. Still, I couldn't imagine life without him. When a woman he had known before, even several years older than I, returned to town, he dropped me for her. I was more devastated than I had ever been before. The year it took me to get over him was perhaps the unhappiest single year of my life.

But eventually I adjusted to living without him and felt the words of Billie Holiday's song:

> You ain't gonna bother me no more, nohow.
> Love goes just so far, no more.
> Woke up this morning and found
> I didn't care for you no more. . . . . .

But my relationships with a couple of other men, while enjoyable to some extent, were less than satisfactory and fraught with various frustrations. I realized that my sense of well-being depended on my being in love, and, even though they provided some degree of companionship, I wasn't in love and had no one I could really call my own.

When I came to Detroit, Paradise Valley and the clubs on East Adams Street were in their heyday. It was not until after my divorce, however, that I was able to enjoy its pleasures. By then the Three Sixes was going downhill, and my favorite place to go was the 606 Horseshoe Lounge. It was there that Don Raphael played popular songs on an organ and seemed to know every song that had ever been written. No matter how old a requested song might be, he always knew it, and I requested favorite old songs frequently. He was always glad to play them.

Whenever one man I went out with occasionally asked me where I wanted to go, I always said the same place. One night when we were sitting at the bar, I was surprised to hear him say that he didn't like music. I could understand that people have their preferences in music, but it was hard to believe that there was anyone who didn't like *any* music. His comment became the subject of my poem, "Poor Reynaldo."

Still at loose ends about my future, I decided to take some classes at Wayne University (now Wayne State University). I had fought the idea of teaching all my life, probably because it was expected of me. Still, looking back on my childhood, some of my play had been teaching an imaginary class. And as I was rearing a child, I came to the conclusion that I was already teaching. I finally realized that I was a natural teacher. I couldn't foresee any time that I could stop working and take the classes necessary for a master's degree and a teacher's certificate, but education was in my blood, and I felt a need to continue taking classes, even if it led nowhere. Because getting a degree in education seemed easier than one in liberal arts, I completed the five core courses necessary for a master's degree in education.

Second Chance

It was a mutual friend, George Higgins, who introduced me to Harold Madgett. We spent our first date at his house just talking most of the night. I thought he was good-looking and very intelligent, and we had a lot to talk about. We continued to see each other, and I soon realized that I was in love with him. He had two sons with Gerry, the woman whom he had married twice. She was in the process of divorcing him for the second time. He seemed cheerful and emotionally normal, and Jill grew very fond of him. We seldom went out to public places, his explanation being that Gerry might have been having him trailed and might use his seeing me as part of the divorce action. We did go to a party at one of my co-worker's homes where his behavior was decidedly antisocial. I should have seen that as a clue, but I didn't.

William Harold Madgett

Once the divorce was over, we got married by the pastor of Second Baptist Church in his study with only my best friend, Agnes

Agnes Duvall, in attendance. Harold's boys were living with their mother. I rented the house on Richter to two sisters and moved into the first floor flat where Harold lived, his mother and stepfather occupying the flat upstairs.

Harold was a foreman at the main post office, but he repaired television sets on the side. He had studied a great deal on his own and knew enough to qualify for a degree in electronics. He was so good at what he did and charged such modest prices for his work that people were willing to wait unreasonably long times for their sets to be returned. They trusted no one else's expertise. The living room at 1505 West Euclid was so cluttered with television sets waiting to be repaired that there was nowhere to sit. What would have been the dining room was the one room where we could read and watch television. He insisted that the blinds stay closed so that no daylight came into the house, and they were so dirty that it took a great deal of effort to clean them in the bathtub. The kitchen was painted a dismal brown.

When we married in 1954, I had worked at the telephone company for six years, but after Mr. Scruggs went to work for AT&T, he was replaced by the only other black man in the commercial department, simply because he was black. He was not qualified for the job. In addition, his attitude and treatment of the service representatives were just the opposite of his predecessor's. Lucille Davenport became so unhappy that she resigned and went back to college to become a teacher. I had several run-ins with him and was extremely tense most of the time. I was not the first person to go over his head and report problems to his supervisor. There were so many complaints that the supervisor eventually called all of us in for individual interviews. I was under such intense pressure that Harold encouraged me to resign and go back to school. In the meantime, Gerry became ill, and young Harold and Gerald came to live with us, all three kids jammed into the same small bedroom, the boys in a bunk bed and Jill on a rollaway cot.

It didn't take long before Harold's psychological problems became manifest. He was a loner who couldn't stand having other people around him and didn't want anyone to talk at the dinner table. I will always regret what I put Jill through during this marriage. He pretty much ignored her as he did his own children except to chastise them for something that displeased him. The boys' salvation was the Boys' Club where they spent a lot of time playing basketball. When he worked the midnight shift, he slept during the day and the children went upstairs with the boys' grandmother. I spent more time at the kitchen table correcting papers than anywhere else. If someone called me on the phone, they knew from the way I talked that I was not free to carry on a normal conversation. I had only two visitors, Agnes and Verona Morton, whom Harold made welcome.

Before he left for work I always warmed up his dinner and kissed him goodbye, feeling free only after he had left. In the morning I always greeted him at the door and served him his breakfast. He told me about his lonely and unhappy childhood. He had been raised by his grumpy grandfather, who had already raised his own children after his wife's death. In light of his past, I made allowances for his behavior as long as I could. He refused to seek help for his problems. He would never explain his frequent two-week angry silences that made me wonder what I had done wrong.

When the boys came to live with us, they didn't own a pair of pajamas between them. They didn't know what it was to sit down at the table and have dinner as a family. They were completely undisciplined. Harold, Jr., who has a cheerful disposition, had suffered from allergies and asthma all his life. He is an orderly person, but he had never had order in his life. After they came under our care and a daily routine was put into place, his asthma attacks ceased, and he has never suffered from them since. He tells me now that, during his parents' marriages, he survived by just trying to ignore his father's physical abuse of his mother and his other peculiarities. I had no way of knowing then what a positive effect my presence would have on Harold during his adolescent years, how grateful he would always be for the normalcy that I brought to his life, and how much like my own son he would be long after our years together came to an end. I depend on him for many of my needs, and I am pleased that he is a happy man with a wonderful wife Mary, who is his perfect mate. Gerald developed some psychological problems of his own, but not nearly as severe as his father's. We are not as close because he lives in Arizona, but when he comes back to Detroit, he always visits me, bringing me gifts and gratitude. They both consider Jill their sister.

Gerald (left) and Harold, Jr. in recent years

223

After Gerry's health improved, my mother-in-law moved her into the upstairs flat while I took care of her children downstairs. On the surface, Harold's mother was friendly, but she was deceitful and made it a point of mentioning Gerry's name frequently. She had never been close to Gerry in the past, and moving her upstairs was an act of spite although I could never figure out what she had against me. If Harold happened to come in contact with Gerry, he never spoke to her. His mother treated her like a servant. I resented the fact that I occasionally ran into her on the porch even though she seemed grateful for my help. One of the neighbors reminded my mother-in-law that Harold was now married to someone else, and Gerry had no business under the same roof with his present wife, but that didn't change anything.

Harold was basically a very good man who had a great deal of integrity. He was generous with me, paying for all the household expenses himself and letting me save what I earned. He never showed any violent tendencies toward me, but he had severe psychological problems which made it impossible to live with him and keep my sanity. I left him once and rented an apartment. When I put a deposit on a house I intended to buy, I informed him that I was filing for divorce. He promised to change and talked me into trying again. I knew he wanted to change but doubted that he was capable of doing it without help. He said, "I know I'll have to change or I won't have a wife." In spite of my doubts, I agreed to a second chance. He knew I would not return to the same flat on Euclid and suggested that we buy a single family dwelling large enough to accommodate the growing children. Since he considered the one I had selected too small for all five of us, I forfeited my deposit, for which he reimbursed me, and I remained in the apartment until we found a much bigger house that I considered ideal.

We had much more room to spread out, but nothing really changed. The required silence at the dinner table, the frequent two-week angry silences, for which there was never an explanation, the closed library door, the fact that, although there was ample space in the basement for him to repair television sets, he still returned to the flat to work—everything indicated that he just couldn't stand to have other people around. When I could no longer tolerate the situation, I left for the second time after six years of a difficult marriage and filed for divorce.

Although he never demonstrated that he appreciated my presence, Harold, Jr. told me that, after I left, he went around the house crying and calling my name. I swore I would never marry again because I couldn't trust my judgment, having gone from one extreme to another. It would be thirteen years before I gave marriage another chance.

A House Called Ugmo

Home ownership is probably one of the strongest and most common aspirations of African American people, moreso, I believe, than other ethnic groups. Perhaps that longing for one's own land goes back to the homelands of Africa and the contrasting sense of homelessness and alienation experienced by slaves in the new world. Later blacks migrating from the rural South to northern cities in search of greater economic security must surely have missed the familiar soil, even amid the excitement and challenge of life in Harlem, Chicago and Detroit. I recall the desperation of many families during the Depression who were on the verge of losing their homes. Physical hunger, forced idleness, and other kinds of need and frustration were never quite so pressing as the desire to hold on to some place they could call their own.

My first four homes as I grew up were parsonages owned by the churches that employed my father. Yet there was never a time when he and Mama didn't own their own piece of property somewhere. During my early years it was the house on North Sixth Street in Richmond, the first floor occupied by my mother's sister Bessie and her family with another family upstairs. Aunt Bessie's sprawling lower flat had large, airy, high-ceilinged rooms that flowed into each other. The bedrooms were furnished with marvelous pieces from another era, marble-top tables and washstands and huge beds with high mahogany head- and foot-boards. We never lived in that house, but Dad was well aware that any one of his Baptist congregations could vote him out of office at a moment's notice, and he wanted to know that he and his family were not dependent on them for a place to live. Because my mother was a Richmond native and all but one of her siblings were there, that seemed a logical place to buy property. Furthermore, Bessie needed whatever breaks in rent or other necessities could be granted her, suffering as she did from rheumatoid arthritis and married to a self-important, politically active alcoholic who was as cruel and abusive a character as ever lived, especially when he went on his binges.

As a child I envied classmates who lived in carefree apartments where all they had to do was pay the rent while a janitor was responsible for general upkeep. They didn't have to get up early, as my brothers did, to shovel coal into a reluctant furnace or remove snow from the doorstep and front walk before they could go to school. They didn't have to cut the grass in the summer. But when I was grown and lived in an apartment for a short time, I didn't like it. Even so, after sharing ownership of two homes during my marriages, I was convinced that I didn't want that responsibility again, especially since I was facing life as a single woman with a child. My closest relatives were seven hundred miles away, and there was no one I could depend on to help me with upkeep and emergency repairs.

After the breakup with Harold, I was pleased to find a nicely decorated lower flat within walking distance of the junior high school Jill was attending. So I didn't have the use of a driveway and sometimes had to lug groceries half a block from a hard-to-find parking place on the icy street. So the neighbor upstairs sometimes became too noisy on weekends and kept me awake. I was still better off, I told myself, than I would have been with a mortgage and a lot of responsibilities.

That was until the landlady decided to disconnect my thermostat on the coldest night of the winter, leaving Jill and me to shiver under the weight of multiple blankets and our heaviest coats to make it through the night. Thinking that a workman had disconnected a wire in error, I had a friend go to the basement and reconnect it. The following day, the thermostat was again mysteriously disconnected at a different location. The basement was cold, and our first floor flat needed more heat than the apartments upstairs, which benefited from the warmth of the first floor. Although my complaint to the landlady brought an apology for this act that I knew was intentional, I was quickly awakened to the realization that I was at her mercy whenever she saw fit to reduce costs at the expense of our health and comfort.

While I knew there were legal steps available to deal with such incidents, the time and expense involved and the possibility of a recurrence in the form of other offenses was something I would rather not have to deal with. Billie Holiday's voice affirming, "God Bless the Child That's Got His Own" took on new meaning and I knew I would have to find a way to buy a house.

Jill would soon be ready for high school, and it was my intention for her to attend the highly rated Mumford a little farther north and west of where we were living. My father, who had been against my renting all along, was happy that I had finally come to my senses and assured me that I need not worry about the down payment. So my search began in neighborhoods which, in some cases, were just beginning to be racially integrated.

I recalled Lorraine Hansberry's play, *A Raisin in the Sun*, and the little house the Younger family purchased in an all-white neighborhood in Chicago. The neighborhood spokesman made an offer to purchase the property back from them at a profit to keep them from moving in, pretending to be concerned about their well-being by saying that black people were happier when living among themselves. Although I deplored the purpose of his statement, I had to agree to the extent that I hoped to find an affordable house surrounded by neighbors my own color. I had no point to prove and had enough battles to fight already without taking on race in a white neighborhood. But the neighborhoods near Mumford High School were predominantly white.

The search began for a house that had certain features I wanted such as a den, a pass hall, a separate breakfast nook, and a first floor powder room. Among the first houses Jill and I were shown was a sturdy looking house built of brick with a front porch supported by eight Corinthian columns. The architecture was immediately impressive and unusual for that neighborhood, and, in spite of the electric blue trimming, my initial thought was, "I wish I *could* afford a house like that." I just knew it was out of my price range.

What a shock I received once we got inside! The rooms had scarcely any furniture, and newspapers were taped over the windows. The ceiling light fixtures dangled precariously from single wires. The ornately plastered ceiling and coat of arms over an unusual fireplace were painted every color in the rainbow. The dining room ceiling showed signs of a leak. It was impossible to tell what color the kitchen was, for the walls and floor were covered with grime. A red stove fueled by gasoline was the only fixture. The gas had been disconnected and almost none of the faucets worked. The refrigerator, built into the house piece by piece, had once been powered by a motor in the basement, but it no longer worked. The entire basement, except for the furnace room, was plastered. The recreation room was also carpeted, what could be seen of the floor. The room held numerous boxes of jars containing some kind of canned food that looked like garbage. It was possible to walk around the edges only. The second floor had no furniture except a soiled twin bed in a back bedroom. The floor of the closed-in back porch, entered from another bedroom, was covered with newspapers on which was spread out to dry some kind of food resembling spinach pasta. The big surprise was the master bedroom that appeared to be freshly painted light blue with a good quality of clean red carpeting that showed no wear. I couldn't understand the contrast between this room and the rest of the house, nor the fact that the wall-to-wall carpeting throughout the house was clean and in excellent condition.

The woman and the house certainly belonged together. She had a short, dumpy figure and was wearing men's shoes. She spoke with a thick Eastern European accent and smelled to high heaven. It was all I could do to contain a sudden sensation of nausea. As we left the premises, I was so busy telling the real estate dealer off for wasting my time that I only half listened to his explanation and the selling price, which could have been five dollars, for all I cared. The for-sale sign in the front yard bore the name of a black real estate company. No wonder the houses on both sides had for-sale signs posted. I'm sure the owners felt that any black family that bought that house had to be trash. That night when Jill and I discussed our day, we laughed about the house she referred to as "Ugmo."

During the following weeks we continued to look at houses, but the more we saw, the more discouraged I became. The ones with the features I wanted were far out of my price range and the ones I thought I could afford were unacceptable. I did make an offer on one house, a thousand dollars less than the asking price. It wasn't quite what I wanted, but I felt I could make do with it. After several weeks of waiting, I learned that my offer had been refused. (Each time I pass that house, which has been sold many times since then, I thank my lucky stars that I didn't get stuck with it.)

Eventually, on one last exploration with a real estate representative from another company, he said with a sigh, "Well, you've seen everything I have to show except a house on Santa Barbara that we can look at now." "Oh, no!" I exclaimed. "Not the house with the jars!" "Oh, you've been there," he said. "But we're right around the corner. It won't hurt to look again."

"Ugmo" in 1961

So for the second time, I entered the weird house with the garage doors and fences falling down, the weeds high in the back yard, the closets devoid of poles for hanging clothes, the medicine cabinets without shelves, the supermarket cart parked in the back yard, and the old man, bent over at the waist, who must have slept in the basement, hovering in the shadows.

But this time I entered the house with the advantage of experience in viewing—and having owned—other houses. This time I brought an open mind and the ability to look beyond the smell, the dirt, and the woman, to see the house itself and its possibilities. What I discovered was that it had all the features I wanted except a pass hall. It was well built and sturdy. The roof appeared to be sound. The walls in the carpeted basement showed no signs of moisture. The condition of the furnace was questionable as was the extent of the obvious plumbing problem, but the carpeting was, unexplainably, clean and of excellent quality and showed no signs of wear. And there was that wonderful sunny master bedroom with bay windows and a window seat, a walk-in closet and a cedar closet. And leading from this bedroom, a carpeted stairway to a pleasant, cozy little room in the center of the third floor—a bonus. In other words, the problems were not basic. Without the woman and her dirt, what was left was basically a very solid house that had all the right features.

Furthermore, the price was right. This time I listened to the explanation. The owner was losing the house through foreclosure. She had listed it with a black company as a last resort. She had a limited time to sell it; otherwise, she would lose all her equity in it. Very desperate now, she was willing to let it go for much less than she could have gotten if she had had the resources to make it more presentable.

At that point my mind came to attention and started making a list. What was basically wrong? What was only cosmetic? How much would it cost to make it habitable? That night I satisfied myself that, for about two thousand dollars, I could correct the most serious problems, taking a chance that the furnace wouldn't break down until

I had had the other work done. I could arrange for money to be placed in escrow to cover the obvious plumbing problems. My decision was made.

Jill couldn't believe that I had actually agreed to buy "Ugmo." One salesman who had shown me other houses less suitable to my needs expressed shock that I would buy a house like that. And my response to him was that if he didn't have the ability to recognize true value and the imagination to see the possibilities, he was in the wrong business.

Since the purchase agreement failed to include specifically such things as wall-to-wall carpeting and other attached items, I fortunately thought to have the agent write in the provision that such attached items were not to be removed, and he had the owner initial the addition in handwriting that was particularly distinctive. That turned out to be a very wise move. It was agreed that she would vacate the premises by a certain date, and I began making plans to do the things that needed doing.

After we had closed the deal, a local department store was having a sale on shades, and I returned to the house to count and measure the windows, but the woman wouldn't admit me. I therefore drove through the alley to count back windows and ordered the correct number of shades at sale price; I would provide the measurements later. A friend who taught with me and was free during the summer agreed to clean up and paint the interior, with the help of one of his brothers who was unemployed.

But the date for the owner to vacate passed and she continued to occupy the house without paying rent. I didn't intend to move in until certain work was completed, and the summer was fast approaching. Even though I cherished my free summers and avoided teaching summer school, I decided to teach that year since my vacation plans were already ruined. The former owner had no telephone and wouldn't come to the door, so there was no communication. I eventually had to go to court to order her out even though I was afraid she might damage the plaster, break the windows, or vandalize the property in other ways out of spite. I consulted my insurance agent, from whom I had purchased a homeowner's policy, about my rights. He informed me (erroneously, it turned out) that I would not be covered until I occupied the house. I crossed my fingers and hoped for the best, but the pressure I lived under for many weeks was almost unbearable.

To let the former owner know that I meant business, I began the work on the outside by hiring a painter to trim the house in a more tolerable color. He had painted houses for several friends, and I liked his work. One Sunday morning he called me with an inquiry. What he had observed through open windows the day before led him to believe that no real damage was being done, but his wife had insisted that he call me anyhow. "The carpeting in that house isn't worth anything, is it?" he asked. "Yes it is," I answered. "It was one of the selling points." "Then you'd better sit down," he warned before telling me that the woman was having all the wall-to-wall carpeting that he could see removed and rolled up. No wonder she had maintained it as the only clean and well-kept item in that shambles of a house!

The last thing I wanted to do in the presence of neighbors and maids gawking from behind curtains was to be seen on a Sunday morning with policemen, but that's what happened. The two officers who met me on the sidewalk wouldn't step up to the porch, advising me that I would be trespassing if I did. "But this is my property!" I protested. "It's my porch!" So I went up anyhow and rang the bell. Of course, the woman didn't answer. I didn't expect her to. But as I passed the powder room on the way to the back, I could see her heading for the kitchen. The policemen followed me to the back yard seeing that I was determined to walk where I pleased on my own property. I called out an empty and unenforceable threat through the open kitchen window pertaining to the removal of any additional carpeting. Told that I could not even file a complaint as long as she was on the premises, I returned to my flat fuming and thoroughly frustrated.

The night before her court-ordered departure, I decided to introduce myself to my next door neighbors. They welcomed me pleasantly, and the grown daughter offered the information she had received from a moving van employee; he had been retained to begin moving the occupant at eight o'clock the next morning. She invited me to her second floor bedroom from which I could see the old woman moving around in the kitchen and stacking things.

The next morning, while I taught my summer school classes, Harold, with whom I was on good terms, arrived early and parked his car far enough down the street to observe what was going on without causing suspicion. Once or twice he drove past the house and around the block, changing his parking place. He kept watch for hours while the garage was emptied of old store fixtures and other odds and ends. Then he saw items that looked from a distance like rolled up carpeting being removed from the house, along with other items he could not identify. He stayed until the van pulled out, with the woman in the front seat with the driver, and followed at a discreet distance to a fast food restaurant on a nearby corner. When they all got out, evidently to have breakfast, he went home to prepare for work.

In the meantime, I got home from school and made contact with him. I was able to pick up the trail and follow the easily identified van to a storefront on Linwood Avenue. I parked a block away and kept watch while the contents of the van were being carried inside. Once or twice I called my lawyer to let him know what was going on. Before leaving, I made a careful note of the address, the license number of the van, and the name of the company. Since Harold worked at the post office, he had found out the forwarding address the woman had provided. It would be simple, I thought naively, to press charges with the information I had.

Not so. Any thoughts I had that the police department was there to serve its citizens was quickly dispelled when I approached the desk of a surly white sergeant at headquarters who didn't write down any of the information I offered. I have since forgotten exactly what did transpire, but I recall that that unsatisfactory interview necessitated my taking off two additional mornings from summer school before he asked, "Oh, you have all that information?" finally taking notes. It was the same information I had tried to give him on the first visit.

In the meantime I had consulted a reputable carpet company whose representative had taken pieces of carpeting left around the radiators, traced it back to the manufacturer, and arrived at the value of the stolen material. When the sergeant, not much friendlier than before, could find no further excuse for delay, he escorted me across the street to file charges for grand larceny and larceny by conversion.

Standing behind a counter in the police station was a black officer whom I had known years before from the neighborhood of the telephone company office. When we began to chat, the demeanor of the white sergeant immediately changed. The fact that someone in the department knew me (or that I knew someone in the department) seemed to make all the difference in the world. Suddenly he was all smiles and affability. More proof, if I ever needed it, that the nobodies of the world are really out of luck, while having any connection at all with a Somebody offers unmerited advantages.

Once the house was empty, we didn't immediately move in. Several weeks of hard work followed. My friend and his brother scrubbed and disinfected. A plumber knocked out walls and replaced broken pipes, followed by a plasterer who raved about the custom ceilings. I hired a high school student to cut the high weeds in the back and pull up as many stumps of old trees as possible. I had the old garage doors hanging by one hinge replaced and the fences temporarily braced until new ones could be ordered. My friends painted the walls and installed the new shades.

Earlier I had planned to take Jill with me to summer school so that if the neighbors wanted to do any damage, she wouldn't be in danger, but by the time we moved in, I knew that wasn't necessary.

235

These people were probably much too sophisticated for vandalism, and several of them, probably out of sheer curiosity, had approached me with signs of welcome. The college student in one house told me tales of what life had been like when the house was an eyesore occupied by the neighborhood witch. It was not long before the for-sale signs on several neighboring lawns came down.

After a year the house across the street was sold to a black family. The following year the one next door was sold. It took another year for the house on the other side to change ownership. Now 45 years later, the neighborhood is probably totally black, the houses and lawns are well kept, and property values have continued to increase. So much for the lies about plunging values when black people move in.

Seeing through externals and selecting "Ugmo" as my permanent home was one of the best moves I have ever made.

My home as it looks today

New Directions

Jill tells me it's my fault that she fell in love with Brazil. When she was in junior high school, I took her to see the movie, *Black Orpheus*. I didn't know it would make such an impression on her, but I'll take the blame. She was graduated from Mumford High School in January, 1965 and entered Michigan State University midyear. A couple of her courses were in three segments. Soon after arriving there she met a young woman from Brazil whose employer had sent her to MSU to take some courses that would be helpful in her work. Her mother accompanied her.

Jill had gotten a book on the Portuguese language and was trying to teach herself. She asked me if I could send her some extra money for tutoring by the student's mother. I did. The next time she came home she told me that, when her friend returned to Brazil, she was going with her. For some reason the girl and her mother went back sooner than they had intended. I breathed a sigh of relief, thinking that was the end of Jill's plan.

At the end of her second semester Jill came home and got a summer job in a telephone company office. When I noticed that she was saving her money, I welcomed the change from her normal spending habits. Toward the end of the summer she started buying summer clothes. When I questioned her, she didn't respond. Then one day when I came home from somewhere, she asked me if I was in a good mood. When I said I was, she said, "I'm not going back to State in the fall; I'm going to Brazil." I tried to discourage her, thinking that she didn't know how to plan for such a trip and I wouldn't help her. What I didn't know was that she had already estimated her expenses; talked her employer into letting her work until December because it would take that long for her to earn the necessary funds; researched and found out that the cheapest airfare was on Argentinas Aerolinas and the ticket could be purchased only in New York; applied for her passport and had it mailed to her office; and made all the other necessary arrangements for her trip. When I tried to convince her that she should go back to college for one semester to finish the third section of her courses, she answered that she couldn't think about anything else but Brazil, and to go back to State would be a waste of money. That was something I could understand as I certainly had no money to spare. When I asked her what she would do if I told her she couldn't go, she raised her hand and waved bye-bye. I decided that, if I couldn't lick her, I might as well join her and began to learn all I could about the country.

In the meantime, a poet friend of mine, a young Jewish lawyer who I suspected was gay, knew some Brazilians including Edouardo, who was living temporarily in Windsor, Ontario across the Detroit River. His visa did not permit him to enter the United States, so Robert took Jill to Windsor to meet him. After that, she visited him several times on her own. His mother was the only other member of his family who knew some English. She wrote to Jill and invited her to spend some time with her family. It was Jill's intention to stay in São Paulo with the student she had met at MSU. They had agreed on how much she would pay for room and board.

When December came, Jill and Robert left by plane for New York where they would catch the plane to Rio de Janeiro. She packed her bags, wouldn't accept any money from me except small change of less than a dollar, and didn't want her father or me to see her off in New York. That didn't worry me because "Billboard" was there, and I knew he would go with her to the airport. I did insist that she send me a cable when she reached Rio. She and Robert stayed in Rio with his friends for several days before she headed for São Paulo. The girl she had met at State, evidently assuming that she had money to spare, reneged on her offer to provide meals for the agreed-on amount, so Jill was on her own for food.

Sporadically I would receive a letter or card from her telling me where she was going for a weekend, leaving me no way of reaching her in case of an emergency. But she had always been very independent. Then she informed me that she was leaving São Paulo to stay with Eduardo's family in a rural area near some other city.

Eduardo's family was well-to-do. His father owned a ranch, and they had a guest house separate from the main residence. It was summer there and school was out. The other children in the family were a 19-year-old girl, a pair of 15-year-old twin sisters, and a baby. Jill stayed in the guest house with one of the twins, unable to speak or understand the language very well, in spite of her study and tutoring. But because the twin spoke no English and Jill insisted that the mother speak only Portuguese, she was soon able to understand and speak the language. The family occasionally rented American movies, and Jill was amused at the frequent difference in meaning in the English dialogue and what was dubbed in or printed across the bottom of the screen in Portuguese.

In the area where this family lived, everybody belonged to a country club according to one's economic status, and unlike Rio de Janeiro, Carnaval was not celebrated in the streets but at the various country clubs. Eduardo's family had two or three servants, one of whom took care of the baby, and a seamstress who came in every day during Carnaval to make the family's costumes for that evening's revelry. One night the family went as circus animals, so Jill and the others had costumes to represent those animals. They spent the night dancing at the club, then slept the next day while that evening's costumes were being created.

When Jill returned three months later, she was speaking Portuguese fluently and ready to go back to State to complete her education. She made better grades after her trip than before and remained there to earn her bachelor's degree.

After seeing the movies my father took in 1934, I had always wanted to go to Europe and the Middle East, but getting Jill through college was a financial struggle, and I assumed that I would not have the money to go abroad until she was graduated and on her own. But when I received her cable that she had arrived safely in Rio, I said to myself, "Naomi, you're a fool. While you're putting your dreams on hold, she's living hers now." That was when I decided to plan my first trip abroad in the summer of 1967.

This trip was annually sponsored by August Kerber, a professor at Wayne State University. The group was so large that it was divided into three subgroups, each with its own director. One group was directed by a woman who was principal of a school in another Michigan city, and mine was directed by a Professor Smith at Eastern Michigan University. Dr. Kerber called several meetings, providing detailed information and instructions on the specific clothing we should take. No bathrobes; a light raincoat could double for that. Two pairs of shoes. One large purse for women and one small one for a dressy occasion. Two dresses, preferably loose-fitting for hot climates; two blouses; two skirts; one sweater. Clothing should be selected for quick drying and ease of packing. Luggage was limited to one 30-inch suitcase.

We would be gone for forty days and would visit eleven countries. We would travel by all means of transportation, including two weeks on a Greek cruise ship. At Northwestern I told another teacher about this trip. She said, "That's the same trip my mother's taking." I asked her if her mother had a roommate. She didn't, so without knowing each other, Lucille Kinchen and I agreed to share a room. Except for optional shore excursions, everything was included in the total price, which was slightly less than a thousand dollars.

Our flight was from Windsor on one of only four turboprop planes that belonged to an English company. The seats were narrow and cramped, and there was only a curtained area where one of the flight attendants could take a nap.

Jill was in summer school at State, but she came to Windsor to see me off. Our friend Saul Bachner was supposed to meet her and drive her to the airport. We were called to board the dinky plane before they arrived, and when I tried to get off to look for them, I was told to stay on the plane. They saw me at the door, but I never saw them, and when we took off, I was in tears because I hadn't seen her. We landed in Gander, Newfoundland to refuel and then headed

240

across the Atlantic, arriving in London.

In most cases, the three subgroups stayed at the same hotel, but several times we were separated. We didn't stay in first-class hotels, but they were all clean and comfortable. In Amsterdam we stayed in a college dormitory. In Paris our quaint little hotel had slanted floors, and we had to share a bathroom down the hall, but each room was equipped with a bidet. In some cities where there were not many hotels, ours was the best.

We traveled to many places including London; The Netherlands; a Rhine River cruise; Germany (Munich, Tegernsee, the Nazi concentration camp at Dachau, and Oberammergau, the site of the Passion Play); and Venice, Italy. From Venice we boarded a Greek cruise ship, the T.S.S. Regina, that took us into four seas, the Aegean, the Adriatic, the Ionian, and the Mediterranean. In Greece we visited Katakolon, Olympia, Athens, Corinth, Mycenae, Patmos, Rhodes, Lindos, Crete, and Corfu. The cruise also included a shore excursion in Ephesus, Turkey; Dubrovnik, Yugoslavia (now in Croatia); and Israel (Jerusalem, Galilee, Nazareth, Capernaum, Caesarea, the Mount of the Beatitudes, the site of the miracle of the fishes and loaves, Tel Aviv, and Mt. Carmel). Our ship returned to Venice where we took a bus up Mt. Titano to San Marino. From there we continued in Italy (Rome, Florence, Fiesole, Sorrento, and the Isle of Capri), Switzerland (Bern), and France (Paris) before returning home.

We traveled by various means—ship, third class train in compartments with live chickens and men who tried to communicate with us in sign language, a bus that wasn't air conditioned, and by donkey to the top of the hill on the Isle of Patmos. In all these places we had excellent guides, many of them university professors. It was worthwhile paying the extra amount for conducted shore excursions, because a good guide can condense a great deal of information into a brief time.

I was not much interested in Germany, mainly because of its Nazi past, my brother's imprisonment there during the war, and the guide's insistence at the concentration camp at Dachau that the gas ovens were never used. I didn't care much for the food. I did enjoy our visit to Lake Tegernsee, though, and even more the little town of Oberammergau. The passion play, which takes place every ten years, was thrown off schedule at some point—by war, I think—so that it was produced in 1934 when my father saw it performed. Everything and everyone in town was in some way involved in the passion play, and we were able to visit the open air theater and go backstage where we saw the scenery, the three crosses, and several robes that the man playing the part of Christ wore. There were many wood carvings and other souvenirs one could buy. I purchased a small wooden cross, the only souvenir I bought in Germany.

My first view of the Parthenon was like walking into the pages of a history book. At that time visitors were still allowed to go up the steps and inside what is left of the building. Our very learned guide pointed out the advantages of the architecture and the slight tilt of the columns.

I found all the structures very impressive and used my visit to Greece in a poem. The weather was so hot and the shore excursions so exhausting that, when we returned to the ship just in time for dinner, we swore we were too tired to go anywhere else the rest of the day. But when someone suggested that we take a taxi back to the Acropolis for the light and sound show, our weariness left us and we knew we had to see the Parthenon at night.

The Isle of Patmos is so small that the ship couldn't dock; we had to take a tender to shore, but we were struck by the beauty of the buildings whose whitewashed buildings gleamed like marble in the sun.

We were not aware that we could have taken taxis to the monastery at the top of the hill. Dr. Kerber probably planned for us to experience the climb the hard way. Someone sat me on a donkey and led him to the top of the hill. We were too close to the edge where the ground dropped off too suddenly for my comfort, and I was afraid, but neither the Greek who led nor the donkey understood English, and I made it to the top. Only a few people in our group had selected this optional trip and, after looking at a lot of old manuscripts, I noticed that no one I knew was still there. One of the monks spoke English, and I explained to him that I wanted to see the grotto where John wrote the Book of Revelation. He advised me to get into a taxi with others and say "Grot" to the driver. On the way down the hill he indicated that this was where I should get off. I walked down a lot of stairs past occupied apartments until I reached a cave at the bottom and entered. The Greek guide was obviously explaining a number of things that I couldn't understand, but I recognized from his motions that the rock ceiling of the cave was divided into three parts. There was a narrow slot in the side of the cave through which I could see our ship anchored. I have no doubt that this was the actual site of John's imprisonment because the island is too small to contain anything similar. I purchased two books written in Greek, thinking that the pictures would be of some use and I might be able to get someone to translate them later.

We were the first ship into Haifa after the Six Day War and didn't know until the night before whether we would be able to land. When we left the ship, we found buses designated for different languages. Some of my friends and I were fortunate enough to board one of the English buses with Benjamin as our guide. He taught us Israeli songs and took us to unscheduled places where the other English buses didn't go. It was his first visit to old Jerusalem since 1948, and his joy at being back spilled over to us as we walked through crowded bazaars and market places. He took us to the Wailing Wall and to the kibbutz where his family lived. This was an extreme kibbutz in which children were separated from their parents at birth and housed with others their own age. Every resident had assigned duties, but for an hour or two every evening, no one worked but spent time with their families. It was late in the afternoon during this free time that we arrived. We went inside a building apparently occupied by kindergarten age children, but they were all with their families, walking, sitting on the lawn, playing, or simply enjoying one another's company. Some of the Americans in our group were critical of this system, but I wondered how many American parents spend an equal amount of quality time with their children, undistracted by other concerns. Those of us who had been on Benjamin's bus promised not to tell others in our group how good a guide he was because we wanted to get on his bus again the next day.

My greatest regret is that we were not taken to the Garden Tomb where Protestants believe Christ was buried. Instead we went to the Church of the Holy Sepulcher which completely turned me off. The church's guide took over as soon as we got inside. Near the entrance was a slab of marble on which we were told the body of Christ lay. Then we were ushered, only two or three at a time, into a small area where we were supposed to light a candle and leave money, which I didn't do. Going to a second floor, we were shown the place where Jesus was supposed to have been crucified. There we saw a rock covered by glass and told that through those very crevices the blood flowed. Directly below this rock was a hole rimmed in silver. The guide said that that was the exact spot where the foot of the cross had rested. Some of the tourists knelt down and kissed the silver rim. How convenient that St. Helena went in search of the place of the crucifixion and suddenly there it was with absolute certainty, in spite of the fact that Jerusalem had been destroyed and rebuilt many times since the crucifixion and burial.

In Athens and other parts of the ancient world, we seemed to follow in the footsteps of the apostle Paul. We were in Ephesus for only a few hours but saw and learned a great deal, thanks to our knowledgeable guide. He pointed to a distant hill and told us that Paul had once been imprisoned there. When I came back home I tried to verify his statement. It wasn't until I taught a course in the Bible as literature that I read recent research that identified one of

244

Paul's letters as having been written from prison either in another city or in Ephesus. The local people knew all the time that the guide was right. In another part of Ephesus, we were shown the area where John was believed to have been buried. The guide didn't say, "In this very spot." He indicated a much larger area and gave the reasons for the belief that John was buried somewhere near there. That I could believe.

Before leaving home I had developed fibroid tumors and my menstrual flow was quite heavy. I couldn't use tampons but felt that I had an ample supply of sanitary napkins. Some of our shore excursions lasted twelve hours as did the one that included the ruins of ancient Corinth. When we left the ship I thought I had enough pads to last me through the day, but the weather was very hot, and walking through old ruins took its toll. By the time we finished listening to the lecture, I was in dire need of a fresh pad but was wearing the last one.

There was a little store nearby where no one spoke English. A young woman came out to wait on me and I used all the sign language I knew to communicate what I wanted, including patting myself in the area of my need. Shortly her face brightened and she went to the back, bringing out what appeared to be one thick pad in a drawstring plastic container. Assuming that it was only one thick pad, I held up two fingers and she brought another. When I went to what I expected to be a toilet, I found just a hole in the ground. Opening the plastic container, I discovered, not a sanitary pad but plain cotton accordioned to fit in the container. No gauze covering. Nothing. What was I supposed to do with it? How did Greek women use it? Perhaps they just tore off a piece and stuffed it, but I knew that wouldn't work for me. So as soiled and wet as it was, I had to remove the contents of the pad I was using and reuse the gauze to accommodate as much of the cotton as it could.

While we were in Greek waters, the ship's store was closed, so on every other island where we landed, I tried to find the kind of

245

pads I was used to. Rather than trying to communicate with a male clerk, I simply went behind the counter and looked for myself. Throughout Greece, this was the only kind of pad available. Fortunately, one of the women in our group had a box of Kotex she hadn't needed yet, and she let me borrow it. I hoped that our ship would get back to Venice before she needed a supply. I was lucky. Back in Italy I was able to replace her box.

While we were in Florence I was happy to learn that there was an optional trip into the little hill town of Fiesole. My interest in going there was that it is mentioned in one of my favorite poems by Robert Browning, "Andrea del Sarto." It pleased me to know that I was walking on the same streets where Browning had walked. On that trip and subsequent visits to Florence I was never able to visit the house where he and Elizabeth had lived, but I did get inside the entrance of the building.

Because gold in Italy was cheap in 1967, I intended to buy some 18k gold jewelry. After visiting the Vatican in Rome, we were taken to the official gift shop. As impressive as the Bernini columns and the interior of St. Paul's Cathedral were, I was surprised at how little emphasis was put on Christ. I was, of course, moved by the Sistine Chapel and Michaelangelo's art, but the church was all about the former popes, Mary, and the saints. At the gift shop it was the same. The thing I was most interested in buying was a gold pendant with the head of Christ on it. All I saw in gold were the heads of Mary, the pope, and various saints. I saw one silver "Christhead," but when I pointed it out to the sales person and asked for it in gold, her reply was, "Oh, no, we don't have anything like that." I went to a jewelry store just outside the Vatican and found the pendant I was looking for, along with a gold cross and chain.

The Italians in general found dark skin very attractive. My roommate, Lucille Kinchen, Zenobia Jones, Margaret Bennett, and I, coincidentally all AKAs, were usually together, and when we walked down a street, men would stare at us with delight and call out, *"Bella, bella!"* Margaret was the darkest skinned, and it was she who got most of the attention. When we were in Florence, one Italian was so impressed with her that he wanted to take her away from the group for a few days and meet up with us later. He couldn't speak English and she couldn't speak Italian, but Lucille, who was a French teacher, could communicate with him in French. In spite of his pleading, she refused his offer. His disappointment was apparent.

My father reported a similar preference for dark skin when he traveled through Europe in 1934. Being light-skinned, he received no attention at all, but he was traveling part of the time with a dark-skinned minister. He said that women would follow him down the street, try to communicate with him, and ask for his autograph. The Italians' fascination with dark skin still exists, but in other parts of Europe, American and English tourists and soldiers have transferred their racism to other Europeans.

Two years after my first trip abroad, I was ready to travel again. Sherry, my former secretary at Oakland University when I was a research associate, told me that she and her mother were going with a group to London, Paris, and several cities in Italy, and I decided to join them. It was a much smaller group than the first, and I was the only African American and one of only three people without a roommate. We went to some of the same cities I had visited before, but our hotels were inconveniently located outside the cities. The one in Rome, though, was where I had stayed the first time, and I had learned to find my way around on public transportation.

In London I skipped the city tour and took a bus to Highpointe to visit Rosey Pool. She was already ailing, but together she and Isa prepared a delicious lunch for me. She had to show me how to eat an artichoke, which I had never tasted before.

In Florence I got my bearing from the hotel near the Arno River where I had stayed before, and while others were shopping for leather, Sherry and I headed for the Ponte Vecchio to look at jewelry;

the prices had gone up significantly in the last two years. In Venice we stayed on one island and took a ferry to the main island. One of the other singles and I visited a night club in Paris to hear Gordon Heath, an African American singer. On a bus by myself on my way to see someone from the States, I dared to try to speak French. I'm sure the words the conductor spoke were curses for my badly pronounced French, but he let me off at the right stop anyhow.

Sherry's mother and I spent a lot of time together. One evening after dinner at a sidewalk café in Rome, a group of us were sitting around the table talking. Sherry's mother said she had always wanted to visit Italy because one of her grandparents on each side of the family had come from Italy. Someone else volunteered the national origin of her family. Jerry, our Belgian guide, looked at me and asked, "And what about you?" I was confused by his question, thinking my race was obvious. I said, "Well, I'm part French, part American Indian, part Spanish—you know how it is with Negroes." Surprised, he asked, "Oh, are you part Negro, too?" "No," I answered, "I *am* a Negro." I couldn't make him understand that in the United States there was no such thing as being "part Negro" any more than a woman could be "a little bit pregnant." The Sicilian bus driver, who spoke very little English, insisted that I was Sicilian. Not wanting to be considered anything other than African American, I decided that, when I got back home, I was going to wear my hair in an unstraightened Afro style. Sherry didn't think much of the idea, which convinced me that that was what I should do.

In Venice I bought a pair of yellow gold earrings with eleven garnets in each one. Jerry complimented me on the way the deep red stones looked against my skin color. His comments were a second reminder that African blood did not have the stigma and concept of inferiority in some parts of Europe that it does in America.

The same single who accompanied me to a nightclub in Paris and I spent time together on a trip to a mountain restaurant. She was a counselor at a high school in one of the midwestern states, and we seemed to have a great deal in common. The view from our mountain of another mountain across a great ravine was most picturesque, and as we talked, I felt a sense of understanding. But I later realized that, in discussions of race, there can be no real understanding. I understood Claude McKay's poem that states, "There is no white man who can write my book." While I have a number of white friends with whom I feel very comfortable and with whom I have shared many experiences and much understanding, I am not convinced that, in spite of all their efforts and empathy, any of them really understands what it is like to be black in America.

I had never had the same compulsion to visit Africa as I had to go to Europe, but when I learned about a planned trip to West and Central Africa sponsored by Operation Crossroads Africa, it sounded too good to pass up. The founder, the Rev. Dr. James Robinson from New York City, would be accompanying us, and I thought there would be no better person with whom to go. The group was small—about 28 persons, including two guides. Clara Jones, a respected friend and the director of the Detroit Public Library, was going, and I thought she would be good company. I knew of my roommate, Louise Grooms, by reputation but didn't know her personally. She was pleasant and congenial company, but I spent more time with Clara. I took with me a small tape recorder, my dependable super 8mm black and white dummy movie camera, and a still camera.

Many of the members of our mostly white group were adult sponsors or supporters of this organization. Dr. Robinson had founded it for the purpose of encouraging American college students to spend a summer living with an African family and building a school. I have heard that President John F. Kennedy got the idea for the Peace Corps from Dr. Robinson's plan but had never given him credit for it. I don't know if that is true or not, but the major difference is that Crossroaders had to earn their own expense money.

We flew from New York on Air France. President Tubman of Liberia had just died, and one of the passengers accompanied his American-made casket on our plane. He insisted that the expensive sterling silver hardware be removed, and he kept it with him all the way. We landed in Senegal just before dawn on July 24, 1972. There to greet us were musicians and dancers. As we got off the plane and walked into the airport, I recorded their sounds. It was amazing to see so many black people in the airport, Muslim men dressed in spotless long white robes. I had never felt this sense of being a part of the majority before. The men carried themselves in a stately fashion. While we encountered several young black Americans loudly affirming, "Africa, we are here!" it occurred to me that Africans have never felt the need to affirm the beauty of their blackness because no one had ever questioned it. They knew who they were all the time and didn't have to discover or be taught a sense of pride. We stayed at the Hotel Croix du Sud, which was very clean, and I felt that I didn't have to fear employees looking through my belongings in search of something to steal.

The women in Senegal were the most beautifully dressed of all the Africans I saw. The market place was interesting and colorful, but one had to ask permission to take someone's picture. Many women didn't want to be photographed. I had been told that everywhere in the world there was someone in every hotel who spoke English, but I found that this was not true. Roommates had only one key between them, so if they were going their separate ways, they left the key at the desk. No one there spoke English, and if you couldn't call your room number in French, you wouldn't get the key. I found French easier to speak and understand in Africa than in France. The syllables separated themselves more neatly. At meals the waiters wrote out our checks in Arabic, which none of us could read, but the cost was included in our services, so we didn't have to be concerned. Those who report the high rate of illiteracy in African nations fail to understand that most Africans speak the official language, English or French, Arabic, and a number of local tribal languages, as well, and are far more literate in speech than Americans. Their need for reading and writing those languages is minimal since history and literature are passed on orally. But the Africans I have met who have been taught in traditional methods are far better educated than Americans.

One afternoon we visited a fishing village in Senegal. Clara and I communicated with two young boys whom we wanted to assure we were of African descent, in spite of our much lighter skin. "*Noir! Noir!*" we emphasized, pointing to ourselves.

There were only a few tiny buildings on the seashore. Looking into one, we saw only a cot and a table. Women bent over open fires cooking food in pots on the ground. They sat in the sand, but their clothing was not soiled. The white robes of the men looked as if they had just come off an ironing board, in spite of their sitting on the ground.

The high point in our days in Senegal was our trip to Gorée Island. We took a ferry there on a Tuesday when the infamous slave house was closed, but it was opened for our group. It was a very emotional experience for most of us as we saw the shackles illustrated and the narrow slits in the walls for light and air. After we left the slave house, we walked to another area of the island where we had lunch and spent part of the afternoon in lounge chairs just relaxing and meditating. I walked to a high wall that had a drop-off point to the water and wondered if this was perhaps the place where Phillis Wheatley's middle passage had begun.

Leaving the island we saw a group of students being taught under a tree. A man approached me with a handmade cotton dress; I still feel ashamed that I talked him down from the price he was asking for it.

My greatest disappointment in our visit to Africa was that we spent too much time listening to lectures at the various embassies and attending cocktail parties at officials' homes, and there was too little opportunity to get to know the ordinary people.

We had at our disposal what we were told was the first Greyhound bus in Africa. Crossing borders was an interesting experience. When we got off the bus, the local residents who had never seen one before gawked, and a few got on and marveled at the toilet in the back.

Our next stop was Ivory Coast where we stayed at the fabulous Hotel Ivoire Continental. Nikki Giovanni was staying at the same hotel, and we met there for the first time. Someone took our picture together.

That Sunday we boarded the bus to visit some historic sites from colonial times. On our way we saw people gathering in a clearing and heard the beating of drums. When we disboarded, the activity stopped, but after we joined the people in their circle, it resumed. What impressed me most was how well behaved the children were. They sat quietly with the adults and enjoyed the events without getting restless or having to be told to sit down. As the music continued, a woman went to the center of the circle with a cloth in her hand and danced alone. Shortly another woman took her place, the cloth passing to her. I don't know what the significance was, but I assumed they were competing with one another to see who could outdance the others. We stayed a while and felt welcome before continuing to our destination.

Hotel Okapi in the Congo was a unit of separate buildings. We didn't spend much time at the hotel, but one free evening a lot of us sat around the pool relaxing. Spontaneously, one of the African Americans started singing "Lift Every Voice and Sing" and the rest of us joined in. I don't know what inspired her to sing the "Negro National Anthem" but it seemed a most appropriate place.

In Lagos, Nigeria I met one of the Crossroads hosts, a young man named Femi Sodipo, ten years my junior, who decided that he was in love with me. We spent a lot of time together. Some years earlier I had met another Nigerian, Tamunoemi David-West, who was studying for his master's degree at Yale. We dated several times, both in Detroit and in New Rochelle when I was visiting my parents. When his mother was killed in an accident shortly before he completed his Ph.D. at McGill, he asked me to write a poem about her so that he could have it published in a newspaper back home. She was the daughter of a chief, but in my poem I took some liberty with that fact. Because of Tom, I felt a closeness to Nigeria that I didn't feel to the other countries.

One day when the bus was not in use, Femi asked the driver to take us to a market where I did some shopping that included a goat-skin bag. He pointed out to me Muslims sitting on a bench who he said had made the pilgrimage to Mecca. He told me a great deal about his life and his father's wives and other children, informing me that he was a prince who had not been acknowledged because of jealousy. He invited me to go to a juju with him, but I declined the offer. While he was confiding in me on the bus, I turned on my tape recorder without his knowledge. When he noticed it in my lap, he asked me what it was and I lied, saying it was a radio that needed a battery.

When we returned to the bus, the driver had left temporarily. We stood at the window looking out as we awaited his return. Some small children were on the sidewalk looking up at the window. Directing their eyes to me, they were clapping and chanting, "*Oynibo, oynibo!*" Femi laughed. "You don't know what that means, do you?" he asked. "It means *white person*." That surprised me. "You mean they can't tell by my hair?" I was wearing it natural. "No. You're not black, so you're therefore white." The children's name for me was not derogatory but chanted because of my difference in appearance. Femi explained that when this name was applied to a Nigerian of mixed blood, the person would say, "No, not oynibo. Black." And that would be the end of it.

The Nigerian men were very well dressed, and one day Femi put on his best outfit for me to take his picture. I'm sure his interest in

253

me was related to his hope of coming to America.

While in Nigeria we visited the oba's palace. The civil war between the Ibo and the Yoruba tribes had recently ended, and we were warned not to mention the subject. Our bus was met by acrobats whose performance was quite impressive. As we got off the bus, the oba, or tribal leader, took special notice of a dark-skinned woman from New York who was wearing a long Afro hair style. Inside the palace, which was really just a house, the oba, who was a pharmacist educated in England, brought up the war himself. At his feet sat an Ibo who had returned to his faithful service after the war. The oba served us refreshments and was very cordial. When we were ready to leave, he invited the dark-skinned woman and her roommate to stay for dinner. She reported to us later that he had asked her to be his seventh wife. His first wife, who was seated at the table with them, had given her approval. She told him she'd let him know, but she had no intention of taking him up on his proposal. When she left he took a gold ring off his finger and gave it to her and gave her and her roommate a pair of wood carvings.

We took a three-day bus drive along the Slave and Gold Coast to Cotonou and then to Lome, Togo and Dahomey (now Benin), stopping for several days at each place. From there we went to Accra, Ghana, where we visited a couple who owned a chicken farm. The woman was from America and Dr. Robinson had performed their marriage ceremony. We also visited Takoradi before returning to Accra.

The high point of my visit to Ghana was a durbar held out in the country. American Crossroaders had been living with African families for several months and building a school. The school was not yet finished for lack of money, but they wanted it dedicated then because of Dr. Robinson's presence. As we approached a clearing, the bus going about five miles an hour, a drizzle began, but it didn't stop people from dancing ahead of us in the dirt road, some shooting guns. The bus driver waved a fly whisk from the window. A woman standing on the ground passed a cloth over each person's face as he or she stepped down off the bus, saying, "Wel-COME! Wel-COME!" We sat under a roof of leaves as the rain fell harder. The chief, handsomely dressed in colorful kente cloth, one shoulder bare, entered with his entourage which included his wives and officials carrying implements that indicated their office. They came to where we were gathered, and someone placed a bracelet of beads on each of our wrists, making us honorary Ghanaians. After this procession, Dr. Robinson and the guides in our group walked to the other side to pay tribute to the chief and his people.

One of the Crossroaders, an American Caucasian, made a speech in the native language, repeating it in English, and then dancing with her African "mother" with whom she was living. Other speeches were made in both languages. The dedication of the school took place, but it was announced that the building could not be completed until they received several hundred dollars. One of the members of our group, an African American woman, quietly wrote a check for that amount. The rain let up and the dancing began, men and women dancing together or with members of the opposite sex. A warrior took my hand, but I took only a few steps with him because I was not adept at their manner of dancing. The chief came to our side and danced with Dr. Robinson. This picture appeared on the cover of a magazine while we were there.

Our last stop was in Monrovia, Liberia where we stayed at Hotel Ducor Intercontinental. I expected to find a statue of Melvin B. Tolson, who was named Poet Laureate of Liberia after writing the book-length poem, *Libretto for the Republic of Liberia,* but no one I talked to had ever heard of him. At our embassy briefing we were told that Liberia, settled by former slaves, had never had the "advantage" of colonialism. I suppose that was intended to explain the backwardness of the country that had always been free. While other countries in Africa were in the process of providing educational opportunities for all children, Liberia had no such plans. If parents could afford to send them to school, the government would then assist them in going to college, but if they were poor, they had no opportunity to pursue a formal education at all.

When we lived in New Jersey, I heard a lot about the Lott Carey Convention and the school in Liberia that black Baptists supported. Many offerings were taken up at church to support this school. It was important for me to visit it and report to my father that I had been there. So my roommate, a Methodist, and I hired a driver to take us to the Baptist and the Methodist schools. The Baptist school was a tremendous disappointment. I wondered where all the money had gone, for I could see no evidence that it had ever been used as intended. We talked to some of the students and found them very well behaved and friendly. From there we went to the Methodist school, which was more impressive, but not much. My roommate said, "I've been sending money to Africa all my life. I'm not sending another penny."

Shortly before Jill and Malaika moved to Brazil in 1980, intending to stay, the government passed a law prohibiting foreigners from getting work permits. Because she had already left her job, given up her apartment and sold her furniture, she went anyhow, feeling that such a law could not exist long. She was right. It was rescinded, but after about nine months she had spent all her savings and would have had to return to the states and apply for a different kind of visa. She was forced to return to California.

But during the Christmas holidays, I spent three weeks visiting. They had been there only three months and, though Jill had been there before and was already fluent in Portuguese, this was Malaika's first trip. She was five years old and after three months, she had learned the language and knew all the popular songs. Jill had put her in school, feeling that if it proved too much for her, she'd take her out, but she adjusted rapidly.

256

They had sublet a tiny apartment in Rio de Janeiro about three blocks from Copacabana Beach. Jill had made friends with several people who were very nice to me, but we couldn't communicate except through Jill and Malaika.

We did all the touristy things, including the ride to the top of Corcovado Mountain to see up close the statue of Christ the Redeemer. Lit at night, it dominates the city. We went to Sugar Loaf Mountain and all the other places Rio is famous for. I was appalled at the poverty. There seemed to be no middle class, only the very rich and the very poor. The huts along the hillside had no city services, and abandoned, extremely dirty children slept on sidewalks. Although there is a great deal of race mixing in Brazil, most of the poorest people are of African descent.

It was extremely hot in Rio, and the sand on Copacabana Beach burned my feet. Women in very scanty bathing suits left the water and sat on buses still wet. It was hard to find a dry seat. The air conditioning in Jill's apartment didn't work, and we could hear the conversation in the next apartment through an open window as clearly as if we were all in the same room. I first removed my slip, then my brassiere until I was wearing nothing but a loose-fitting dress and panties. Rio is such a relaxed city that women didn't care if others could see the bare outline of their bodies.

My visit to Brazil was the only overseas trip I have ever taken without being a part of a group, the first one where I stayed with someone who lived there. We spent one day at a house in the country that had a huge outdoor swimming pool. Another day we visited a family whose house had tile walls and a tiled front yard. A huge turtle that might have been a pet made its way across the tile yard. Jill and Malaika conversed with the family members and manicured each other's nails, but I had no idea what they talked about. Now and then they would look at me, indicating that I was the subject of discussion. Sometimes Jill would summarize in English what they were saying, but I was otherwise a complete outsider. The food they served was tasty and different from my usual fare.

Celebrating Christmas in Brazil was interesting. Light poles were decorated with colored lights and strung at an angle to represent trees. On Christmas Eve we visited a department store, and parents were busy buying gifts for their children as in North America. Santa Claus was Papei Noel. Jill cooked dinner in her tiny kitchenette and invited a lady in the same apartment to join us in the small dining area. The guest gave me a silver box which I still treasure. But it wasn't like any other Christmas I've ever experienced.

On New Year's Eve, people shot guns into the air, rang bells, and put bottles holding candles or other items in the gutters. These rituals evidently had something to do with African traditions. They also bought paper boats, cheap perfume, wine, and other objects. By the time evening came, the streets were wild. Jill said that Brazilians who didn't live near water always came to a city where there was water to celebrate the end and beginning of years. We met at the home of a couple Jill knew to accompany them to the beach. The streets were so crowded that it was impossible for traffic to move. If Carnaval is any wilder than New Year's Eve, I never want to witness it.

One man at Jill's friends' house spoke English and asked me who our goddess of the sea was. I told him we didn't have one, and he couldn't understand how we could have a country without such a deity. The African culture was evident in many aspects of Brazilian life in Rio. At about ten o'clock we joined the crowds at the beach. People dug holes in the sand to hold their paper boats. Some Afro-Brazilians held religious ceremonies. Everybody, it seemed, was drinking beer and having a noisy good time. I have never seen the kind of fireworks displayed there, including white fire streaming down the sides of hotels a sidewalk away from the beach. At midnight, everybody tossed their paper boats and their contents into the ocean, paying tribute to Yemanjá, the Yoruba goddess of the sea.

On New Year's Day, we took a plane to Bahia where we stayed for six days. Alberto, a friend whom Jill had met on her previous visits there, met us at the airport and drove us to our little hotel in old Pelhourinho, the oldest part of the city on the upper level. (A street elevator is available to transport pedestrians between the two levels, but drivers may take the long way around to reach another level.)

The sidewalk in front of our hotel entrance was so narrow that two people couldn't walk abreast. The entrance was one step up from the sidewalk. Jill, Malaika and I slept in one bed on a thin mattress. There was nothing luxurious about the hotel, but it was old Pelhourinho, which was more typical of the real city than other hotels where most tourists would prefer to stay. The hotel was located on a steep hill of cobblestone streets and buildings several hundred years old.

Because it was New Year's Day, Alberto insisted that we go to his mother's house where she had prepared food. The entire house was no bigger than one large room, and it was filled with children and flies. I had to make some pretense of eating, but nothing I saw was appetizing, and the beverage looked and tasted like a mixture of beer and red wine. I have no doubt that it was there that I got shigolosis.

African culture is stronger in Bahia than anywhere else in the country. Slavery didn't end there until 1888, and this is the area where most of the former slaves settled. Africa was present in the appearance of the people, their clothing, the food, their dancing, and many other aspects of daily life. Around the corner from our hotel was a small museum showing life-size figures of Yoruba deities in their particular regalia and adorned with their special implements. We visited a place where capoeira and dancing were performed and saw all the sights that were characteristic of the area. We visited churches, including The Church of the Good End, where we tied on our wrists souvenir ribbons that were supposed to be worn until they fell apart. Felinto, a friend of Jill's who owned an art store, insisted that I accept his gift of a carving made from a single piece of wood. It stands about three feet tall and the branch that parts in two represents a crucifix. The ankles are twisted unnaturally around each other, and under the feet is an African mask, depicting the close relationship between the Catholic and African religions. He wrapped the carving very carefully so that I could take it on the plane

Back in Rio I still felt extremely warm but attributed the heat to the outdoor temperature. Each morning I had diarrhea, but it didn't reoccur until the next morning. I suppose that was due to my taking Lomotil.

My three-week visit to Brazil was like experiencing Jill's dream firsthand. Aguiar and Iracema, Jill's friends, drove us to the airport, and I boarded the plane to Miami where I would have to claim my luggage and change to a plane to Detroit. In Miami I waited as long as I could for the wood carving to come through. Fearful of missing my connecting flight, I rushed from one end of the airport to the other, thinking I would never see the gift again. Once on the plane, I still felt very warm and thought it was from rushing.

When I arrived in Detroit, my husband Leonard met me with a winter coat, gloves, and boots. It was about six degrees below zero. After settling down for a few hours at home, I realized that I had a fever and went to the emergency room at Ford Hospital where some tests were taken. The next day I went back to work. Leonard called me to say that the hospital needed me to get back there immediately. That was when I found out I had shigolosis, which would have run its course naturally if I hadn't taken the Lomotil for diarrhea. I was told that this infection was contagious and advised to be extremely careful about my toilet habits. The hospital even sent a public health nurse to the house to make sure my mother and Leonard hadn't caught it. My temperature went back to normal and the problem soon ended.

Leonard and I went to Mexico twice, visited Nassau and Puerto Rico at different times, and cruised the Caribbean. We also went to Italy, France, and Greece, spending one week in Athens and cruising the Aegean the next. Since his death I have been to Egypt and Thailand. I would like to visit northern Africa, Spain, and Portugal but probably never will. I have been to most of the places overseas that I wanted to visit and, except for a possible cruise, I am at the point that another such trip would be too strenuous. I still hope to cross the Atlantic on a ship. I have not seen as much of my own country as I would like. I would very much like to follow the civil rights trail. I still do readings and attend conventions and conferences in other states and visit those few relatives I still have but, with those exceptions, my traveling days are probably over.

V.
Bringing the Light

Preparation for Teaching

It was only after my marriage to Harold in 1954 that I was able to leave the telephone company and continue my full time preparation for teaching. I knew that, with my love of literature and composition, I would not be happy teaching small children. I admired those who had the patience to take on the difficult and extremely important task of building a solid foundation for future learning, but I didn't feel qualified to do so. At that time there were almost no African Americans in administration and very few teachers in high schools. Several friends told me that I was foolish to insist on secondary education as the chances of my being hired were slim. I should take courses in elementary education where I stood a much better chance of getting a job. But I was entering the field late and under the handicap of household duties that now included a husband and three children, and I had no intention of pursuing a career in which I knew I would be unhappy. I felt that if I was qualified, I would be hired on the level of my choice.

Because I had been so stubborn about my course work in the past, I was required to take several undergraduate classes in education to qualify for a teaching certificate. At the same time, I signed up for a full load of graduate classes, majoring in something the catalog called "English Education." But the only classes Wayne University offered in English education were on the elementary level. Therefore, all the graduate courses I took were designed for English majors in the liberal arts curriculum. That suited me fine except for the time and hard work required of my double-duty schedule.

I didn't find the undergraduate courses in education stimulating at all. Nevertheless, my days were hectic. A typical morning found me preparing breakfast for the family and leaving the house in order to do my student teaching at Hutchins Junior High School, one of the toughest schools in the city. After the class and an occasional conference with my critic teacher, I would rush back home and wash the breakfast dishes before dashing out to my late morning and afternoon classes on campus. Often I had an evening class that permitted me to come home for a hastily prepared dinner before leaving again. One of the neighbors who was illegally running the numbers observed me as I drove off and returned home, notebook in hand, with such frequency that he assumed I was involved in the same business he was. He said to my father-in-law, "Tell your daughter I don't care what kind of deal she has; I'll give her a better one." He replied, "That girl is going to school." The numbers probably would have been a lot easier than what I was doing.

My most time-consuming and dreaded class was one called Bibliography for English Majors. It was reputed to be also the dullest of classes, but fortunately, the professor who normally taught the course was on sabbatical leave. Taking his place was Bill White, a journalism professor who, while following the original format, nevertheless breathed some life into the course with his breezy teaching style and his anecdotes about famous plagiarisms. Our one assignment for the semester was to identify 35 quotations. The purpose was to force us to learn firsthand what kinds of information could be found in which resource materials.

No matter what time of day or night I went to the library, I found half of my class there wandering about more or less aimlessly like kids looking for Easter eggs in a dense forest at midnight. As soon as someone did find an answer to one of the 35 questions, he or she was generous enough to share it with whoever happened to be nearby at the time. I thought that was pretty decent of them and was happy to reciprocate. With one exception.

One night I was deeply absorbed in my search for one particular quotation but, as usual, was aware of the other unsolved mysteries as I perused every likely book. This is how I lucked up on my prize answer. One of the quotations was about Byron; I had looked for his name in the index of many books only to be disappointed. That George Gordon, Lord Byron proved to be so elusive was a particular annoyance as I had once felt such a close kinship with him as an undergraduate that I wrote a sonnet about him. But one index, unlike the others I had perused, listed not one Byron but two! Excitedly turning to the page listed after the name of this other Byron, whom I had never heard of, I found the quotation. How clever a trick Dr. White had played on us, knowing all the while that we would make the assumption that I had made! I was so pleased with myself and so amused by his cleverness that I kept the secret of my discovery to myself. .

When the time came for us to report our answers, I was the only one in the class who was able to identify the critical quotation about an obscure dramatist whose last name just happened to be Byron. Years later when I was a research associate at Oakland University where Bill White's wife Gertrude taught, I had the pleasure of attending a dinner party in their home, and we had a good laugh about my adventures in the deadliest class for graduate English majors on campus.

My undergraduate courses in education, while far less challenging, still held some warm acquaintances and bright moments and, with my heavy schedule, I was grateful for whatever relief the easier courses gave. I feel no particular sense of accomplishment, however, for being able to ace my way through them since chance often paved my way. My advisor, a man who carried a walking stick and an acquired English accent, was a lover of poetry. On more than one occasion, he began to quote some of his favorite lines and, seeing my lips move along with his recitation, he would point to me to finish the stanza.

One day this professor was discussing ways of designing examinations and, to demonstrate whatever point he was making, related that he had once studied at Yale under Dr. William Lyon Phelps. Dr. Phelps had given an examination that ended with a single quotation; the instruction was that anyone who could identify the quotation was exempt from the rest of the exam. My professor recalled hearing Dr. Phelps discuss the colors in this particular poem and knew that if he thought hard enough, he would remember the title. Eventually he did. He wrote his answer to that one question and left the room, much to the dismay of the other students. Ending this anecdote, he challenged us to identify the line, "A common grayness silvers everything." After a few stutters, I shouted, "'Andrea del Sarto' by Robert Browning!" Completely shocked, he asked, "How did you know that!" One of my classmates with whom I had shared another class had seen me scribbling bits of poems on scraps of paper when a class was particularly boring. She responded, "Oh, she knows all of Browning's first lines," to which he answered, "But that's not a first line!" What he didn't know was that the same professor whose exam he was describing was the author of the book on Browning that Dad had used at Upsala College and which I had read and reread. Dr. Phelps had made the same observation in the book as he had made in my instructor's class.

It was by such means as this that I came to the conclusion that colleges of education should spend more time on the acquisition of subject matter than on methodology. I have also learned from experience that the teachers most in need of knowledge of teaching methods—university professors—are never required to take such a course. Teachers eventually find their own style and method; what works for one doesn't work for another. Teachers teach more than subject matter; they teach themselves.

At Hutchins Junior High School, my critic teacher was so nonchalant that he attempted to talk over students' conversations and didn't seem concerned that they weren't listening. One boy sitting near some cabinets in the back kept slamming the door open and shut. Nobody had to tell me that this wasn't the way to run a class. When I took it over, I demanded quiet while I was talking and, if others were talking, I simply waited in silence until they stopped. If I ever had any doubt about teaching, I soon realized that I was a natural at it.

My second semester I was assigned to Northern High School with the department head, Mr. Whitmer, as my critic teacher. I had a good eleventh grade class in American literature, one of the students being Edward Boyer who would eventually marry my daughter. Mr.

Whitmer and I got along very well, and he had great confidence in my ability. He never stayed in the room to observe me for more than a few minutes, and when we had our required conferences, we talked about poetry and other matters that didn't pertain directly to my teaching. I was happy there and wanted to stay. I don't know if he asked for me or not, but after completing my degree requirements and earning certification to teach, my first assignment was to Northern High School. Among my classes was one in English literature, composed of college-bound students. I couldn't have been happier.

Then a few days after the second semester began, Mr. Whitmer told me that the enrollment had dropped and, as the low man on the totem pole, I was being transferred to Burroughs Junior High School the next day. Actually, I was the "low man" only in the English Department. I cried buckets of tears and, for a long time, couldn't pass Northern without wanting to cry

I will always believe that I was selected to integrate the faculty at Burroughs. When I arrived, there were no classes for me to teach and no classroom ready for me to occupy. I spent the first three days doing nothing but sitting in the teachers' lounge. I was then assigned to a room in the mathematics section and given a class in math and one in social studies, along with the three in English. On paper I was qualified to teach social studies but didn't feel competent, reading a chapter ahead of the students. In English, on the other hand, I could have taught with no textbook at all. As for mathematics, I had taken no courses in college and was still adding and subtracting on my fingers. Math had always been my worst subject. There was no way I could teach these students what I didn't know myself. That evening I called my supervisor and explained the situation. She advised me to do the best I could if the department head insisted but to tell him that I was not qualified. The next day I was given an English class that was being taught by a math teacher.

Two weeks later, a second black teacher was transferred to Burroughs, and he took my class in social studies, leaving me with only English. But I didn't feel that I could really teach in that atmosphere. The best I could do was keep order. I don't approve of junior high schools or middle schools because the students in that difficult age group have no older students to look up to and emulate; they simply reinforce each other's age-related behavior.

Again I called my supervisor to ask for a transfer to Central, Northwestern, or any senior high school. She commented that she would normally advise me to try it awhile longer, but since I already had a master's degree, she would do what she could. If I had not received a transfer at the end of the semester, I would have stopped teaching and looked for another type of employment. There was no way that I would continue to teach in a junior high school. My transfer was to Northwestern High School.

Northwestern High School

My happiest years of teaching were at Northwestern High School where I began working in September, 1956. The department head, Miss Beatrice Merriam, had begun there as a young teacher the year after the school was built. As were most of the teachers and administrators, she was white while almost all of the students were black. Most of the few white students were enrolled in a special citywide class for those with extremely poor sight. Since I was a fairly inexperienced teacher, Miss Merriam assigned me to composition classes and the lower grades in literature, promoting me to higher level classes as she came to recognize my ability better. Eventually she urged me to take the examination for department head, but I was happy as a classroom teacher and had no desire to be an administrator.

During my years of high school teaching, I saw a number of excellent teachers move from the classroom to administrative positions which they didn't enjoy, but the lure of a higher salary was too much for them to resist. I could have used more money, too, but I never associated my paycheck with the work I was doing. I would have put the same dedication into teaching even if I hadn't been paid at all. When I received my paycheck, it simply seemed like a gift. I don't approve of merit pay *per se*, but I do believe that there should be a position for master teachers for which one must qualify by interview and examination, just as counselors, department heads, assistant principals, principals, and district supervisors qualify for their promotions, and that such a promotion should pay a higher salary. There are arguments to refute such a plan, but members of a department already know who the most effective teachers are. Why should they be required to stop doing what they do best, and why should the students be deprived of their best teachers simply because of a difference in salary?

I enjoyed the company of most of the other members of the English Department, and at one time some of us became such close friends that we had impromptu gatherings at each other's homes after school. We had some excellent English teachers, several of whom eventually moved on to college teaching. Some others we lost during a period of forced transfers after three years at the same school. That is not to say that all of the teachers were excellent. One white teacher, in particular, was obviously afraid of the black students. Unwilling to admit that she was hard of hearing, she spent the whole period writing verb conjugations on the blackboard while students in the back ignored her and talked or played radios softly.

The English office was equipped with desks, each shared by two teachers. This seldom presented a problem since we didn't all have preparation periods at the same time. But those of us who were there during the same periods got to know each other well and shared stories about our students.

The students, who came from a broad spectrum of socioeconomic backgrounds, were in general polite and cooperative. Their parents, when they visited, were also cooperative, wanting the best for their children. I realized that, if I treated my students with respect, they would treat me the same way. If I saw young men in the hall with their hats on, all I had to say was, "Gentlemen, your hats" or just point to my head, and off they came. Our beginning students were normally tenth-graders; after finishing ninth grade in junior high school, most of the best students chose to attend Cass Technical High School, which was considered to be one of the best high schools in the city and was selective in the students it accepted. But occasionally we got a class of ninth-graders, and, after a year at Northwestern, many of the best students decided to stay, having discovered that Northwestern was a better school than they had been led to believe. I had the pleasure of teaching some of the best college-bound students in the city.

The level of my teaching was closer to college than high school. Miss Merriam wanted the teachers to give her copies of our final examinations. One of mine consisted of four essay questions; I turned it in after the exam had been given. Her comment was, "You can't give an exam like this; it's college level." I replied, "But three students made As." I taught to that level, and many of the students were capable of learning what I taught.

Miss Merriam had originated a class called Essay, probably the only such class in any high school in Detroit. It was an extremely rigorous course for college-bound seniors. Each week the students were assigned a certain number of pages of reading in a specific type of essay. At the end of the week they had to turn in a bibliography of their reading, along with their own original essay of the same type. When Miss Merriam assigned me to teach that class, I knew how highly she thought of my teaching. Going over the bibliographies and correcting the papers for this class alone consumed all my time at home, compelling me to stay up late many nights to complete my work and return the papers as a new batch came in. But as difficult as the work was, it prepared the students well for college.

I insisted that all assigned essays be turned in. I informed my graduating seniors that late papers would be marked down but they must be turned in anyhow by a certain date. One student evidently didn't believe I was serious and, when the deadline arrived, he had several assignments still missing. True to my word, I gave him a failing grade. His older brother, whom I had taught earlier, came to see me, pleading for leniency. The student had paid for graduation pictures and invitations, and he must graduate on time. I held firm, getting the student to admit in his brother's presence that he had had fair warning but had ignored it.

That summer was the only time I taught summer school. At August graduation, when the student I had failed did graduate, I'm sure I clapped louder than anyone else. He came up to me afterwards and kissed me on the cheek, saying, "I've been getting away with things all my life; if you hadn't stopped me, I would have gone on doing the same thing."

In another very good English literature class of seniors, one girl, who had not achieved the level of the other students and probably should not have been there, went to her counselor and asked him to transfer her to another class; she just knew that she would fail. Knowing me, he refused and sent her back, advising her to ask for help when she needed it. I had already recognized her deficiencies and felt that receiving help from her classmates might be more effective and less intimidating than dealing with me alone. I divided the class into groups, making sure that an excellent student was a part of each group. As they worked together, they read and discussed the form of various poems and essays and their possible interpretations. My thinking was that, even if another student interpreted a poem for her, if she remembered that interpretation on an examination, she had learned something. The method worked well and she received a *C* plus at the end of the semester.

In one class of composition and grammar, I had a student whose last name was Parks. She was a quiet, sober-faced girl who seldom had much to say and was not a part of the "in" crowd. I got the impression that her family was struggling financially. She was always clean and neatly dressed but not in the latest fashions. It was the practice for teachers to collect money from the students and order the textbooks from the bookstore. On the day that the money was due, she had only half of what she owed. She promised to bring the balance the next Friday. When Friday came, she brought me the money without being asked. I learned that she was dependable and had good work habits. Although she rarely earned a higher grade than a *C*, her homework was always turned in on time, and it was obvious that she was doing the best she could.

There was one thing that bothered me, though. Whenever she turned in an assignment, she spelled her name at the top of the paper with an apostrophe between the *k* and *s* in *Parks*. One day when I was returning papers, I told her quietly that her last name should not be spelled with an apostrophe. I could feel her bristle as she replied, "That's the way my mother spells it."

"That's all right then," I said, adding: "We're going to study punctuation this semester." I tried to let her know that I didn't intend to contradict or criticize her mother. I admired her loyalty—a precious thing I didn't want to tamper with.

She didn't volunteer to speak during classroom discussions and sat stony-faced when I explained rules of grammar and their application. But as time went by, I sensed a softening in her expression and she eventually raised her hand to ask a question. There was no further discussion about the spelling of her name even when we got to the chapter on punctuation. We went through the explanations and exercises on the apostrophe with no more emphasis than we had placed on the comma and semicolon. And the papers continued to be signed: Renonnia Park's.

Some weeks went by and, when the change came, I almost missed it. She had dropped the apostrophe in her name, and my heart leapt with joy because I knew that she had come to trust me.

Renonnia gradually opened up to me to the point that we sometimes talked a few minutes after class. I tried to let her know that I was interested in her as an individual and cared about her progress and well-being. We eventually became friendly enough for me to learn that she was looking for after-school work, and I asked her if she wanted to come to my house to do some ironing one day a week—with her mother's permission, of course. She did. She turned out to be an excellent worker, a little bit slow but thorough and painstaking. She took enough time with each item of clothing to make sure it didn't have any wrinkles before folding or hanging it neatly. I was always pleased with her work.

Putting one's best effort into any given task is a rare and wonderful thing. Taking pride in one's work, whatever it may be, is more to be valued than money and prestige. I never met Renonnia's mother but was grateful for the personal traits she had instilled in her daughter.

All these years I have remembered Renonnia and revered her as the kind of person I think of as a plodder, one who works up to his or her potential. Not imbued with brilliance, not one to excel in activities usually associated with success, she and her kind are nevertheless the ones who have a right to be proud of their achievements. I'd trade people like her any day for the gifted ones who can earn *A*'s with little or no effort and therefore have no incentive to struggle. Not accustomed to everybody's easy praise, the plodders are likely to enjoy their rewards more because they have put so much of themselves into earning them. Not being offered money on a silver tray, they are likely to handle it responsibly because they understand its relationship to hard work.

I have seen many persons more amply endowed end up in frustration and a sense of *ennui* and aimlessness—sometimes even complete failure—while the middle *C*s of the world pass them by and live successful and emotionally rewarding lives. I don't know what became of my former student, but whatever she is doing, I'm sure she is doing it as well as she knows how, and I hope she is feeling tremendous pride in that.

Remembering Renonnia brings to mind the tenuous relationship that often exists between teacher and student and how carefully that teacher must tread to respect the sensibilities of youngsters while, at the same time, trying to guide them. Long live the plodders of the world! And long live teachers who can make a difference in their lives, even to the point of eliminating superfluities as tiny as an apostrophe.

Fourteen years after our first meeting, I received a letter from a Northwestern graduate who had entered as a senior, having always before attended parochial schools. She was a Seventh Day Adventist who didn't feel comfortable in her new school with its different values and made few if any friends. She talked to me about her discomfort, and I took special time with her whenever I could.

Remembering Constance Grayson in New Rochelle, I respected her adherence to her religious beliefs and the fact that most Seventh Day Adventists that I have come in contact with were much more serious and knowledgeable about their beliefs than most other Christians I knew. When I came back from my travels in the fall of 1967, I shared with her a small portion of the bottle of water I had dipped from the Jordan River. I had forgotten this incident and had not thought of her until she wrote me from Michigan State University fourteen years later. It was a long, handwritten letter in which she recalled our relationship and said that, after all these years, she was about to receive her degree and become an English teacher because of the influence I had had on her life.

When she later married and her first child was christened in Detroit, she insisted that my husband and I stand with the family during the ceremony. For a while we stayed in touch and I visited her family in their home.

I continue to run into former students from Northwestern, many of whom didn't show particular promise of success at the time I taught them. They are now grandparents and great-grandparents. Most are retired. I see them in stores, on the street, at social functions, almost everywhere, and most of them remember me by name. It is a great pleasure to learn how successful many of them have been in their chosen careers. I would not have predicted such success for some of them. Some have told me things that I said or did that inspired them or changed their lives. These meetings have convinced me that the effect of doing one's best may not be immediately evident and, if I hear words of praise from the former students that I meet, there must be others I will never see again who were also influenced in positive ways. It is impossible to know what effect one has on others; it is therefore imperative to me to live my life in service to others, be the best role model that I can be, and hope that, following my example, others will make positive and meaningful contributions to society.

277

During my years at Northwestern, the principal sometimes brought visitors to my class unannounced and sat in the back of the room to observe my teaching. I had student teachers assigned to me as their critic teacher, and one year, on a special program, I was given only four classes to allow me time to supervise and instruct beginning teachers. I gained a reputation for being tough but fair. Colleges considering applicants often rate them according to the high schools from which they are graduating and do not give the same value to an *A* or *B* from some schools as they do from others. I felt that many teachers at Northwestern gave inflated grades, and students who went to college realized only then that they were not as well prepared as their grades indicated. But I didn't give North-western-type high grades. Any student receiving an *A* or *B* from me would have received it at Cass or any of the other schools considered to be among the best in the country.

On the lower end, I was somewhat more lenient. Seldom did anyone fail my class who had turned in all his or her assignments, even though they might not have done them well. Most of those who failed simply had not done all the work assigned. I realized that many had come from such educationally deficient lower grades that they were incapable of doing any better in high school; they just didn't have the necessary foundation. I recall one girl who had taken the same course twice before with different teachers and failed. When she pleaded with me to pass her, she said, with tears in her eyes, "If I take it a fourth time I still won't be able to understand it." Since she had turned in all her assignments, I passed her.

For many years I have believed that American education is in deep trouble. One of my ninth grade composition and grammar classes had in it a significant number of students who had gone to elementary school in the rural South. They were, for the most part, better prepared than those who had gotten their foundation in northern schools. I think the reason is that the southern schools had never changed their methods of basic teaching, while the more "progressive" schools changed with every new theory that came along, losing effectiveness with most of these changes. Change is not always improvement; that should be obvious, but evidently it isn't. Students who learned to read using the phonics method were better readers and spellers than those who learned to read by the whole word method. Those who learned handwriting by a particular method grew up writing legibly. Those who learned the parts of speech, formal grammar, and the relationship of parts of a sentence by diagramming could reason out the proper pronoun to use and understand why a composition did not earn an *A*. But teachers were forbidden to diagram sentences on the board (which I did anyhow, omitting only the lines) and were instructed not to put a lot of red marks on students' compositions because they would discourage them from writing at all. As if continuing to write voluminously would lead to improvement! Today we have a generation of "educated" adults who speak publicly as television anchors, public officials, and even some professors, who don't know how to speak their native language and have no educational basis on which to decide when *I* is the proper pronoun and when *me* is called for. Many don't know that a verb agrees in number with the subject of a sentence and not what follows. And the English teachers—sorry, it's no longer English but "language arts"—can't teach their students what they never learned themselves. Few people know any geography anymore except what is learned from news of wars and other catastrophes; China could as easily be in Texas as it is in the Far East.

Our curricula at Northwestern included some subjects that were not taught in any other high school in Detroit. I introduced the first accredited course in creative writing and was allowed to handpick my students and limit the class size to twelve. Now famous Pearl Cleage was one of these students. Mrs. Eula Gayle Cutt taught four years of Latin although the classes were small and sometimes combined. We had a class in Russian, and Don Thomas, the only qualified teacher in the city, taught radiation biology. Beginning in 1966-67 I taught the first accredited course in African American literature. Mrs. Cutt was also a scholarship committee of one, matching scholarships to the individuals she felt were best qualified for them.

The course in American literature used a textbook entitled *Adventures in American Literature.* I was accustomed to textbooks that had a paucity of material by black authors. This edition contained "The Creation" by James Weldon Johnson, "One Wants a Teller in a Time Like This" by Gwendolyn Brooks, an article about Mary McCleod Bethune, and an essay on Dr. George Washington Carver which included his photograph. Other than several of the happier Negro spirituals, there was no other mention of African American contributions to American literature. When I discovered that not one of the students in my all-black class had ever heard of a black poet, not even Paul Laurence Dunbar or Langston Hughes, I began dividing the students into groups, bringing in personal copies of books by six black poets and letting them use them in class to prepare reports. I also mimeographed material to distribute. I assigned outside biographical information about the poets whose work they were studying. When one young man's response to a poem I read to them was: "You mean a Negro wrote *that*?" I realized how sad it was that he and others had accepted the myth of racial inferiority.

I struggled for several years in this way supplementing the textbook and, at the same time, informing other teachers in the English Department of these literary contributions of which they, too, were unaware. Some of them were happy to follow my example and asked me for direction.

When I read the advertised contents of the new edition of this same textbook, I was appalled to see that even the few items concerning black people in the edition we had been using had been removed except "The Creation" and the spirituals. I decided that I would not use the new edition. I perused several other high school texts and found that they were no better than this one. I wrote to the

280

editor of *Adventures in American Literature* and informed him that I would not use the new edition of their book, explaining my reason. Shortly I received a call from him at home explaining that, when they removed material from an older edition, they were not aware of the race of the authors. I replied: "Nonsense! George Washington Carver was a dark-skinned man. There is no way you could have removed his picture and not been aware that he was black." His other lame excuse concerned the removal of the poem by Gwendolyn Brooks. "We try to include something by a young author, and we realized that she is no longer young." That she had won a Pulitzer Prize was not reason enough to include her, but her age was sufficient to exclude her. How absurd! I wrote letters of complaint to the publishers of other American literature textbooks but received no reply from any of them.

Teachers had no part in selection of textbooks, but, without asking anyone's permission, I went out and found a set of four paperback American literature anthologies on the college level and purchased them with my own money. Then I had my students buy them from me instead of ordering them from the bookstore. These were what I taught from every semester after that.

In 1971 I was on the program to speak at a National Council of Teachers of English convention in Las Vegas. I don't recall the main topic of my paper, but I did discuss at length my objection to the omissions in the textbooks. I mentioned several that I had examined without disclosing their titles. After my talk, a woman came up to me and said, "I think you were talking about our book." She was an editor of a book that included something by Frank Yerby, who many readers believed was white, and an untypical essay by James Baldwin and nothing more. The editor said, "I agree with you, and the senior editor does, too, but we have to be aware of sales potential. Because we included James Baldwin, 'that rabble rouser,' in our book, one whole school system in the South canceled their order for all of our textbooks." What she was saying was that publishers are not educators, and they will include and exclude anything that will get their books adopted by school systems across the nation.

Evidently my objections had some effect nevertheless. Gradually I began to see minor changes. One white teacher at Northwestern, using a textbook with some inclusion of African American authors, asked her students to turn to a certain page to read a poem by Phillis Wheatley. They turned to that page, but the poem wasn't there. The teacher took one of the copies from a student's hand and, sure enough, something else was on that page. Without any designation that there were two simultaneous editions of the same book, the publisher had produced a northern and a southern edition. The students had copies of the edition intended for the South while the teacher's was the northern edition.

It should be apparent that, if students of all races are to receive an adequate education in the whole area of critically acclaimed American literature, they cannot depend on the general textbooks to supply their need. If it takes a separate course in African American literature, then such a course needs to become a part of the curriculum.

In 1965 I was allowed to teach an experimental course in African American literature during summer school. It was held at Northwestern High School, but students from other schools participated. Fewer than ten students enrolled, but the class proceeded. While it was in process, poet Melvin B. Tolson came to Detroit for a visit. Only 25 dollars was available to pay him to visit our class. He was not concerned about the money but was gracious enough to come. A professor who used the Socratic method of teaching, he asked the class two important questions. The first was, "What is a Negro?" Each student replied with an answer that had to do with the usual descriptions. When one student defined a Negro as having nappy hair, Mr. Tolson put his hand on the head of a boy whose hair was straight. "Is this a Negro?" he asked. Someone else said a Negro had dark skin color, to which Mr. Tolson turned the head of a light-skinned student, asking the same question. With each reply that related to thick lips, broad nostrils, and other stereotypical images, Mr. Tolson put his hand on another student's head, negating the answer. Finally, one of the students volunteered, "There is no such thing as a Negro."

His second question was, "How many oceans are there in the world?" All the students tried to remember their geography lessons, one trying to recite the various oceans' names. He asked where the Atlantic Ocean begins and ends. Eventually, the answer came that there is only one ocean in the world, all the water being connected.

I had preached so much black consciousness, black achievement, and black pride to my students and other teachers that, when Dr. Benjamin Mays, the black president of Morehouse College, came to speak to selected classes in the auditorium, I was very happy. It was the first time to my knowledge that a black college president had been invited to speak there. I was teaching a class in English literature with a heavy concentration on the poetry and philosophy of Robert Browning. I had made my students memorize lines from some of his poems. Since Dr. Mays was speaking during my preparation period, I was free to go to the auditorium to hear him. I hoped that some of my students, attending other classes that period, would have the opportunity of hearing him speak. During his remarks, what did he do but repeat one of the Browning quotations I had had my students memorize:

> Ah, but a man's reach should exceed his grasp
> Or what's a heaven for?

One of my English literature students later told me that, after hearing that quotation, she said to one of her classmates, "I don't know if Ms. Madgett's in the auditorium or not, but if she is, she's going to be the first person on the stage to speak to him." And I was. I was especially pleased that Northwestern students had had an opportunity to hear a black college president.

In 1964 there was a statewide competition for the first Mott Fellowship in English. It required the entrant to describe a project he

283

or she would complete if granted the fellowship. The project I proposed was an American literature textbook that would combine the appropriate African American contributions with those of white authors. It would have both a chronological and thematic approach. The selection committee was made up of faculty members and administrators at Oakland University. After they had read the entries, they invited me for an interview. I don't know how many other applicants were interviewed, but I was the person selected for the fellowship. So after my summer class was over at Northwestern, I secured a leave of absence from Detroit Public Schools and made preparations to commute the 25 miles to Rochester, eager to begin the 1964–65 school year on the campus of Oakland University as a resource associate.

My total stipend, to be paid monthly by the Continuing Education Department, was $10,000, more than my salary as a teacher. I was provided an office in North Foundation Hall and a part-time student secretary. At first I felt very lonely there, but I gradually met other faculty and staff members who were very congenial, and Sherry, my secretary, and I got along very well. I was not told but later learned that another $10,000 had been designated for my expenses. Once I found out about the expense money available, which the department possibly intended to use for its own purposes, I tried to spend as much of it as I could. As the book was intended for inner-city students similar to those at Northwestern, I decided to travel to schools all over the country, staying in good hotels and spending one week at each inner-city school that would accept me. I wanted to try out some of the finished chapters to test their effectiveness. I made three such trips, each one to three cities, continuing to write and sending finished chapters back for Sherry to type.

My last trip included Vashon High School in St. Louis, a multiracial, multicultural school in San Francisco, and a school in the Watts section of Los Angeles. I had never been to California before, and since the funds were available, I decided to go by train and see as much of the country as I could. I went from St. Louis to Kansas

284

City, where I changed trains, then rode to San Francisco. For most of the trip I was the only person in the sleeping car. The porters were very attentive, bringing me something on which I could write and waking me up for my first view of a desert.

Los Angeles presented the only problem I encountered because of the difficulty of public transportation. As soon as I checked into my hotel, I called my cousin Giles who had recently married for the second time. He told me to pack what I needed for an overnight visit with him and "Ever" and he would pick me up. Early the next morning he received a call from Minnie in Richmond that his father had died, so Ever and I took him to the airport and our visit was cut short.

Ever made arrangements with several friends for each to take me a portion of the way to the high school because no public transportation was available from the hotel where I was staying. It was therefore impossible for me to spend a solid week there trying out my material, but I did get a chance to observe the classes of an excellent teacher. This was the same high school where Bubba's twin daughters from his first marriage, Yvonne and Yvette Jackson, were students, and the counselor called one of them to the office to meet me for the first time.

One class I observed was making oral reports on Shakespeare as the teacher sat in the back of the room. Whenever a student made a grammatical error, he quietly gave the proper form, the student corrected himself or herself without embarrassment and continued. I had been taught that teachers should never publicly correct a student who was speaking. After class I asked the teacher how he got away with doing this. He said, "At the beginning of the semester I asked my students if they wanted to learn the correct way to speak or continue to speak as they normally did, and they all answered that they wanted to learn." If his manner had seemed to be critical, they would have reacted differently, but they knew that he loved them and wanted to help. I learned that it is not what the teacher does that matters but the manner in which it is done and the personal relationship between student and teacher. In my own classes, I did something similar. When I heard a grammatical error, I would simply repeat it with a question mark in my voice, and the student usually made the correction.

Oakland University was then still a part of Michigan State University and had a chancellor rather than a president. Dr. "Woodie" Varner called me into his office one day and asked me if I planned to work toward a Ph.D. He really wanted to keep me there, and if I had agreed to begin doctoral studies, he would have hired me. But at the time I didn't feel that I wanted to take time away from my creative writing to earn a higher degree. I had continued taking graduate courses but toward no particular end. Education was just in my blood, and I was too close to the University of Detroit and Wayne State University not to avail myself of their courses in literature, writing, and philosophy.

Oakland University provided me with the desire to teach on the college level. At the beginning of the school year, the freshmen were welcomed with a ceremony in which the faculty and staff members wore caps and gowns. The newspaper picture of me in line wearing academic attire and the campus atmosphere in general convinced me that, as soon as Jill graduated from Michigan State, I would apply for a position in a community college where I would not need a doctorate.

I returned to Northwestern in September, 1966. My project was completed and I sent the manuscript to Follett in Chicago, the company that had published *Success in Language and Literature/B*, a textbook for high school slow learners that I had co-authored with Henry B. Maloney and Ethel Tincher. We signed a letter of intent to publish my new American literature textbook, and Follett began work on the editing of chapters.

Late in 1967 I took eight weeks off from teaching for surgery and recuperation. Ed Boyer, my former eleventh grade student at

Northern High School and my future son-in-law, substituted for me. I was almost ready to return to school when it was announced that Dr. Martin Luther King, Jr. would be the speaker at one of the noonday Lenten services held annually at Central Methodist Church downtown at Grand Circus Park. I had never met him, but he knew members of my family. I had met his father many years earlier. When my daughter was quite small and we were still living on Richter Street, Dr. King, Sr. came to my house to visit my father when both were in Detroit attending a convention. At that time, his son was probably still in school and had not yet become well known. Dr. King, Sr. needed several letters typed, and I was happy to oblige him. Another year, Dr. King, Sr. and Dad were in Detroit again to attend a convention downtown. When I went to pick Dad up, I recognized the face of Dr. King but not his name. I said, "Who is that man over there? Don't we know him?" He said, "Oh, yes, that's King," and we went over to speak. It was not until many years later, reading *Parting the Waters* by Taylor Branch that I learned how these two Baptist ministers had become close friends. The book detailed Dr. King's 1934 trip to the World Baptist Alliance in Berlin and his travel following the convention; it was the same itinerary my father had taken.

I had never seen Dr. Martin Luther King, Jr. although I had marched from my church to the auditorium downtown where he delivered his first version of "I Have a Dream." My church group was so far behind the beginning of the long line that there was no room for us in the auditorium, and we sat on the grass outside and listened to his speech over a loudspeaker.

On this return to Detroit, I didn't want to miss the opportunity of hearing and perhaps meeting him. As it turned out, the overflowing crowd was disappointed because he had been delayed and would not appear until the following day. I wanted to give him a copy of my book, *Star by Star*, in which one of my civil rights poems, "Alabama Centennial," appears. Even though the poem does not mention him by name, it is easy to recognize his as "the quiet voice" in the poem.

I knew that if I was fortunate enough to get close to him and shake his hand, I would have no time to talk. I wrote a note on my business stationery which contained my address and phone number, identifying my family and directing his attention to this particular poem. I inserted the note in the book.

Every day a different high school choir sang for the noon Lenten service. I had tried so hard to raise my students' level of awareness of black pride and black achievement that I was tremendously pleased, when I returned the next day, to learn that the Northwestern High School choir would sit on the platform with Dr. King that day, sing, and listen to his sermon. I sat in the balcony and listened intently to his marvelous sermon on hope.

When the service ended, I pushed my way through the crowd and past television cameras to get in line to greet him. I held out the book, and he looked at me questioningly. I simply said, "This is for you," as I shook hands with him. In a little while I headed down a hall to the room where the choir was disrobing. I was anxious to see them again after my long absence from school and to get their reaction. Dr. King was walking ahead of me with the minister of the church. As I passed by them, he turned his head and looked at me, and that was all.

The following week I returned to school, taking a short nap after I got home every day. The week after that, Martin Luther King was assassinated. The next day at school, an impromptu program was put together in the auditorium, and the choir sang the same selections they had sung at the church, some of the students singing through their tears. I struggled through an emotional reading of "Alabama Centennial." I wondered if he had had a chance to read my poem, assuming I would never know.

The day before his funeral, I was taking a nap after school when the telephone rang. A man identified himself by a name I wish I could remember saying, "I was a friend of Martin Luther King, and he wanted me to give you a message." Those were his exact words, and they shocked me, making me feel that this message was coming from another world. He continued, "I read your poem to him and he asked me to be sure to call you and thank you for it. He appreciated things like that." Then he went on to say, "We expected something to happen either in Memphis or [whatever the next place was on his schedule] but when it came, I just couldn't take it. I'm getting ready to leave now for the funeral." I thanked him for calling, satisfied that Dr. King had had a chance to share my poem.

My daughter, a member of the Black Students Association at Michigan State University, and another member went to the president's office demanding representation at the funeral. Told that there were no funds available for such travel, they insisted that funds could be found. Soon after, I received a phone call from Jill's roommate telling me that she was on her way to Atlanta to the funeral. There were no hotel rooms to be had, and she shared a room with one of her black professors and his wife. The men fended for themselves. They were unable to get anywhere near the church and watched the service on television, but at least, they were there.

It was some months, or perhaps a year later, that I was invited to Memphis to do a reading and workshop. I took along my trusty "dummy" movie camera with which I had taken excellent pictures in Europe and the Middle East, as well as at home. The super 8mm. camera was simple to operate, requiring no adjustments. If you couldn't see the object through the eyepiece, you couldn't take the picture. It was almost impossible to make a mistake, but on one or two occasions when I didn't take the entire film or failed to so some other simple thing, the Kodak Company where I had to send it to be developed included a slip of paper indicating what I had neglected to do.

Arriving in Memphis, I asked my hostess to drive me to a florist; I wanted to place a vase of flowers in front of Dr. King's hotel room, which at that time was easily accessible to the public and had not yet become a museum. Arriving at the Loraine Motel, I showed my hostess how to hold the camera, and she filmed me as I walked up the steps and placed the vase of flowers at the door. Rev. Ralph Abernathy had had the biblical quotation placed on the door in brass letters: "Behold, this dreamer cometh. Let us slay the dreamer and see what will become of the dream." ("Come now therefore, and let us slay him . . . and we shall see what will become of his dreams." Genesis 37:20). I could not get far enough back on the balcony where he was killed to film the entire quotation so, taking back the camera, I panned the lettering on the door. Knowing that some of the local people disagreed with where the shots had come from, I photographed the entire area. Then I returned the camera to my hostess, who filmed me coming back down the steps. By that time, the reel had come to an end, and I had to insert another cartridge. As we left the parking lot, I took another picture of the motel sign through the back window.

When the Kodak Company returned the film, the first reel was completely blank, and there was no slip of paper with an explanation. All I had was the second reel taken as we were leaving. I have always believed that this film was confiscated and sent to some government agency. J. Edgar Hoover of the F.B.I. was so intent on getting as much information about other women in Dr. King's life to discredit him, even after his death, that I think someone saw this picture of a fairly attractive young woman and was determined to find out my identity and my relationship to him. I wouldn't be surprised if Kodak and other companies that developed film had been instructed to turn over any photographs that might involve him. There are other possible explanations, but I hold firm to my belief. I know for a fact that the federal government had records on my stepson and his gay rights activities.

Not knowing if the copy of *Star by Star* I had given to Dr. King ever reached his family, I gave his father a copy when I had a chance to talk to him at a convention, and on another occasion, when Mrs. Coretta Scott King spoke at Oakland University, I gave her a copy, too.

One year I was invited to read some of my poems at a local P.T.A. meeting. I didn't know that a special guest had been invited. Just as I was about to conclude, in walked Mrs. Rosa Parks. It was a great pleasure to read "Alabama Centennial" in her presence before I sat down. I had met her once in Detroit before her importance to the civil rights movement had been fully acknowledged. She needed a ride to some program, and my husband and I had picked her up at her home. I never met her husband, but I think he was still living.

When Margaret Walker was at the Shrine of the Black Madonna Cultural Center and Bookstore some years later, Mrs. Parks was present and couldn't understand why her young companion did not know who I am. Oliver LaGrone had created a bust of Mrs. Parks which was stolen from his van. Upon his return to Detroit, his daughter, Lotus Joy, gave a birthday party for him—I think it was his 87th. Mrs. Parks was already there when Leonard and I arrived, and Joy made it a point of seating us at the same table with her. We had ample opportunity to converse. What a lovely, modest, genteel lady she was! While many other southern women had refused to give up their seats on buses and move to the rear to accommodate a white person, most of them, with different personalities, images, and backgrounds, would not have been as likely to gain sympathy for the cause as Mrs. Parks was. She was the right person in the right place at the right time. When she died in 2005, she had truly come into her own, and the entire nation mourned. I have never before seen such crowds as those that lined several city blocks to view her body at the Charles H. Wright Museum of African American History in Detroit during a full day of viewing and throughout two nights. After her seven-hour funeral, thousands of people lined the streets for ten miles as her body was transported to the cemetery.

The mood at Northwestern changed after the rebellion of 1967. (I call it a rebellion for lack of a better word. It was certainly not a race riot, as the one in 1943 was, and, though there were many

291

conditions in Detroit that justly could have started a rebellion, I don't know what to call it when people burn down their own homes and burn and loot their own businesses.) Returning to school in September, I found that some students who claimed to have wanted classes in African American history and literature enrolled in those classes but did not attend. I had always found our students courteous and cooperative, but many now showed disrespect. One excellent white teacher, who had taught there for many years, was well liked, and always had the students' welfare as her primary goal, told me that, for the first time in all her years, she did not feel welcome. It seems to me that the real "rebellion" was the senseless aftermath in our students' attitudes. For the first time I felt frustration. In addition, the present principal had not been supportive of his teachers as former principals had been.

During that school year I had occasion to go to the Schools Center Building where I ran into the department head at the University of Detroit. We stopped in the lobby to talk, and he asked me if I would consider teaching a course in African American literature at the university during the summer. Just then, Frank Ross, who had once been the supervisor of high school English teachers, moving from that position to one in Oakland County, and was now a professor of English at Eastern Michigan University, saw us as he was getting on the elevator. He got off to join us. I knew that he had always admired my teaching and my professionalism. Frank asked me if I would like to teach at Eastern Michigan University in Ypsilanti. I was surprised at his question since, without a Ph.D., I didn't feel that I was qualified. The U of D department head said: "I was just asking her about teaching a summer class at U-D." Frank responded, "But I'm talking about a full time position." I exclaimed, "Would I ever!" still thinking that I didn't have a chance. But Frank followed through on his word, and called me to keep me up to date on the thinking of the outgoing and incoming department heads of the English Department at EMU. When I finally received a call inviting me to come in for an interview (without my ever having applied), Frank told me in advance that they were considering offering me a position as an assistant or associate professor, but he felt that, if I played my cards right, I could be hired as an associate professor. On the basis of my poetry and what Frank knew of my teaching, I was asked to begin teaching as an associate professor of English in September, 1968. Because my salary as a high school teacher was meager and I didn't have a Ph.D., the university offered me only a little more than I had made as a high school teacher.

During negotiations, I had told only a few people at Northwestern of the possibility that I might be leaving. When the principal got word of this, his response was: "That's impossible. She can't teach on the college level." But after the contract was signed and my resignation became a certainty, he called me out of class during the Honors Day program in June, borrowed one of the student's caps and called me to the stage as another "graduate," announcing my new position and placing the student's cap on my head.

So it was that my early determination never to teach was proved wrong, and my hope of teaching on a higher educational level became a reality that I had never dreamed was possible.

Eastern Michigan University

My parents were extremely proud of my new position which was announced in an article in the New Rochelle *Standard Star*. When I began commuting to Eastern Michigan University in Ypsilanti, almost forty miles door to door, in September, 1968, I was ecstatic. I had bought a couple of neat fall dresses, not realizing that those who taught on college campuses were more relaxed in their dress than high school teachers, many wearing blue jeans and sport shirts or slacks and sweaters. My first year I shared an office in one of the older buildings with two other teachers, an office so small that, if one of us had a student in conference, there wasn't room enough for the others to move back our chairs. There was an opening in the wall between our office and the one next door, so that everything said in one office could be heard in the other. One of my classes was in another building, which required bundling up during the winter to move there from my office or another classroom. But I was happy to be teaching three classes instead of the five I had taught in high school, and the classes met only three days a week instead of five.

My second semester there, I taught a course equivalent to the high school methods course I had taken at Wayne University. It was designed for junior and senior English majors who were preparing to teach in secondary schools. I appreciated the fact that this course was a part of the English curriculum rather than in the College of Education, but I was appalled at the lack of preparation of most of these students. They seemed to know little about classical literature and less about writing and grammar. They were incapable of critiquing each other's compositions intelligently. I was discouraged that they would enter the classroom and inflict their ignorance on their students. What I was teaching them is what they should have learned in elementary and high school. I was so disheartened that I asked my department head not to assign me to this class again.

The following year we moved to a newly constructed building, Pray-Harrold. I selected a single office without a window rather than sharing a brighter office with a colleague. I felt I could get more accomplished that way. The sixth floor was taken up by the mathematics and English department offices, each of several units having its own lounge with a small refrigerator-stove combination, so instead of having to walk up the hill for lunch in the cafeteria, we all brown-bagged it. I got to know a group of other professors in my department whose schedules often placed us in the lounge at the same time. I occasionally attended cocktail parties in their homes and once hosted one in my home in Detroit.

Often my first class was not until ten o'clock, but I usually arrived by eight in order to get a parking space in the closest lot and to have time for student conferences and extra preparation before teaching. No restrictions were placed on the subjects I could teach, which included one in Victorian literature, poetry, creative writing, and other courses in literature. When the professor who created the class in the Bible as Literature retired, no one else in the department felt qualified to teach it, but two professors took it over anyhow and shared their notes as they learned. Eventually I had the opportunity of teaching the class, reading and studying as I taught.

The English Department head at EMU was evidently interested in having a course in African American literature introduced into the English Department curriculum. My having introduced this course into the high school curriculum in Detroit may have been one reason that I was hired, another perhaps being that the largest department in the university did not have any African American teachers. The summer before I started teaching at EMU, the incoming department head, Dr. Milton Foster, called to ask if I would be interested in attending a seminar on African American literature at Cazenovia College in upstate New York at the department's expense. I was happy to agree. It was there that I first met Ishmael Reed and his sidekick, Steve Cannon, Dorothy Porter, head librarian at Howard University, and Darwin Turner, an outstanding critic and scholar. Although I was no stranger to African American literature, I found the seminar extremely helpful. The small town where the college is located was so conservative that when a showing of Leroi Jones's film, *Dutchman,* was scheduled, the directors could not let it be known outside the campus, and we had to identify ourselves before being admitted.

Because I have published under three different names, Dorothy Porter advised me to never change my name again. "It took me years to figure out that Witherspoon and Madgett were the same person," she said. I took her at her word and, when I married Leonard Andrews in 1972, I continued to write and function professionally as Naomi Long Madgett.

During my second or third semester, I proposed an undergraduate survey course in African American literature which had to be approved by the other members of the English Department. I had no difficulty getting this approval although some members of the department evidently felt such a course was not legitimate. One of my colleagues said, "I don't know why you want to teach all of those third-rate writers." I asked him if he had read any of Robert Hayden's poetry. He hadn't. Had he read Zora Neale Hurston or Melvin B. Tolson? No. I answered, "Then brush up on your education before you label excellent authors as mediocre and not worth studying." The former department head's knowledge of literature by black authors was limited to the few offerings included in one of Louis Untermeyer's anthologies published in the 1940s. The general attitude of some of my colleagues was that they had received Ph.D.s in English from the best universities of the country, and if any of these black authors had been worthy, they would have been included. But if a race is considered inferior, of what possible value could be their literary creations? Nevertheless, the department approved the course and the next semester I taught it for the first time.

In the process, some members of the department who had faith in my judgment became sensitized to the need for fairer representation of African American contributions to literature. When they were considering textbooks to adopt for their courses, they would bring them to me for approval or dismissal based on representation of African American authors whose names they depended on me to recognize.

The first time I taught the course, the majority of the students were white. Several of the few black students seemed to have enrolled for the purpose of castigating "whitey." Once they realized that this was a legitimate literature class requiring reading, several of them dropped the class. As the semesters continued, more and more black students enrolled so that the classes were evenly divided. Many of the white students expressed anger at the educational systems that had deprived them of knowledge of any of this outstanding literature. Eventually the majority of the students became black. When I retired the racial representation seemed to becoming racially balanced again.

One semester when there were only two or three white students enrolled, most of the members of one class were not reading the assigned material, depending on the several who did read and contribute to the discussions to help them get by. Aware of this, I included in my first examination questions that we had not discussed in class but were so obvious that anyone who had done the reading would have no difficulty discussing. I gave them explicit instructions on how to study, but the majority of the students failed the exam. The same thing happened on the second exam. When I handed the papers back, there was a great deal of grumbling and eyeball rolling. I knew I had to comment.

I said, "We're going to have a family discussion today. I am making those of you who are not black honorary African Americans." The hall between our offices in the English Department was narrow, and we usually kept our doors open, so it was easy to hear my colleagues talking among themselves. Afraid of being considered racist, one occasionally came to me and asked my advice about a black student's final grade. It was always a student who seldom attended class, did not do the required assignments, and did not pass examinations. "On what basis could you possibly pass him?" I would ask, knowing that the grade of a similar white student would be failure. To my class I continued, "I hear my colleagues talking about you. If you have received a grade that you know you didn't earn, that professor was trying to tell you something, and you didn't get the point. He or she was saying, in effect, that it didn't matter what grade you were given because you were doomed to failure anyhow." I continued, "I realize that some of you have come from an inadequate educational background, and some are in college on probation, but that only means that you have to study harder. You have my conference hours in your syllabus and they are posted on my door. Not one of you has ever been to my office to say that you needed help. I refuse to accept the notion that you are inferior. Even though some of you are not well prepared for college, I will accept nothing but your best. I am here to help you, but you must show some indication that you want my help." The room was absolutely silent.

After that, students began coming to my office. One said, "I know I read on the fifth grade level." I told her that I could help her only if she read the assigned material. Then if she didn't understand it, she should come to see me and we would discuss it. One of the students who appeared to be older than the others came to my office one day. She was capable of reading and understanding the assignments but just didn't do it. "That day you told us off, my opinion of you hit rock bottom," she said, pointing her finger downward. "I had never had a teacher talk to me like that before. But then I realized that you were right." She came to my office several times after that just to talk, and we became friends. Once the students accepted the fact that I was not to blame for their failure, the entire situation improved.

Under the pressure of a number of students for more studies in African American culture, a Black Studies Committee was formed and I was a member. Dr. Mary Frances Berry, a history professor who later held a national position on the Civil Rights Commission, also served. The university sent her and me to Nashville, Tennessee to observe what was being done in the black colleges there. Since she is a native of Nashville, she was glad to go home for a few days. We shared the same room in a motel, and I got to know her and admire her brilliance, her wisdom, and her incredible achievements. Author of a history book, she held doctorates in both history and law. Together we visited her high school and went to lunch with a former teacher named Minerva whom she obviously adored. Mary Frances told me something of her background, indicating that she had come from the wrong side of the tracks and had a lot of rough edges. It was Minerva who recognized her potential and made a crucial change in her life. Mary Frances left Eastern shortly thereafter, and I have not seen or talked with her since, but I have kept up with her progress and heard her speak on television. She is one of the most articulate, intelligent, levelheaded, and capable persons I have ever known. As the result of the committee's findings, additional courses were added in African American studies, but when I retired there was no separate department for such studies.

It is hard to find many black English majors in colleges across the nation, and that was certainly true at EMU. Pamela Cobb was one of the few at EMU. She was an excellent student who earned both her B.A. and her M.A. in English at Eastern. I taught her on both the undergraduate and graduate level. When *Pink Ladies in the Afternoon* was published in 1972, the English Department sponsored a book signing, and I saw Pamela sitting in a corner alone reading her copy. I learned that she was writing poetry of her own, and eventually she started bringing me individual poems to be critiqued. We became friends and talked frequently outside class. Since Lotus Press had already been founded and I had bought a color duplicator, I asked her permission to publish her small collection, *Inside the*

Devil's Mouth, to encourage her. But more about that later.

Pamela, who changed her name to Baraka Sele, later asked me to be her godmother. I was deeply honored by her request and gladly accepted. We have stayed in touch through the years, and I have witnessed her incredible success as the program director of several institutions for performing arts. She continues to travel widely and is currently the program director of the New Jersey Center for Performing Arts.

The most difficult aspect of teaching the Bible as Literature was to convince the students that it was a class in literature, not theology. I realized that, in spite of this, many were enrolled because of the course's theological aspects. I encountered several Jewish students who felt that they already knew it all, and one very well read African American nurse who took all of the Bible literally and frequently argued about information. We used an excellent handbook that contained the most recent scholarship on the Bible, along with the standard text, *The New English Bible with the Apocrypha, Oxford Study Edition*, which provides copious helpful footnotes. I had acquired about every translation and edition of the Bible in print and was able to make comparisons, noting how the meanings of words had changed over the centuries, affecting the meaning of certain passages.

Some of the students belonged to The Campus Crusade for Christ. When we were studying *Daniel*, one of them asked permission for one of their members to speak to the class. I insisted on talking to him first, insisting that there be no sectarianism in his remarks. Some of the students hadn't purchased the textbook since they already had copies of other Bibles including the Schofield Bible and didn't feel it was necessary to have another copy. In spite of the Crusader's assurance, he did proselytize and interpret the book of *Daniel* from a theological standpoint. The main point was whether this book was true prophecy or a book written after the fact in the form of prophecy. His views differed widely with those of the author of the handbook. Rather than argue with him, I let him take the whole period to answer questions.

When the class met again, I realized that I would have to deal with the Crusader's remarks on the level that he had made them. I asked the students who were using the Schofield Bible to locate the names of the editors and contributors. None was listed. Then I asked those using the Oxford Study Edition to do the same thing. I had one of them note aloud the number of Biblical scholars and their degrees. Then I asked them to reread the introduction to the handbook, which indicated that the author was an outstanding scholar and a devout Christian. I asked what purpose these great scholars would have in denying truth? What would their motives be? They were simply interpreting what was once believed in view of recent scientific and literary discoveries. "If you built a little house out of match sticks or toothpicks," I asked, "and the first time a door opened, the wind blew it down, how well built was the house in the first place? If your religious faith is not strong enough to stand up in the face of newly discovered fact, how strong is it? How much does it matter whether *Daniel* is true prophecy or events told after the fact? Are the basic truths changed in any way?" After class one of the students thanked me for clarifying what the Crusader had made confusing.

The books of the Bible were written by individuals of their time who wrote what they believed to be true. They didn't have the scientific information that is now available. I have never believed that science and the Bible are in contradiction of each other. In fact, the more we learn through modern research, the more that learning reenforces the Bible.

I am reminded of the Rev. John Jasper, a former slave and pastor of Sixth Mount Zion Baptist Church in Richmond, Virginia. I first heard of him from my mother whose mother or grandmother had heard him preach. Though not formally educated, he had become a thorough scholar of the Bible. Based on its contents, he developed a sermon that brought him his greatest fame. Whenever it was announced that he would preach this sermon at his church or outside the city at an all-day camp meeting, crowds of people would throng to hear him. In spite of his scholarship, he never learned to speak standard English, so the title of his famous sermon, "The Sun Do Move and the Earth Am Square," was grammatically incorrect. I have a book about Rev. Jasper written by a white contemporary, also a minister. In it the author reported going to hear John Jasper preach this famous sermon. He detailed how thoroughly the preacher offered proof from the Bible that the sun moves and the earth is flat and square. So convincing was his argument and so dramatic his style of oratory that when, at the end of his sermon, Rev. Jasper asked how many believed what he had said, the author reported, "My hand shot up instantly — and I was not being hypocritical." He knew that the Bible, limited by the knowledge of its time, was sometimes inaccurate. Yet for the moment, he believed the "proof" the preacher had offered.

In the summer of 1970 the University of Iowa sponsored a two-week conference on the Harlem Renaissance, a period in which I had always been particularly interested. The English Department paid my expenses to attend. Dr. Charles T. Davis was the main lecturer, and his work took the art of lecturing to the highest level I have ever experienced. Arna Bontemps and Saunders Redding also contributed, and it was a joy to spend time talking with them, hearing them lecture, and sharing the beauty of the campus.

As a result of that conference, I proposed a graduate course in the Harlem Renaissance at EMU. The only problem I had getting it accepted was that I had to call it The Harlem Renaissance and Beyond because my colleagues didn't feel there was enough worthy material published in that brief span of time to justify a course. I enjoyed the opportunity of teaching this course but was surprised at how poorly prepared some of the English majors were in basic writing and grammar. They were in the process of receiving master's degrees in English, and some would no doubt go on to earn Ph.D.s. Once a student advances this far, it is assumed that the basics of the language have already been mastered, but I learned that this was not always true. Graduate students become experts in one narrow field of knowledge, and that is evidently considered enough. It's no wonder that American education is in so much trouble.

One year I received an invitation to teach one section of African American literature at The University of Michigan in Ann Arbor. Darwin Turner taught one section, and the professor who normally taught the other had been detained on a visit to his home in Africa. I agreed to teach the class, which met for three hours one evening a week, in addition to my normal class load at EMU. The class consisted of seniors and graduate students. Unfortunately, the information that should have been mailed to me in advance had been placed in a mailbox I didn't even know I had. I was therefore late ordering books and had to spend the first session giving a general lecture. Furthermore, the classroom was much too small for the number of students enrolled and had to be changed. I expected the students to be much better prepared than most of those at EMU. There were more who were, but there were also many on the same level. One Ph.D. candidate was outstanding, but another was marginal. Perhaps he was not an English major.

For the major written assignment, I asked the students to turn in their topics and thesis statements for my approval before proceeding. Three students didn't comply. One of them, an African American, didn't participate in discussions but was earning a *B* and was to receive her M.A. at the end of the semester. When she turned in her paper, I found that some of it was plagiarized. We had read and I had lectured on Richard Wright's *Native Son*, and the entire class should have been aware that I had read all the criticism on it that had been published. Another M.A. candidate who didn't turn in her topic and thesis statement, a young white woman, turned in a paper comparing *Native Son* to Wright's *The Outsider*. I would not have approved this topic. I knew Nick Aaron Ford from the College Language

Association and went straight to his critical essay from which this student had lifted entire paragraphs without giving credit. I gave both students failing grades. I think that, after I left, both were given additional work and probably passed, but I don't know.

The best part of my one semester at U-M was the friendship I cultivated with my graduate assistant and the fact that my borrowed office was next to Robert Hayden's although I saw him only once since he was usually not on campus that late. I also renewed my friendship with Carlton Welles who, if I recall correctly, had retired from teaching but was working at some other position on campus. Some years before, while I was still teaching in high school, I had participated in a panel discussion at U-M, and Professor Welles had been so impressed with my presentation that he asked me to return to talk to his classes. He had taught there for many years, hired at a time when a Ph.D. was not a requirement. I asked him what the chances were that I could be hired at the college level without the degree, and he told me that things had changed and it would be highly improbable. I keep a vision of him walking me to my car after class as he recited a poem by Emily Dickinson and the wind tousled his white hair. When I did eventually begin teaching at EMU, his letter of congratulations was the first communication that I received.

English majors and minors at EMU had a choice of courses, expository writing, journalism, or imaginative writing. To many the last seemed the most interesting, but the majority of the students were not particularly gifted in writing. We concentrated on the traditional short story and poetry. The excellent textbook we used on short story writing went out of print and I couldn't find anything else suitable, so I was left to my own devices. I found myself writing and duplicating chapters that contained exercises in short fiction. I had taken a graduate course in creative writing at the University of Detroit some time earlier and patterned my course after the one taught there by John Schmittroth. The procedure was to study the various techniques of the initial situation, dialogue, character, plot, stream of consciousness, flashbacks, and other aspects of a traditional short story before putting them all together in a completed original story. I also included exercises in poetry. I eventually realized that, put together, these chapters made a book. It was later published as *A Student's Guide to Creative Writing*. At the end of each section (the short story and poetry), I included some of my students' writing, realizing that they had already read professionally written examples and could not hope to equal them. The writing of other students, I assumed, would serve as an encouragement for the best writing they could do.

Each student was asked to select a pen name that only I would know. Assignments were turned in with pen names on masters which the department secretary duplicated for discussion. I felt that, in this workshop atmosphere, students would be freer to discuss their classmates' work if it was anonymous than if they could identify the author, and that the class would learn more from their peers' comments than they would from mine alone.

I had a hard time convincing the class that the grading system in that class would be different from that in any other course they had taken. If a final grade were to be based on a student's ability to write well, I would not have to teach the class. I would know after the first assignment who would get *A*'s and who would receive lower grades. But how unfair that would be! Instead, the students' grades would depend on effort and improvement. I tried to impress on them that they were not in competition with each other but with themselves. They received credit in the form of cumulative check marks for completed assignments involving writing exercises. These check marks added up to numbers that fell into certain letter grade ranges. The student who turned in all the assignments, however inadequate some might be, received more credit than one who neglected to even try. Writing creatively is such a personal matter that I wanted them to feel free to exercise their imagination and make mistakes without being penalized for them.

On the first draft of their completed short stories, assigned with staggered due dates so that I could give more attention to each, I spent a considerable amount of time carefully reading each paper and writing voluminous comments and suggestions along the margins, on the back, and everywhere I could find space. I assigned a letter grade but only as a guide; it would have no effect on their final grade. When the second and final draft came back, accompanied by the original draft for comparison, my only consideration in grading would be the degree of improvement made in view of my comments.

I don't think my students believed me at first when I explained the system, and even later on, some of them complained that their *B* or *C* story was better than one that had received an *A*, and that may very well have been true. But I reiterated that the *A* represented improvement, the only fair basis on which I was willing to judge. As a result of my comments, the final drafts of most of the stories showed remarkable improvement, and several, I felt, were publishable. I encouraged these authors to submit them to magazines for consideration.

One story stands out in my mind. Its author rarely participated in discussions, turned in his assignments on time, and didn't make any particular impression on me. When he turned in his short story, it was so good that I was convinced it was plagiarized. It took place in the old West, and I looked for historical errors and anachronisms but couldn't find any. It did not include all the traditional elements on which our exercises had been based but was freer; still, I could find no fault with it and found it hard to believe that anyone in that class could have written it. Not wanting to accuse him of plagiarism, I told him that the story was excellent but that I had hoped he would incorporate the elements on which the exercises had been based. He offered no protest and turned in another story not quite as impressive as the first but nevertheless very good. How bored he must have been in my class!

Loren Estleman is now the famous author of sixty novels, and around 200 short stories. We talked once at a writers' conference and had a good laugh. He said he knew I thought his story was plagiarized, but he was encouraged because I had thought it was so good. Recently he wrote me, "It was my first rave review." I didn't think I had taught him anything he didn't already know, but in a more recent letter he stated:

> . . . I learned character development at your hands. You won't recall, but you bounced three character studies I submitted for that first short story before accepting a fourth. My first novel . . . was high on style at the expense of character, but your lessons had kicked in by No. 2. I've long considered plotting far less important than character. Put enough interesting people in a room and sooner or later, they'll do something.

I had already ascended to the top rung of the academic ladder without a Ph.D., receiving tenure as soon as I was eligible and then being promoted to full professor. Other than an increase in salary, I had nothing to gain by pursuing a higher degree. Nevertheless, when I read about a nontraditional degree program at the International Institute for Advanced Studies in Columbia, Missouri that did not require residency and gave credit for experience and graduate courses taken at other universities, I decided to apply. I had accumulated enough class credits and a proficiency in written French, I felt, to qualify for consideration. After submitting my various transcripts, I was accepted as a degree candidate. My only requirement was a dissertation. I was assigned an advisor, who sent me back critical comments as my dissertation progressed, and once it was finished, I had to defend it to an academic committee of my choosing. In 1980 I received a nontraditional Ph.D. The Institute later became a part of Greenwich University located in Hilo, Hawaii. I earned this degree simply for my own personal satisfaction. I hasten to say that I do not equate it with the same degree earned by other academics in a traditional program, but neither do I apologize for it. The institution is not and never was a diploma mill, and I feel that the course work I took beyond my master's degree and my experience are as legitimate a qualification as the work of some others I know who earned Ph.D.s and D.A.s from traditional accredited universities.

Eastern Michigan University was good to me. When I had invitations to read in libraries and colleges across the country, the department head encouraged me to go. My activities as a poet and lecturer made me one of the most newsworthy members of the department. When my parents and brother died, my paycheck was never docked for overstaying my time out of town, and when I returned a week late from a visit to Brazil between semesters, I was never penalized. During my almost sixteen years at EMU, two other black faculty members were added to the department, but I remained one of only a handful of black full professors on the entire campus.

My class in The Harlem Renaissance met from seven to ten on Monday nights, and I didn't want to drive back to Detroit that late. At first I stayed overnight at the conference center, taking a brief nap after my last undergraduate class, then going to dinner at Haab's or another nearby restaurant. But sometimes the room wasn't made up when I arrived. Later, students were housed in the center, and their noise was disturbing. I began staying at a cheap motel instead. But when I figured up what it was costing me to stay over, I realized I was losing money. That wasn't the reason for my leaving, though.

For one thing, after my accident in 1978, I dreaded the winter drive to and from Detroit. For another, Lotus Press was consuming more and more of my time. When the trimester ended at the end of April, I spent most of the summer working on new books. And after classes started, there was still a growing amount of work I had to do to keep up with Lotus Press book orders. Finally, I was becoming discouraged that my teaching efforts were bearing so little fruit. During my first years, freshman composition classes were taught by part-time instructors. Eventually these instructors were eliminated,

308

and each professor had to teach one of these elementary classes. Mine was considered one of the better ones, but testing the students at the beginning and end of the semester, I became frustrated that, after all my efforts, they seemed to know little more at the end than they did at the beginning.

The clinching factor was an article I read by Sidney Harris, a columnist for the *Detroit Free Press,* who wrote, in effect, "Money that doesn't buy you the time to do what you really enjoy doing is not worth earning." I clipped the article and reread it, and on the spur of the moment, I decided I would retire at the end of December, 1983. I was sixty years old, not yet old enough for Social Security, and I hadn't taught there quite long enough to qualify for a special retirement incentive offer, but I knew that whatever pension I received would be sufficient for my needs. I reasoned that anybody could teach, but no one else I knew would make the sacrifices I was making to keep Lotus Press alive.

My last class was in African American literature. During our last meeting before the final exam, Dudley Randall was on campus and came to my class to visit. Someone took a picture of us standing together on the podium.

Before a final examination I had a good idea of what a student's grade would be, based on the semester's work. I don't believe that one day's performance on an exam should outweigh the work of many weeks. The exam should simply confirm the grade already earned or, in some cases, elevate it or lower it but not to a great extent. So I told my students what to study for, believing that the study itself was more important than demonstrating what they had learned on paper. The day of my final exam in African American literature was my last day of formal teaching, and I wanted it to be special. I did prepare a very difficult exam but had no intention of giving it. Instead, I wrote a poem dedicated to my class and, after reading it, distributed copies to the students. I then announced that there would be no exam; they had already earned their grades.

Most of the students were relieved, but one or two protested and wanted to take the exam anyhow. I assured them that, if they did, they wouldn't pass it, and failure would lower their grade. They were wise enough not to insist.

As I walked up the hill for the last time to turn in my grades, I looked forward to packing up the carloads of books in my office and taking them home. Once the office was empty, I took my name off the door of Room 13E and replaced it with a sign, "Gone fishing." When the first snow fell, I was happy to turn over in bed and go back to sleep.

VI.
Flower of a New Nile

Stumbling Into New Waters

It was not something I ever intended to do, but it happened anyhow. Sometimes we stumble into areas of activity that we would never dream of entering if we had any idea what we were getting into. Still, I should not have been surprised. My childhood involvement with books predicted that I would do something more with them than read or write them. For no particular purpose that I knew of, I purchased two significant items. I already had two typewriters and certainly didn't need another, but while I was looking for something else in an office machine store, I saw a used typewriter that had proportional fonts. Like most typewriters, the two that I already owned printed each letter in the same width, but with proportional fonts, I could type material that looked like real printing. I had no idea what I would use it for, but it offered possibilities. The second purchase resulted from an advertisement I received in the mail regarding a duplicator that came with tubes of various colors of ink that could be interchanged. The idea of being able to print in color fascinated me.

In 1972 I completed my fourth poetry manuscript, *Pink Ladies in the Afternoon,* and was looking for a publisher. There had always been a problem for black poets seeking publication by major white-owned companies that considered poetry by African Americans either "too black" (meaning "not universal enough") or "not black enough." Injustice, suffering, and alienation were universal enough when those of the same skin color wrote and read about them, whether in the USA or Europe, but if those conditions were reported by people of color, the reader suddenly could not identify with them. At that time the market was being deluged by books that either titillated the reader with the lurid details of ghetto life, crime, prostitution, and broken families or discovered the glories of Africa and black identity while playing on the collective conscience of Whitey by flagellation and insult. The prospect of getting a book of quiet, reflective poetry that dealt with race in more subtle ways, as well as the experience of being a woman, a divorcée, a single mother, a sister, a daughter, a friend, and an observer of life as a total human being, stood less chance of acceptance than before.

By now the small press movement was under way and several independent companies had been established by African Americans, but the response I got from their editors was hardly better than from their fairer-skinned peers. (The divisiveness created within the race by those who would distinguish between "knee-grows" and "true" blacks is the subject of my poem "Newblack" in *Pink Ladies in the Afternoon.*) One of these editors told me years later that he selected manuscripts on the basis of their ability to make a profit. Most of the books he published were more politically direct and "relevant" than mine. The mood of the times was one of militancy and rage, and *Pink Ladies* didn't fit the mold. Harlo Press, which had published my last book, *Star by Star*, had stopped publishing books and resumed its earlier practice of printing only.

One day during a casual conversation with three friends, I expressed my frustration over the future of this manuscript. One of them, who had always been supportive of my work, mentioned the possibility of publishing the work as an independent project. The others were receptive to the idea but felt that they lacked the necessary experience for such a task. Some weeks and several conversations later, it was decided that they would contribute the funds if I would do the leg work. I agreed. In thinking of a name for the press, I ran across some information about the lotus plant in Egypt, so late that year *Pink Ladies in the Afternoon* was published by Lotus Press, with the motto, "Flower of a New Nile." I had learned something about promotion from the 1956 publication of my second book, *One and the Many,* by a subsidy or "vanity" publisher. That was before the advent of the small press and widespread self-publishing. While I was fully aware that I would never get back the money this company charged, which was at least five times more than the printing cost and the scant services they provided, I felt that having something tangible to show for my efforts was important. I was actively involved in public readings, and there were always persons in attendance who wanted to carry away more than a memory of the poems they had heard. My first little book had gone out of print, and I had grown beyond it anyhow. I was well aware that this publisher's acceptance was no indication of the literary value of my work. They would accept any material, however poor, as long as the author had ready cash. But I didn't have to depend on my own judgment as assurance that my poems were worthy of publication. Some had already been included in anthologies such as *The Poetry of the Negro, 1746-1949*, edited by Langston Hughes and Arna Bontemps, and *American Literature by Negro Authors*, edited by Herman Dreer. Others had been published in respectable national journals. And Countee Cullen, after reading some of my work, had assured me that I was indeed a poet. J. Saunders Redding would later confirm that opinion in his favorable review in the *Afro-American Newspapers*. So it was a desire for more than just seeing my name on a book cover that drove me to this act; I had already had that thrill fifteen years earlier.

As with *One and the Many*, I was responsible for managing all the details of publicizing the book, supplying names for a mailing list, contacting persons at television and radio stations in all the cities where I had lived, and providing a list of editors of black periodicals throughout the country.

In exploring possible printers, I learned about the offset or lithograph method of printing and was told that we could save money by preparing "camera-ready" copy. So I prepared my poems using the typewriter with proportional letters. A mutual friend had brought to my home a young man named Peter McWilliams who was producing and peddling his own very attractive books of facile, greeting-card type verse and making a fortune from them. That was before he got involved with writing for the computer industry. His cover art on each book was an appealing geometric design that I discovered anyone could do with construction paper and a pair of scissors. So I followed his example and cut out some odd shapes that I combined for my own cover. Naturally, with the word *pink* in the title, I had to use that color. Combined with black ink on glossy white cover stock, the cover turned out to be attractive.

During its first two years *Pink Ladies* did reasonably well but only because of my readings. I thought that it should have gotten stronger promotion, but my benefactors evidently felt that they had fulfilled their mission and became involved in other interests. They agreed to let my husband and me take over the name and the existing stock for a minimal amount which did not begin to reimburse them for their investment. We parted company on friendly terms. By their request they have remained anonymous.

Because we had no reason to see beyond publication of *Pink Ladies in the Afternoon*, it never occurred to us that we should register the name of the press, thereby preventing its use by future publishers. If we had foreseen our later activities, we could have prevented the confusion created later by other companies on both sides of the Atlantic that called themselves Lotus Press.

I had no intention of publishing additional books, but while I was teaching at EMU, it occurred to me that, since I owned a duplicator, I could encourage Pamela Cobb (now Baraka Sele) by producing a small collection of her work. I typed *Inside the Devil's Mouth* on the same typewriter with proportional fonts, using letter-size sheets of blue paper folded in half. All I had to do, I thought, was duplicate them, collate and fold them, and then staple them with a saddle stapler my brother had given me when he closed his printing shop in New Rochelle. I used medium blue ink, combining it with red for the cover design. After all, what was the point in having a machine that printed in color if I didn't take advantage of that feature? And wasn't the object to attract the attention of potential buyers?

But was I in for a surprise! After printing the pages and collating them, I discovered that the pages didn't follow in sequence. I had never thought about the fact that only the middle pages would follow in order. So I had to discard all the pages I had duplicated, make a

316

"dummy" with the pages properly numbered, and separate them to learn which pages faced and followed each other. Starting again from the beginning, I finally had a completed chapbook. I was very proud of myself, and Pamela was happy to see it, but the colors were awful and the collection looked very unprofessional and as "mammy-made" as anything I had done since the penciled "books" I had held together with safety pins as a child.

Another early project was a collection of "poster-poems" by twenty living black authors, entitled *Deep Rivers*, published in 1974. It was intended for use in secondary schools as a means of demonstrating the rich variety in African American poetry at a time when one white teacher told me, "If you've read one, you've read them all." I believe that many children's early love of poetry is killed inadvertently by teachers who don't feel comfortable with it. Having no enthusiasm themselves, they cannot elicit any from their students. Yet, there it is in the textbook to be "taught." What to do? Some resort to the pursuit of interpretations, hidden meanings and symbols. Some assign written reports on the poets' lives and works. Some require their students to write a poem and recite it in front of the class. Memorizing some of the old standbys of the teacher's choice is another favorite assignment. There is also the sentimental teacher who becomes so absorbed with his or her personal favorites that the only result is the embarrassment of the gawking teenagers who have not been invited to participate in the poem themselves. These and similar activities may very well succeed in producing the desired letter grade on a report card but result in a lifelong fear or hatred of a reading experience that easily might have become the thrill of new discovery, mature understanding, and perhaps even sheer joy. It was for the purpose of giving the teacher uncomfortable with poetry some guidance that I included in the portfolio of *Deep Rivers* a teacher's guide that included several discussion questions for each of the poster-poems, suggestions for related writing activities, and a method of introducing a unit of poetry into the secondary school classroom. The National Council of Teachers of

English purchased several hundred copies of this portfolio for distribution. I printed these, too, on the color duplicator using different colored ink on colored paper but with much more success than with the chapbook. I paid very small permission fees to the authors who agreed to let me reprint their work.

While participating in a Melvin Butler Poetry Festival at Southern University at Baton Rouge, Louisiana, I met a veteran poet, May Miller, who was also reading there. We immediately recognized each other as kindred spirits and hit it off very well, in spite of her advanced years. I liked her style, her mature wisdom, and the quietness of her poems. Through continued correspondence, we became close friends. I learned that she was the daughter of Kelly Miller, once the dean at Howard University on whose campus she had grown up, that Paul Laurence Dunbar had once lived in her parents' home before she was born and had written some of his books there, and that, as she grew up, people such as Booker T. Washington and W.E.B. DuBois had been frequent visitors. I also learned that she had been a playwright during the Harlem Renaissance but had later turned to poetry. Several of her chapbooks had already been published. I expressed a desire to publish her new poetry manuscript, *Dust of Uncertain Journey,* and she was happy to oblige. It came out in 1975.

In 1976 a young white woman then living in Richmond, Virginia, Beverley Rose Enright, sent me a manuscript of poetry written by a black prisoner with whom she had become friendly. She had illustrated this short collection and sent it to me camera-ready. I was not extremely impressed with the poetry itself but felt that this poet should have a chance to be heard, and the finished project was so impressive without any additional work on my part that I couldn't refuse to publish it. Beverley and I remained friends for years. She later illustrated *O Africa, Where I Baked My Bread* by Lance Jeffers (1977), as well as my book, *Exits and Entrances* (1978).

It went on from there. On one occasion I was on the staff of a black poetry workshop held at a church in Detroit. The participants had been instructed to turn in their work ahead of time but few of them did. When I arrived in the crowded classroom where my session was scheduled, I was appalled to find the desk overflowing with poems I had not had a chance to read. What was I supposed to do with them? What could I say to those waiting, hopeful neophytes when I really knew nothing about them or their writing? In desperation I started aimlessly shuffling papers on the desk hoping perhaps for a miracle. Then one came. One poem separated itself from the rest and seemed to jump off the cluttered desk into my hands. I read it carefully, then read it again. It was a very good poem entitled, "Big Maybelle," and signed by someone named Paulette Childress White. After reading the poem aloud, I soon found myself talking about what made it successful, what the author had done right to achieve the effect the poem had on me. It was easy from that point on to talk about some of the attributes of a successful poem and the time allotted for my workshop went by quickly.

After the discussion ended, a strikingly beautiful young woman came up and identified herself as the author. With her was her husband, Bennie White, who, I was told, was an intense and successful visual artist. (They have since divorced and she no longer uses the name White.) Somewhere along the way, as our friendship developed, I learned that Paulette had interrupted her education to raise a family of five sons and had gotten bogged down with domesticity. Nevertheless, although no one had ever assured her that she was talented, she had always felt that she could write and had continued to nurture her interest in poetry.

The other poems that she later shared with me were not as polished as the one I had seen at the workshop, and she seemed to want guidance. I spent a considerable amount of time now and then going over her work with her. She was very open to criticism and listened attentively. She would test a remark I made about one poem against others to see if it also applied to them. We stayed in touch, sometimes talking on the phone at night for more than an hour as I shared my work in progress with her and welcomed her comments as she welcomed mine.

Eventually I heard her read one of her poems at a public event and felt that it was probably time to think about a book. Lotus Press published *Love Poem to a Black Junkie* in 1975.

Up to this point all the poets whose work I had published had been African Americans, but I seemed to have a soft spot for good poets whose work did not necessarily follow current trends and was therefore not likely to get published, in spite of literary merit. An independent publisher once told me that his company had stopped publishing poetry because it didn't pay. My response was, "But somebody has to do it anyhow." Louie Crew was gay, and at that time there was no network of publishers producing work by gay writers, so the first of several manuscripts I published by Caucasians was *Sunspots* (1976). Over the years Lotus Press published books by four other white poets who were not gay simply because I liked their work a great deal and felt that they should have an opportunity to be read. They include Agnes Nasmith Johnston (*Beyond the Moongate,* 1987), Eugene Haun (*Cardinal Points and Other Poems,* 1981), Gilbert Allen (*In Everything,* 1982), and Gunilla Norris (*Learning from the Angel,* 1985). I also published books by two African poets and one Brazilian.

Early in the game I had decided not to get into debt. Paying for services as they were rendered was the way I had always tried to handle my personal finances, and it felt good not to owe anyone anything. I simply took on another responsibility each time I accepted a new book, using part of my own salary or small savings to pay the printer. The last thing I wanted was to require the author to pay. I didn't want ability to pay to influence my selection of material.

320

Furthermore, subsidy publishers had such a bad reputation, and my one experience with one of them had been so enlightening that I didn't want the name of Lotus Press tainted with that kind of operation. If I couldn't afford to pay the printer upon completion of a manuscript, I just postponed publication until I could. In each of the early years I spent between $3,000 and $5,000 a year to keep the press going and continue to publish books.

Except for occasional volunteers and two short-term interns, I worked alone handling all the details of reading manuscripts, making editorial suggestions, doing occasional workshops, corresponding with aspiring poets, typing up pages, doing layout and cover design, writing promotional material, invoicing, bookkeeping, packing and shipping books, and sending out review copies. An instructor at the University of Detroit gave his students an assignment on publishing, and two came to talk to me about Lotus Press. After turning in their reports, the instructor gave them an unsatisfactory grade with the comment, "No one person could possibly be doing all those things." When they called me back, I invited them to go through a mini-version of the process with me, showing them around the premises. "Go back and tell your instructor," I said, "that one person is indeed doing it all."

Lotus Press was located in the recreation room in the basement of my house on Santa Barbara Drive, but boxes of books were stored in the basement of my husband's house to which I had moved when we married in 1972. My parents continued to live on Santa Barbara, five minutes away from the house on Inverness Street. During and between her pregnancies with her two youngest sons, Paulette came over one day a week and helped me collate material or assisted me in any other way should could. We were still printing and collating our own books.

In 1976 Lotus joined a group of local independents who combined to form the Associated Black Publishers of Detroit, Inc. I served as treasurer of that group which included Agascha

Productions, Pamoja Press, and Black Graphics. We met in one another's homes and exchanged information and techniques. It was through one of the members that I learned an alternative to saddle stitching. Librarians prefer "perfect bound" books, books with a spine whose title can be read on the book shelf. However, perfect binding was expensive, and most local printers didn't have the equipment to produce books this way. But as most of us were putting our books together by hand, we learned a do-it-yourself method of achieving the same effect as perfect binding. Spreading a standard sheet of paper horizontally, we dealt with it as two pages, but after these pages were printed, instead of folding them in the middle, we cut them in half. This required a heavy duty paper cutter that could cut through the pages of several books at a time. The pages had to be carefully numbered so that they would follow in sequence when one half of the book was folded over on top of the other half and stapled together on the outside. A heavy duty stapler was required. Then with a sharp instrument and a ruler, we scored two parallel lines in the center of the cover to insure a clean fold, being careful not to cut through the cover stock, folded the cover over the stapled pages, and applied a thin coat of commercial glue to the back of the cover. After the glue was dry, we again placed several copies of the book on the paper cutter to trim the pages evenly. The result could be very professional looking and much stronger than a truly perfect-bound book. I was really proud of the job I did on Herbert Woodward Martin's *The Persistence of the Flesh* in 1976. The Associated Black Publishers occasionally sent representatives to book exhibits in other cities and, in June of 1977, we rented space at the Alexander Crummel Center, located in the basement of a black church in Detroit, and put on a quite successful poetry festival.

When I accepted Toi Derricotte's first book, *The Empress of the Death House*, for publication, she expressed a desire to have it professionally typeset, offering to pay the difference in cost. This was, of course, long before the time that computers and laser printers became standard equipment in many households and home offices, but I found Bob Muhn, who had his own typesetting shop. I liked the appearance of Toi's book so much that I continued to use his services. He would typeset the manuscript and a set of page numbers and print them out in galley proofs, making an amazingly few errors. He had an excellent grasp of grammar although we sometimes disagreed on a fine point until I brought in proof to back me up. Knowing that he could depend on immediate payment, he always gave my work priority, usually completing it overnight. I would take the work home and, cutting the long strips into more manageable pieces, carefully proofread his pages against the original. Then I would return with the errors and wait while he cut in the corrections.

Still pasting the pages up myself, I bought a light box, a photo blue pencil, some graph paper, a T-square, a Scripto knife, and some Scotch tape, all of which I used to align each poem on the page, attach it to the graph paper, and place the page number in its predetermined position. The appearance of my camera-ready copy would never have been mistaken for the work of a graphic artist, but I knew what would photograph and what the camera would not pick up. The finished book told no secrets.

While I was working on Toi's book, I was also in the process of completing the work on James Emanuel's *Black Man Abroad: The Toulouse Poems* (1978). He had not yet retired from teaching but was going to Paris for an extended stay and wanted to take a number of copies with him. I had spent the night on campus in Ypsilanti and, on my way back to Detroit, had an automobile accident in which I fractured a vertebra in my neck. I still had corrections to make on the pasted-up pages of both books and worried about being able to meet the deadline I had set for completion.

After I was released from the hospital in a rigid metal neck brace that kept my chin tilted upward and permitted me to move only from the waist, Paulette Childress brought over a drafting table that she wasn't using and adjusted it to a height that permitted me to barely see the pages I needed to work on. In that way, I was able to complete the work on both books on time.

A generous donation permitted us to purchase our first computer system, and when we were able to acquire a laser printer, I felt that we had finally arrived. This equipment eliminated the need to paste up pages. Some poets have supplied the art or photography for the front cover themselves, and photographers and professional artists have donated their work. Even so, I still have some part in designing the cover myself, if not designing it totally.

I have always felt an intense need to respect the independence of the individual artist. Never one to follow current trends in my own poetry, I resent the assertion sometimes fervently stated by African Americans that the black artist has an obligation to his or her people and their cause. I think we are in very deep trouble when some self-appointed prophet, no matter how legitimate his or her cause, seeks to determine the direction or mode of anybody else's creative expression or the degree of emphasis that should be placed on what political messages or agenda. As editor of Lotus Press I have vigorously protected the freedom and sanctity of all our authors' expression. As a result, the poetry published by Lotus Press over the years demonstrates a remarkable variety in subject matter, tone, and style. It ranges from the extremely political to the serenely pastoral. When we celebrated our fifteenth anniversary with a three-day series of readings at Wayne State University, one of our authors, standing to read, observed: "We have absolutely nothing in common here except the person of Naomi Long Madgett." The statement took me by surprise, but it didn't make me sad. On the contrary, I felt that I had succeeded in my intention of allowing for differences, of not dictating to prospective authors what kinds of writing they would have to produce in order to be acceptable for publication. When asked, as I often am, what kind of poetry I'm looking for, my answer is and can only be, "Good poetry"—poetry which, in my necessarily subjective opinion, is worthy of its place on the book shelves of the world now and for many years to come—poetry which, like any successful work of art, invites the senses to experience new possibilities in sharing, understanding, and living life to its fullest.

For this commitment to other poets I have been willing to forego time and effort I could easily have used to develop and promote my own career, money I could have spent more enjoyably on luxury travel and vacations. I never had any illusions about making money from the publication of good poetry. If being "successful" as it is commonly understood had been my goal, I certainly could have achieved that with relative ease. I could have quit teaching long before I did and developed a lucrative subsidy company, publishing the poorly constructed poetry of everybody who wanted to see his or her name in print; even providing better services than can be expected from such existing companies, I still could have made money. Or I could have published black romance novels to pay for one or two books of poetry a year and still realized a handsome profit.

But those are things that others would not hesitate to do since there is little risk involved. Since I was doing this the hard way, I could see no point in wasting my life doing something I didn't believe in. Several years ago at a conference of black publishers in New York City, one of the participants, who obviously thought my whole operation was stupid, attributed my lack of profit to the absence of proper planning and business sense. He simply couldn't understand that I would rather work for nothing than to compromise my standards. What has been accomplished through my sacrifice and determination has proved to me that my work as a publisher has been much more important than the career of one individual poet. Yes, I regret that my career as a poet has not brought me the kind of recognition I wanted for myself, but I made my choice a long time ago, and I do not regret it.

325

After years of supporting the press out of my own pocket, I realized that another arrangement needed to be made. In 1980 Lotus Press became a non-profit corporation, with my husband, my daughter, Paulette, a former teaching colleague, and a current one forming the first board of directors. The following year we were granted tax exempt status by the federal government under Internal Revenue Code 501(c)(3).

The more books we published, the more our reputation grew, and our new classification permitted us to apply for grants and solicit tax-deductible donations. The financial burden I had been carrying alone grew much lighter, especially in terms of the outlay of cash. But I continued to work without any monetary compensation, thereby keeping the company in the black. With a computer system we were now able to prepare camera-ready copy for a book printer. Eventually the task of packing books and carting them to the post office became too much, and we began using the services of a storage and fulfillment company in Ypsilanti. Nevertheless, we still had to prepare the invoices and shipping labels ourselves. (I use *we* and *our* in the editorial sense as, more often than not, I have been the only person working. While there have been a few volunteers and interns, Lotus Press, Inc. has remained much more a one-person operation than it should be, mainly because of a shortage of funds.) We have always needed a salaried staff person to relieve me of the day-to-day operations, but the funds have not been available. I have neither the time nor the temperament to write grant proposals and plan fund-raising activities, and I am afraid that doing so would divert me from my real purpose. At any point I would have welcomed help from those who professed an interest in the press, but little has ever materialized. We were consequently able to remain independent of bureaucratic influences and requirements, but the cost of that independence is great. Even now I continue to pay some of the ongoing expenses from my own personal funds. Except for my donations and the generosity of a few other individuals, Lotus Press would have gone out of existence many years ago.

In spite of its ongoing struggle, Lotus Press, Inc. has enjoyed 34 years of dependable and uninterrupted service with the publication of ninety titles, many of which are still in print. These books have small but worldwide distribution, and some are being used as required reading in high schools and colleges across the country. Many have received excellent reviews in prestigious journals. Some of the authors' careers have flourished as a direct result of their having been published by Lotus, a name which commands respect from those who are familiar with the quality of its offerings. The highly acclaimed twentieth anniversary anthology, *Adam of Ife: Black Women in Praise of Black Men*, represents a timely breakthrough in the way the African American male is viewed, especially by African American women.

The Before Columbus Foundation recognized my contributions as a publisher and editor by selecting me for a 1993 American Book Award presented in Miami Beach at the American Booksellers Association Convention.

Eventually I realized that I owed a debt to myself that had gone unpaid for many years. The age of seventy was fast approaching and there was much of my own writing that I felt the need to do. It was my desire to keep the books we had published available by having another press take over their distribution. Sadly I concluded that I could no longer afford the luxury of publishing and promoting books by other poets while continuing to neglect my own career. Therefore, I intended *Adam of Ife* to be the last book to be published by Lotus Press. However, we did publish one other book after that. We established the Hilton-Long Poetry Foundation to sponsor an annual award in my name. The Naomi Long Madgett Poetry Award was in celebration of my seventieth birthday, However, this foundation was short lived since this project could be handled by Lotus Press, already established and well known, so Lotus Press took over the sponsorship of the award. It was my intention to offer a cash amount of $500 and a plaque for an outstanding book-length manuscript by an African American poet. The first year's award was specified for an author at least 65 years old. Since then we have made no stipulation concerning age or previous publication. While many of our winners have been first books by young authors, the award was never intended for a first book or for a young poet. There were already enough of those being offered.

My intention to cease the publication of books was aided by a chance meeting with the assistant editor of Michigan State University Press during a writers' conference where both of us were presenters. A later meeting with the director resulted in an agreement effective June, 1993 for Michigan State University Press to distribute Lotus Press books. Under the terms of a separate contract with me, I became editor of the newly established Lotus Poetry Series of Michigan State University Press. With this development I was now able to devote more time to my own writing while continuing to work with and present publishing opportunities to other deserving poets.

To introduce this new poetry series, Michigan State University Press published my eighth volume, *Remembrances of Spring: Collected Early Poems*, in the fall of 1993. In addition, the press offered to publish the winning manuscript of the annual Naomi Long Madgett Poetry Award; Lotus Press continued to be the sponsor, and we continued to pay the author the cash amount of $500. We also continued to handle the entries and select the judges for the award. After the editing process, which was still my responsibility, Michigan State University Press published the first five award-winning manuscripts.

There has been a great deal of confusion about the university's association with Lotus Press, especially because they added all the Lotus Press books published before our agreement to the Lotus Poetry Series, even using the Lotus Press logo, which has since been changed. That was not supposed to have happened, but I wasn't sharp enough to prevent it. The university press was only intended to distribute books already published by Lotus Press. The Lotus Poetry Series was meant to include new books I selected for publication by Michigan State University Press. Their contract with me as poetry editor was entirely separate from the one with Lotus Press.

Although Lotus Press did not publish any *books* during the five years of our relationship, we kept active by publishing several sets of poster-poems (broadsides) on laminated specialty papers, the most important one being *The Fullness of Earth,* 100 copies of a set of ten signed and numbered collectors' copies. Having established the company, I had no intention of letting Lotus Press go out of business or become completely inactive.

Unfortunately, the arrangement with Michigan State University Press turned out to be quite disappointing due to poor leadership and accounting. Their royalty payments to Lotus Press were irregularly reported, some six-month periods omitted altogether, and the amounts paid were so miniscule that, based on their own figures, I once called for a meeting with their staff. I estimated that, even if all the Lotus Press books they sold were at a forty percent discount, which I knew was not true, we should have received over $1,000 more than we had been paid. The director never properly oversaw the entire operations and did not respond to my letters, calls, and fax messages. When I finally caught up with him, he informed me that they had changed their computer system and he didn't think they could access the figures, but I was persistent. Since Lotus Press had records going back to its beginning when we had no computer, I couldn't accept his response. When I arrived for the meeting and distributed the report I had prepared, they had indeed accessed the figures and discovered that they owed Lotus Press over twice as much as I had estimated.

After they settled this account, I thought the problem was solved and would not occur again, but I was wrong. We continued to encounter the same problems which, I am convinced, will never be settled. The amount of money they still owe Lotus Press is anybody's guess, but I estimate that it is probably well over a thousand dollars, and I am convinced that, without a law suit, we will never be fully compensated.

I resigned as poetry editor after five years. Lotus Press resumed the publication of books with the sixth winner of the Naomi Long Madgett Poetry Award, and we stopped sending new Lotus Press books to MSU Press for distribution even though the contract for distribution of our older titles continued until 2003.

Prior to our anniversary celebrations, one of our authors, Dolores Kendrick, a resident of Washington, DC, organized a joint reading and book signing at the Martin Luther King Branch Library in the nation's capital. At that time she was a professor at Philips Exeter Academy in New Hampshire. The event took place for one evening only, and about ten Lotus Press poets participated. She had done a superb job of planning the event which was well attended and very successful. Dolores is one of the Lotus Press poets who have moved on to bigger and better things. She is now Poet Laureate of Washington, DC.

We celebrated our fifteenth anniversary with two evenings of readings, June 25 and 26, 1987, and one morning reading on June 28 in the Afro-American Heritage Room in Manoogian Hall at Wayne State University. We received no grant for this event, and our out-of-town poets came at their own expense. We found a nice but inexpensive motel for those who needed a place to stay and furnished local transportation. Others were guests in the homes of local poets. The readings were recorded on videotape, and the event concluded that Saturday afternoon at the press headquarters on Santa Barbara Drive with a barbecue and other refreshments for the poets. Roy Faust, the husband of one of the poets, took photographs, including one of the group in the back yard. The participating poets (pictured back row, left to right, middle row, and front row seated) were Philip M. Royster, Samuel Allen, Haki R. Madhubuti, Mwatabu Okantah; Dolores Kendrick, Paulette Childress, Naomi Long Madgett, Jill Witherspoon Boyer, Naomi F. Faust; Pinkie Gordon Lane, May Miller, and Agnes Nasmith Johnston. (Not pictured are illustrator Beverley Rose Enright, Ray Fleming, and Herbert Woodward Martin.) Subsequent to this event, we published an anthology, *A Milestone Sampler: 15th Anniversary Anthology*, which includes photographs and poems by poets who participated in the Detroit and/or Washington readings. Such a heavy burden of planning fell on my shoulders that I swore I would never get involved in such a venture again.

Fifteenth Anniversary participants

When *Adam of Ife* was published, I intended to make the celebration of our twentieth anniversary much more low-key, involving only readings from this groundbreaking anthology. Of the 55 women whose poems were included, enough were local that I felt we could sponsor a program and reception with only the local poets reading, with a reception following. Plymouth United Church of Christ (Congregational) offered us the space. But some of the out-of-town poets found out about the celebration and asked to participate. Sixteen contributors to the book were present. The members of the board of directors and local Lotus Press poets hosted the visitors in our homes. On the evening of the reading, male members of the Plymouth Renaissance Choir, to which I belong, removed the pulpit furniture, leaving only sixteen chairs for the poets and a podium. Because some of the poems, whose authors were not present, were essential to the theme, I assigned those poems to be read by poets who were. The poems were to be read in the order of their appearance in the anthology, and I asked the poets to keep any comments they felt were necessary to a minimum. After Dr. Verona W. Morton, then chairman of the board, introduced me, I made a few remarks about the concept of the book. Then I introduced the fifteen other poets. After that, each poet went to the podium and read her poem or the one assigned without any commentary at all.

After the last poem was read, the senior minister, the Rev. Nicholas Hood, II, made brief remarks and asked the audience's support by passing the plate for donations. As he prepared to give the benediction, Dr. Wright, founder of the Charles H. Wright Museum of African American History, stood and interrupted the minister saying, "I just have to say something." Invited to the microphone, he talked about how wonderful it was to hear this positive poetry supporting African American men. Several days later he wrote me a letter of approval and congratulations.

Our thirtieth anniversary, "A Feast of Poetry," also took place in the sanctuary of my church over a two-day period of readings. The

332

Go-Getters Circle, one of the church organizations, provided an opening Friday evening reception, and the YMCA Writers Voice, through the efforts of fellow poet M.L. Liebler, paid for the poets' lodging at the St. Regis Hotel. The church provided a van for transporting the poets to and from the hotel. Each poet was to read for only five minutes on Friday evening, but because two had other commitments the next day, they did their longer reading the first night. Desiree Cooper, a columnist for the *Detroit Free Press*, served as mistress of ceremonies. Saturday morning began with a catered continental breakfast, followed by four poets' longer readings in the morning. Then after a catered luncheon, the remaining poets read Saturday afternoon. Members of the board of directors and volunteers attended book tables in the narthex, and purchases and signings took place at all convenient times. Mr. J. Clifton Graham was master of ceremonies the second day.

We had invited all the poets published by Lotus Press and winners of the Naomi Long Madgett Poetry Award that we could locate to participate, letting them know that we did not have the funds for honoraria or travel expenses. Eighteen poets participated, only three of whom were local, coming at their own expense from California, Massachusetts, Illinois, New Jersey, New York City, Pennsylvania, Ohio, Washington, DC, Maryland, Missouri, and Mississippi. I was meeting most of them for the first time, and they were meeting each other for the first time, too.

I insisted on reading in alphabetical order. I did not want this event to be about me but about Lotus Press. Nevertheless, most of the poets introduced their first reading with kind words about my contributions as a publisher. A crew of videographers and a regular photographer made pictorial records of the entire event. One of the videographers also interviewed the poets for a documentary film still in progress.

After the program was over, the board of directors hosted a dinner for the poets at Sweet Georgia Brown, an upscale black-owned restaurant in Greektown, where we had a chance to socialize and get to know one another better. It makes me very happy that a few of the poets who met at this celebration have kept in touch with and supported one another, one inviting another to read at the university where he or she teaches. Several have since won awards and had other collections published elsewhere. The poets who participated in this event were Jill Witherspoon Boyer, Kiarri T-H. Cheatwood, Paulette Childress, Toi Derricotte, Bill Harris, Nubia Kai, Ruth Ellen Kocher, Monifa Love, Naomi Long Madgett, Haki R. Madhubuti, Herbert Woodward Martin, Adam David Miller, Mwatabu Okantah, Baraka Sele, Peggy Ann Tartt, Jerry Wemple, James R. Whitley, and Claude Wilkinson. We had applied for several grants, and upon their receipt and with other donations, we were able to reimburse the poets for their travel expenses.

At the end of the readings, the board of directors gathered in front of the sanctuary. Diane Reeder, chairman of the board, announced that the Lotus Press Board of Directors had commissioned a bronze bust of me to be created by renowned artist and sculptor Artis Lane. She then introduced a representative from the Charles H. Wright Museum of African American History who announced that this bust would become a part of the permanent collection at the Wright museum.

The necessary funds were raised by soliciting friends and organizations to which I belong. The bust was unveiled on June 4, 2005 in the rotunda of the museum.

We have never gotten back the volume of orders from wholesalers and other booksellers that we had before our association with Michigan State University Press, and much of the expense of running the press again falls on my shoulders and those of other contributors. It is my intention to publish only one book a year from now on, the winning manuscript of the annual award.

334

I see no one on the horizon to take over my duties, and, when I am no longer able to carry on my work with Lotus Press, it is likely that it will cease to exist. I am hopeful that the award will be continued, however, and that another press will assume the distribution of our existing titles.

I do not regret my decision to offer other poets an opportunity to be read rather than to promote myself. I have watched a number of them move to major publishers that are able to provide them more exposure than I could give, and some have won major awards and become well-known and well-respected names in literary circles. I am pleased that I have had a part in their rise and see myself as a ladder upon whose rungs they have climbed. I have been amply rewarded. When we published May Miller's cloth-covered *Collected Poems*, she called me after receipt of her first copy and said, "I never thought I'd live to see the day that I could hold this book in my hand." She was then in her early nineties or closely approaching them. Remarks like hers and the appreciation that poets across the nation have expressed have made the task worthwhile.

My bronze bust created by Artis Lane, now a part of the permanent collection of the Charles H. Wright Museum of African American History

Adam of Ife

Because of my high regard for my father and because I have known many other good African American men, it bothers me that the black male has been so often viewed negatively in general and in novels by black women. Too often I have heard women say, "A black man ain't shit." Since I had seen no books contradicting this opinion, as a publisher and editor I had the means to produce one. I envisioned an anthology of positive poems about African American men—not famous ones, but men in everyday life—and I felt it was important that these poems be written by African American women.

When I mentioned my intention to a young acquaintance, she replied with a grunt, then asked, "Do you think you'll get any material?" The response of another young woman was a short, brittle laugh, followed by: "You must be expecting a teeny-tiny little book." I said, "Why? You must know some good men. Your father is a good black man." Her response was: "And he's the only one." I do not deny that many black women have found their experiences with black men disastrous, and daily media reports remind us of the depth to which too many have fallen. Nevertheless, I believe that, for every negative example of black manhood caught in the public spotlight, there are numerous others who are quietly living exemplary lives without ever seeing their names in print. I felt the need to bring them out of the shadows and tell them, "We see you; we know you are there, and we appreciate your presence in our lives." Still, I thought that if I received enough poems for a book of about 75 pages, I would be lucky.

I set out to reach as many black female poets as I could locate, either through direct contact or *A Directory of American Poets and Fiction Writers.* I wrote personal letters, and some periodicals published notices. By word of mouth, other poets heard about the plan and eventually poems started pouring in. Selecting only those that I thought worthy as literature, I was surprised to find that 55 poets, including me, would be represented.

I felt that an introduction was necessary. While concentrating on positive images of black manhood, I did not want to forget our other brothers who have fallen by the wayside. They did not arrive at their present state without help. When I was teaching, I discovered as one of the recurring themes in African American literature the emasculation of the black male. The short stories, "Truant," by Claude McKay and "Health Card," by Frank Yerby are just two examples. The American system has conspired, since the first African set foot on this soil, to deprive him of his humanity. What other immigrant in world history was ever legally defined as "three-fifths of a man"? White fiction writers have traditionally stereotyped him in so many demeaning and sometimes vicious roles that it would be difficult to recognize him as a man among men. Sterling Brown's essay, "A Century of Portraiture in American Literature," includes some of these stereotypes.

During slavery, the black male had little opportunity to shoulder responsibility. Since it was believed that only women could nurture children, the presence of a man in a household was deemed unnecessary and perhaps even dangerous. As much as a black father might have wished to care for and train his children, he was often permitted little or no contact with them. Even when families were kept intact, the father was powerless to protect his wife and daughters from sexual exploitation by masters and overseers. What degradation and shame he must have suffered to find himself in a position of such impotence! The segregationists who railed against race-mixing certainly did not object to the union of a white male with an African female; the variety of skin tones, hair textures, and other features apparent among African Americans today attests to the popularity of the southern man's most noble sport! It was, of course, the reverse of this arrangement—the involvement of a black man with a white woman—that always has been the most widely protected taboo in this country, for sex is indeed power, and the black man must never be granted the privilege of competing with a white man on this level. Furthermore, the myth of racial inferiority could not stand to be put to a test, for if it were, it would be necessary to answer the question of why a white woman would *want* to sleep with a black man. The black man had to be portrayed as subhuman and deprived of his freedom of choice and movement in order to prevent his becoming a threat to the white male ego.

From Emancipation to the Civil Rights Movement, the power structure used any means necessary to keep the black male from occupying his rightful place in society, fearing that, given an equal opportunity, the black man might surpass his white brother. By the beginning of the twentieth century a pattern of inequality of opportunity had been firmly established. If education was the key to advancement, then it must be rendered useless to the black male. Therefore, if a struggling family, by pooling all its resources, could manage to send only one child to college, a daughter was likely to be chosen even though a son might have been older, for experience had proved that, while a young woman could sometimes find employment commensurate with her training and ability, her brother would not be so fortunate. From my youth I recall a number of black men who had impressive ability and/or had earned college degrees but were forced into specific types of manual labor or service jobs that were considered beneath the dignity of their white neighbors who were not as well prepared as they. Except for self-employed professionals, the most prestigious kind of employment for black men in northern cities was postal work. Even the professionals were limited; the black medical doctor, not permitted to practice in white hospitals, was forced to either send his patients to white doctors for specialized care and surgery or join forces with some of his colleagues to establish their own inadequate hospitals.

The African American woman, on the other hand, posing no threat in the work place, could often use her education to advance as teacher, nurse, social worker, or secretary, professions traditionally reserved for females. The result in this inequality of opportunity between the genders led to a family structure in which the wife was often better employed and better paid than her spouse. That such a disadvantage could lead a man to try to boost his own self-esteem by attempting to "knock down to size" the female who had surpassed him does not come as a surprise, considering that, in spite of women's liberation, we still live in a male-dominated society.

Within recent years I have witnessed a dramatic change in the employment opportunities available to young black men. Yet as a group, they are worse off than ever before. Reading the statistics on school failure, drug addiction, family irresponsibility, and crime, we might easily conclude that the fault is not in these men's now plentiful stars but in themselves. While agreeing that, in some cases, no better explanation is available, we must also concede that history and its effects cannot be erased easily, nor are its scars quick to heal. Many young males are trapped in a syndrome of failure and despair so familiar to them that only a will stronger than they possess could liberate them.

Considering the disproportionate number of young black women who are currently rearing families alone, one might be tempted to blame them for their sons' failures. No one would deny that home training and parental discipline are extremely important to a child's development, but I am wary of generalizations. From my experience and observation, I find that having both parents present is no guarantee that a child will turn out well, even when those parents provide an ideal moral environment. The "broken home" has too long taken the blame for problems whose roots may lie elsewhere. I am convinced that, in spite of those very visible parents who are neglectful, if not downright abusive, the majority of single mothers are doing an admirable job of bringing up their young. Many rise early to drop them off at child care centers, hold down responsible positions, come home to cook and clean, and still manage to find quality time to spend with their offspring. Many more of them than we are willing to recognize are doing their best to teach the same moral values they learned from their own parents. Many men, too, are rearing children alone, often with as much success as women.

But this is not the same world of generations past, and today's youth face outside pressures and perils far more critical than those of bygone days. All American youth today are at risk, but it is the least prepared of them who are the most vulnerable. The absence of positive male role models in the lives of many young men must be addressed with community response.

When we take into account the omissions and distortions inherent in traditional education, it is hardly surprising that many little black boys can perceive nothing in their universe that can thwart their sense of hopelessness and futility. Until quite recently, very little that they learned in school related positively to their own identity or encouraged a feeling of self-worth. As far as they could determine from their textbooks, their kind simply did not exist. School systems and textbook publishers have made progress toward correcting past sins, but the changes have not come soon enough to make a difference to those who have already adopted an attitude of no expectation. Until the educational system catches up and teaches the whole truth about black people's contributions to history, literature, art, and science (without the need for separate courses), all American children will continue to be educationally and culturally deprived.

The title of this collection came to me quickly. Ife (pronounced EE-fay) is a city in Nigeria where, according to African legend, the deity Odudua (OH-doo-DWAH) created the first man. Since that moment of creation, many men of African descent have forgotten their heritage. During the 1960s, Harold G. Lawrence (later Kofi Wangara) wrote a poem entitled, "The Mirror," in which he pictures such a young man looking at his reflection with shame and self-hatred. The speaker in the poem raises the question, "Why do you look at you like that?" knowing the answer very well. Referring to this African creation story, the speaker continues, "When Odudua went to Ife, / he went to make you—you." It was my hope that this book and its title would serve as a reminder to others of their heritage as first man and view themselves more positively.

341

I have only admiration for those generations of black women who gave support and encouragement to their men, forgave many trespasses against them, and kept on going, disciplined their children and held them together as families, and gave unstintingly of their strength and love. One of them in particular comes to mind. Recall the son in Lorraine Hansberry's marvelous play, *A Raisin in the Sun.* Walter Lee Younger, frustrated by his lack of opportunity, has lost his family's inheritance through a scatterbrain get-rich-quick scheme that failed. Recall his college student sister's disgust as she reviles him for being less than a man. To her insults, Mama replies:

> Child, when do you think is the time to love somebody the most; when they done good and made things easy for everybody? Well then, you ain't through learning—because that ain't the time at all. It's when he's at his lowest and can't believe in hisself 'cause the world done whipped him so. When you starts measuring somebody, measure him right, child, measure him right. Make sure you done taken into account what hills and valleys he come through before he got to wherever he is.

I did not find the organization of the poems accepted for inclusion in *Adam of Ife: Black Women in Praise of Black Men* difficult. They fell into eight categories which I called Fathers; Brothers, Sons, and Other Youth; Lovers; Street Scene; Beacons; Music-Makers; In Light and Shadow; and "In This Sad Space." I procrastinated as long as I could asking the late portrait artist, Carl Owens, if I might use some of the faces he had created to illustrate each of these sections. Lotus Press could not afford to pay for his services, and I was afraid he would refuse. But he quickly responded on a card that contained some of the faces I had in mind, saying that he didn't think he had anything that would serve my purpose, but I could visit his studio and look around. When I went, I took the card he had mailed me and said, "I can use more like these if you have them." He reached behind some other items and brought out three large boards of small drawings. "I forgot I had these," he said. "You can take these with you and select anything you want." He suggested that, since the images were small, I should group four to a page. I thanked him for his generosity and left.

Shortly after my visit, he called me to say that he had spoken to his friend and fellow artist, Paul Goodnight, in Boston to tell him about my project and ask him about a possible painting I could use on the cover. Paul's response was: "Any black man who wouldn't be willing to contribute to that would be crazy." Paul sent me slides of eight of his paintings from which to select—at no cost. One of them was perfect for the title. It shows a young black man wearing a cap with an African male sculpture superimposed. It is the perfect cover to illustrate the theme of the book.

The response to the published book was overwhelming. Reviews and feature stories, including pictures and quotes from some of the contributors, were published all over the country. It was shortly before Christmas when the book came out, and many people bought multiple copies to give as gifts. And men, looking at the subtitle, were pleasantly surprised. "You mean the sisters have something good to say about *us*?" they asked. The book went into a second printing within a matter of months.

The book was published in 1992, and I still have not seen any similar collection. I feel that it is as necessary today as it was then, and I consider it my most significant contribution as the publisher and editor of Lotus Press.

I am grateful to all the poets who contributed to this anthology and to the artists whose work added so much to its appearance. I also gratefully acknowledge permission to quote from "The Mirror" by Harold G. Lawrence (published in *The Negro History Bulletin,* October 1962, page 52) and the estate of Robert Nemiroff to quote from *A Raisin in the Sun* (copyright © 1958, 1959, 1965, 1966).

VII.
The Written Word

Integrating a Writers' Club

During the year I spent as a research associate on the campus of Oakland University in Rochester, Michigan, I met one of the members of the Continuing Education Department who belonged to an organization of professional writers, Detroit Women Writers. They held an annual writers' conference in October at Oakland University. Knowing that I was a published poet, this member invited me to be a speaker. On another occasion I spoke or held workshops for one of their conferences. One day when I was talking to her, she made a comment and said, "You know; you're a member of DWW." When I responded that I was not, she seemed a bit embarrassed and responded, "Well, I know they're going to ask you to join." I didn't know at the time that normally writers were not invited to join but went through a process of applying or being recommended by an active member.

I thought no more about the conversation until I read an article in the *Detroit Free Press* concerning the Women's City Club located in downtown Detroit. Detroit Women Writers had been holding their meetings there but had begun to meet in the main public library instead.

I don't recall the exact sequence of events, but there were several other articles concerning the Women's City Club and its policy of not permitting African Americans in its building. Mrs. George Romney, wife of the governor of Michigan at the time, was a member of this club. I learned that the Women's City Club planned to vote on whether to change its policy. When the vote was taken, it was decided that the club would continue to prohibit African Americans from its premises. The governor's wife resigned. I was convinced that this issue concerned me. It was shortly afterward that I was invited to join Detroit Women Writers, becoming its first African American member. Years later one of the members told me that they had agreed not to burden me with the circumstances of my membership, but I had already figured it out.

On one occasion we were having boxed lunches prepared for our meeting at the library. I was riding with a member who picked up these lunches at the Women's City Club. After we had eaten, one of the members commented on the quality of the food. I replied, "Yes, it was well prepared, but I almost choked on it." She understood what I meant and tears welled up in her eyes.

Since those years, numerous African American professional writers have become members and officers, including Darlene House, one of the most efficient presidents we have had in recent years. The organization, of which I am a life member, has made every effort to be as inclusive as possible and is represented by other minorities as well. Over one hundred years old, it now includes male members and has recently changed its name to Detroit Working Writers. I commend DWW for taking the stand it did in the mid-1960s, and I am glad that I had a part in their move toward justice and equality.

A Fellowship of Poets

In the first few years of my arrival in Detroit I became moderately active as a lecturer and reader. A friend of mine who was a member of the Detroit Study Club, which had been organized at the turn of the century as the Browning Study Club, asked me to present the annual Robert Browning lecture, which I did on at least two occasions. I also lectured at a church in Windsor, Ontario and read my poetry at various places including the Detroit Unitarian Universalist Church. It became important to have a book available, so in 1956 my second book, *One and the Many*, was published by Exposition Press, a subsidy company.

Nationally it was a very dry period with few collections of poetry by black authors being published, and I didn't know of any other African American poets in Detroit. This was the year that Dudley Randall returned to Detroit, but I hadn't met him yet. The publication of my book was so refreshing an event during this drought that all the black newspapers, *The Michigan Chronicle*, the *Pittsburgh Courier* (Detroit edition), and the short-lived *Detroit Metro* carried feature stories about me. I was interviewed on the Dick Harris Show, aired on Station WJR in Detroit on December 11, and a lady who had read about my book invited me to do a reading for her literary club in Grand Rapids. A glowing review by critic J. Saunders Redding appeared in the national *Afro-American Newspapers* on January 5, 1958, and I made my first commercial flight on Febraury 21 to do a reading in Philadelphia.

I later met Oliver LaGrone, a poet and sculptor. He was author of a chapbook, and his poetry had received some national attention. It was good to make contact with a kindred spirit who, as far as I knew, was the only other serious black poet in Detroit. On several occasions we were interviewed together and conducted dialogs on radio.

349

On the night before Thanksgiving in 1959, I was visited by Dr. Rosey E. Pool, a Dutch scholar then living in London. She was in Detroit doing research at Wayne State University and had been told of my work. During our conversation I learned that she had become interested in African American poetry in 1925 when she discovered Countee Cullen's first book in the University of Amsterdam library. Time spent in a concentration camp during World War II led her to a deeper identification with the plight of African Americans. She later began to correspond with several authors, including Langston Hughes and James Edward McCall, lectured on African American poets on British radio, and edited a series of anthologies published in London and Amsterdam. She gave me a copy of one of them, *Ik Zag Hoe Zwart Ik Was* (I Saw How Black I Was), and I reciprocated with a copy of *One and the Many*. On December 14 she ended a television lecture with the first stanza of one of my poems, "Not I Alone." The next day I attended a program at Northeastern High School to which the assistant principal, Wesley Rhea, had invited me. Students and faculty members, including David Boone, presented James Weldon Johnson's *God's Trombones*, and several Negro spirituals were sung under the direction of a Jewish teacher. Again Dr. Pool closed her lecture with "Not I Alone," a practice that she continued.

Her presence in Detroit was the catalyst for a significant period of local literary activity. A number of things happened. Her series of lectures and readings on educational television, entitled, "Black and Unknown Bards," drew together other local black poets who had not known each other before. A verse choir publicly performed poems by black authors, and dance teacher Vera Embree directed a video performance that featured local black artists representing various disciplines, including a dance which she choreographed. At some point several of the poets visited Dudley Randall's apartment for a purpose I don't recall. A small group of black poets began to meet in each other's homes for informal discussions and workshops. In addition to Randall, LaGrone and me, they were James W.

350

Thompson, Harold Lawrence, Edward Simpkins, Alma Parks, Betty Ford, and a talented high school student, Gloria Davis. I don't recall at what point Margaret Danner joined our group.

Dr. Pool's first visit to Detroit was interrupted by a trip to Mexico, Margaret Thomas hosting a gathering for her on December 27. When she returned she brought gifts for some of the poets, following the Dutch tradition of giving rather than receiving birthday presents. Her gift to me was a piece of unpolished jade which an archeologist friend in Mexico had just excavated. After one of our discussions I wrote "Midway," giving her a copy to use as she saw fit. Soon after that, she returned to London, having gathered material from the poets she had met here for a new anthology, *Beyond the Blues*, published by Hand and Flower Press in Kent, England in 1962. She also included poets in our group in *Ik Ben de Nieuwe Neger* (I Am the New Negro), a bilingual volume published in the Netherlands in 1965.

Margaret Danner had left her husband and sixteen-year-old daughter in Chicago and come to Detroit, probably early in 1960, the year after receiving a grant from the American Society of African Culture to visit Africa. She became poet-in-residence at Wayne State University and lived at 81 Orchestra Place. According to an article in the *Detroit Free Press*:

> After a series of July lectures at McGregor Memorial Building, she will sail for Africa and on October 1 will watch as Nigeria celebrates its independence from Great Britain. Mr. Whitney's' award, plus $700 from the American Society of African Culture and $350 from the African Culture Studies Association should last through Christmas in Africa.

But instead of going to Africa, she received permission from the Rev. Theodore S. Boone, pastor of King Solomon Baptist Church on Fourteenth Street, to live in an unoccupied house next door to the church and use it for her own writing and as a community art center. Her occupancy in what has come to be known as Boone House lasted from 1962 to 1964 during which time she and Dudley Randall worked on the poems for a small cooperative collection.

We poets met there each month on Sunday evenings and took turns reading our work to each other and to a handful of people who rarely numbered more than five or six. The most regular attendants were the late Ron Milner, who shared the house with Margaret for awhile, and Arthur and Carolyn Reese, educators and civil rights activists. Only Danner and LaGrone had published chapbooks, and I had published two collections of poetry, the second full-length, but we met as equals who shared the spotlight and were qualified to be mutually helpful in our critiques. No one individual stood out as a leader or star. To my knowledge, these readings represented the most visible activity of the house. Except for a few children's drawings I once saw on display, I don't remember any other significant community arts activities. (Though Randall, in a 1971 interview by A.X. Nicholas, mentioned jazz sessions and creative writing classes for children, he later didn't recall any such activities. He was also mistaken in that interview about the name of the church which owned the house, naming instead the one where Aretha Franklin's father was pastor.)

The old house was beautiful in its details but in poor condition. The furnace was evidently inoperable, some of the lights didn't work, and the toilet lacked a seat, but we were glad to have this meeting place and to huddle together good-naturedly in front of the fireplace in cold weather. Rosey Pool returned to Detroit in the spring of 1963. Except for her lecture and reading there on May 11, celebrating the publication of *Beyond the Blues,* and Langston Hughes's very brief visit on February 8, 1964, with no readings or other activity going on, I know of no connection that any other poets such as Robert Hayden, who was living and teaching in Ann Arbor, Hoyt Fuller, or Owen Dodson had with Boone House. (This disputes erroneous information and assumptions made in an entry written about Dudley Randall in *A Dictionary of Literary Biography.*) At Rosey Pool's lecture on May 11, she read my poem "Alabama Centennial" (except for the reference to Selma that I added later), which I had just written that day, and Harold Lawrence's "Black Madonna," which he wasn't present to hear.

Edward Simpkins edited the October, 1962 issue of *The Negro History Bulletin,* which focused on Detroit writers. Featured were Margaret Danner, Harold G. Lawrence, Alma Parks, Betty Ford, James W. Thompson, Edward Simpkins, Dudley Randall, Oliver LaGrone, and me, all members of our group. Also included was the elderly poet, James Edward McCall. Two beginning poets who were not a part of our group were also represented, along with several other writers and playwrights, including Woodie King and Powell Lindsay.

On March 22, 1963, our group presented to a large and enthusiastic audience at Hartford Avenue Baptist Church a joint performance of our work entitled "Poetry Unlimited" and reported in the *Michigan Chronicle* as "An Exposé in Talent."

In April, 1963, I entertained Rosey Pool at my home on Santa Barbara Drive. Among the guests were Irma Wertz, Margaret Danner, Tamunoemi David-West, a Nigerian who is the subject of one of Danner's poems and later one of mine, and Oliver LaGrone. Margaret brought a photographer to record the occasion. He took a photograph in my living room of Margaret, Oliver handing Rosey one of his sculptures, and me. Danner's collection, *To Flower,* came out in October of that year. Shortly after the gathering at my home, Rosey left Detroit to lecture at black colleges in the South. The poets continued to meet periodically at each other's homes to critique each other's work. In my journal I noted a meeting at Betty Ford's house December 28, 1963, and on another occasion we met at Oliver LaGrone's flat to meet Owen Dodson, who was visiting Detroit.

The elder Detroit poet, James Edward McCall, blind newspaper publisher and author of the early poem, "The New Negro," died. On December 31, 1963 Oliver and I attended his funeral at Plymouth

353

Congregational Church, and Oliver read a tribute from the Boone House poets.

In late July, 1964, Ebenezer AME Church presented a Festival of Arts which was reported in an article in *The Detroit Courier*. LaGrone, Randall, and I participated.

Earlier in 1964, the group began to disperse. Margaret Danner suddenly dropped out of sight. (A year or so later, a front page article in the *Detroit Free Press* reported that her disappearance from the current scene was due to her having spent the grant money intended for her trip to Africa. She was finally planning to make the long-delayed voyage.) James Thompson moved to New York, and Harold Lawrence changed his focus to history and his name to Kofi Wangara and moved to Africa.

Nevertheless, those of us who were left continued to thrive individually. Hughes's anthology, *New Negro Poets: USA*, included some of our work in 1964. In 1965 Oliver and I began our participation in Detroit Adventure, forerunner of the Michigan Council for the Arts and its Creative Writers in the Schools program. My poems continued to appear in anthologies, journals, and magazines such as *Negro Digest,* later named *Black World.* That year my third book, *Star by Star*, published by Harlo Press, went into the first of two printings, to be followed in 1972 with the first of several printings of a second edition by Evenill, Inc. By the time the cloth first edition was published, I already had orders for almost 200 signed copies. Dudley sat with me in my den while I signed the copies I had ordered. (At that time, Harlo Press was publishing books, not just printing them, and my book was published on a royalty basis.)

I won the statewide competition for the first Mott Fellowship in English and began the school year as research associate at Oakland University. Dudley Randall founded Broadside Press that year with the publication of his poem, "Ballad of Birmingham." In 1966 his first chapbook, *Poem Counterpoem*, with which he and Margaret

Danner had been collaborating, each contributing ten facing poems, was published.

Eventually a second informal workshop group was formed to include from the old group LaGrone, Randall, Gloria Davis and me, in addition to Joyce Whitsitt and a few other newcomers, including Wardell Montgomery. We were joined by several white poets—Juliana Geran, a brilliant and talented young Romanian Jew, Professor Louis J. Cantoni of Wayne State University, Ethel Grey Seese, Sheila Pritchard, and Robert Honigman, a young Jewish lawyer. From our association came the anthology *Ten: Anthology of Detroit Poets* published in 1968 by South and West, Inc. (Contrary to what has been recently published, we did not pool our money and have it printed ourselves.)

Such workshops were a boon to us who for a while found a wonderful companionship to buffer the loneliness of our profession. We had moved a long way forward from the dry period in which *One and the Many* was born.

The "Midway" Story

A poem can be like a willful child determined to live its own life. Once the labor is over and the baby delivered into print, it no longer belongs to you, regardless of how you may try to direct its ways. Revisions are always possible, but the first version will always be out there somewhere roaming the streets of its own choosing. And what you meant to say and didn't say well enough or clearly enough or maybe just differently, or what you left out and wish you had included can never be changed.

That's a disconcerting thought, in a way, but even more disturbing is the realization that you have no control over which offspring gets noticed and appreciated, which misunderstood and scorned, or which completely ignored. "Look!" you want to cry out. "Pay attention to this one. This is my good girl, my pretty girl, so talented, so well behaved. See how she shows off her careful upbringing. This is the child who deserves your praise." But no one pays attention. It's the one with the errant eyes and undisciplined heart who is likely to climb to the stage, flip her wild hair in the spotlight, and grab all the applause. Sorry, Mom. There's nothing you can do about it. It isn't up to you.

"Midway" is my unrestrained offspring, determined to lead her own life, in spite of me. I wrote the poem in late 1959 during Rosey E. Pool's first extended visit to this country. We had had an intense discussion on race relations and the change of attitude of black people following the 1954 Supreme Court school ruling (Brown vs. Board of Education, Topeka, Kansas) and their determination never again to accept things the way they used to be. At home that night, I summarized my thoughts in this fifteen-line poem whose form was determined by the first line as it came to me. It was rhythmical and forceful, and the lines that followed just seemed to fall into place naturally, creating their own rhyme scheme. But almost as soon as I had finished writing it, I was dissatisfied. Perhaps it was the obtrusive jump-rope rhythm that hammered on the ear too relentlessly. It was certainly, too, the inconsistency of the diction which ranged from a stilted formality to something more relaxed and fitting. I had struggled with one line in particular, unsure how to finish the thought. Finally, I had simply filled in with words that had no real justification for being there except that they fit the poem's form. It was probably a combination of all these factors that caused my dissatisfaction with the poem as a whole. Though I knew what was wrong, I could think of no way to make it better. When I read it to my husband, he immediately singled out the flawed line and asked me what it meant. "Not anything really," I had to admit. He agreed that this poem was not up to my usual standard.

Nevertheless, my department head at the time insisted that the line did indeed have meaning, and Rosey Pool liked the poem. When she left Detroit, it was one of a sheaf of poems I gave her, granting her permission to use them as she saw fit. Because she was gathering material for her next anthology, I hoped she might choose something from this group to include.

I put the poem out of mind until two years later when the phone rang and the voice of my good friend and fellow-poet, Oliver LaGrone, without a greeting, thundered the vaguely familiar line: "'Mighty mountains loom before me and I won't stop now.' I see you've been published in *Freedomways*," he said. "Congratulations!" I told him that he must be mistaken, but he insisted. "It's right here in the new issue," he said. "I'm looking right at it."

How could it have gotten there? A few days later, Oliver dropped off a copy of the fall 1961 issue of the journal. Sure enough, there it was on page 258. It was not until I saw Shirley Graham listed as editor that I was able to make the connection. Rosey was a close friend of Ms. Graham and her famous husband, Dr. W.E.B. DuBois. She had taken me at my word and submitted the poem to *Freedomways*, assuming that no further permission was necessary. She must have had second thoughts about the quality of the poem later, though, because she didn't include it in *Beyond the Blues*. Edward Simpkins did include it in *The Negro History Bulletin*. Most

357

of the other poets in my group evidently liked it, too. Harold Lawrence would often quote a line or two as a greeting.

There were others, however, who had reservations. Although Jessie Ketching's review of *New Negro Poets: USA* (edited by Langston Hughes, 1964) in *Publishers' Weekly* singled out this "rhythmic song of freedom" as "rating special mention," J. Saunders Redding, whose critical opinion I valued highly, did not agree. In his June 20, 1964 *Afro Magazine* review of the same Hughes anthology, he wrote that "Mortality," my other poem included, was "so much better than 'Midway' that it is hard to believe the same poet wrote it." Nevertheless, praise comes so seldom, deserved or not, that I did not permit myself to linger over my own assessment of the poem. There was nothing I could do about it anyhow.

When *New Negro Poets: USA* came out, I was shocked to see that someone had made changes in its form without my permission. Langston Hughes, the editor, had said to me earlier, during a visit to Detroit: "Naomi, I think you'll be pleased with the appearance of your poems on the page." I smiled and nodded, anticipating perhaps some special lettering or design. When I saw it I was stunned. The stanza breaks of both poems had been eliminated, and the six indented lines of "Midway" had been brought out to the margin. In addition, the longer lines had been broken into two so that the fifteen original lines had now grown to 23. I couldn't believe that any thinking person, especially another poet, would take such a liberty.

I have said that the poem is rhythmical. While I had viewed this quality negatively, others have evidently found it an asset. Modern dance groups and verse choirs across the country have performed it with increasing enthusiasm. If the rhythm worked for them, so be it, for it is apparent not only to the ear but also to the eye. The poem as I wrote it has a visual rhythm which is apparent the minute one sees it on the page. The visual image is appropriate to and reinforces the sound. This is as it should be. The version in *New Negro Poets: USA* destroys that image and therefore diminishes the impact and integrity of the poem.

The same change had been made in "Mortality," but I felt that minimizing the regularity of the beat in this poem was an improvement, and I have continued to use the poem in its revised form.

I am not sure that Langston himself made these changes although it is clear that he was aware of them. Nevertheless, I had such deep respect and love for him that I refrained from writing. I'm glad I did. I later ran across two notes from him, several months apart, commenting on the review in *Publishers' Weekly* and congratulating me on the reception of "Midway." I eventually did write, couching somewhere in the middle of some comments about his last visit to Detroit my tactfully-worded displeasure with the changes made in my work. I could not be angry with him, but I had to let him know that I felt the integrity of my work had been violated.

I didn't hear from him again, and I realized later that he was ill. As we were not regular correspondents, I didn't consider that strange. Still, I have wondered about his reaction to my letter. It was not very long after that that he died.

Printers' ink tends to be highly durable, and once an error gets published, it is almost impossible to destroy. In spite of my admonitions and instructions, the Hughes version of "Midway" got reprinted in several more anthologies. Even now I occasionally receive a request to reprint this version of the poem, and I am quick to insist that the original version be used.

Some time in 1965, Dudley Randall, who was working as a librarian in the Wayne County General Library, called to tell me about another problem. He had been perusing new books that came in when he found a few lines from "Midway" at the beginning of one chapter of a book with which I was not familiar. It is a non-fiction account of the Mississippi Freedom Summer, *The Summer That Didn't End,* by a Washington, DC attorney, Len Holt. My feathers were only slightly ruffled to learn that a part of my poem had been used without my permission or knowledge. The next day Dudley brought me a copy of the book, directing my attention to page 76, the beginning of Chapter Five. Just under the chapter title, "Supporting Organizations," were the last five lines of "Midway" with the word *the* omitted and my indentations ignored but otherwise accurately quoted. My name—misspelled—was tacked on at the end, followed by the identification: "Greenwood, Mississippi, Freedom School." I was only slightly annoyed, having never been to Mississippi for any reason. Nevertheless, I began formulating a mental note to the publisher correcting the errors and chastising him or her for their occurrence.

Idly leafing through the rest of the book, I made another discovery. On Page 150 appeared the title of the poem, followed by an inaccurate, but nonetheless recognizable version of the first portion of the poem. This was attributed to an "Unknown Student of the Mississippi Freedom Schools." The line breaks were those that appeared in the Hughes version.

It didn't occur to me until later what must have happened. Some time prior to this discovery, Bob Fletcher, a young man who had once been my student teacher at Northwestern High School, had come back to the school to visit. He related some of his experiences as a worker in the South during that first "Mississippi Freedom Summer," telling me of the popularity of my work there. Arthur and Carolyn Reese, who had spent that summer in Mississippi at their own expense directing some of the activities, had been regular attendants at the poetry readings at Boone House in Detroit and were familiar with my work. I concluded that they or someone else who had access to the poem might have made a copy of it for someone who, in turn, made another copy. This would account for the inaccuracies. It is further likely that the copy Mr. Holt found had been torn in two from handling since he was obviously unaware that the two parts he had quoted were from the same poem. There is some doubt that the author of the book was present during the events of that summer. If he gathered his material from secondary sources, the possibility of inaccuracies was intensified.

At any rate, I began a slow seethe while Dudley sat patiently waiting for me to calm down. My letters to Morrow and Company, the publisher, brought not so much as an apology at first. When I threatened a lawsuit, they became somewhat more attentive. However, after talking to an attorney I knew, I learned that most of the copyright lawyers are retained by publishing houses, and a lawsuit would be very costly and nonproductive. The publisher finally settled for three hundred dollars and a promise that a correction would be made if the book went into a second printing.

When *Star by Star* was published in 1965, I included "Midway" as the final poem, realizing that this poem has popular appeal, and I wanted to make sure the accurate version was available.

When I began teaching at Eastern Michigan University in 1968, one of my colleagues showed me a clipping about a local African American woman who had recently recited this poem on a program. In another instance, the July 30, 1970 issue of *Jet*, under the title, "Black Beauties Denied Rewards," discussed the thwarted efforts of one Theresa Smith of Oakland, California, a student at the University of California at Berkeley, to be fairly considered for the "Miss America" title and other benefits earned as winner of a beauty pageant. Under the subtitle, "Calif. Officials Ban Her Use Of The Word 'Black,'" the article reads in part:

> Miss Smith, a svelte, stately beauty . . . won the Miss Oakland title after performing an interpretive dance to a poem by Naomi Madgette *(sic)* that details the Black man's struggles. She entered the contest, she says, because she needed the experience and "was interested in modeling." Easily out-pointing the competition . . . she moved into competition for the Miss California title in the state finals at Santa Cruz. She lost . . . . Officials at the Miss California State pageant refused to allow Miss Smith to perform unless she dropped the "offensive" word, "Black," from her recitation.

My, how times have changed!

One night in 1973 I received a call from the editor of a small-town paper in upstate New York. He asked if I had heard about the turmoil this poem was causing at the local high school. He wanted to get my reaction. I had never heard of the city or the incident. After talking to me, he agreed to send a copy of the article he was writing.

"A Poem and Pride Split High School" (Bob Wacker, *Newsday,* Wednesday, May 9, 1973) tells how a disagreement about the recitation of "Midway" caused the cancellation of the variety show that for fourteen years had been a fundraiser at Newfield High School. "Midway" was to have been recited by one of the school's thirty black students (out of a student body of 1,750) while three other members of the Afro-American History Club danced. But after receiving approval, the students were notified that the poem was too serious for the show; they could perform the dance but not include the words of the poem. One student, Dale Boyd, 16, went to the principal and protested the cut. Her father, former president of the local NAACP, could not understand why the poem was rejected since it had already been accepted, and for a day and a half, the black students picketed the school. White parents threatened a counter protest if the poem was included. The show was finally canceled, bringing on a protest by 300 picketing white students angry over the loss of expected funding for the senior prom, which the variety show would have provided.

Several days after publication of the article, I received a detailed letter from Dale Boyd, the astute student who had planned to recite the poem. Quoting from one of the dancers, she said: "They like to see us niggers jump up and down, but if we open our mouths and say something which in essence means that Black people . . . have moved on up, are moving on up, and will continue to move on up, they don't want to hear it. Or to put it another way: We can dance to the music, but we can't say the words."

In 1981, a young man who lived in Flint, Michigan called me, extremely excited to have reached me. He identified himself as

Gerald Savage, a graduate of a university in Indiana where he had set "Midway" to music and performed it with a campus group in a moderate gospel mood. He insisted that I listen while he played the piano and sang it over the phone. I invited him to visit and when he came, he brought me a copy of the music, which was published later that year with his permission. I have heard his song, under the title, "I've Come This Far to Freedom," publicly performed on several occasions, once receiving a standing ovation when Samuel McKelton sang it at Plymouth Congregational Church in Detroit during Black History Month.

One of the more recent anthologies to include this poem is a beautifully illustrated book for children, *Pass It On* (Scholastic, 1993). I was much impressed with the colorful volume and the selection of poems which, except for mine, seemed suitable for children in about second or third grade. "Midway," however, seemed strangely out of place, and at first glance I wondered why Wade Hudson, the editor, had chosen it. Would children that young be able to relate to it? But it was this poem that one reviewer singled out for special mention. On second thought, I wondered if, even at their tender age, young black readers had already experienced enough racism to understand the spirit of the poem if not all the history behind it.

Wherever I go there is bound to be someone who claims to like my poetry but has seldom read anything I've written except "Midway." Most readers don't include much poetry in their diets, and when they do, they are likely not to be as concerned with artistry as with content. It is the message, most of all, that appeals to them, and the message in this poem is clear and accessible. The form, however blatant, makes it easy to remember. In addition, this poem expresses the racial mood during a particular period which, strangely enough, has not been addressed in many other poems.

When I went back to St. Louis to my fifty-year high school

reunion, one of my classmates insisted that I go with her to visit her minister who admired my poetry and was eager to meet me. I was not surprised that it was "Midway" that had drawn him to my work. What did surprise me was that, instead of reading it as a civil rights poem, he interpreted it on a highly personal level. He told me that it reflected the details of his own harsh life in the South and his determination to rise above them. So affected was he by this poem that he had required all of his children to memorize it.

That's one of the wonderful things about poetry. Poets write out of their own experience, but readers bring to a poem something of their own and interpret it in the light of their own experiences. Seldom are poets present to tell the reader what they had in mind, and I think that's good because such knowledge would rob readers of other possibilities. This minister's interpretation was certainly a valid one, which is borne out by the words. He wanted copies of *Star by Star* and all my other available books, but I'm afraid he was probably disappointed if all he wanted to find was another "Midway." Maybe not. Perhaps he saw in some of the other poems, too, meanings that I did not intend when I wrote them but which related to his own unique experience. I hope so.

Maybe I am protesting in vain. Who reads literary poetry anyhow but other poets, critics and scholars? Who buys books of poetry? Unlike other cultures, Americans do not consider poetry as vital to life. Most people don't care about art, and what poetry they do relate to is often frowned upon by the elite as being mediocre or just plain bad. Performance poetry is in; literary poetry still has little appeal for ordinary readers. But maybe it's the people's choice that should prevail. Perhaps those of us who toil over the precise and multiple meanings of the words we choose, the sounds and rhythms of the language, the totality of the emotional-intellectual experiences of our poems may be wasting our effort. But I am not willing to give in to such a notion, and if holding my ground dooms me to oblivion, so be it.

More recently the author of *NBA Rookie Experience*, Mike Monroe (Harper, 1998), contacted me to verify that I am the author of "Midway." The last place that I expected to see this poem was in a book about athletes. But in Chapter 6, "The Poet," concerning an athlete named Jacque Vaughn, the following quotation appears:

> He had come to poetry as a grade-schooler, when he memorized a poem a classmate had impressed him by reciting. He had been inspired not only by the fact of a young contemporary's ability to memorize the verse, but by its message.
> "I don't know who wrote the poem," Vaughn said, "but I still remember it." It went like this:

> *I've seen the daylight breaking high above the bough.*
> *I've found my destination and I've made my vow*
> *So whether you abhor me*
> *Or deride me or ignore me,*
> *Mighty mountains loom before me and I won't stop now.*

> It is a message Vaughn has taken with him the rest of his life. He would turn to poetry, which so many youngsters sarcastically deprecate, as a source of delight and inspiration.
> "That was the start of my poetic life," Vaughn said.

So I am not sorry I wrote "Midway," and I will not disown my willful child. The message is important. I only wish I had crafted it better. I am deeply gratified that something—anything—I have written might possibly live on and continue to touch people's lives long after I have been forgotten.

It is the editors of anthologies who determine what the public comes to know as the work of individual poets since most people do not buy books of poetry by individual authors but will sometimes purchase an attractive, beautifully illustrated anthology. Unfortunately, many of the editors of these anthologies are lazy. It annoys me no end that, even though my poems have been included in more than 180 anthologies in this country and abroad, they are the same few, usually at least forty years old. I think what most of these editors do is simply gather together all the anthologies they can find and select from them some that they like. Seldom do they go to primary sources to view the entire body of a poet's collected work. Even less frequently do they ask a poet to send a sampling of more recently published and new, unpublished poems to be considered. Abraham Chapman, editor of *Black Voices*, was one of the few editors I have known who asked for newer poems when he was collecting work for *New Black Voices*. Even when I have made it a point to send copies of several of my books to editors, most have made their selections from the first one they picked up, unwilling to take the time to look at the others. As a result, many people, including students, who tell me they like my work are limiting my 66 years of published work to the same ten or so old poems which, in many cases, I feel I have outgrown.

Therefore, I have come to be known by something less than my best work, and, especially in the case of "Midway," I want to protest. But this offspring refuses to budge from center stage, defiantly flinging her hair in the face of Mama's good upbringing, Mama's more disciplined ways.

Irresponsible Scholarship

Although I taught for many years, most of them in higher education, I chose to devote most of my time to creative rather than scholarly writing. Having been a full professor of English, however, I know what good scholarly writing is and am capable of producing it. I am appalled at the number of scholars who are just plain lazy and publish material that is not researched as carefully as it should be. Once something erroneous gets into print, it is difficult, if not impossible, to undo the damage. Errors keep getting repeated by other scholars who are not willing to make the effort to consult primary sources.

Entries concerning my life and work appear in numerous resources. Many, such as *Who's Who in America*, provide only minimal information, but their publishers give the subject an opportunity to update the material and verify its accuracy. It is not these publications that I am criticizing. It is the other resources that contain more detailed information, along with critical comment.

I am commenting now on only one of these. I have purposely omitted the title because it is not my intention to embarrass anyone, and I have never known which of the several contributors was responsible for this example of ineptitude. I will begin with a quotation, then add my comment.

"[Madgett] was a part of a rare but representative upper-middle-class black family . . . ."
My father was a well educated man and was the pastor of churches for most of the 63 years of his ministry, but his salary never exceeded 300 dollars a month. There were other benefits; we lived in parsonages so had no rent to pay, the churches gave him an allowance for gas to visit the sick, and we ate a lot of free chicken dinners at members' homes. During the Depression, his church managed to find the money to send him to Berlin as a delegate to the World Baptist Alliance. If the writer had said that my family had

middle-class values, that would be true, but "upper-middle-class" is a sociological term that refers to wealth, and we certainly didn't have that. I realize now that we were relatively poor, but we didn't know it then because Dad had a job and we were therefore better off than most of the black families we knew. Dad often traveled throughout the country, often to visit relatives, but he knew ministers who would, at his request, permit him to preach at their churches, taking up an offering for him, so he was able to earn the money for his travel by preaching. My parents had no social life outside the church, and their tastes were simple. They knew how to make do with little. Mama could take a cupful of leftovers, cut up some onions, potatoes, and celery, and end up with enough food to feed an army. Some of our members who were domestic workers brought us food from their employers' homes, and others who were on welfare gave us extra government-provided food that was in excess of their needs. I grew up in other people's hand-me-down clothing and wore Wil's outgrown overcoats to school until I was in seventh grade when I received my first store-bought everyday coat.

"... her mother was a teacher ...."

This statement gives the impression that there were two incomes. The truth is that my mother went to normal school at the age of thirteen, graduating in 1902 at sixteen, and for several years she taught in one-room country schools in Virginia. She was a very intelligent, well-spoken woman, but this was the extent of her formal education. After her marriage, she never again worked outside the home.

"... [Madgett] was able to attend the all-Black Sumner High School, where she was even more immersed in African American literature."

I was not "able" but was forced to attend an all-black school because the schools in St. Louis were still legally segregated. My attendance there was the best thing that could have happened to me, but I had no choice in what school I would attend. Sumner did not teach any courses that related directly to African American history or literature. The classical curriculum was almost identical to that at the predominantly white high school in East Orange that I attended for two months before we moved. So the assumption that, because the school was black, I was "even more immersed in African American literature" is completely false.

" . . . [Madgett] was able to publish her first book of poetry, *Songs to a Phantom Nightingale,* **in St. Louis."**
My first book was published in New York City, not St. Louis.

" . . . [Madgett] worked for *The Michigan Chronicle* **from 1945 to 1946."**
I did not arrive in Detroit until April, 1946. I wrote for this weekly for several months in 1946.

"She continued to work intermittently for the Detroit public school system . . . ."
My teaching was not intermittent. I began in September, 1955 and took one school year off, 1965-66, as the first Mott Fellow in English at Oakland University. At the end of that year I returned to Northwestern High School and continued to teach there until I became an associate professor of English at Eastern Michigan University in 1968. I continued to teach there until my retirement. One semester's medical leave and a sabbatical do not qualify as "intermittent" teaching.

"Her *One and the Many* **came out in 1956 before white American critics understood or accepted the political aesthetic of African American protest poetry . . . . Obviously, the critical establishment was not ready for a strong voice of protest against the endemic racism . . . ."**
My poetry has never been considered political, and this comment

certainly does not describe my book in any way. Of the 66 poems included in this volume, only nine have any racial content, and those that do could not, by any stretch of the imagination, be called protest poetry. The writer evidently read a comment by a white critic who completely overlooked the majority of the poems and saw only the nine with racial content, probably labeling them propaganda.

Regarding *Pink Ladies in the Afternoon* (1972): "**. . . the national scene was somewhat different. The Civil Rights Movement was at its zenith, and black protest poetry was in vogue . . . .**"

Here again, this book was anything but "black protest poetry" and was not in any way similar to the poetry then in vogue. It was because it didn't fit the mold that even black publishers were hesitant to publish it and Lotus Press came into being. It would have been helpful if the person who wrote this essay had read the books him/herself. This book contains 48 poems, one of which deals with the accidental death of an African woman; one deals with my impressions of Africa after my visit there; two concern racial pride and beauty; one is in memory of Langston Hughes; and two others are only obliquely racial. The only protest poem, "Newblack," is a protest against the divisiveness within the race by those who made a distinction between "true" black people and Negroes. In no way can this be considered a book of protest poetry.

"Not only was Madgett's literary career greatly advanced by ownership of a major publishing company, but scores of other budding black writers—Houston Baker, Tom Dent, Gayl Jones, Pinkie Gordon Lane, and others—were able to launch literary and academic careers because of their early association with Lotus Press as well."

My first three books were not published by Lotus Press, nor were two of my later books. In addition, all four of the poets named were already well established, three in academic careers and all as writers and/or critics. It is true that Lotus Press published the first books of *poetry* (several each) by Gayl Jones and Houston Baker, but they were already well established writers in other genres, as well as successful academicians, and Tom Dent was also an established poet and writer. The statement is more true now than when the resource book in which it is contained was published. Many newer Lotus Press poets, some winners of the annual Naomi Long Madgett Poetry Award, established in 1993, have indeed moved on to major publishers and outstanding national awards.

"During the seventies and eighties, Madgett's work shifted from a general ethnic focus . . . ."

My books never had "a general ethnic focus." *Exits and Entrances* (1978) has a *more* ethnic focus than any of my earlier books, which is in direct opposition to this statement.

"*Octavia and Other Poems* . . . celebrates her great-aunt Octavia . . . ."

Anyone who has read this book knows that Octavia was my father's sister, making her my aunt, not my great-aunt.

" . . . this neglect stems mainly from the delicacy of the poet's aesthetic style. Over the years Madgett has emphasized her lyric poetry at the time when such poetry, regrettably, had been regarded lightly . . . . Madgett has tended to downplay her Afro-American verse.'"

Didn't the person who wrote this essay detect the contradiction in this last statement, quoted from Robert Sedlack's essay, and the earlier statements about my protest poetry?

My books are available for reading, and I am easily accessible and willing to answer questions. Unfortunately, this is not the only "scholar" who has published bio-critical essays about my work, relying only on mistaken secondary sources, assumptions, and speculation. In the cause of responsible scholarship and truth, I appeal to those who take on the task of writing about literary artists and their work to do their homework. If the subject is still living, obtaining accurate information should not be difficult. They should avoid the trap of reprinting what others have written, which is often false. Find out the truth and write it.

Recreating Octavia

I still have guilty visions of the full trash bags on the curb in front of my parents' house in New Rochelle that summer when my sister-in-law and I met there to help organize their move to Detroit. My father had retired as pastor of Bethesda Baptist Church although he continued to preach somewhere almost every Sunday and still attended the ministers' conference in New York City. But it had become obvious that the house was too large for them to care for properly, and I didn't want to be called there in an emergency that might occur in the midst of my final exams. After several years of my urging, they had finally agreed to sell the house and move to Detroit to spend their remaining years with me.

Painstakingly, my sister-in-law Laverne and I had separated linens, tagged furniture, thrown out tons of used gift wrapping and ribbons that my mother had planned to recycle, and perused the contents of two old trunks in the basement. It was this last venture that was most challenging.

In one trunk we found neatly folded linens edged with lace, fascinating old photographs, records and documents, and the largest collection of letters I had ever seen. We saved the pictures and most of the other material but, after reading some of the letters from family members, decided that there were just too many to keep. There were already numerous books and other items to be transported; who would ever look at these letters again? So after awhile we began to dispose of what we considered excess clutter. If I have ever regretted anything in my life, it was that decision. Those discarded letters would have answered a great number of questions whose answers no one now will ever know.

It was not until some years later that I came to realize the value of the material we had saved. I did ask Dad at one time to identify some of the people in the photographs; I wrote the persons' names in pencil on the back. By that time, however, his memory was sometimes faulty, as I later found from the handwritten notes he left about his life. By the time he died in 1976, my interest in family history had been confined to putting the extant letters in chronological order and printing out copies for my brothers' and cousins' families. In doing so, I was amazed at how much they revealed. What the family members wrote to and about each other provided a great deal of characterization and a sequence of events that read like a narrative.

I never knew my paternal grandparents or Aunt Octavia. My mother once told me of Grampa's visit to Norfolk either before or shortly after I was born, commenting on how studious he was and how absent-minded about things that had no importance to him. She described his complexion as an unusual *café au lait*. We had seen Uncle Robert on several occasions. It was not until I was thirteen that we met Aunt Ethel, her husband William Johnson, and our cousins, Harold, Kenneth, and William, Jr., on the campus of Wilberforce University. I had met two of my father's cousins, but my knowledge of them didn't compare with the familiarity of my mother's family in Richmond, whom we visited every summer. So the letters that various members of my father's family wrote to each other were extremely revealing. What a shame it is that in today's world of e-mail and cell phones, we have lost the fine art of letter writing!

After my father died I found two new notebooks on the covers of which he had written: "The Story of My Life." Inside both were only blank pages. The only thing I could find that he had written was two sheets of paper on which he tried to record from memory family dates and places where they had lived. He had felt extremely frustrated by his having let the years get away from him without following through on his intention. Because of him, because of my cousin Kenneth, and because it was I who was the keeper of records, I felt an obligation not only to preserve what I had but to put these treasures into some more accessible form.

It may seem strange that my creative interest centered on Octavia. She had died of tuberculosis at the age of 34, three years before I was born, but though I never knew her, she was not a stranger to me. Throughout my childhood I had heard a great deal about Dad's sister. I was said to have looked like her as a child. Dad wanted to name me Octavia Cornelia, but my mother felt that my having her name would be too constant a reminder to my father who was still in grief over her early death. But I was given her middle name, Cornelia, which was also the middle name of my mother's sister Minnie.

Because I was underweight, Dad was forever cautioning me about my health and my careless habits. If I didn't wear my boots or scarf, if I didn't improve my appetite, I, too, would go to an early grave. To avoid such a catastrophe, he made sure that I took plenty of tonic. One such concoction had a horrible taste and was so thick that I had to almost chew it to get it down. Whenever I could get away with it, I tried to pour it down the drain, but it was so thick that it just sat there in the sink, and Dad would come back and see it. Then I'd get scolded for being so hardheaded.

Throughout my childhood I overheard comments about Octavia that told me a great deal about her personality. I knew that she had been a teacher. I also got the impression that, although not exactly wild, she was strong-willed and somewhat liberated for her day, sometimes defying rules of proper behavior for a young lady. She dared to ride with a young man in an open carriage without a chaperone! When she married, hers was a quiet wedding without the fanfare or previous planning of her sister's, and the marriage soon ended. I sensed that my mother held some resentment toward her. And somehow I came to feel that in some ways other than appearance, I was like her in disposition. By the time Aunt Ethel gave me her gold ring containing two small pearls, my fifteen-year-old mind was convinced that I was Octavia's reincarnation.

As I grew older and moved away from the family setting, the sense of identification with her receded and I seldom thought about her, gradually learning to feel that I was very much my own person. What revived my interest was an invitation during the 1980s to submit some poems to a special issue on African American writers to the literary journal at the University of Kansas. Aware that Octavia had graduated from there, I began a poem about her which I planned to submit. But the poem kept growing and growing, and I could never succeed in limiting its scope. I ended up not sending in anything.

The continuing poem began to consume me. I reread family letters, all written during the years that my grandmother and her four children lived in Guthrie, Oklahoma, Grampa having left to work as principal of a high school in Hot Springs, Arkansas. I noted how and what Octavia wrote to others and what others wrote to and about her. Sometimes these letters provided more questions than answers. Who in the world was Mrs. Green whose name was frequently mentioned? "Mrs. Green was not feeling well yesterday." "Be sure to write to Mrs. Green." And who was the Evelyn who was also mentioned occasionally. Why did letters sometimes come from two different addresses in Guthrie with such references as: "Octavia was home last night"? I also studied Octavia's photographs intently. People never smiled for the camera back then, but the facial expressions were revealing nevertheless, especially her wedding pictures. The difference in her personality and her sister's became remarkably clear. Octavia became the main character in a real-life drama involving the entire family, and I felt compelled to provide the dialogue.

Section followed section, not always in the order in which they were later placed. Late at night, after I had finished whatever work I was doing on the computer, her picture on the dresser communicated with me and I communicated with her in fragments of poems. The first line that came to me became the first line of the poem, "When as a child I wore your face, Octavia . . . ." This prologue, in several parts, is directed to Octavia and deals with my sense of identification with her. In the main section, I drop out of the picture and the anonymous speaker recreates her life, illness, and death, as well as the lives of other members of the family, beginning in about 1900 in Guthrie and ending with Octavia's death in 1920 in Charlottesville,

Virginia. To my knowledge, Octavia did not write poetry, but one poem in the main section, printed in italics, is attributed to her as I imagined what she might have written. In the epilogue, I reenter the picture and the poem discusses my visit to Guthrie and the people I met who knew her. The poem ends at Octavia's grave in Richmond, Virginia with my new sense of my own individuality.

Octavia Cornelia Long (1885-1920), taken in 1909

377

Having been told that Octavia had taught fifth grade in the same building where her mother taught first grade, I began one poem that showed her walking to school on a blustery morning (without a hat, to suggest the lack of precaution that might have contributed to her ill health). I hadn't gotten far with a reference to the weather when I realized that I could not create an authentic setting because I had never been to Oklahoma, let alone the city of Guthrie my father had always referred to as home. I knew I had to go there and see it for myself if I wanted to make the ongoing poem authentic.

With some of the grant money I had received to complete the book, I flew to Oklahoma City and rented a car, having made reservations at a small motel. For good luck, I wore Octavia's little pearl ring. I took with me letters from the four addresses from which they had come, a picture of a house I assumed was one of them, a studio picture of Octavia with three younger persons I could not identify, several class pictures showing my grandmother with classes of her young students, and a card signed in pencil by someone whose name seemed to be Dounda Wigley. The card, showing an address, looked as if it might have accompanied a gift.

I drove my rented car from Oklahoma City thirty miles to the motel down the hill from town. I asked a black waitress in the dining room where most of "us" lived, and she told me the southern part of the city. This is where I would begin my journey. My first act after dinner was to look up the name *Wigley* in the tiny telephone directory. I would call each of the persons listed in an effort to track down some information on "Dounda."

Because Octavia had been the last member of the family to live in Guthrie, I didn't expect to find anyone who knew anything about the Longs. All I wanted to know was if any of the old houses were still standing and if not, where they had been. My main goal was to get the "feel" of the place, to absorb its atmosphere so that I could place Octavia in an authentic setting. To know how the sky looked, what the pavement felt like beneath my feet, the architecture. To walk and observe and absorb. To sense the place as a distinct locality.

378

When I first drove up the hill into the city the next day, I was not prepared for its size. Immediately a water tower with the name Guthrie loomed over everything. Simultaneously, I noticed a street sign that said "Drexel," the street from which some of the letters had come. It couldn't be that easy! Unwilling to believe, I passed it by and kept driving around until I found Springer Street. The place where I assume the house of my grandmother's last extant letters had stood was now a garden behind a private residence. It was at the top of a hill whose street was rocky and unpaved. The soil was copper-red. I talked with a woman who occupied the house with the connected garden. She recalled the last residents but knew of no one named Long. At the foot of the hill, an elderly man named Mr. Tucker took an interest in my search and talked with me at length. The only name he could associate with the house on the hill was Jones. I had expected no more so wasn't disappointed.

My next stop was East Grant Street. Where the house numbered 324 had evidently stood was now the length of a church yard and parking lot. Across the street were the remains of two destroyed buildings, one of which appeared to have been a school gymnasium.

Then I doubled back to South Drexel Street just a short distance away. I slowed down to note house numbers. Had the city changed them at some point? If I found 202, would it be the same house that bore that number in 1910? As I approached the water tower, the house numbered 202 came into view. It was easy to see that this was the house in the photo I had brought with me. There was no longer a front porch, but the position of the chimney, the line of the roof, and the number and placement of the windows were the same. I stopped the car and almost ran up the several steps to the front door which was standing ajar. Nobody answered the doorbell. After ringing again and waiting, I pushed the door a little farther open and, without entering, took a picture of the living room. Was that the room where Aunt Ethel had gotten married in 1910 and Octavia had played the piano and sung a solo? The discovery of this house was an unexpected reward. I vowed to return and return until I found someone at home. Closing the door to its original position, I began my search for the last house on my list.

All the houses, I now sensed, had been close to each other. Finding South Second Street confirmed that, but the street looked desolate. Beyond the railroad tracks nothing was visible but one white shingle house and a lot of trees and wild shrubbery that cast a heavy shade. I came upon two other houses before I realized they were there. The windows of both of these tiny structures were boarded up. On one I read the number 707. The house across the street was unnumbered but, by reason of its position, must have been 708. By now my heart was pounding wildly. It seemed impossible that I could find the house that the family had occupied in 1900 with so little effort. A short distance beyond, I saw a little bridge over a muddy creek. Beyond that was a well kept area that I assumed was a park. Making every effort to be calm, I grabbed my camera from the seat and scrambled out of the car. Then for several minutes, all I could do was stand and stare.

The house was covered with some kind of siding which hid its original material. Looking through a partially exposed side window, I could see what must have been the living room. The last occupants had left an old sofa, and rags and other debris littered the floor. That's all I could see from that position. In the back was a second door better secured than the window and front door. A curious kitten poked its head through a wooden back fence. A small cloud of insects stirred the air near me. I finally got my emotions sufficiently under control to take pictures.

As I headed back to my car in the front, a man came out of the white house and looked in my direction with curiosity. Why would any stranger be interested in that deserted old shack? To put him at ease, I approached him and introduced myself, telling him my purpose for being there.

708 South Second Street in 1987

"You need to talk to Frank Smith," he said. "Get in your car and follow me up the hill." We drove two or three blocks along Second Street into a more populated area, stopping in front of a house where an elderly lady wearing a house dress sat on the porch. It was May. My new friend introduced me to Mrs. Smith and explained my mission. "I can't help you," she said, "but maybe my husband can." She called inside. While we were waiting for him, I said, "My grandparents were named Frank and Sarah Long. They had four children, Octavia—" She interrupted me. "Octavia Long was my high school English teacher." While I tried to recover from my shock, she continued. "She was my aunt's (or sister's or cousin's?) best friend. Her name was Dorinda Wigley." Remembering the gift card I had brought, I could see how the "r" and undotted "i" could be mistaken for a "u." I had not recognized the address on the card because it was abbreviated, but once she mentioned it, I knew that I had made a connection. Mr. Smith, it turned out, had a problem remembering things and was of no help. But I had heard enough, only wondering if the old lady was mistaken about the grade inasmuch as I had never heard my father associate Octavia with a high school.

Mrs. Beulah Wigley Smith directed us to a house diagonally across the street where we found Mrs. Loletta Finley, walker nearby. She too had been one of Octavia's high school students. With her was her husband who, though he hadn't grown up in Guthrie, knew a great deal about its history and who used to live where. According to him, the family I had often heard my father mention had lived in a large two-story house next door to my family between their house and the creek.

From there my willing guide took me around the corner to Vilas Street to a large, well-kept house with a wide enclosed porch. There we were greeted by Mrs. Ollie Matthews Fried, 95 years old and still glowing. Between steady fingers whose nails were painted bright red, she held a thin brown cigarette. I was later told that she still wore the highest heels in town. "I knew the whole Long family," she told me. "Marcellus tried to go with me, but I was too young for him." "Marcellus was my father," I said. She smiled warmly. "I ought to cook you a chicken dinner." She certainly seemed capable of doing so for she still worked as a seamstress for special clients. As she recalled her three marriages, it struck me that she must have been quite a belle in her day.

Our last visit that day was to the nearby home of Miss Minnie Tilmon and her sister. Miss Tilmon, too, had been in Octavia's class, and her sister had known her. By now I was convinced that Octavia had indeed taught in high school even though my father had never mentioned it. It later occurred to me that, by the time Faver High School, the first high school in Guthrie for African American students, was built in 1912, Dad had already left Guthrie. While he must have known that Octavia was one of its first teachers, that fact was not as vivid in his memory as seeing her prepare for elementary school while he was still a boy at home. We were given several other names of people to see, but I was so intoxicated by the events of my first day that I headed back to the motel to put my impressions on paper. I made an excited call to Laverne to tell her what I had learned. She was surprised. "I thought you were going on a wild goose chase," she said.

Other days of my week in Guthrie brought other discoveries. I met additional ladies whom Octavia had taught, including Mrs. Katherine Jackson Chadwick and Vivian Hamilton. I also visited the Oklahoma Territorial Museum, so named because, when my father's family moved there, Oklahoma was a territory, not yet a state. When I entered, a group of school children was being given a tour. I looked around and waited. Eventually Wayne Woods, the curator, was free to talk. When he saw the picture of my grandmother with her first grade class, he became very excited and wanted to borrow it and the other pictures to duplicate. I promised him I would have them copied for him; I didn't want them to leave my hands. From the style of clothing in the picture of my grandmother's class he assumed that it had been taken around 1900. "We don't have much information on early black families," he said, "but we might be able to find something." He led me into a small office where an Indian woman was working. Together they pulled down a large dusty ledger that listed families by street address. Turning to 708 South Second Street, I read, "F.C. Long, colored, principal, Lincoln School, 1900." Mr. Ward himself was surprised to see that other members of the family were also listed over a period of several years. Uncle Robert was shown one year to be working for the daily newspaper. My two aunts were listed either as students or teachers, depending on the year. My father was variously listed as student or printer. In another book we found an outline of the house on Second Street which once had an L-shaped porch. The slight doubt I had that the house I had seen was the right one was quickly dispelled.

One of the former students I met had been taught by Octavia in high school and by my grandmother in first grade. She had one of the same class pictures I had and identified herself, her sister, and several other first graders.

Doris Thames, the Native American at the museum, offered to drive me around the city one evening so that she could show me some historical sights. During our drive she pointed out fields of grain with deposits of sand still visible. She told me that Cottonwood Creek had once been clear but that the flooding of the Cimarron River had eventually muddied it.

Each night when I returned to my motel room, I sat on the side of the bed and recorded what I had learned that day. At times I simply sat there, reflecting and meditating, perhaps looking out the window or watching the sky. In that mood I sometimes became so much involved with the place that I became a witness to the past. I could see my father at about the age of twelve tossing a ball to his little brother. I could feel the heat from a passing train and catch on my skin flecks of soot coming from the open windows behind the engine in the Jim Crow car. I could join Octavia in her discontent, walking the few steps from the house to the backwaters of Cottonwood Creek and hear her sighs as she leaned against the bridge. Being there was a very spiritual experience.

After Aunt Ethel's death, my father had had the family piano repaired and moved to his home in New Rochelle. I recalled his saying that it had been in floods in Oklahoma. One evening while I sat on the bed writing and half listening to the news, the weather reporter predicted a flood and warned families living in the vicinity of Cottonwood Creek to make plans to evacuate. In that instant I realized that it was in that house on Second Street that the family piano had been flooded. Two weeks after I returned to Detroit, Oklahoma City and Guthrie were in the news because of heavy floods.

One of Octavia's former students showed me a 1917 yearbook from Faver High School which included photographs of faculty members. Octavia's picture was one I had seen before in Dad's collection. The next year would be Octavia's last in the classroom because of her declining health. The lady permitted me to borrow her book long enough to have the pages duplicated.

I met another lady named Nona whose mother had continued to correspond with my father until his death. I recognized the name at once as I had often heard him mention her. Nona's father had published his own newspaper in Mississippi and, having been run out of town for his outspoken editorials, he had founded a black weekly newspaper in Guthrie. It was for him that Dad had once worked as a printer between the time he graduated from the preparatory program at Bishop College in Marshall, Texas and his leaving for Virginia Union University in 1909. During our conversation I showed Nona the studio picture of Octavia with the unidentified young people. "Oh, those were the children Mrs. Green was raising." She pointed out the taller of the two girls as Evelyn who she said was then in a nursing home in California. The children, she thought, might have been part Mexican. More mysteries were being unraveled.

Mrs. Green, it seems, was married to a man still remembered among the old-timers in Guthrie as "Sergeant Green" because he had fought in one of the wars. He was black but spoke with a foreign accent which might have been French of Caribbean. The family had lived across the street from the original building of Faver High School, which was later destroyed by an explosion. When Octavia returned to Guthrie from a brief residence in Washington, D.C. to become one of its first teachers, she had lived with the Green family. That explained the letters from two different addressees during the same period. That was the house where church grounds were now located. From Nona I also learned which church the family had attended.

That Sunday morning I made it a point to attend services at First Baptist Church, the present building located on the site of the original one. Before going in to the service I took pictures of the exterior. I was introduced as a visitor and had a chance to tell why I was there. One elderly lady recalled that Octavia had taught her daughter in fifth grade. I discovered that my father's recollection was

385

faulty and that it had been Ethel who taught with her mother at Lincoln School while Octavia taught at Douglas School. (This error along with several others is reflected in my book-length poem, "Octavia.")

Outside the church after the service, one couple introduced themselves and offered to show me the site of the present Faver High School, built there after the explosion. While I was talking to them, my eye happened to fall on the original cornerstone that read, to my surprise, "S.S. Jones, 1899." The minister who had evidently founded the family church in Guthrie was the same one who baptized my father as a youth, the same one that my father held dear as his spiritual father, who had visited Europe and the Holy Land in 1924–1925 with a movie camera and came to visit us the following year, taking moving pictures of us.

I kept returning to the house on Drexel Street, learning from a white neighbor that people in Guthrie remodeled old houses instead of tearing them down. He showed me through his own house, pointing out the changes he was making, and told me when I was most likely to find someone at home across the street. I was eventually successful.

When the door was finally answered by a young Caucasian woman whose family now lives there, I showed her the 1910 photograph of her house, along with a letter with that return address and explained my interest. It took her a few minutes to catch on to what I was saying. Then she became quite excited. She and her husband have since purchased the house and, on my second visit, permitted me to see the papers dealing with the title, but at that time they were renting. She put me in touch with the owner who had always assumed that the house was built in the 1920s. The occupant would not permit me to go through the house because she wanted to clean up first, but eventually I was allowed to explore and take pictures.

I assumed that the bedroom on the front of the house downstairs had been my grandmother's and that Robert, the youngest, had occupied the tiny room off from the living room. The stairway led to a single room on the second floor not visible from the street. It is a pleasant, sunny room looking out on the back yard. In it is an alcove with a built-in ledge that could easily be used for a bed. Some of the original plaster was still visible near the ceiling. I feel certain that Octavia and Ethel shared this room for the short period after they moved from Second Street and before Ethel's wedding. I feel that this was the room where Octavia anguished, experienced fits of bitterness or anger, and suffered the loneliness caused by her sister's departure until the time she went to Washington and entered into a brief marriage that ended about the time Faver High School was completed.

During my week in Guthrie, I retraced what I believed was probably Octavia's route to Lincoln School, which no longer exists. I retraced Dad's steps from the house on Second Street to the little railroad station a few short blocks away, still unchanged from the way it must have looked that day in 1909 when he left home to attend Virginia Union University. He often told the story of leaving Guthrie with one suit to his name, a summer suit in the winter, his other belongings in a cardboard suitcase. Arriving in Richmond with only 25 dollars, he went to the president and told him he had no money but wanted an education and was willing to work at whatever jobs were available to pay for his tuition. The president put him to work and let him stay. The next year he got his brother Robert in under the same conditions. Eventually Dad was able to pick up extra money by preaching in country churches.

The summer that I was writing the book, Leonard and I drove east to visit relatives. I put a typewriter in the trunk of the car, and everywhere we stayed, I set up the typewriter and worked—at his daughter Sharilyn's house in Westfield, New Jersey, my brother's house in New Rochelle, and my sister-in-law's house in Washington. Being among relatives and sharing the poems helped me to write. Their interest spurred me on. What I could not support with letters, information I had acquired in Guthrie, and matters I had heard discussed during my childhood was written purely from my imagination.

Dad had saved numerous photographs which included what I assumed to be Octavia's high school graduating class. As there were only about five African American students in the class, along with some Native Americans, I supposed that the school was in Kansas, which was more advanced than a number of other southwestern states, and the family had once lived there. A name, which I thought was the school's, was printed on the bottom of the picture. I called all over Kansas trying to identify it to no avail. I later learned that the name was not the school's but the photographer's.

I appended to the poems some family photographs, short biographies, and a chart listing birth and death dates of family members and their offspring, beginning with my grandparents. *Octavia and Other Poems* was published by Third World Press In 1988.

After the book was published I returned to Guthrie to read at the Oklahoma Territorial Museum. Since my first visit, two of Octavia's former students had died, and two more were out of town, but one, then in her nineties, attended the reading. I had sent copies of the book to those who were a part of it, one of whom was the couple I had met the year before at the family church. They were also present, along with the Native American woman who worked at the museum and her son, who presented me with a pair of beaded earrings she had made for me.

Before the reading, the lady from church called me to tell me about surgery she had had many years earlier which left her unable to stand or walk straight. She described the substandard conditions to which black patients were subjected in the local hospital. "When I read the poem about your sick aunt being confined to a damp barn," she said, "I immediately understood her feelings as you described them, because they were the same feelings I experienced at the hospital." Others have indicated to me their identification with certain parts in the poem, and I am deeply moved by their words.

Before returning to Guthrie I had indicated to the curator at the museum that, if one of the tentatively placed boards could be removed, I would like to go inside the house on Second Street. The evening before I left for home, I waited at the museum while he made copies of some of the old photographs. He said, "By the way, did you go around to the back of the house?" I said I hadn't. He replied, "Well, it's open." He asked me if I had anyone to go inside with me. I didn't. He offered to accompany me there. Along the way we stopped to get a battery for his flashlight.

Standing inside that tiny shack was an extremely emotional experience. There were only four small rooms, one of which was a bathroom, which I'm sure did not exist when my father's family lived there. Where could five people sleep and still find space for a piano? Yet this had been the most permanent residence in my father's life as he was growing up.

In my parents' last years in Detroit, they were cared for around the clock by two women who took turns staying with them. One of them, Lillie Mae Jackson, had received little formal education but was very intelligent. Knowing that she would know how to handle any emergency, I felt free to go to Europe with Leonard for three weeks, showing her where I had put the payment for each week's service. She was very fond of Dad and had met Uncle Robert when he came for a visit.

So when she read a feature story about the book in the news-paper, she called to say that she wanted a copy. When she came by to get it, she said: "I don't read much, especially poetry, but I'll put the book on my shelf and treasure it." I said, "Don't do that. Start at the beginning and don't skip around. Read it!" A few days later she called me and said in amazement, "How did you do that! I started reading the book and couldn't put it down. I felt like I was there." I still consider this the most significant compliment I have ever received concerning the book.

In 1988 *Octavia and Other Poems* was selected as co-winner of the College Language Association's Creative Achievement Award, along with a collection of poetry by Pinkie Gordon Lane. During the same year, Detroit Public Schools made it required reading for high school students. Each public high school ordered a set. It was the first time that a collection of poetry had this honor, and to date, I have heard of no other.

Riverlight, an organization in Battle Creek, wrote a script based on "Octavia" and invited me to come for a week of workshops and presentation of a documentary film we would produce. I stayed in the historic Kellogg House. In the video, one young man read the male voices and I read the female voices. I was not entirely pleased with the results but appreciated the effort.

Then John Prusak, a filmmaker I had met at workshops in which we both participated, expressed an interest in creating a film about me, along with his partner, Kathy Vander. At first it lacked focus, and I felt frustrated because the reels of film ran out so fast that I didn't have sufficient time to answer questions. It eventually occurred to Kathy that a documentary film could be made based on "Octavia." Knowing that I had received the Michigan Artist Award (also known as the Governor's Artist Award), she asked for and received permission to film the ceremony which took place at the Detroit Institute of Arts on October 28, 1993. Even though the sponsoring organization has changed, to date no other poet has won the Michigan Artist Award.

During the reception preceding the ceremony, I heard that James Earl Jones was present. "You mean I'm supposed to make a speech in front of James Earl Jones?" I exclaimed. He was not on the program but had an engagement the next day in Ann Arbor. His only function was to escort sculptor Marshall Fredericks, who was feeble, across the stage to receive a Lifetime Achievement Award. I had written out my acceptance speech so that I wouldn't forget what I wanted to say. It read:

Poetry is probably the most neglected of all the arts; yet it holds a place of distinction in the souls of people everywhere, even when they're not aware of it. Many who claim they don't like or understand it are nevertheless moved at times by vocal music, without realizing that the song that sends their spirit soaring cannot be sung unless some poet writes the words.

Poetry reaches to the depth and breadth of human experience, expressing our loftiest aspirations, our greatest joys, our ~~must~~ crushing disap- *most* pointments. It sustains us through our most devastating griefs.

Following the assassination of President John F. Kennedy, the *New York Times* received hundreds of original poems, many from people who had never tried to write poetry before, indicating the emotional need that this art form fulfills. Torn from the shores of Africa, how would slaves have survived their dehumanization in an alien land except through the noble poetry of their spirituals? And who of us today, in our own hour of need, has not turned to the poetry of the Psalms for comfort? Who has never been sustained, uplifted by the words of some more modern David who interprets the human condition as most of us cannot do for ourselves?

So I feel humble this evening—and deeply grateful—that my lifelong dedication to poetry, spanning more than half a century, is being recognized and honored by Governor Engler and the Concerned Citizens for the Arts in Michigan.

On behalf of all my fellow poets who have contributed so much to the spirit that makes us human, I thank you all.

When the program was over I had a chance to talk to Mr. Jones in the back of the auditorium. He said, "I had never heard the story about the poems sent to the *New York Times*, but it confirms what I have always believed, that poetry is a universal language." While we were conversing, Kathy joined us and asked Mr. Jones if he would agree to be filmed standing beside me and say a few words about what poetry means to him. He graciously agreed.

Vander Films received a grant to film, *A Poet's Voice*, which includes this cameo appearance of James Earl Jones taken at the awards ceremony, and combines my reading and discussion of poems from the book with music and ten local artists' interpretations of the poems. When the film, transferred to videotape, premiered at the Scarab Club in Detroit, there was standing room only. This film was nominated for an Emmy and received the Gold Apple Award of Excellence from the National Educational Media Network. It has been aired on public television and continues to be shown with some regularity on local cable.

Before the third printing of *Octavia and Other Poems* was published, I was searching for something I had put in my father's filing cabinet, thinking that I had removed all the items he had left. To my surprise, I found a number of documents rolled up in the back of one drawer. Among them were Octavia's 1904 high school diploma from Lawrence High School in Lawrence, Kansas, her 1909 diploma from the University of Kansas, and some of her teaching certificates.

In October, 1989 I was requested to read at the University of Kansas. Dr. George Wedge picked me up at the airport in Kansas City to take me to his home. Knowing that I wanted to continue research on Octavia, as well as Langston Hughes, he invited me to spend a week with him and his wife Margaret. On the way to Lawrence, we passed a sign that read "Hugoton." I mentioned that my grandmother's farm was in Hugoton. He said, "That's oil country." I assumed that the land provided to the other members of the family as part Indians was also in Hugoton. Dr. Wedge's remark gave credence to my brother's saying that oil had been found on Octavia's land. If that was true and she sold her land, that would account for her having enough money to attend high school in Lawrence and graduate from the University of Kansas in 1909.

I read from *Octavia and Other Poems* on the evening of October 23 in the Jayhawk Room, Kansas Union. Then I did a second reading on October 26 in the Alderson Auditorium, Kansas Union, with five poets from Kansas City.

Professor Wedge provided me with the use of a car and showed me how to get around the city and the campus. It was difficult to find, but I finally did locate Octavia's high school class card, which listed her address as Hot Springs, Arkansas, an indication that her father must have provided some financial support. The principal made a copy of this record for me.

On campus I was able to find Octavia's yearbook, *The Jayhawker*, 1909. Her photograph was placed, not alphabetically with the white students in the College of Liberal Arts, but at the back of the section, along with the two other black students in her curriculum. Her photograph in the yearbook is the same one that I had kept on my dresser while I was writing the book and used on the front cover. Beneath her picture were the words: "A hard working student, always striving for the best grade in her class."

When only a few copies of the original book were left, Lotus Press reprinted the title poem without the "Other Poems" in 2002 under the title, *Octavia: Guthrie and Beyond*. For this edition I wrote an introduction and, having done further research, especially on my grandfather, updated the appended biographical information and the chart of births and deaths.

While I was writing "Octavia," one of my father's former church members in New Rochelle said, "I wish your father had lived long enough to know that you visited his home." Somehow, I think he does know, and I hope that my poetic record of part of his family history helps to compensate for the empty notebooks he left behind.

VIII.
Family Matters

Paternal grandparents,
Frank Cornelius Long
and
Sallie E.K. Mumphord Long

In Search of Grampa Long

Having become involved in family history through the poetic recreation of Octavia's life, my curiosity about my paternal grandfather increased. Who was this man who had dragged his wife and children all over the Southwest, never seemingly satisfied in one place, moving them to Guthrie, Oklahoma where he was principal of a black elementary school for only one year, then leaving the family there while he moved on?

Early in my life I had heard my father speak proudly of his accomplishments. I knew, for instance, that he was born in New Orleans where he was the first male graduate of Leland University. I knew that was where he met my grandmother, also a student there. I also knew that he had been the first full-time black instructor at Bishop College in Marshall, Texas and that he had "built" a high school in Hot Springs, Arkansas, which he served as principal. I had often seen his picture, and I knew that a large copy of this photograph was hanging in one of the libraries at Bishop College. I remembered his death in 1928 when we were forced to sit in silence during the hour of his funeral. I was told that he was in his seventies when he died. I had no other dates, however, and, except for my interest in Octavia, probably would not have been curious to learn more about him. I never heard my father say anything negative about him, but it was his mother that he spoke of with highest praise, the parent who had held the family together and made do with little after Grampa followed other pursuits. I knew that Rev. S.S. Jones, who had baptized my father as a boy, once signed himself "Your other, better second father" and was more of a real father to him than Grampa Long was. Grampa's letters, in which a great deal of his personality and values were apparent, became the basis for some of the poems in "Octavia."

Among Dad's papers I had found some of his father's notebooks containing sermons, a class book, several of his personal books, and a copy of his transcript from Leland University. I was eager to learn more about him.

I decided to spend a week in New Orleans to discover what I could. Leland University had moved from New Orleans to a different location after he left and eventually closed. Nobody seemed to know what happened to the records, but before my husband and I left Detroit, I was put in touch with a woman who told me that a few of the Leland University papers had been found in an old drawer somewhere and were purchased for the Archives and Manuscripts Department of the Earl K. Long Library of the University of New Orleans. (No known family relationship.) Upon arrival, this was the first place we went.

After I signed the necessary forms to examine these papers, I was brought two small boxes of material. The first one contained a hardcover ledger in which were recorded students' names, dates of enrollment, places of birth, dates of conversion to Christianity, and dates and places of baptism and baptizing ministers' names, along with a notation of whether or not the ministers were ordained. Most of this information was handwritten, apparently by the same person, but the students' names were in their own handwriting. On the first page I was elated to find the signature of Frank C. Long. From this ledger I learned that he entered Leland University in October, 1876, was born March 2, 1857 in New Orleans, became a Christian December 28, 1874, and was baptized in Augusta, Georgia in January, 1875 by Henry Watts, an ordained minister.

Flipping over a few pages, I found that Sallie E.K. Mumphord, my grandmother, had entered Leland University in December, 1878, was born in DeWitt County, Texas on April 27, 1860, became a Christian in 1871 and was baptized February 7 of that year in Victoria, Texas by Mitchell Harrison. What a find! I noticed that a large number of the New Orleans students had been baptized by the same ordained minister, George W. Walker. None of the other material in that narrow box was helpful.

In the second box, which held no other pertinent information, I found a printed program. It was one folded page whose cover read:

"The Annual Exhibition of The Ciceronian Literary Society of Leland University at Austerlitz Street Church, Tuesday, May 24, 1881." The program printed inside included prayer, music by a chorus, speeches and recitations, a debate ("Shall the President of the U.S. be elected for Life?"), a bass solo, a song, music by a male chorus, and a tenor solo by F.C. Long, "The Ivy Green." The final address was "Farewell" by Sallie Mumphord. I was ecstatic.

I have no knowledge of what my grandfather was doing in Augusta, Georgia, but a letter written to my father during his later illness saying that he might seek medical assistance in a government hospital suggests that he might have spent some time in government service.

From another source (*Standard History of New Orleans* edited by Henry Richton (Chicago: The Lewis Publishing Company, 1900, page 246), I learned that Leland University was located near the present site of Tulane University on the corner of St. Charles Avenue and Audabon Street. It was founded in 1870 by Holbrook Chamberlain, who retired as a shoe merchant in Brooklyn, New York and moved to New Orleans the same year. Leland received aid from the Freedman's Bureau and the American Baptist Mission Society. It offered both a preparatory program and college courses, and there was no charge for attending except for the instrumental music program and a small fee for fuel and care of students' rooms.

Another important source of information about Grampa Long was the copy of his Leland University transcript which Dad had kept. This copy was made by C.A. Priestley, registrar, on June 27, 1916. It indicated that Grampa's curriculum included mathematics, history, science, philosophy, literature, composition and rhetoric, six courses in Greek, seven in Latin, and three in German. He maintained close to a 4.0 grade point average. To this copy is appended Priestley's typewritten notation: "Mr. Long spent eight years at Leland University, after which he did two years post-graduate work at University of Michigan (Ann Arbor), and two years work in education at Kansas State Normal. This institution, in addition to his scholarship Degree A.B. in course of time conferred A.M. upon him, merited by his long training and tireless service in the schools of the South." The eight-year stay mentioned here does not correspond with the ledger information. Perhaps he took preparatory courses before being considered a student on the college level. I can't really explain the difference.

From a local resident I learned that Leland University had a connection with Austerlitz Church whose pastor was the minister who baptized many of the Leland students listed in the ledger. One entry in the New Orleans city directory lists F.C. Long's address as W. Austerlitz with the abbreviation "clk" after his name, indicating that he possibly worked for the church as a clerk and lived nearby.

My husband and I made a trip to the church, which was closed during the week, and took pictures of the exterior and the signs outside listing its founder and early ministers. During a Sunday morning visit to the church several years later, I saw a photograph of this former pastor on the wall. I was hoping to learn more of the history of the church, but nobody there seemed to know as much about it as I did.

The day after our visit to the University of New Orleans, Leonard and I went to the Amistad Research Center. I didn't expect to find much information since this institution is relatively new, but I did think there would be something about Leland University. The employee in attendance was as helpful as he could be but found nothing about my grandfather or about the university that was a part of New Orleans history. We had walked such a long distance from the streetcar to the center that my husband sat down to rest while I browsed randomly through books on the shelves. The employee kept asking me questions and looking for information, always coming back empty-handed. Then he asked me if I knew when Grampa died, and I told him 1928. A few minutes later he asked, "Frank Cornelius Long?" "Yes!" I shouted. He had found him listed in *Who's Who of the Colored Race,* published in 1915.

In this entry, he is listed as clergyman and teacher. Contrary to the year of birth in the Leland records, it is listed here as March 2, 1860. Due to his seeking a different position in 1915, I think he deliberately indicated that he was younger than he was, and I am inclined to believe that the 1857 date is the accurate one. His parents are listed as Alexander Dumas Long and Anna Mae (Hawkins) Long, information that I'm certain my father didn't have. The entry also indicates that he was educated in the public schools of New Orleans and was the first male graduate of Leland University in 1881, "A.M. later." He also lists "post-grad. Courses Univ. of Mich. and Kan. State Normal School; B.D., Union Theological Seminary, Morgan Park, Ill, 1884; grad. Stenographic Inst., Chicago, 1900; married Sarah E. Mumford [note change in the spelling of her name], of Victoria, Texas, June, 1881." Then the four children's names are listed. The entry continues: "Was first colored teacher in Bishop College, Marshall, Texas, serving as instructor of mathematics, 1881-2; principal Langston High School, Hot Springs, Ark., since 1907; this is a first-class Colored High School; its course covers 4 years each in Latin, English, science, history, mathematics; graduates have easily found entrance into freshmen classes of leading American colleges. Republican. Baptist. Member Knights of Pythias, Knights of Honor, United Brothers of Friendship, Mosaic Templars. Home: 132 Silver St., Hot Springs, Ark.:

According to an article in *The Bishop Herald* by Dr. Melvin J. Banks (Volume 96, No. 1, Summer 1977):

> The first faculty consisted of five full time teachers, a student assistant, and a matron of girls. With the exception of one teacher and the student assistant, they were white and came from the East and middle West. Their coming caused great excitement among Negro Baptists of Texas. Abe Lincoln had freed their bodies and now they looked to this group to lead the way in the emancipation of their minds and spirits.

Under the heading, "Frank C. Long," the article continues:
> The first full-time Black teacher was Frank C. Long, a graduate of Leland University. He taught

English and penmanship. He insisted upon exactness in oral and written expression. He was a stickler for correctness in grammar and the best manners in stage decorum.

Long and the President sponsored the Marston Literary and Debating Society which met every Friday evening. These meetings were educational and inspirational. The critic's report was scathing. Grammatical errors were pointed out. The manner in which the speakers presented themselves was a subject of rigid analysis. Many a country lad was inspired by this erudite Black teacher. Although he was with the College for only a year, leaving for graduate study at Chicago, Frank C. Long left a deep impression upon those who studied with him.

Family letters indicate that he had one brother, or perhaps a half brother, named Robert Johnson who died, leaving a wife and six children. (He may have been a full brother, even though his last name was different because women who remarried often unofficially changed their existing children's last names to the name of the second husband.)

Grampa's reason for leaving Bishop was evidently to pursue a degree in theology, in which he earned a Bachelor of Divinity degree in 1884. I don't know whether his wife was with him in the Chicago area or elsewhere completing her own education. I am also unaware of how long it took him to complete the requirements for graduation from the Stenographic Institute of Chicago in 1900 and where he spent the intervening years.

It is probable that the couple moved several times during the birth of their four children: Octavia Cornelia, born in Waco, Texas in 1885; Ethel Elizabeth, born 1887 in Waco; Clarence Marcellus, my father, at his maternal grandmother's house in Victoria, Texas in 1888; and Robert Elliott in Fort Smith, Arkansas in 1892. Other cities of residence mentioned in my father's notes were Independence, Missouri and Emporia, Kansas.

Records kept by street address in the Oklahoma Territorial Museum indicate that "F.C. Long, colored" was principal of

Lincoln School in Guthrie, Oklahoma in 1900, residing on Mansur Avenue between Fourth and Fifth streets. No further city records mention him. Perhaps his family joined him shortly after his move to Guthrie. It is possible that he never completed the year as principal and left Guthrie before it was over.

When Grampa left Guthrie, I can only speculate on the reason his family did not join him. It seems likely that my grandmother was simply tired of moving and wished to settle down and provide a stable home for her children. I can imagine her saying to him, "I don't know why you can't be satisfied in one place, but if you feel you have to move on again, please feel free to do so. The girls and I can teach here and find some stability."

Having successfully completed her normal school training, Grandma Long taught kindergarten and first grade at Lincoln School for a number of years. In due time, Ethel joined her, while Octavia, after graduating from the University of Kansas with a Bachelor of Arts in English and taking additional courses and teaching at Bishop College, taught fifth grade at Douglas School, the other of the two black elementary schools in town. Then, when Faver High School, the first high school for black students, was built in 1912, she taught English there. While Grampa kept in close touch with his children and expressed concern about their progress, he never lived with the family again.

The school in Hot Springs where Grampa was principal originally contained elementary grades and was named Rugg Street School. In 1984 when we visited there, an elderly resident with whom I spoke remembered his year in first grade and described Grampa as a strict disciplinarian, a distinguished gentleman with a cultured voice, silvery hair, and dignified bearing who often punished him for mischief.

In 1913 a fire destroyed the Rugg Street School and the Hot Springs high school, evidently housed in the same building. In 1914, still under Grampa's administration, "a rather imposing building was erected on Silver Street and was renamed Langston High School in honor of John Mercer Langston, a black United States Congressman during Reconstruction and great-uncle of poet Langston Hughes."

Perhaps no longer feeling challenged after the completion of the new building, Grampa began seeking other employment. During the year 1915-1916, he seems to have applied for the position of principal of the normal school in Pine Bluff (now University of Arkansas at Pine Bluff), soliciting letters of recommendation from influential persons. But for some reason I do not know, he never worked there. It is difficult to imagine that he could have been rejected in view of the many letters written in his behalf expressing highest praise. Could he have appeared too erudite to some who were in position to influence the decision?

A letter from a member of the Board of Directors of the Hot Springs School Board, dated March 29, 1916, states: "It is largely due to [Long's] untiring efforts that the school was built up until it is considered among the best in the states." He is described here as "well educated, an earnest worker, a good organizer, and has a great many friends here who are delighted to see him advance in his chosen profession."

Mr. J.W. McClendon, mayor of Hot Springs, also recommended him in a June 26, 1915 letter, stating: "His work as teacher, principal and organizer is of a superior order and commands the highest respect and commendation of all citizens. He is a college graduate, a christian *(sic)*, well connected socially and fraternally and his community interests are very marked. I cheerfully recommend him to any Board of Trustees desiring to employ a man with the foregoing qualifications." And George B. Cook, superintendent of the State of Arkansas Department of Education, also wrote a very positive recommendation.

My grandmother having died in Guthrie on April 21, 1914 and her body returned to her native Victoria for burial beside her mother, Grampa soon married Sarah Baker, an employee of one of the white bath houses in Hot Springs. In what appears to be a pattern of leaving his wives behind, he moved without her to Memphis, Tennessee sometime in 1915 or 1916. There he taught but may not have been certified as a principal until 1922. His class records and notebooks reveal the high standards to which he held his students, his disappointment in the performance of many, and his sometimes scathing remarks about their lack of preparation.

In 1924 he was incapacitated by the first of a series of paralyzing strokes. His wife brought him back to Hot Springs and cared for him with tenderness and deep concern in their rented house at 215 Silver Street. Under considerable financial strain, she moved him to 6 Helem Street, a house owned by her family, to avoid the necessity of paying rent.

Frank C. Long died on November 15, 1928 and was buried in Greenwood Cemetery in a section then owned by two black churches, one of which was Union Baptist Church of which he was a member. While my father's notes mention a marker, his wife's niece believed that there was none, reporting that, when Sarah Baker Long died in 1967, her family could not afford a memorial stone but buried her beside my grandfather with both graves unmarked.

When I returned to Arkansas ten years after my initial visit, my search for Grampa Long's grave turned out to be as easy as it had been difficult before. One call to the cemetery, now managed by a different company, brought the information that there were indeed records and that, when we arrived, we would be shown to the grave site. This part of the cemetery was now so well kept that we couldn't recognize it as the same area where we had stood before. While the second Mrs. Long's niece had not been aware of it, someone (probably Dad) had placed stones at the heads of both Grampa and his wife, whom Dad loved for the care she had given Grampa during his lengthy illness.

I leaned down and touched the broken stone, slick with rain.

405

Then we went back to the manager's office and looked through catalogs to find the proper new stone for this man whose educational accomplishments had been as overlooked in books as they were minimized on the stone that identified him only as "husband of Sarah Long." I arranged for the original marker to be shipped to me; that slab of broken marble is now buried in my backyard. I didn't want some future scholar to find the original stone cast away in another location and think that that was his burial site. At the head of his grave now stands a proper monument that reads:

Frank Cornelius Long
1857-1928
Pioneer Educator

The story in not over, though. There are many more questions left unanswered. What was Grampa doing those years before he enrolled at Leland University? Why was he in Augusta, Georgia? How did he qualify for care in a government hospital? Who was Alexander Dumas Long, his father? This was evidently where the French blood came from. Was my great-grandfather related to Alexandre Dumas, father and son, celebrated French writers of African descent? If not, what kind of education provided Grampa's parents with the knowledge of who the original Alexandre Dumas was that they should name their son after him?

On the other hand, Dumas is a very common name in New Orleans, and the descendants of many of those who bear it, I have been told, came to the United States from France by way of Haiti. Every answer leads to more questions. Will the quest ever end? I never thought it would happen to me, but when the genealogy bug bites, it bites hard and relentlessly, and there is no cure except to continue the search.

I learned much more about Grampa's personality from family letters than from any other source, not all of them positive. In one letter that he wrote to Dad in 1909 from Hot Springs, he stated his delight that Dad planned to enter the ministry but expressed doubt that he could qualify for admission to the "Union Theological College" (Virginia Union University), to which he had applied. He further stated, in reference to Octavia's imminent graduation from the University of Kansas: "She is the only child of the family that I ever expect to see graduate from college, for the rest of you have not put the same value on education as she has." Nevertheless, in a letter he wrote Octavia in 1912, he cautioned her about her careless usage, suggesting that she review a good grammar handbook lest people with less education than she make unpleasant remarks about her speech.

Once Dad had been admitted to Virginia Union University, Grampa urged him to attend Harvard or Yale after he was finished there. He later congratulated him on his grades. In spite of Grampa's stated doubts, Dad earned three academic degrees and received an honorary Doctor of Divinity, and Robert was graduated from Meharry Medical College and became a physician. Had their father's negative expectations spurred them to prove him wrong?

While he was apparently never the pastor of a church, preaching only on occasion, Grampa held certain views about the delivery of sermons. His absence from the pulpit on a regular basis may not have been by preference; his style might well have been too scholarly for the tastes of the people. ("I am always dignified," he wrote in 1910, "and try to impress my hearers with the fact that I am somewhat trained and learned.") He cautioned my father to avoid "the whining or moaning habit of preaching" characteristic of many black preachers who were less educated. In another letter he criticized a preacher named Watson for having "too much of the nigger whine" in his sermons. Somewhat like William Edward Burghardt DuBois, he seemed not to have the common touch, nor did he seem to appreciate even from afar, as DuBois did, "the souls of black folk." Yet he as surely earned his place in history for stretching (and sometimes embarrassing) black youth toward excellence, accepting nothing less than their best, for heading a first-class educational institution which moved its students upward, for being the first male to graduate from Leland University, and for becoming the first African American to teach at Bishop College. He set a family standard that has been passed on to all the succeeding generations of the Long family who have from childhood viewed the attainment of a college education as an expectation.

Lineage

According to recently reviewed 1870 census records, Sarah Mumford, age 10, was one of a number of children born to Claiborne and Elizabeth Mumford. (Census takers were not always careful to spell names correctly.) Her age agrees with Leland University records that state her birth date as April 27, 1860 in DeWitt County, Texas. Her place of birth is also listed as Victoria, Texas, where her mother lived and where both are buried. Both parents are listed as mulatto, both originally from Virginia. I always assumed that her father was a Cherokee Indian, whether full-blooded or not, and he still may have been since people, either black or white, with Indian blood were classified as mulattos. Sarah or Sallie had a half sister with the last name of Arthur who had at least two children that I know of, James and DeLois. I have been told that Sallie's mother, my great-grandmother, was once a slave.

The 1880 census indicates that Sallie E.K. Mumphord, the name and spelling she used in the Leland University listing, was living in Texana, Texas with a family named Jackson and teaching there. Did she leave Leland University and then return in time for the May, 1881 program at Austerlitz Street Baptist Church?

In 1910 Sallie sold her farm, evidently in order to buy the house on Drexel Street in Guthrie where Ethel married shortly after the move.

Next to Octavia Cornelia, the eldest child who had no known children, was Ethel Elizabeth (1887-1965) who married William Johnson from Xenia, Ohio. They lived in Brooklyn for some years before moving to the campus of Wilberforce University where he worked as custodian of buildings and grounds, church side. (Wilberforce had the equivalent of two colleges on the same campus, but they were both a part of Wilberforce. One was "state side" and the other "church side." They have since divided into two universities, "state side" becoming Central State University.) William and Ethel had three sons. Harold Eugene (1912-1981), the

409

eldest, married Camille Cotter Taylor, and together they had two children. Sylvia Penelope Johnson (1947-   ) married Robert Aulston, and they had three sons, Alexander McKenzie (1973-   ), Damon Taylor (1977-), and Nicholas Jay (1980-   ). The second child, Harold, Jr., married Cathrine Berry, and they had one son, James Morris (1987-   ). Kenneth Lowell married Evelyn Belle Lewis, and together they had two children: Kenneth, Jr. 1944-   ) who married Mary Dell Parker, having together a son Kenneth, III (1971-   ) and Marilyn Elaine (1949-1978). The youngest son, William, Jr., (c. 1920-1972) married, but no one seems to know his wife's name. They had one son, William Eugene, III (c. 1950-   ).

My father, Clarence Marcellus, married Maude Selena Hilton of Richmond, and together they had three children. Clarence, Jr. (1918-1978) married Laverne Stansbury, and they had three children. Cheryl Marie (1949-), the eldest, has not married and serves as a federal judge in Superior Court in Washington, DC. Patricia Ann (1950-), an assistant superintendent of schools in Washington, DC, married Michael Wyatt Tucker, and they became the parents of one son, Michael, II (1976-). Clarence, III was married and divorced and has no children. Wilbur Franklin (1920-1998), the second son, married Katie Marie Butler and together they had two daughters. Kathy Etolia (1956-1997) married Severol Antonio Bonilla and together they had two daughters, Victoria Marie (1990-) and Alexandra Antonia (1992-). Karen Octavia (1958-), a marine biologist, married Peter C. Rowe, and together they had one son, Cody Quentin (1996-). I married Julian Fields Witherspoon and together we had one child, Jill Annette (1947-). Jill married Edward Jay Boyer and together they had one daughter, Liliana Malaika (1975-). My grandparents' fourth child, Robert Elliot, married Shirley (maiden name unknown). They had no children,

Although I've known my mother's family all my life, I know little about the names of generations earlier than my grandparents. Grampa Hilton was a slim, dark-skinned man with keen features. He was shorter than my grandmother. I have only one snapshot of him, but I remember him from our annual visits to Richmond. His name was Sidney Ham Hilton (1855-1929), and he was self-employed as a roof tinner. His mother's name was Martha. I assume her last name was Hilton, too, but I can't be sure. It is likely that both Grampa Hilton and his parents had been slaves. I recall seeing him come home from work and deposit his tools in the brick house behind the main one at 747 North Fifth Street. I don't remember anything about his personality. I was six years years old when he died. My mother and I went to Richmond for his funeral which took place in the living room, where his body had lain in state. The younger grandchildren were dressed in white but were not allowed to go downstairs for the ceremony. We did go to the burial. My cousin, Giles ("Bubba") cried profusely when Grampa was buried. In those days the family watched while the casket was lowered into the earth.

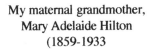

My maternal grandmother,
Mary Adelaide Hilton
(1859-1933

Grampa and Grandma Hilton

I didn't know until I was grown that Grandma, born Mary Adelaide Saunders (1859-1933), also known as Addie, had a white father. She was light-skinned and had fairly straight hair. It is possible that her mother, Mary Jane, was a slave. Whether Saunders was her own last name or the name of the slave owner I don't know. I probably saw my white great-grandfather on one or more of my visits there but didn't know who he was. He visited her and kept in touch, and I was told that he gave her a great deal of the furniture in the house. Grandma worked as a practical nurse. Her mother married Jefferson Mosby and they lived on Decatur Street in South Richmond where my mother was born. Grandma was raised by her mother and stepfather who was the father of Uncle Junius Mosby whom I remember.

Sidney, Jr., the eldest of the Hilton children, left home and lived in Philadelphia where he died young and was buried before his youngest sibling was born. My mother, Maude Selena (1886-1982), was the second born. We always thought she was born August 2, 1888, but documents I found after her death indicate that she was born two years earlier. Bessie was the third child, but she seemed older than Mama because she was crippled by rheumatoid arthritis. She looked more Indian than any of the others and had long, wavy hair. She married Roscoe Jackson whose father, Giles Beecher Jackson, was famous. They had four children. Eleanor, the first born, married Sylvius ("Sid") Moore who taught and was a coach at Hampton Institute. They had one son, Sylvius, Jr. When I tried to compile a family record, young Sid was not interested in supplying information. He has been married three times, I think, and has several children by at least two of his wives, and grandchildren whose names I don't know. Ruth (1914   —) and her twin were born next; the twin died soon after birth. Ruth was so faithful in caring for her mother that she didn't marry until she was past forty when she met and married William Paxton who had moved next door with his mother. They had a very happy marriage that lasted many years until his death. They had no children. Giles Beecher Jackson, II was the last born. With the encouragement and financial assistance of Aunt Minnie, he became a lawyer and a judge in California. He married Gwendolyn Lackey, and together they had three children, Mignon, and twins Yvonne and Yvette. The marriage ended in divorce, and he later remarried Mary Jackson ("Ever"). They had no children together.

Minnie Cornelia was the next born of the Hilton children. She never married. She taught the early elementary grades in Richmond public schools and cared for my grandparents during their illness.

Sadie Mae was the next born. She married Jacob Milton Sampson, a lawyer, who taught at Virginia Union University. I believe his father was a white man who left him a great deal of property. Sadie and Milton had one daughter, Helen Mae, who married John Brooks, and they had one son, Milton Earl, who married and had two daughters, one of whom died as a young child. Milton and his family moved to Chicago where he evidently thought he could earn more as a lawyer, but he did not do well. When he needed money, he sold one of the houses he had inherited. Sadie pleaded with him not to sell the last one in which Helen was born, but he sold that one, too. It seems that Sadie and Milton's marriage was dominated by his mother. Sadie divorced him and brought Helen to live with us in East Orange. After they moved back to Richmond, Milton went back, too. When Helen was ready to begin college, Milton and Sadie remarried. He got a job as manager of a housing complex on Charity Street to which the family moved.

Wilbur Ellsworth, the "Billboard" of my childhood, was the youngest of the Hilton children, born thirteen years after my mother. He formed a half generation between his sisters and my older cousins, Eleanor and Ruth. He worked most of his life in New York as a personal courier for the Standard Oil Company. He married Estelle Victoria Morton, a registered nurse from Brooklyn, and bought a home on Long Island. After Vicky's death he remarried but soon divorced. He had no children. After retirement he moved back to Richmond where he lived the remainder of his life.

When Octavia died in 1920, Dad and Mama's parents bought a burial plot together in Mt. Olivet Cemetery in Richmond. In the center is a marker with Long on one side and Hilton on the other. Grampa and Grandma Hilton, Minnie, and Wilbur are buried on the Hilton side. On the Long side are buried Octavia and both my parents. It is there that I intend to be buried.

The family burial plot in Richmond, Octavia's headstone on the right

Lessons

My father was the greatest single influence on my life. Whether I was born with a disposition like his or developed it because of my admiration I don't know. I suspect it was a combination of both. When I was in grammar school I talked about him so much that one of my classmates asked me if I had a mother. It was partly that he was constantly in the public eye as a minister and that he had such a great impact on other people's lives that I was tremendously proud of him and the respect that he commanded. I adored him and always wanted to be like him. Although as a teenager I came to realize that he was not perfect and thought of him as my god dethroned, and as an adult we often clashed because our personalities were so much alike, I have always been proud to identify myself as "Rev. Long's daughter."

I think his father's absence from home as he was growing up made him the good and responsible father that he was and made him determined to succeed to prove his father's low expectations wrong. His father lived long enough to witness Dad's success as a husband and father, a brilliant student, and a pastor of several prominent churches.

Dad had a somewhat complex personality. One of my high school friends saw him as stern as an Old Testament prophet. He could be stern. He demanded obedience and was always in complete charge of his household. As we were growing up, he sometimes reminded my brothers when they wanted to have their own way, "I'm running this ranch." He nevertheless encouraged and valued my mother's opinions. Sometimes when she disagreed with him on something, he would come back later and say, "Maude, yesterday you said [so-and-so], and I think you were right." He was also a disciplinarian. Mama never spanked us, leaving that job for him, but when she said, "I'm going to tell your daddy," we knew we were in for it. He shaved with a straight razor and kept a razor strap for sharpening it on a hook behind the bathroom door. When he whipped Clarence and Wil, this is what he used. If I was the offender, he spanked my bottom with his hand. But the spankings weren't nearly so dreaded as the reprimand that went with them. We wished he'd just spank us and get it over with, but a half hour later he'd think about the offense again and start fussing all over. When he cleared his throat and called you into his study and shut the door, you knew you were guilty of some major misdemeanor.

But he enjoyed playing, too. We weren't allowed to have playing cards in the house, even for trading, and we were forbidden to dance, but all of us played dominoes and checkers and did magic tricks with the boys' set. Dad couldn't resist joining my brothers and their friends in a game of baseball or horseshoes. And he liked to tickle me and make me laugh. One summer we played a game of tag that lasted all season. He often attended the Negro League baseball games in Newark, and several times he took me with him, leaving me in the park outside to play on the swings and slides.

He had a great sense of humor and liked to tell jokes. He enjoyed talking to people and was very outgoing and friendly. I used to like to listen to his conversations. We were not a hugging-kissing family, but Dad showed his affection for me in other ways. Often he'd touch his finger to his lips and blow me a kiss. I always knew I was Daddy's girl, but I was quite introverted and uncomfortable with demonstrations of affection. Sometimes Mama would say, "Don't be so touchous." (I think she made up the word but I knew what she meant.) It wasn't until I married Leonard that I became comfortable hugging and kissing family members and friends.

Having grown up in a female-dominated home with a working mother and two working older sisters, he believed in the equality of women although he sometimes showed signs of being a chauvinist. He thought that women should be feminine but believed in equal rights and encouraged them to pursue careers and be successful in them. He couldn't have been prouder when I became a professor. He encouraged Mama to take driving lessons so that she wouldn't have to depend on him for transportation. She took the lessons and got her driver's license but never used it. She preferred to walk or take the streetcar or bus when necessary.

Dad valued education highly. There was never any discussion about *if* we were going to college; it was taken for granted that we would. But he wanted no more for his children than he wanted for the children of other families. He was responsible for having at least three of the churches he pastored make sizable contributions to the educational expenses of members, including William Bailey, who eventually became pastor of Calvary in East Orange. He started the practice of including a "children's sermon" in the worship service. It consisted of a short narrative with a moral. While addressed to children, it was beneficial to adults as well. When Clarence became a minister, he continued this practice at his churches.

Perhaps because I spent more time in the house than the boys or he considered me more apt, Dad taught me many things including how to write a check properly, explaining the details. He also taught me a great deal about handling money. He urged all of us not to spend all that we had. If we had ten cents, he insisted that we save at least a penny. At that time the Woolworth Tower was the tallest building in the world, and he was quick to remind us that the Woolworth Tower was built on nickels and dimes. He also advised us to stay out of debt whenever we could, no matter how little we had. He didn't like to pay interest. He reminded us that the practice of borrowing and lending often led to a loss of friendship. And under no circumstance should we ever, ever cosign a loan for anyone, no matter how close the friend!

He didn't like to pay rent and believed firmly in home ownership. Except for my parents' generosity, I would not have been able to purchase my first house in Detroit and the present one which I have owned for 45 years now. He never made much money, but he knew how to manage what he had. "It isn't how much you have that matters," he'd say; "it's how well you handle it." I have taken those lessons to heart and have been able to do more with my meager salary as a single working parent and now with my pension than a number of professional couples I know whose combined incomes far exceed mine.

Dad also taught me how to write business letters and trusted me to compose them after summarizing what he wanted to say.

Sometimes when I needed information on something, Dad would tell me where to go to find it. At other times he told me what I needed to know. One summer in vacation Bible school I was assigned a report on Martin Luther about whom I knew nothing. He told me the story of the Reformation and Martin Luther's influence on the establishment of the Protestant Church.

I thought Dad was the best preacher I'd ever heard. From his sermons I learned a great deal about the organization of ideas and the effective use of language. I hung on his every word, and some of his phrases found their way into my early poems. As for singing, he could carry a tune and stay on key, but that was about all. He encouraged young ministers who sang well to use this talent in their sermons. I think the only time Dad ever sang during a sermon came as a complete surprise. When he nodded to the organist in New Rochelle, Mama said, "Oh, my God! Don't tell me he's going to try to sing!" But the hymn he chose was very appropriate to the point he was making, and his solo, ordinary as his voice was, proved quite effective.

Dad didn't allow us to use poor grammar. If he was in the bathroom with the door closed and I knocked, he'd ask, "Who is it?" If I answered, "It's me," he corrected me. The open sesame was "It's I."

My father taught me integrity. He pointed out the difference between reputation and character. If you developed good character, that was all that mattered, no matter what people said about you. You must always do the right thing even when you know that no one is watching you and you're certain you won't get caught. When we were teenagers, we seldom left the house to attend a social function

419

without Dad's admonition, "Remember who you are." Sometimes I wondered if he didn't really mean to remember who *he* was so that we wouldn't do anything to reflect negatively on him. There were times that one or the other of us failed to take his advice and, if caught in some indiscretion, told lies as big as a whale to try to conceal our guilt. As I matured, I began to understand the value of a good name. As far back as I know, my ancestors were good and productive African Americans whose names and reputations I was proud to inherit. That is why, when a friend asked me during the early 1970s when I was going to renounce my slave name and claim an African identity, I responded that I liked my name just fine and had no intention of changing it. Names are a very important aspect of our truest selves, and I understand and appreciate the need of many African Americans to identify themselves with names of their own choosing, more symbolic than the ones they were given at birth, but I have never felt that need.

During the Depression, beggars, as often white as black, frequently came to our back door asking for food or money. Mama had no money to give them but would always prepare something for them to eat, if only a sandwich. I don't know if I remember it or if I just heard her tell the story, but one day before I started school, she and I were the only ones home when she invited the man at the door to come in and eat at the kitchen table. When he lifted his hand she saw that he was wearing a sawed-off handcuff. It turned out that he posed no danger, but that was the last time she let a stranger inside the house. On another occasion she made a sandwich for a man who had asked for money. He evidently wasn't hungry but wanted money to buy bootleg booze. Later that day she found the sandwich discarded in the bushes on the side of the house. When Dad came home she told him she was tired of giving her good food to men who didn't want it. His reply was, "No, if someone tells you he's hungry and he isn't, that's his problem. If he really is hungry and you don't feed him, it's *your* problem."

As children will, we often dropped a toy on the floor and left it there. Dad would tell whichever one of us came along first to pick it up. Not being the offender, we'd say, "I didn't drop it." His response would be: "It doesn't matter who dropped it. Pick it up. If somebody stumbles over it and hurts himself, you're responsible for the injury." I have carried these lessons with me all my life.

Dad was what would have been called back then a "race man." He taught me a great deal about black achievement and black pride. He supported black businesses as often as he could and bought books by black authors.

He taught me a great deal about responsibility and priorities and about the value of work. He encouraged us to do whatever job was at hand, no matter whether we wanted to do it or how menial it might be, to the best of our ability. Nothing should be done carelessly, and he deplored a D-minus attitude, doing just enough to get by. We should take pride in everything we undertook, whether it was sweeping a floor or cleaning the toilet. Do it well. "If you say you're going to do something, do it," he insisted. "And when you use something, put it back where you found it."

He didn't like to see us idle. Work in itself, he felt, was its own reward. After he retired from his church and he and Mama moved to Detroit, he immediately joined the Council of Baptist Pastors of Detroit and Vicinity and attended the Tuesday meetings regularly. At each meeting one member was assigned to preach. Sometimes the assigned preacher was unable to attend because of a funeral or some emergency. Dad would usually be called on to take his place because all the members knew that he was always prepared with many sermons stored in his mind. Almost every Sunday, until the last year of his life, he was the guest preacher at some church in Detroit. He told my minister once, after delivering a sermon at Plymouth, "I didn't hit my stride until I turned eighty." I, in turn, have found work to be therapeutic. If I didn't have several jobs to do, I'd have to invent them. Nothing beats the doldrums like work. When I was in high school I read an essay by Thomas Carlyle, "On Labor." I have a quotation from it attached to the wall above my computer. It reads:

> The latest gospel in this world is, Know thy work and do it. "Know thyself": Long enough has that poor "self" of thine tormented thee; thou wilt never get to "know" it, I believe. Think it not thy business, this of knowing thyself; thou art an unknowable individual; know what thou canst work at, and work at it like a Hercules! That would be thy better plan.

Dad trusted us and didn't believe we would lie to him. That trust was often misplaced. He never hesitated to give advice, whether it was asked for or not. As an adult I smoked for a number of years but never in his presence. When he smelled smoke on my breath or in my clothes, I always got a lecture. Long before tobacco was proved to be harmful, he insisted it was, and when I denied it, he'd say, "Well, it isn't doing you any good. You might as well burn up a dollar bill." I rebelled by continuing to smoke. Nobody was going to tell me what to do with my own body. But later, after I started teaching, I realized that cigarettes were contributing to my postnasal drip and decided I would cut down, smoking only after nine PM. One evening I was smoking as I corrected papers. About eleven o'clock, I noticed that the ashtray was full of butts and all the gook that went with them. Without hesitation I took the rest of the pack to the basement and incinerated them. I never told Dad, but I made a silent promise to him that I would never smoke again. I think if I were ever to break that promise, I would instantly drop dead.

It's interesting that all three of us followed in Dad's footsteps. He had learned printing at the academy at Bishop College, and once when Wil, who at that time had his own printing company, hurt his hand, Dad still remembered enough about typesetting and the other details of the trade to finish the jobs he had on hand. Clarence became a minister. Dad had taught two adult education classes during the Depression, and I became a teacher.

Although Mama's formal education was limited to three years in normal school, she was a very intelligent and wise woman and had a lot of common sense. She and Dad shared the same values, and she was the ideal minister's wife. She was friendly and outgoing with everyone and completely absorbed in the work of the church. And she could make a speech at church at the drop of a hat, usually beginning, "Dear Christian friends." She organized the Junior Missionaries, high school students and graduates, who gave food baskets to the less fortunate and performed other missionary duties. She told them that, when they bought a gift for someone, it should always be something that they themselves would enjoy and like to own. Many of the girls confided in her and sought her advice on personal problems. They considered her a trusted friend.

Mama taught us respect for Dad's needs. If he was taking a nap prior to the evening service, we knew we had to be quiet and let him rest. When I ironed his handkerchiefs, if one had a hole or tear in it, she made sure I folded it so that the flaw was apparent on the outside. She didn't want him to open a faulty handkerchief in the pulpit.

I was inclined to be aloof and not speak to people as enthusiastically as she thought I should. She reminded me, "These people are your bread and butter. Speak as if you mean it." She impressed on me that nobody was any better than anybody else. Everybody was just as good as I was, and I needed so show them respect, no matter who they were and what they did or didn't have.

Many words of wisdom came from my mother's mouth, sometimes disguised in the homey and picturesque language of her native South, sometimes crouched in cryptic imagery that took me years to figure out. I sometimes heard her say, "If you have to tell somebody who you are, you aren't as important as you think." At other times she'd say of someone, "Self-praise is half-scandalous." Another expression she used was: "Fools' names, like fools' faces, are often seen in public places." Perhaps I had been denied permission to go somewhere where, I assured her, just everybody in the whole world would be, and if I couldn't go I would be extremely deprived. Or maybe one of us would indicate how impressed we were by huge crowds that witnessed the performance of some popular entertainer and the amount of applause and money he or she had received. When she repeated this rhyme she certainly didn't mean that only fools made public appearances and all the right-minded people lived in modest seclusion. I heard her repeat this phrase in so many different contexts that I finally understood what she meant. She was teaching me the distinction between notoriety and renown, between glittering popularity and true worth. Transitory popular acclaim was not as good as lasting achievement; character was more important than reputation. She was instilling in me an understanding that fame with neither substance nor responsibility is unworthy of emulation and that it is more honorable to make worthwhile contributions in the quiet shadows than to make a big splash in the glare of public approval.

Both parents taught us by example what a good marriage is. They represented unity. We couldn't pit one parent against the other. If we asked Dad's permission to do something, thinking he was more likely to approve, he'd say, "Ask your mother." If we asked her first, she'd say, "Ask your daddy." If it finally came back to her, she seldom said an outright yes. It was more often, "We'll see," which usually meant yes. I never heard my parents raise their voices to each other. If they disagreed about something, it was done quietly and with respect for the other's opinion.

Mama taught me how to recite with expression. As a P.K. (preacher's kid), I often had to recite something in church, and she drilled me and drilled me until my presentation met with her approval. I think I read my poetry today with more expression than many poets I know because of her careful instruction.

I learned from her the unimportance of material things and how to make do with little. She had little social life outside the church.

She always looked nice but seldom bought new clothes. The only fur coat she ever owned was one that Mrs. Allen was discarding when she bought a new one. Church members often gave her clothing or other objects, and she always thanked them with enthusiasm, never letting on that she didn't like or couldn't use them. She appreciated their thought-fulness. "You have to take what you don't want to get what you do want," she'd say.

We were taught respect for our elders. I don't know how we got away with calling my maternal aunts by their first names without *aunt* in front of them, but they were the only exceptions. If we called an adult by her first name, it was always preceded by "Miss." And we always responded to a question with "Yes, sir" or "No, ma'am." If we didn't understand a question Dad asked, we didn't ask, "What?" It was "Sir?"

My mother taught me dignity and morality, but she also taught me what altruism is. She was not unique in this way. Most mothers would sacrifice everything for the sake of their children; that is the nature of motherhood, but not all mothers possess this quality. Once during my teens when I was suffering from a severe case of menstrual cramps, she went to the local drugstore and purchased a small bottle of whiskey to mix with some other ingredients. This was an old-fashioned remedy that she knew would offer me immediate relief. Since alcohol was not allowed in our house, this defiant act to relieve my pain is an example of how far she, a respected preacher's wife, would go for her child's comfort. I idolized my father so much that it took me many decades to fully appreciate my mother and her sacrifices. Now when I think of her, the words of a song, whose source I don't know, come back to me.

> One bright and shining light
> That taught me wrong from right
> I found in my mother's eyes.
>
> Those baby tales she told
> Of streets all paved with gold
> I found in my mother's eyes.

Just like the wandering sparrow,
One lonely soul,
I walk the straight and narrow
To reach my goal.

God's gift sent from above,
One real unselfish love
I found in my mother's eyes.

Of all the blessings I have received throughout my life, I consider the good Christian parents I had the most important one by far. They taught me by example and word what honor and integrity are and shaped my life.

The complete Long family in 1963.
Back row: Clarence, Jr., his wife Laverne, Dad, Mama, Wilbur, his wife Katie, my daughter Jill, and me.
Front row: Clarence, III, Clarence's daughters Cheryl and Patricia, and Wilbur's daughters Kathy and Karen.

Loss

The longer we live, the more family members and friends we lose in death. I am now the last member of my generation on my father's side, and I have only one first cousin on my mother's side still living at the age of 92. I have lost many friends who were in high school and college with me and other newer friends, some of whom were younger than I. Leonard died in 1996, and all five of his siblings are now deceased. Harold died in 1997 and Julian in 1998. One of my nieces died young, leaving behind two little daughters. The most recent loss was Laverne in November, 2005.

Although the death of parents is not easy to bear, it is the natural order of things for them to die first. I grieved for my father, who lived to be 87, and my mother who died at 95, but they had lived full and exemplary lives and their time had come. Except for the death of a child, I think the loss of a sibling is the hardest to bear. When a brother or sister dies, it is a part of you that dies, too. Siblings are close in a way that parents are not.

When we were children both of my brothers teased me a great deal, but Clarence's barbs were more taunting than Wil's. He often got me in trouble, blaming me for something he had done, and I was punished because he could outtalk me. When we were in our teens he was always watching over me and protecting me, and while I objected to it then, I later realized that he was concerned because he loved me. When we were in college I discovered that we shared many things, including an adoration of Dad. I think his decision to go into the ministry had something to do with the fact that he idolized Dad and wanted to be like him. He also enjoyed poetry. We shared favorite poems with each other, sometimes both of us memorizing the same one. One that I remember was Byron's "When We Two Parted." One year I gave him a copy of Walt

Whitman's *Leaves of Grass* for his birthday. We liked some of the same popular songs, too. Every time I hear "Don't Blame Me" and "There, I've Said It Again" on my car radio (tuned to a station that plays songs from earlier decades), I think about Clarence. In spite of occasional loud arguments, I loved him, too. He was my "Nonnie."

My brother Clarence before his fatal illness.

After I moved to Detroit, it was always a joy to visit our parents in New Rochelle at the same time Clarence and his family were there. One year we took our children to a cabin in Hyannis, Massachusetts for a week's vacation. I loved being in his and Laverne's company. When I visited their first home in Washington on Webster Street, my sense of family was strong in their presence. One night after the children had gone to bed, Clarence was stretched out on the bed in his pajamas, picking at his toes. I sat on the edge of the bed and Laverne was in a chair nearby. As we talked I felt complete and at home with them.

When Clarence showed his first symptoms of illness, the doctor, who was the chief of staff at Howard University Hospital, a neighbor and friend, could not find the source of his problem and attributed it to grief over Dad's death. As the symptoms increased, diabetes was diagnosed. Cancer of the pancreas is often very difficult to detect. Laverne's sister in Mississippi was dying of pancreatic cancer and asked the doctor if that could be Clarence's problem. He said he could find no indication of that. Still, Clarence couldn't stand the smell of meat cooking and couldn't lie down in bed. He slept sitting up in a chair. We were still inclined to believe that his problem was psychological.

That Christmas Laverne planned a trip to Mississippi to see her sister and suggested that Clarence come to Detroit to see Mama. We didn't tell her he was coming. When Leonard and I picked him up at the airport, I was shocked to see how bad he looked. He was practically dragging himself and complained that he had had to stand up on the plane for long periods. We took him to a seafood restaurant where he ordered lobster, and by the time we were ready to leave, he seemed to feel better.

When we got to the house on Santa Barbara, a lady from East Orange, then living in Detroit, was visiting my mother. She noticed how bad he looked and mentioned it later. Always heavyset except for his adolescent years, he had lost a lot of weight. Mama claimed that she thought he looked fine, but the next day, the woman who was caring for her told me in her presence how Mama had screamed uncontrollably the night before. Mama didn't deny it or try to explain, but I think she knew she would never see her firstborn again. When he got back to Washington, his legs were so swollen that the doctor decided to operate. It was only then that the cancer was detected and determined to be terminal. The doctor said he might live for weeks or perhaps as long as three or four months.

It was a month after that that I broke my neck in an accident. Because I couldn't work, I was able to spend quality time with him and Laverne. Laverne advised me not to upset him by disagreeing with him on anything, but she didn't have to tell me. In the face of his present condition, all differences were forever laid aside, and pure love and the reality that I was going to lose him were all that mattered. I made seven additional trips to Washington, staying a considerable amount of time with each visit. Sometimes he was at home and sometimes at the hospital. If he was in the hospital, Laverne and I went in the morning and stayed with him until evening visiting hours were over. If he was really feeling bad, she had a private nurse to stay with him at night. He was in good spirits most of the time. When he was at home, I'd come down to the second floor in the morning and ask how he felt. "I'm feeling pretty good," was his usual reply. He was optimistic about getting well and highlighted in green a passage in the Bible that he read as an assurance that he was not going to die. No one dared to tell him otherwise. I watched him reduced to a skeleton of his normal weight. I wouldn't show Mama the last snapshot of him and Wil together. It was too painful to see him that way.

He lived longer than the doctor's estimate, celebrating his sixtieth birthday in September. I had gone back to work the same month for the fall trimester. Then a sudden call came that Clarence had taken a turn for the worse and Wil and I should come right away. He had been taken to the hospital almost dead, but the doctor ordered a blood transfusion, and by the time I arrived, he had perked up. For several days Wil, Laverne and I visited the hospital together and took turns afterward treating each other to a restaurant dinner. Clarence was doing so much better that I considered returning to Detroit, but I knew that the end was near and I would have to come right back, so I

431

decided to stay until it was over. He still hadn't faced the fact that he was dying.

One night, one of the hospital employees, thinking Clarence was asleep, said to another, "I don't know why they're doing all this. They know he's dying." Overhearing this, he finally had to accept his terminal condition.

Early the next morning, the private nurse called to tell Laverne what happened. She had spent the night praying with him and talking to him about dying with dignity. She urged Laverne to come first, then the children, and then Wil and me.

When we got there, he was seated on the side of the bed, his back supported by a nurse's hand. He was vomiting what I assumed to be bile and was in great discomfort. I couldn't bear the sight. Before I started crying, I left the room and went into a vacant one across the hall where I wept uncontrollably. Karen, the private nurse, came in to try to comfort me. When I finally forced myself to return to the room, I had regained some composure, but I know my eyes were red and puffed. I'm sure he was too sick to notice. "We'll take good care of Laverne," I assured him. "She's in our hearts." When we left, one of the nurses said, "It won't happen tonight," but how could she know?

After we had dinner, we went back to the house where Wil and I sat up for hours talking and drinking rum and coke. As soon as we had settled down to sleep, the phone rang, telling Laverne that Clarence was dead. What an eerie silence there was in the streets of Washington as we drove back to the hospital after 1:00 AM! The private nurse told us which locked door to come to, and she met us there to let us in. On the way to Clarence's room, she told us that he died with a smile on his face. Did he walk through a tunnel? Did he see at the lighted end Dad waiting to greet him with open arms? Did he take one last look back to wave goodbye to Laverne, then walk forward with joy?

Only when Laverne saw him dead did she let her tears flow freely as I tried to comfort her. All the next day I sat in a reclining chair while visitors came and went unnoticed. Wil drove back to New Rochelle to get different clothes, pick up Katie, and drive the other car back for the funeral.

Even though we had ample time to prepare for Clarence's death, it didn't help. There is no way to prepare emotionally for a death, no matter how long expected it may be. Clarence was buried in a cemetery in Maryland near a statue of a doe feeding her fawn, a statue he had photographed earlier and hung on a wall in their home.

After the funeral one of Clarence's college classmates and a lifelong friend, Thomas Brackeen, invited Wil and me to come to his house for a visit. Even though I never went to Lincoln, I knew a lot of people who did. It helped to talk about the old days in Missouri and laugh at some of the foolish things we did. But one never gets over losing a sibling, and every October 1, I relive that silent night ride through the streets of Washington.

When we were children, I idolized Wil and followed him around like a puppy. He was like a magnet drawing to himself all the boys in the neighborhood. He didn't talk much, but he had a dry sense of humor, and when Wil laughed, everybody laughed. He didn't tease me as much as Clarence did and stopped when I learned how to tease back.

During our years in St. Louis we became closer. It was his apparent unconcern that made me enjoy going out with him and his friends, and he seemed to want my company. After his discharge from the Army Air Corps, he shared a third floor room for a while with Myron, my friend from St. Louis, who was enrolled in college in Manhattan. They used to play records and cards in their room. After Myron left and he was alone, Dad went to his room one day and found him playing solitaire. He didn't say anything to him but complained to Mama because cards had never been allowed in the house. Mama's reply was: "After all he's been through, if I knew how to play cards I'd go up there and play with him." That was the end of Dad's complaint.

He later married Katie Butler in New Rochelle. We seldom communicated, but I sometimes called him, knowing that he wouldn't call me. It didn't matter; that's the way he was. I enjoyed my visits to his and Katie's house in New Rochelle tremendously. One of my favorite places to be in all the world was on his cabin cruiser in Long Island Sound.

Wil in front of his boat in New Rochelle

One summer when I was visiting my stepdaughter in New Jersey, I informed Wil and Katie that I would drive to New Rochelle on a certain date. They were going out of town but said they would be back before time for my visit. Packed and ready to leave, I called only to get their answering machine. Numerous calls brought the same results. I eventually learned that they had extended their vacation, neglecting to inform me and evidently unconcerned about my plans. My first impulse was to drive back to Detroit, but I didn't want to leave without seeing him, so I stayed at Noel and Sharilyn's longer than I had planned and went to New Rochelle when they returned. I had no hesitation admitting that it might have made no difference to him, but I desperately needed to see him. There were only two of us left of the original five members of our immediate family. Although I didn't want to die, I hoped that he wouldn't leave me behind.

One evening in February, 1998, I had an engagement to read at the main public library in Detroit. Because I didn't want to go alone, I asked a young friend of mine to pick me up, cautioning him to be on time. I wanted to get there in time to catch my breath before the program began. It's a good thing he came a little early because five minutes later I would have received Katie's distressed call.

When I returned home, I checked my voice mail. Katie had left a frantic message that Wil had been rushed to the hospital and there was grave doubt that he would live. I immediately called New Rochelle Hospital and was told that he had been transferred to the county hospital. I was given the phone number.

When I called the county hospital, an attendant called Katie to the phone. She filled in details and then was called away. The attendant came back on the phone and told me the doctor was coming out of the room and it didn't look good. A few minutes later, Katie came back on the line to tell me Wil was dead. His abdominal aorta had ruptured, and by the time the doctors could locate the source of the bleeding, it was too late.

After I had finally stopped wailing, I realized that I had to do something constructive. I asked Katie if she would give me the necessary information and let me design the funeral program and have it printed in Detroit. She was glad to have me take over that responsibility. I had his picture with his Tuskegee Airmen's class enlarged for the back cover. He is kneeling at the end of the front row with his hands showing. I had to include his hands; they were so much a part of him. On the front of the program I had another photo of him in uniform. There was room on the back to include a short poem, "White Cross" that I had written when he was missing in action. Then on separate specialty paper, sky-blue with white clouds, I typed on my computer "To a Man with Wings," which I wrote when he got his wings as an Army Air Corps pilot, changing the archaic diction of the original version. The last lines of the poem seemed as appropriate in death as they were at the beginning of his career as a second lieutenant.

> God give you wings not of a silver cast;
> God grant you altitude not found in air
> And happy landing in smooth fields at last:
> This is my prayer.

Seeing him in a casket was almost more than I could bear. The long ride in a limousine to the national cemetery in Long Island and the military ceremony didn't help. If I wasn't prepared for Clarence's death after his long illness, I certainly wasn't ready for Wil's sudden departure. His death has been the hardest loss I have had to bear. Now when I'm driving, I look up at the sky a lot and feel his spirit tunneling through a cloud.

Wil as a young pilot

Late years

IX.
Providential Timing

Providential Timing

The longer I live, the more I tend to believe that there is no such thing as coincidence. I have experienced too much to doubt that there is something providential in the timing of things.

When as a youngster I attended Saturday serial movies, each episode ended with a cliffhanger, sometimes literally. The hero might be left barely holding on to the branch of a tree, his grasp quickly weakening with nothing to prevent his fall to a painful death on rocky terrain many feet below. The next exciting episode would show his miraculous rescue, perhaps by a large bird that suddenly swooped down from nowhere just in the nick of time to carry him off to safety in its claws. Only in movies like these would such *deus ex machina* salvation be dared.

Nevertheless, truth is stranger than fiction, and actions that a good storyteller could never get away with with any credibility do sometimes occur in real life. These circumstances might be considered coincidence if they occurred once in a lifetime, but when they are repeated again and again, I think they must be viewed in a different light. The juxtaposition of some events in my life has convinced me that more than mere chance is at work.

On a cold morning in February, 1978, I was driving to Detroit from Ypsilanti on Interstate 94, having spent the night on campus. I was due to begin a poetry workshop at Redford High School and was trying to decide which exit I should take. Planning to exit at Telegraph Road, I began moving into the left lane just as another vehicle was entering the highway from the left, causing the driver in front of me to apply brakes. When I, too, applied brakes, I hit the only patch of ice on the bridge over Ecorse Road. My car slid across the road to the right. Somehow I was able to change its direction and slid back across the road. The car was completely out of my control and I knew that I was going to hit the guard rail. That was all I remembered until I became aware of a hissing noise and a distant voice saying, "Is she alive?" By that time I had regained consciousness and hastened to say, "Yes." I was later told by a witness that the car had turned upside down and, when the door was pried open, I was found lying face down on the ceiling. In addition to a temporary but painful eye injury, bruises, and a cut on my leg, there was a fracture of one of the vertebrae in my neck, which caused me to be confined in a rigid brace for the next three months. It kept my chin tilted upward and permitted me to move my body only from the waist.

Miraculously I survived the accident alive and was not paralyzed. I was the most cheerful patient at Heritage Hospital as I considered the alternatives I had escaped. But was the result simply good fortune or was there some other significance?

A month before this accident, we had learned about Clarence's terminal pancreatic cancer. My husband and I had made one trip to Washington, D.C. to see him shortly after his surgery. If I had not been forced to take a medical leave, I would not have been able to visit him again except perhaps for a weekend because of my teaching schedule, but due to my injury, I was able to visit him eight more times, each visit for a week or more, spending quality time with him and Laverne. It was on one of these visits that Robert Hayden, Poetry Consultant at the Library of Congress, invited me to record a reading there.

During my recuperation, another significant event occurred. I received a phone call from a lady who said she had been given my number by a mutual friend who told her that I published poetry. She had a fourteen-year-old daughter who had written a group of poems that she wanted to have printed. I told her that her young daughter's poetry probably would not meet the standard for publication by Lotus Press, but I would be glad to look at it and give her my opinion.

When the lady brought the poems to my home, I was pleased to see that they showed a great deal of sensitivity and some knowledge of traditional form. I could certainly understand the mother's pride and her desire to encourage her daughter. Because there were only about fourteen poems, I began to explain how the collection could be prepared for the printer on an electric typewriter and how she could use pressure-sensitive lettering, available at an art supply store, for an attractive cover and title page. She did not really understand the details of this procedure, so I offered to prepare the manuscript for her and get the collection camera-ready. I also offered to take it to a local printer I frequently used if she was willing to pay him. She was relieved and quickly accepted my offer. After all, I had the time to help out, and I felt that it was important to give this teenager whatever support and encouragement I could.

However, because my chin could not be lowered, I was unable to see the top of my desk or the typewriter keys, nor could I look down to read the manuscript. Paulette Childress brought me a drafting table and set it up so that I could see the keys, so I was able to type the poems with some difficulty and get them ready for the printer.

When the mother, who planned to give copies of the collection to friends and relatives, came back to pick up the printed copies, her daughter was on a field trip out of state with her class. I gave the mother a signed copy of my most recent book for her daughter, asking that she have her daughter sign and send me a copy of her little collection. Shortly after her return, I received the copy in the mail. The mother called again to thank me and to let me know that their minister had reprinted one of the poems in the church bulletin and that her daughter was very pleased to see her poems in print.

It was about six weeks after that, as nearly as I can recall, that I received another call from the mother, saying that she wanted to have the poems printed again, but this time with her daughter's picture on the cover. I was only half listening because the addition of a photograph did not present a problem. But suddenly my ear picked up two words that demanded my full attention and, thinking that I hadn't heard correctly, I almost yelled, "What did you say!" She repeated the sentence that contained the words, "pronounced dead."

The girl had been hit by a car and killed while riding her bicycle, and the mother assumed that I had seen the article in the paper.

This was the second indication that my injury had a purpose that could have been served only with the right timing. If I had not been on medical leave, I would have been too busy reading short stories from my creative writing class, preparing literature lectures, or correcting examinations to perform this service. As much as I would have liked to help, I simply would not have been able to do more than offer a few words of advice. If the mother had waited to follow through on her intention or until I had more time to help, the young girl would have died without experiencing the joy of publication.

The weather on the morning of my accident was not noticeably bad. It had not snowed or rained the night before and there was no need to clean my windshield even though the car had stayed out in the parking lot all night. I was not aware of any ice on the streets or freeway. Signs do warn of the possibility of ice on bridges and overpasses, but why was I on the only spot on the highway that was icy at that particular time? When Leonard went to retrieve my belongings from my totally damaged car, he was told by one of the men who had towed it that they had difficulty walking near it because of the ice although the rest of the road was clean.

Why was I spared? People have died from accidents not nearly so severe as mine. Others unfortunate enough to fracture a vertebra are commonly paralyzed. This experience and its implications have had a lasting effect upon my attitude and my priorities. I feel an added obligation to make my gift of years full of meaning, to spend my time in positive endeavors that will make a difference to others and justify my being allowed the privilege of continued life and movement.

There have been other indications of that eerie combination of timing and destiny. In 1983, my cousin Kenneth, whom I had seen only three times before, called to say that he and his wife Evelyn, both retired from teaching at the University of Arkansas in Pine

Bluff, were in Detroit. They had just returned from a reunion of the U.S. Army group that he had commanded during World War II and were stopping overnight at the Pontchartrain Hotel. Leonard and I drove downtown to pick them up for a short visit. I was shocked to see how much he resembled my father. Once we arrived at home, he started asking questions about the family, indicating that, with both parents and both brothers dead, he had become interested in family history. After Aunt Ethel's death, his father had moved to Boston to live with his eldest son Harold, and in the move most of his personal papers and memorabilia had been lost. Kenneth had been left almost no family information.

Because I still had my father's papers, I was able to supply him with much of the missing information on his mother's side of the family. I knew from the family Bible, for example, that his mother's middle name was Elizabeth, which he didn't know, and I showed him a photograph of her and her three siblings as children. He had never seen the picture. "Naomi," he said, "you've traveled all over the world, but you can't get down to Arkansas to see us." "We'll be there within a year, Kenneth," I promised.

In the spring of 1984 we kept that promise, taking with us the letter our grandmother had written to my father describing Kenneth's parents' wedding in 1910, a piece of material from his mother's wedding dress, and several other items of particular interest to him. Those two weeks were among the most memorable in my life as we talked a great deal, laughed a lot, and thoroughly enjoyed each other's company. I bonded with him and felt that he was more a brother than a cousin. We met his son and grandson for the first time and slept in the bed where their daughter Marilyn had lain in a coma for fifteen years. We visited her grave and were told the burial arrangement on either side of her that they had agreed on for themselves. Kenneth and Evelyn entertained us royally, arranged a poetry reading for me at a museum and a signing at a bookstore, and gave a reception at their home, inviting friends in to meet us.

Knowing that I, too, was interested in learning more about the family, Kenneth and Evelyn introduced us to a friend who was an alumna of Langston High School in Hot Springs, the school where our grandfather had served as principal for many years during the early part of the century. She was able to provide some very helpful leads such as names of persons in Hot Springs to contact and a printed history of the school.

Kenneth and Evelyn owned resort property ten miles away from Hot Springs, so we spent a wonderful weekend there, two days of which we went to Hot Springs and interviewed people. At the funeral home from which Grampa Long had been buried, we were discouraged by the news that they had no records that went back that far and that that section of the cemetery, originally owned by two black churches, was now neglected and overgrown with weeds. Nevertheless, we returned the next day, planning to inquire at the office, but forgetting that it was Saturday, we arrived just after the office closed at noon. Driving through the grounds we asked an employee where the oldest section was, and he directed us to that area. As a slow drizzle began to fall, we got out of the car and walked around, looking at tombstones whose names sounded as if they might have belonged to African Americans. Having been told that there were no headstones on the graves of Grampa Long and his second wife, who was buried next to him, we took pictures together standing among the weeds, and I said, "Kenneth, I think this is the closest we'll ever get." He replied, "No, I'll come back one day when the office is open. There must be some information." But four months later, Kenneth bled to death unexpectedly following successful surgery.

I have often thought about the timing that brought my cousin and me together so close to the end of his life. Another year would have been too late for me to come to know and love this considerate, fun-loving, wonderful man whose blood I shared. I would have been the poorer for that lost opportunity.

Another series of events demonstrates my belief. Early in 1984 I happened to discover in a drawer a small, inexpensive radio equipped with an earphone. It was a free gift with a purchase I had made. I had never listened to it, assuming that such radios produced a tinny sound. I wondered why so many teenagers seemed unable to walk down the street without this auditory attachment. But one night I decided to see what it sounded like. What a pleasant surprise I had when the majestic strains of a symphony coming over an FM station invaded my very being! It was not like any listening experience I had been accustomed to. It was more like being one with the music, feeling it in my very veins.

The next time I saw my friend, Irene Williams, at church, I asked her if her husband Al had his own personal radio, she said, "Yes, he has a radio." "No, not just any radio," I said. "Does he have a little one with earphones?" She said he didn't, so I bought him one.

Al and Irene were my daughter's godparents who were living with us when Jill was born. Al was always jolly and fun to be around. He was diabetic and had suddenly gone blind, and their close marriage was only strengthened because of his increased need of Irene's help. In spite of the inconvenience of his condition, he remained the jolly, optimistic, wonderful person he had always been and made the necessary adjustments to his condition cheerfully. After I gave him the radio, Irene called me to say how much happier it had made him. "He dances around the room," she said, "with that thing in his ear and just has a natural ball all by himself. I can't tell you what it's done for him." I was pleased that my little effort had been so deeply appreciated.

While Jill and Malaika were home on vacation from California that summer, Irene called to invite us to lunch at their home. "Tomorrow's my birthday," she said. "I'll be 65. I want both of you to come and help me celebrate." On such short notice, nobody took the time to buy a gift, knowing that she wasn't expecting anything and deciding that we could get her something later. Jill's friend from elementary school, Toni Eubanks, was in town from New York, and we invited her to go along, knowing it would be all right with Irene.

Alfred and Irene Williams

We had a wonderful time in what turned out to be the last happy day of Irene's life. After a delightful lunch, we sat on the screened back porch that they had added on to their house because they always enjoyed ours so much when they came to visit. Irene had picked out the furniture about which Al teased her because she hadn't gotten the bargain she thought. They had installed a brass and wood ceiling fan which Al asked us to describe. We talked of many things, mostly old times together during Jill's childhood and teens. Al recalled, as he often did, cute things that she had said at one time or another. We laughed a great deal.

Eventually, we went outside to the back yard at the request of Jill and Toni as both, serious photographers, had brought their cameras. Basking in the loveliness of the July afternoon, we grouped and regrouped ourselves for various poses, the sun shining joyfully on our faces and myriad flowers swaying in a gentle breeze behind us. The garden was glorious still in spite of Al's no longer being able to plant and tend his roses and daylilies of every imaginable variety and hue. One of the pictures Toni took was of Jill with Malaika's arm around her mother's waist.

Returning to the porch, Al expressed some concern about a test he was scheduled to take the following day to determine the cause of a sore toe that didn't want to heal. A previous test related to his diabetes, different from this one, had caused a violent reaction. We tried to assure him, having been told that this one did not carry the same risks. When we finally said goodbye, I'm sure we all felt fulfilled by the warmth and love we had shared.

The following day Al postponed his test and Jill and Malaika returned to California as planned, all of us vowing to send Irene belated birthday gifts. I thought the best gift I could give was a verbal expression of how I really felt about her, the warmth and dependability of our friendship, and my appreciation of the fine example of womanhood she had been as my daughter's godmother. I knew that, in spite of her creativity and intelligence, Irene had a deep-seated feeling of inferiority which stemmed from her unhappy early family life and the fact that her formal education had ended with the passing of a GED exam some years after dropping out of high school. It was difficult to convince her of her worth, but I certainly tried. With a thoughtfully worded letter I enclosed a small ruby pendant which I had purchased for myself some time before. We shared the same birthstone, and I thought it would be appropriate to give her something that had belonged to me.

Al's test went well, but several days later his heart started playing tricks on him. When I visited him in the hospital, Irene said she could hardly wait for Al to get better so that she could share my letter with him. But it was not to be.

It was my difficult task to call Jill and tell her that Al had died. Nine days after our birthday afternoon, she was back in Detroit for her godfather's funeral. Irene's close friend Alazeen, who lived in Los Angeles, also came for the funeral and stayed with a local friend, Bea Jackson, because Al's relatives were occupying all the available space in their home. But during those difficult days when many relatives and friends came to the house to pay their respect, Irene missed no opportunity to produce the letter I had written her and ask someone to read it aloud. Clearly I had given her the perfect gift.

Several weeks went by and Irene adjusted as best she could, but she wasn't very successful. Her loneliness was devastating, all the more so because of Al's dependence on her. Furthermore, the depth of his love for her, a woman with low self- esteem, had been the most supportive force in her life. Without it she was only a shell. She told a friend that she wouldn't mind dying if she could be reunited with Al.

Toward the end of August I decided to drive to Washington to my nephew's wedding. Leonard had another commitment, so I invited Irene to accompany me. I thought it would be good for her to get away. Instead of driving straight through, we stopped overnight in Pennsylvania. I enjoyed sharing with her the routine I had been observing for years on my trips back to New Rochelle—having a leisurely dinner at a motel, walking, and getting a good night's rest before completing the journey.

My sister-in-law had arranged for us to stay at the same waterfront motel in southwest Washington where Wil and Katie, my cousin Ruth, and other relatives would be. But as we unloaded our bags in the underground parking lot and started to our room, I injured my foot on a dangerous step just inside the entrance. Since it was close to the time of the wedding, we had no time to spare. After greeting relatives and arranging rides to the church, we make a quick change of clothing and left, I hobbling painfully on my way to the car. By the time the wedding ended, I was unable to stand. The bride's brother carried me to my niece's car, and she took me to the hospital. My foot was broken, and I returned to Laverne's house in a cast and on crutches. In the meantime, Irene had been enjoying the camaraderie of my family, fitting in as if she had always been a part of it.

That night in the motel room we shared, I found out how difficult it was to handle crutches and take care of natural functions at the same time. Once seated on the toilet, I was unable to rise without assistance. When I called Irene into the bathroom to help me get up, she suddenly burst into uncontrollable tears and recriminations. Perhaps this was the first time since Al's death that she had really let it all hang out. She hated God for taking Al from her, knowing how much he had loved her and how much she needed that love. She couldn't understand why anyone, especially the God she had faithfully worshipped, could play such a dirty trick on her. Nothing I could say consoled her. Finally, in desperation, I began to pray aloud. I can't remember what I said other than some reference to His sacrifice in the form of His own Son's crucifixion, but something must have done the trick for soon she became calm and seemingly at peace.

Obviously I couldn't drive my car back to Detroit, and Irene, who avoided city freeways whenever she could, would have been emotionally unable to undertake a long journey on an interstate highway even if she had known how to shift the gears with which my car was equipped. My complaint to the owner of the motel about the dangerous step and my threat of a lawsuit produced a solution. He would have one of his employees, a licensed taxi operator, drive us back, but we would have to leave that day. We had planned to stay longer and spend more time with the family, but I couldn't afford to pass up this offer.

The young driver, a native of the Dominican Republic, drove much too fast for my liking, but he was witty and personable and the trip back was a lot of fun, Irene in the front seat with him and I in back with my injured leg stretched out across the seat. When we arrived at my house, I insisted that Irene spend the night, promising her that Leonard, who was at a meeting, would drive her home the next day. Our special time together was thus extended a few more hours, making this the longest period of time we had shared since the old days on Richter Street forty years before. That was the end of August.

One night in early December, Irene's godson, Melvin Stringer, called to ask me when I had talked to her. One of her neighbors had not seen her car or any recent activity and was concerned. I told him that we had last talked Sunday at church and later that day on the phone. "She isn't answering the phone," he said. "We're going to drive out there and check on her. If there's a problem I'll call you back." It was about eleven-thirty at night. I said, "Call me back anyhow, Melvin. I'll be worried if I don't hear from you."

In less than a half hour the phone rang. It was Melvin's wife. "Well, the back door's open," she said "—and she's in there." It took only a split second to know that she had been murdered. After my first hysteria subsided, I rushed my husband into the shoes and socks he had removed in preparation for bed and we headed toward Irene's house.

I will not go into the grisly details of Irene's vicious murder by a teenager she had befriended, but they are recorded in my poem, "The Last Happy Day."

Once again—when I had time to think about it—time had played out its eerie drama in what some might think of as coincidence. I never dreamed, when I gave Al the radio that made him so happy, that his life was almost at its end. As close as we all were, I had never before given him a gift. Why, after all those years, had I been led to the perfect gift while he could still enjoy it? And what possessed me to write Irene the letter expressing things that I had never told her before, things that made her feel better about herself perhaps than she had ever felt before? And why had I urged her to accompany me to Washington on what turned out to be a last-chance opportunity to share? Providential timing or, as the Bible calls it, "the fullness of time," I am convinced, plays a significant role in our lives. Nothing will ever convince me otherwise.

X.
A Sense of Home

A Sense of Home

At my insistence, my stepdaughter Sharilyn drove me from Westfield, New Jersey to East Orange to the first home I remember. We pulled up close to the house at what is now 75 North Clinton Street and turned into what was once the driveway of the Purcells' house next door when it was still standing. The vacant area seemed to be anybody's parking lot.

I got out of the car and clung to the chainlink fence that separated the lots. A lethargic dog stared at me across the dirt back yard devoid of greenery. He seemed disinterested and made no sound nor did he move. The steps to the back porch that held our ice box had disappeared. The pear tree, whose knot hole once made it easy to climb to the lower branches, was gone, too. So was the cottonwood tree farther back in the yard and the mound where wild flowers once burst in colorful profusion. The metal garage door looked the same. I stared into the nondescript back yard and at the battered pickup truck deserted in the driveway as if it had nowhere in particular to go. Apparently the house was now a rooming house with a fire-escape leading to the attic. It hardly looked like the same house, the one still recognizable exterior feature being the bay windows in what was the dining room. The front porch was now enclosed. I longed to go inside, but I didn't know what kind of people lived there, and I didn't dare to ring the bell. I clutched the fence in desperation and nostalgia, leaning toward memory, trying to reclaim the closed rooms, the vanished years. My home was no longer home. Still, I go back to it whenever I can.

The first people I ever knew were in East Orange, the first church, the first school, the first neighborhood. I grew to adolescence there and lived in the same house for twelve years. I still remember where every tree in the block was and the place on the slate-like sidewalk that was buckled by roots so that you had to be particularly careful when roller-skating. One of the Banks girls still lives in the same house in the next block where she grew up, but most of the people I knew have moved away or died.

I have always enjoyed reading novels and poems that have a strong sense of place, of land. I like reading about the rural South although—or perhaps because—I've never lived there. After my father died, I found a comment he had written at the top of a newspaper article he had saved: "I dearly love the South." I was amazed to learn of that love, especially in view of the treatment that African Americans received there. But that love goes beyond the segregation, injustice and racism; it is an irrevocable relationship with the very earth itself. My poems are devoid of that sense of place and land.

I have never lived in a city where I had relatives such as aunts, uncles, cousins, or grandparents except for the short periods when Wilbur Hilton, Sadie and Helen lived with us in East Orange and Dad's cousin, James Arthur, in St. Louis. But there were never any relatives in the same state for us to visit and share a meal with on holidays or any other time.

When people ask me if Detroit is my home, I give them the whole story. I was born in Norfolk, Virginia but moved to East Orange, New Jersey when I was about seventeen months old. I went through grammar school and started high school there. We moved to St. Louis, Missouri near the end of the first semester of my freshman year in high school and stayed there long enough for me to graduate and spend the summer working. During my freshman year in college my parents moved to New Rochelle, New York. After spending only a part of four summers there, I married and moved to Detroit, where I have now lived for sixty years, virtually all of my adult life. I have certainly been here long enough to feel that it is home, but there is something missing. I didn't grow up here, I didn't go to school here, and nobody knew my parents or other members of my family. I came a stranger. While I am not a stranger now, I still have a sense of being rootless.

East Orange was the only place I ever felt was really home. St. Louis was a four-year interlude, and I never felt at home in New

Rochelle. I felt closer to it after I left than when I was living there, simply because my parents were there. Instead of identifying with areas and land, I have an ongoing compulsion to revisit houses where I have lived.

I vaguely recall a childhood visit to Norfolk, but the only thing I remember was that Dad took us to the *Journal and Guide* building and Mr. P.B. Young, the publisher, showed us around the plant. Later, when I was a student at Virginia State College, James A. Eaton, with whom I had become friends when we worked together on *The Virginia Statesman*, invited me to spend a holiday weekend with him and his family in Portsmouth. I was ready to decline until he told me that Portsmouth was just across the river from Norfolk. I accepted his invitation.

The memories I carry of that weekend are warm with the hospitality I received from the Eaton family and the closeness I felt toward James, but I couldn't remain among them until we rode the ferry across the river to Norfolk. Our first visit was to Bank Street Baptist Church, the same building where Dad was pastor when I was born. It was from that pulpit, I was told, that Dad announced that Naomi Cornelia Long had entered the world. The minister, a Reverend Henderson who knew Dad, escorted us through the spacious, impressive sanctuary which I was seeing for the first time. We went from there to 627 Bank Street where I introduced myself to the occupant. She remembered my family and showed us through the house. In the master bedroom, she said, "This is probably the room you were born in." I'm glad I had the opportunity to see my birthplace before the church and the parsonage were torn down.

Years later, the Chesapeake/Virginia Beach chapter of Links, Inc. invited me to present a reading at their annual luncheon held on a Saturday in March, 1980. From my window at the Omni Hotel I could see naval ships in the harbor and recall my mother's description of Norfolk as a seaport town. Dr. Thelma Curl, whom I knew through the College Language Association, asked me if I would like to stay until Sunday and accompany her and her husband to Bank Street Baptist Church where they were members. Would I ever! This newer building is at a different location, still in Norfolk but near the Virginia Beach border.

Before the service began, Dr. Curl introduced me to two Dungee sisters, daughters of one of my mother's best friends in Norfolk. I remember their mother's visit when we lived in East Orange and still have a book of poetry written by their father. Doris and Helma had baby-sat with me. My mother had often told me how much like Doris I was. And here she was in the flesh. During the service the minister graciously introduced me to the congregation and invited me to the pulpit to say a few words. I was so overwhelmed that I haven't the slightest idea what I said. Afterward several people introduced themselves, telling me that my father had baptized or married them. One lady recalled some cute thing I used to do. I tried to gain some sense of wholeness to help me piece the segments of my life together, but it was useless.

Leonard and I attended the 45-year reunion of my high school class in St. Louis. When the activities were over, most of those who had come from all over the country headed homeward, but Leonard and I had decided to stay a few extra days. On our way back to the hotel from our closing brunch, my classmate, still a resident of St. Louis, asked if there was anywhere in particular I wanted to go. "I want to see my house," I told her. As we neared it, I was aware of the many changes in the neighborhood. There was a school across the street now, the streetcar tracks were gone, and many of the houses had been replaced with empty lots and overgrown weeds. But 4219W Finney was still there.

We parked in front and got out of the car to take pictures. All I intended to do was stand in front of the fence (which wasn't there before) and have someone snap me with the house in the background. But my classmate said, "Why don't you ring the bell?

458

The house looks so well kept. It may still be a parsonage." I knew that it was no longer a parsonage, but I took her advice and rang the bell, noticing a heavy commercial-type security gate protecting the front door. A woman about my age came to the door, and I introduced myself and explained my presence. To my surprise, she quickly unlocked the gate and invited us all in.

We had lived there for only four years, and I had forgotten many of the details. I had forgotten the very wide front door with beveled glass that had been replaced with a standard size door and badly patched gaps on either side. I had forgotten the wide staircase that split at the landing so that one part entered the kitchen and the other went upstairs. I had forgotten, too, the butler's pantry and the window in the dining room that looked out into the back yard where the garage no longer stood. But I remembered the fireplace in the living room, the parquet floors, and the place where our piano had been. I also recalled the alcove under the stairs, now converted to a powder room, where I used to sit on the trunk Mama kept there and talk to friends on the downstairs telephone extension. Sitting in the living room, I happened to glance at the ceiling and found the light fixtures familiar.

Mildred Griffin, the owner at that time, had attended the other black high school, Vashon, which accounted for my not knowing her. Her mother had bought the house after the minister who succeeded my father moved out, and she lived there until recently. (Her daughters, who live in other states, felt that it was no longer safe for her to live there alone as she aged, so the house was recently sold.) I was extremely grateful that she permitted me to wander all over the house. Many people would have said, "Oh, I haven't cleaned up upstairs" or "The bed isn't made up," but she knew I wasn't interested in her housekeeping, only the house itself. The third floor was now blocked off because of the absence of a fire escape, but otherwise, I found the memories coming back—the fireplace in my room, the two places where I had located my bed, where my desk used to be, and the view from my back window.

On several later visits to St. Louis, I always went back to my house, the last time spending an afternoon with Mildred, sharing two meals, and taking a nap in what used to be my parents' bedroom. She and I have become friends; she once visited me in Detroit and invited me to stay with her on future visits to St. Louis. The last time I was there, she said, "I think I have something that belongs to your family." She brought out a nondescript small table which I didn't remember, but when I looked at the back of it, I saw written in chalk, "December 1937." "Yes, that was ours," I said, remembering that Dad had bought some used furniture for this much larger house to which we moved during that month.

I was flooded with memories of the front porch, Dad's study (much smaller than I remembered it), the piano behind which mice had once made a nest in the sheet music that had fallen behind it and reproduced. When we heard the newborn squeaks, Mama had quickly gathered up the pink creatures and disposed of them. I remembered sitting on the floor playing Pick-up Sticks with Robert McFerrin when I was not yet allowed to go out with a boy. This was the house I didn't want to move from in the city that I did and didn't want to leave—the house where I fell in love with John, wrote numerous melancholy poems, along with my later-destroyed novel, the house from which I had taken long walks at night and suffered through the anguish of adolescence. I wanted to think of it as home, but it never was. And yet I keep returning, hoping in vain to gain a sense of home.

I have never thought of New Rochelle as home. The longest time I ever spent there was from August, 1945 to the end of March, 1946, never a full year. After I moved to Detroit, I returned almost every summer to visit my parents, but except for Laura, my former college roommate in Manhattan, there were few people to call or visit. Even though Wil married and settled there and Clarence and his family lived there for a while, it was never home to me.

Even so, after my parents died, I had a burning desire to go inside the house on Lathers Park. One summer when I was visiting Wil and Katie, I was fortunate to find someone at home and was able to see the first floor, now hardly recognizable. For some inexplicable reason, the airy wide veranda with a swing suspended from the ceiling had been enclosed to make another room—as if the house needed any more. The kitchen was now a kitchen again and had been remodeled. Having been back once, I have no desire to enter this house again.

Strangely enough, a house and a city in which I never lived were my most stable home. Every summer when I was growing up, and occasionally in the winter, we visited my maternal grandparents who lived at 747 North Fifth Street in Richmond. It was usually near the end of August before the concord grapes in the arbor behind the house were ripe. All my mother's relatives except Wilbur Hilton (who eventually did move back) lived there or on Sixth Street, the next street over. I enjoyed spending time with my aunts and cousins. I remember all the details of that house and knew the children in the neighborhood and all of Helen's friends.

I don't really remember Dr. Rachael Keith who has lived in Detroit for many years, but I do remember her name. She lived on Fourth Street, the next block over, and was in Helen's graduating class at Armstrong High School. I knew from Dad that her father had been a missionary in Africa. All I remember was what we chanted on the sidewalk. Several years ago, she and her husband, Judge Damon Keith, were attending a social function. I knew she didn't know me, but I went behind her chair, leaned over and repeated the chant we used to say as we played on the sidewalk: "Rachael Hannah Celestine Boone. Rip-a-dop-a-dip-bop, Celestine Boone." She turned around and laughed saying, "I know you're from Richmond."

Even after the house was gone, Richmond continued to feel a great deal like home. During my college years I spent a great deal of time with Helen at their new location. I try to get back as often as I can to visit my only living first cousin, Ruth Paxton, whose house is in an area where no black people lived in the old days. All my mother's relatives except Giles are buried in Richmond, as well as Octavia and my parents.

I loved the house at 747 North Fifth Street so much that I wrote a poem about it after it was torn down for a freeway ramp. I also wrote a descriptive essay about it in a textbook I co-authored. After the freeway was built, I always made my way back to the brick sidewalk across the street, one year bringing back to Detroit one of the loose bricks. On my last visit, though, I found that a new building occupies the spot where I used to stand to view the ramp where the house was, and I will never be able to stand there again.

I have returned, too, to my first home in Detroit, 9381 Richter Street. Any time I am on the east side of the city, I drive by it. The street is only a block long and the garage and houses on both sides are no longer there, but I go out of my way to make sure the house is still standing. One Sunday afternoon I was fortunate enough to find a young woman and a boy working in the yard, and I stopped the car. "Do you live here?" I asked. When she said she did, I got out and told her, "This is the house to which I brought my newborn daughter fifty years ago." She was excited to meet me and, like Mildred in St. Louis, invited me inside. The small bedrooms still have curtains in front of the closets instead of doors, but she has changed the position of the sink in the single large bathroom. The antique ball-and-claw tub is still there. When she told me her mother had raised fourteen children there, I wondered where they had all slept. Perhaps the unfinished attic was eventually finished. Many of her siblings must have slept there although they probably weren't all at home at the same time. The present owner bought the lot next door and is keeping it well. She has recently had the fake brick siding covered with vinyl, a vast improvement in appearance.

This was the first home of my own, shared briefly with Julian until after the divorce. I lived there from February, 1947 until 1954 when I remarried. This is the home that Al and Irene Williams shared with me. We had some good times together there. But life as a single parent on a very small income was extremely challenging, and I was often lonely and very unhappy there. Still, I have a special love for this house where I spent my young adult years.

When Jill and I moved to my present address on Santa Barbara Drive in 1961, I had a feeling that this is where I would spend the rest of my life. She was about to begin high school, and I felt that this house would become my real home.

Then, several years after Dad retired from his church in New Rochelle, I convinced my parents that their house in New Rochelle was much too large for them to care for. We had received reports that both of them had been sick at the same time and were in need of care. Dad was still driving locally but had someone else take him to New York City for the weekly ministers' conference and preaching engagements. On one occasion, it was already snowing on Sunday morning when he and his driver left for the church in New York where he was to preach. By the time the service was over, the snow had turned into a blizzard. They found themselves on the freeway unable to move and had to spend the night there. Clarence frantically called New York from Washington trying to get information from the police, then called me. The calls back and forth went on for hours with no information except that the weather had tied up traffic. Dad didn't get back until the next morning. After that experience I was able to convince my parents that they should move to Detroit and spend their remaining years with me. Of the three children, I was the logical one to make a home for them. Neither brother had extra space with growing children still at home. I was alone, Jill having graduated from college, gotten her first job, and moved into her own apartment. Furthermore, I would not have been able to buy this house without my parents' financial assistance.

I hadn't forgotten what it was like to live in the same house with my father. In whatever house he lived, he was in complete control. In addition, he couldn't abide idleness. Whenever the three of us were sitting in the living room in St. Louis on a summer day listening to the radio and saw his car pull up in front, we would all scatter. Later, in the parsonage in New Rochelle, if I was just sitting on my bed and thinking about something, I would quickly open a drawer and pretend to be busy when I heard his footsteps heading toward my room. Satisfied that I was engaged in some activity, he would go away. I only hoped that, now that I was grown, he would grant me some leeway. Still, I knew what an autocrat he was and had no expectations of significant change. So I rented a studio apartment in the vicinity of Wayne State University even before they arrived, knowing that I would need some time to myself. I had a second telephone installed at home, remembering that whenever I was conversing with someone Dad was likely to listen in on the extension. I had to instruct both of them not to answer my phone.

I soon found out that he still considered me his "little baby girl," said affectionately enough, but an admission that, in his sight, I would never grow up. If someone came to visit me, he sat in the living room with us and engaged in conversation. If a male visitor stayed past midnight, I heard about it the next day. I wasn't free to offer anyone a drink or take one myself although I figured my way around that. I had given my parents the master bedroom and moved into the room that Jill had vacated. A door from Jill's room leads to a closed-in back porch. I kept any wine I might have had well concealed out there, and if he saw me drinking in my room as I corrected papers, he couldn't tell what it was.

Because of glaucoma and cataracts, his night driving in New Rochelle had become so atrocious that he once knocked down a street sign. I asked a police officer who was a member of his church why the city didn't revoke his license. "Nobody's going to bother Rev. Long," he responded. So when he talked about bringing his car to Detroit, I insisted that he get rid of it. Another minister always picked him up and brought him home from his Tuesday conference meetings. I drove Dad and Mama to the various churches where he

464

preached most Sundays on my way to my own church, knowing that someone would bring them home. But for other places he had to go, he refused to call a taxi. He often called Jill to come from the other side of town to drive him to the barber shop that was only four blocks away. I taught on Monday, Wednesday and Friday and used the other days for reading, correcting papers, and preparing lectures. But every Tuesday and Thursday without fail, there was somewhere he needed me to take him. As soon as he had finished his business one place, there was another place he had to go, then perhaps a third. By the time I brought him home, it was usually three o'clock, and I still hadn't had any time to prepare for the next day. I dropped him off and went to my apartment where I usually worked until after the eleven o'clock news. My mother suspected that I was seeing some man away from home, and I never let her know where I was actually spending my time. Dad and I sometimes locked horns, engaging in heated arguments after which he was the one who always broke the silence that followed. On one such occasion, commenting on my willfulness, he added: "But I guess I can't say anything. You're just like me." Clearly, this house was no longer my home but my father's.

I am not sure I would have gotten married again if my parents hadn't moved in with me. After two failed marriages to two men who were exact opposites, I no longer trusted my own judgment. When Leonard and I began to see each other after his first wife's death, I had no freedom at home and spent more time at his house than he did at mine. Between visits we spent an amazing amount of time on the phone. If I had been living alone, I think I would have preferred to continue seeing him without marrying, but it soon became apparent that he was the marrying kind and wouldn't settle for anything less. And he was too good to pass up.

When Leonard asked my father for my hand in marriage, he gladly granted it because he liked Leonard. On the other hand, he was most displeased. Though his best friend, Joe Henderson, on a visit to Detroit, had tried to prepare him for that possibility, he felt that I had betrayed him. He expected me to be with them and care for them until the end of their lives.

A couple of months after our marriage, Jill and Edward Boyer got married in a simple ceremony performed by my father in our living room. Three years later their daughter, Liliana Malaika, was born. When she was just over a year old, they moved to California; Ed was a journalist on the staff of *Time Magazine* which transferred him there. (He later wrote for *Los Angeles Times* from which he eventually retired.)

It never occurred to Leonard and me to buy another house; mine had been paid for many years before, thanks to my parents' generosity, and Leonard's payments were almost complete. It didn't make sense to go into debt again. We had to decide which house would accommodate everyone. Leonard, Jr. was still in college at Eastern Michigan University and needed a room at home, and Kathy, the youngest daughter, not yet a teenager, needed a room. We needed one, and so did my parents. And I needed a study. Dad insisted that he did, too. My house on Santa Barbara is not large enough to accommodate that many people. We could have made do at Leonard's house, but Dad wouldn't hear of moving, and when the subject was brought up in my mother's presence, her eyes teared up. "I've never lived in any man's house," she said, "except my father's and my husband's." Even if they had agreed to move, the arrangement would not have been amicable because Dad would have insisted on being the boss. So it was agreed that they would stay in the house on Santa Barbara and I would move to Leonard's house on Inverness Street.

I was not at all concerned about living in the house where Leonard's first wife had lived and raised their four children. I never felt in competition with her and felt that, if he didn't still love her memory, I wouldn't want him. I did have some concern, however, about his children's reaction. When I mentioned it to him, he said, "My kids aren't like that," but he didn't know what his kids were like or how hostile three of them could be. After her mother's sudden death when she was only ten, Kathy was sent to live with her mother's brother and his family, which included two male cousins close to her age. Leonard was in no condition to care for her, and her two older sisters, both married, each with a young daughter of her own, lived some distance away in other cities. Kathy came to Inverness some Saturday mornings when I was there, and I received a strong indication that there would be trouble with her. Still, it was only through our marriage that she would be able to return home to live.

I knew Leonard and his first wife and the children, except Sharilyn, from the church we all attended, but it was Sharilyn, the only one who didn't know me, who said of the marriage, "If this will make my father happy, I'm all for it." It was she who cooked food and left it in the refrigerator so that when we returned from our honeymoon in Chicago, I wouldn't have to be concerned with preparing a meal on my first day there.

I will not go into detail about the opposition to my presence in that house I received from the other three children, the eldest of whom used the occasion of our marriage to leave her husband and move back to Detroit with the intention of moving in with us with her three-year-old daughter. I wouldn't accept this arrangement, and we found her an apartment elsewhere, but that didn't stop her from spending as much time at our house as she could, trying to assert her ownership of the space that I was usurping.

It took a long time, but she and her brother finally came to accept my presence. It has been only recently that I have sensed a change in the youngest child's attitude. In the years I lived there, I was determined not to let her drive me away. I learned to coexist only by being courteous and saying as little to her as possible.

Did I ever feel at home in that house? Only after we were alone.

Leonard was a good man, gentle and kind and with a great sense of humor. He was my "Sunday kind of love." I enjoyed his companionship, traveling together and playing backgammon or scrabble or doing crossword puzzles after dinner, and he gave me the time alone that I needed for my work. He was very proud of me and supportive of my work. After Dad's death, we moved my mother in with us, and the same two ladies who took care of her came in every day, but they no longer stayed at night or on weekends.

During the next few years, I rented the house on Santa Barbara to a friend for a very small amount since I still had furniture there, my father's study on the third floor was still intact, and I needed access to the basement office of Lotus Press. After she left, I moved the office to the master bedroom and used the house for Lotus Press and my own writing. I always had a feeling that I would some day live there again.

The house on Inverness had some serious structural problems, many of which had existed for all the years that Leonard and Marilyn had lived there. Leaks on the first floor returned every two or three years in spite of all the work done to eliminate them. Water pipes froze and broke inside walls whenever the weather became severely cold, and water flooded the basement from the ground up. Leonard was not as diligent about making repairs as he might have been. In addition, we had several burglaries. Once during the night, the intruder came into the room where we slept. Fortunately, we didn't wake up. Another time someone broke in through the front door on a Sunday morning. I found myself looking over my shoulder every time I entered or left the house. The neighbors were wonderful, the houses and lawns in the block were well kept, and we had a very strong and congenial block club. But we were near the corner of a main street that had several questionable businesses on it, and people with ill intent could easily drift off this street to see what trouble they could get into in that first block.

Two years after my mother died, I suggested to Leonard several times that we move to Santa Barbara, and he would almost agree and

468

then decide against it. But gradually I began to see in him signs of physical or mental problems. He forgot to pay bills and then wondered why the amounts doubled or tripled. I realize now that he suffered several mini-strokes from which he seemed to quickly recover. When I came home one day and saw him sitting in the living room with the television off, I sensed that something was wrong. He said he needed something from Sears. I didn't notice whether the car left the garage or not, but he later came back to the door without his keys or any merchandise. We looked everywhere for the keys. The next morning we found them still in the ignition. Then he started having hallucinations. If I was going to have to take care of him, I knew I could do it better in the house with which I was more familiar. In addition, I was tired of living in fear in a house with so many problems. One day I announced, "By spring I'm going to be living on Santa Barbara. I hope you'll join me." To my surprise he said, "Okay."

Now that the decision was made, I didn't wait until spring. In December, 1994, we moved only a few pieces of furniture and clothing that we needed immediately, thinking that we could go back and gradually get rid of the things we didn't need, clean out the furnace room where some of his children's possessions had collected for years, along with his own clutter, and get better organized. However, his condition worsened so rapidly with hallucinations and some form of dementia, misdiagnosed as Alzheimer's, that that didn't happen.

He was with me on Santa Barbara from December until July 4, 1995. The hallucinations got worse, and he was constantly falling. I had difficulty getting him back on his feet. Sometimes he was unable to stand without assistance. When he suffered a cerebral hemorrhage that put him in the hospital, I knew I couldn't handle him at home in this condition. When his doctor informed me that I needed to make arrangements for his care, I had already found a very good facility that had a vacancy. Before his discharge from the hospital, an X-ray, necessary for his admittance to the skilled care facility, revealed lung cancer. He was too sick to cooperate for some of the tests, and the hospital couldn't begin radiation treatments in his condition.

Leonard with me in California

Eventually his mental condition improved, and I realized that whatever form of dementia he had, it was not Alzheimer's. His improvement was so marked that he was now able to have the radiation therapy, so for six weeks, five days a week, I picked him up and drove him to the hospital and back to the nursing home. For a while he was doing so well that he was moved to assisted living within the same facility. But gradually his condition deteriorated. He was taken to the hospital for a collapsed lung in May, 1996. As soon as that was inflated, another problem occurred with his blood. Then a paralyzing stroke, a seizure, and another stroke. He died on May 29, 1996 after 24 years of marriage.

Lenora, Kathy, Leonard, Sharilyn, and Leonard, Jr.

I have had recurring dreams about additional rooms in houses that don't exist. I often think of extra space as "my undiscovered room," which is the opposite of what I really mean. When I bought the house on Santa Barbara Drive, I was looking for certain attributes which were all there. The thing I think of as my "undiscovered room" was a bonus. It is a small third floor unheated room whose

471

stairs lead up from the master bedroom. It was Dad's study. I seldom use it now except for storage and special projects, but it has a small chest of drawers, a leather chair, a bookcase, a studio couch, and an oil-filled electric radiator, along with a powerful window fan on the landing, which make it possible for sleeping comfortably in any weather when I need extra space.

But the rooms I dream about are not this very real third floor room. In one house there are so many extra rooms and lavatories that it could almost be a hotel, and I have a choice of which one I want to be mine, often changing with a change of dream mood.

The more frequently dreamed house has a raised platform on the first floor near the kitchen. It can accommodate a desk or podium. Behind it is a room that can be used as a bedroom, with another somewhat smaller room inside it. On the second floor are several empty rooms, but in my dreams I always choose a large one with high windows, reminding myself that I have to decide the color of the curtains I intend to buy and what furniture I intend to include.

I don't know what psychological need compels these dreams of houses and the possibilities of empty rooms, but it confirms my attachment to houses and a need to find or make a home.

I live alone now with my dog in the house on Santa Barbara Drive. I have come to realize that, with parents, brothers, and cousins gone, making a home depends solely on me. I have to do my own planting, establish my own roots. If it is ever to be anywhere, it has to be here. This house and I are one, and I have finally found the home where I hope to end my journey.

XI.
Reach and Grasp

Reach and Grasp

Earlier in my life I hoped to make a name for myself as a poet. While I have achieved some degree of success, it has not been enough to satisfy my ambition. In anthologies where my work appears and some of the better known authors' names are listed on the cover, I am usually relegated to the "and others" category. I have never won a major national award except as a publisher and editor, and many people who read poetry have never heard of me, or if they have, the only poems with which they are familiar are the same few, most of them written thirty or forty years ago, that keep getting reprinted.

I read a great deal of contemporary poetry that I don't care for, but there is also much that I admire greatly and recognize as better than anything I am capable of writing. In spite of the inclusion of many of my poems in major magazines, journals, and anthologies, I suffer from a lack of confidence in my own ability and have often refrained from submitting individual poems to journals for fear of having them rejected. Most of the poems that appear in more than 180 anthologies were solicited by the editors. I sting from the omission of any of my work in an anthology widely used as an African American literature college textbook. When a similar anthology was compiled for use in high schools with input from outstanding members of Detroit high school personnel, even here my work was omitted. Nevertheless, Detroit Public Schools did select *Octavia and Other Poems* as required reading in all eleventh grade public high school classes, and *A Poet's Voice*, a documentary film combining my reading and discussion with ten visual artists' interpretations of the poems, won a Gold Apple Award of Excellence from the National Educational Media Network and won rave reviews in *Library Journal*.

I have been inducted into three halls of fame. One is at Sumner High School in St. Louis, which boasts a number of graduates who have established national and international fame in their chosen careers. Another is the International Literary Hall of Fame for Writers of African Descent at Chicago State University. The most recent is the Michigan Women's Hall of Fame.

Honorary degrees include a Doctor of Humane Letters from Sienna Heights College, as well as one from Loyola University-Chicago, and a Doctor of Fine Arts from Michigan State University. I have received several Lifetime Achievement awards as well.

Other recognition as a poet includes (to mention only a few), appointment as Poet Laureate of Detroit (2001); the Michigan Artist Award (1993), the only poet to date to have won this state honor; an Award of Excellence from *Black Scholar* magazine; a Literature Award from the Arts Foundation of Michigan; two awards from Alpha Kappa Alpha Sorority, Alpha Rho Omega chapter; an "In Her Lifetime" tribute from the Afrikan Poets Theatre in Jamaica, New York; and most recently inclusion as an honoree at the Detroit Historical Museum, as well as at the Charles H. Wright Museum of African American History. In addition to receiving the Mayor's Award for Literary Excellence (2005), my life-size bronze bust is now a reality. Except for a $3,000 grant from the city, most of the funds required for the creation of the art, a custom-made pedestal, and a reception at the unveiling ceremony (June 4, 2005) came from individuals I know across the country and several organizations to which I belong. Their generous response to letters of solicitation was both surprising and humbling. This bust is now a part of the permanent collection at the Charles H. Wright Museum of African American History.

Some of my poems have been translated into European languages, and three have been set to music and publicly performed.

So why am I dissatisfied? My books might have received more critical attention if more of them had been published by major companies, but since I chose to publish most of them through Lotus Press, they were not widely reviewed, even locally. A larger company would have advertised them and reviews would have appeared in major journals. That is not to say that no interviews or feature stories have appeared in national publications, but not enough. I have never promoted myself as many poets I know have done, spending my time and effort instead on promoting the work of others. I made my choice, and I should not be disappointed that I have not been as well recognized as a poet as I hoped to be.

Poetry was my first love, and it was as a poet that I wanted recognition. *Star by Star*, published by Harlo Press, first in hard cover and reprinted in paper, was published again in a slightly revised version by Evenill, Inc., before Lotus took over the reprinting. And *Pink Ladies in the Afternoon* and *Exits and Entrances*, both published by Lotus Press, went into second printings, received favorable reviews, and had wide distribution, in spite of the lack of adequate advertising. Poems from *Star by Star* continue to be reprinted in textbooks and anthologies, and *Pink Ladies*, as well as *Octavia and Other Poems*, were made required reading in at least two universities that I know of. So they must have found favor in some knowledgeable individuals' eyes. And I am assured in a number of ways that many of the poems have had a positive impact on readers' lives.

Nevertheless, it is as a publisher and editor that I am best known. Poets across the nation, especially African Americans, whether I have ever published their work or not, send me their signed books and express gratitude for my encouragement and the opportunities I have offered through my determination to keep Lotus Press alive. The annual Naomi Long Madgett Poetry Award, established in 1993, has given many young poets hope, as well as an opportunity to be heard. I have lived and worked according to the hymn, "If I can help somebody as I pass along, then my living will not be in vain." It is students and poets to whom I have tried to offer that help.

Lotus Press and I are inseparable. Because I have operated the press for 34 years with only occasional volunteer assistance, I *am*

Lotus Press. Before the press was established, Ann Allen Shockley, special collections librarian at Fisk University, asked me to donate my papers pertaining to my career as a poet to that collection. I was flattered by the invitation and was happy to comply. However, I stopped sending material when I realized, after her retirement, that Fisk no longer has the funding and personnel to catalog and preserve material adequately. Recognizing the inseparable nature of my work as a poet and publisher/editor, The University of Michigan Special Collections Library purchased the Lotus Press and Naomi Long Madgett Archive in 2003. In addition to newer material, this archive includes some copies of early material, the originals still at Fisk.

I have come to terms with my belief that my poetry does not compare well with what I consider the best contemporary poetry, and I am honest to admit that some of the poets I have published are far better than I will ever be. Sometimes I think my life has been too sheltered, that I haven't suffered enough misfortune or tragedy to be a better poet. I have never been a very political poet or followed current trends in style and content. Many of my poems are not considered "relevant." But I write what I write in a wide variety of styles and subjects, apparent in my most recent collection, *Connected Islands: New and Selected Poems.* I write as well as I can, and I write for myself, but I hope that others will appreciate and identify with individual poems. I know that many people do.

In "Rabbi ben Ezra" Robert Browning wrote: "What I aspired to be, / And was not comforts me." And his "Andrea del Sarto" reminds me that "a man's [or woman's] reach should exceed his [or her] grasp, / or what's a heaven for?" I console myself with that thought.

Epilogue:
In the Time of Age

Four generations:
Mama and me standing
Jill seated holding baby Malaika

In the Time of Age

When my daughter first noticed that a few strands of my hair had turned gray, you would have thought it was the end of the world. In an animated voice, she urged me to run, not walk, to the nearest beauty salon to have the gray tinted out. I quietly replied that I had no such intention. Those gray strands were mine; I had earned them and intended to keep them as battle medals of victory.

Now, many years later, I envy young or middle-aged women with prematurely silver hair and wish that mine would change faster than it is doing. But both of my parents grayed slowly, so I should not be surprised that the color of my hair is still only mixed gray. My feeling about my hair is symbolic of my general attitude.

I feel sorry for eighty-year-olds with faces that show their age who insist on dyeing their hair a harsh, unnatural black that makes them look older than they are. I wonder what youth held that was so wonderful they can't bear to let it go—or what it withheld that they are still feverishly groping to capture. Don't get me wrong; I'd like to discover a magic elixir that could smooth the ever-deepening creases in my face and remove the occasional pains that slow me down and send me more frequently than before to my medicine cabinet. Yet, I willingly accept the changes brought by age as completely natural and a new experience in which I should rejoice. Consider the alternative; I'd rather be old and active than dead. An automobile accident in 2004 in which my pelvis was fractured, in addition to two internal injuries, makes me even more grateful than I was before to be alive and active.

My most difficult birthday was the thirtieth. Over the telephone my best friend and I commiserated late into the night as we related to an article in a popular women's magazine that discussed the advantages and disadvantages of reaching that ripe old age. The trauma I suffered had much to do with the turmoil of my personal life. I often felt overwhelmed by the formidable responsibility of raising a child alone, my closest relative being more than seven hundred miles away. In addition, I was experiencing a tremendous struggle trying to make ends meet on a very small salary as a service representative for the telephone company. And I couldn't seem to find the key to unlock the door to the right romance. Life was fraught with myriad complexities and frustrations and seemed to offer no hope for a smoother existence. But I survived that traumatic birthday and moved on, vowing that forty wouldn't throw me for the same kind of loop. And I almost carried it off until the onset of latenight meditations.

After that, birthdays didn't present a problem. I think I was most pleased with my life from forty through 55. Having looked younger than my years for so long, I welcomed the physical and emotional mellowing that transformed me from the girl I was used to seeing in the mirror into a mature woman.

The changes came gradually—the clothing that didn't fit quite as well around the waist as it used to, the filling out with flesh (and little pouches of fat) where there used to be only muscle and bone. I saw the frown line in my forehead deepen and flesh loosen around my mouth. And I won't lie and say I didn't mind, but I began to embrace a philosophy of healthy acceptance. Although death claimed someone I knew now and then, I seldom thought about the fact that I wouldn't live forever, especially as I enjoyed good health. A medical concern or two, but nothing that wasn't easily resolved.

But once I realized that the seasons were now changing much more swiftly than they used to and each summer brought me closer to sixty, I actually found myself looking forward to the next phase of my life. I had remarried and my life had somewhat settled down. I was happy commuting to Eastern Michigan University in Ypsilanti, and my writing-related activities kept me invigorated. I expected to teach until the age of seventy when I would be forced to retire.

But several factors caused me to rethink my intention. The near-fatal accident I survived in 1978 brought increasing apprehension about the forty-mile drive to the campus, especially when winter was at its iciest worst. The pressures of juggling the duties of teaching and publishing also complicated my life. I felt some frustration, too, over the nonchalant attitude of some students who seemed to consider the pursuit of higher education a joke. Sometimes my efforts seemed like pearls being tossed into the pigpen of languor. I was sixty and eager to work at publishing and editing full time, reading some of the books I had never found time to get around to, and spending more time writing. I longed for the day that I would reach 62 and could supplement my meager retirement checks with Social Security. When the first check came, I celebrated by buying myself the ruby ring I had always wanted.

At 65 I felt that I had finally grown up. I still preferred sweaters and skirts or slacks to any other kind of clothing and would have gladly rushed out to buy a pair of saddle oxfords in every available color if I could have found them. Psychologically, I will always be eighteen, nineteen, or twenty whenever I feel girlish, or forty-five when I feel mature.

But reaching seventy was also great. I celebrated that birthday by investing in a fund that would ensure the continuation of an annual national poetry award in my name. And Michigan State University Press brought out *Remembrances of Spring: Collected Early Poems*. I received several important honors that year. It seemed like a year well worth waiting for.

I happily embrace the age of 83 and am humbly proud to be considered by some, especially younger poets, as an elder, with all that that connotes. If life hasn't brought me all the rewards I hoped for, I have at least learned something from those deprivations and grown wiser and more philosophical because of them. My mother used to say, "Old fools are worse than any," and I admit I'm still foolish sometimes, but the secret of growing old gracefully is learning not to waste anything and putting all experience to use.

Aging also provides an opportunity for assessing one's purposes in life, for learning what is important and what it is that one lives for. I once assigned my students the writing of their own obituaries. Doing this while one is young can be useful in providing the chance to consider goals and sometimes redirect them, but even in advanced years, it's not too late. What is it that one wishes to be remembered for? What can it be said has been the value of her life?

Several years ago I attended a memorial service for a lady I knew only slightly who had lived long past expectation, and while her name was well known and there were many who had loved her, I came away feeling sad. Friends talked about their acquaintance with her, evidently considering that she had enjoyed a wonderful life. In a sense, she had. She was a physically beautiful woman. She had married well and lived a life of ease. Well educated, she had the distinction of being the first African American to hold a certain important position. But most of all, she was remembered for having entertained lavishly, traveled widely, and enjoyed her life thoroughly. "When we were kids," the person sitting next to me said, "she used to let us play on the private beach of her summer home."

But throughout the recitation of many words of acclamation, I sensed a deep hollowness. I got the impression that she had played a lot of bridge, worn a lot of expensive clothes, entertained all the right people—and little more. Nobody mentioned that her life had been anchored in any kind of faith, that her character had been marked by integrity, that she had contributed to any worthy cause, that she had helped anybody. Nobody said that this socialite had been or done any of that. All I could think of to sum up what I had heard of her was the irreverent sentence, "She was a good-time gal." Maybe that was her goal, and who am I to impose my values on her life? But the words of a song sung by Peggy Lee kept ringing in my ears: "Is that all there is?"

I was blessed with the best parents anyone could ever have, and brothers and cousins of good character who made significant contributions to society. And I couldn't wish for a more wonderful daughter who is beautiful in every way. I am thankful for a granddaughter who has brought me great joy, an extended family which includes stepchildren, grandchildren, and great-grandchildren, and some faithful friends of many years, as well as several newer ones. How could I have known when I was raising Harold's two sons, with whom the prefix *step* was never used, that Harold, Jr. would become my true son on whom I can always depend for help, along with my wonderful daughter-in-law Mary.

Moving on down the line has caused me to take stock of my life and try to make some sense of it all, to determine what was frivolous in it and what was of enduring value, what to cast aside and what to embrace.

I find myself now scurrying to tie up loose ends while I still can. What of myself can I still give away? Whose life can I still help to make better in some small way? What young person headed down a destructive path can I still redirect? How can I still be an inspiration and a model to someone by the way I speak, the things I do, the way I carry myself? And how can I pass on to others some measure of the goodness and helpfulness that provided the basis for my own good life?

Old age isn't a party by any means. It is the negative aspects that are most frequently associated with it. The death of family and friends, loneliness, failing health, the increasing dependence on others. I was made acutely aware of that through my daily visits to the nursing home where my husband of 24 years was a resident for ten months before his death. I realize that the time is closer than it used to be when I, too, will grow increasingly dependent on others for my needs. But this is a part of life, and all life is good. And I have faith that I will no more walk alone in whatever dusk of adversity I may find myself than I did in the sunlight of my earlier years. I trust that I can face advanced age with a courage and cheerful acceptance that life has taught me. I have seen that happen with people who faced death as beautifully and positively as they did life because their souls were anchored in eternal values and they knew that their supplication would be heard: "Cast me not away in the time of age; forsake me not when my strength fails."

In "Rabbi ben Ezra," Robert Browning writes: "Grow old along with me / The best is yet to be." But he told only part of the truth. The best in life is never "to be." The best *is,* at whatever age one happens to be. Life is a balance, and each age, I am convinced, has its compensations.

I am not ready to hang my hat up and don't think I ever will be. Like Tennyson's "Ulysses," I shall forever hope "to seek a newer world," embarking on new projects as others come to a close. Work is my life, and I have found fulfillment in it.

I know that I am not as foolish as I once was. I will never have a chance to undo the mistakes I have made, but I have sense enough to understand now why I made them and to forgive myself. I can't undo the waste—of time, of energy, of tears, of misplaced trust, of dead-end pursuits, of foolish yearnings—but I can know from having followed those false and hopeless road signs that I was not afraid to take chances and therefore did not resign from life.

I have learned that happiness should never be pursued. It is an elusive bird whose swiftness in flight increases in proportion to the fever of the quest. There is no magic salt that will halt it in midair and bring it to our outstretched hand.

It was only when I gave myself away that I began to find myself. Service, I have learned, is where true happiness lies. It has provided me with a compassion that I didn't have in my youth. It has permitted me to walk in the shoes of many and feel the warmth of their feet as well as the pebbles that injured them. I have discovered that cheerfulness, kindness, and helpfulness bring as much joy to the one who extends them as the ones who receive them—perhaps a great deal more.

The problems the world faces don't offer much reason for

optimism, and the melancholy person I used to be would have declared the earth's doom decades ago. But while human nature daily manifests its beastliness in various ways, and the world seems wildly determined to destroy itself, I remind myself that humankind survived being outcast from Eden, as well as the destruction of Sodom and Gomorra, and still hasn't succeeded in completely demolishing itself. The God in all of us may save us yet, and I am hopeful.

The clock is winding down, but I have a Friend who has been close to me "all along my pilgrim journey," and I am not alone. I go to sleep at night soothed in the blessed darkness of rest and renewal. While I sometimes succumb to loneliness and mild depression, most of the time I embrace the dawn and believe in ever-renewing day, waking with an increasing sense of serenity and grace.

Jill, Malaika, and Edward Boyer after Malaika's high school graduation

Daughter Jill
in recent years

Granddaughter Malaika
in recent years

Lotus Press Poets and Publications
1972-2005

Books of Poetry

Samuel Allen, *Every Round and Other Poems*

Gilbert Allen, *In Everything*

Monifa Atungaye, *Provisions*

Houston A. Baker, Jr., *Blues Journeys Home*
.... *No Matter Where You Travel, You Still Be Black*
.... *Passing Over*
.... *Spirit Run*

Jill Witherspoon Boyer, *Breaking Camp*

Beth Brown, *Lightyears*
.... *Satin Tunnels*

Kiarri T-H . Cheatwood, *Bloodstorm: Five Books of Poems and Docu-Poems Towards Liberation*
.... *Elegies for Patrice*
.... *Psalms of Redemption*
.... *Valley of the Anointers*

Robert Chrisman, *Minor Casualties*

Pamela Cobb (Baraka Sele), *Inside the Devil's Mouth*

Louie Crew, *Sunspots*

Selene de Medeiros, *This Is How I Love You*

Tom Dent, *Blue Lights and River Songs*

Toi Derricotte, *The Empress of the Death House*

Abba Alethea (James W. Thompson), *The Antioch Suite-Jazz*

James A. Emanuel, *Black Man Abroad: The Toulouse Poems*
.... *The Broken Bowl: New and Collected Poems*
.... *A Chisel in the Dark: Poems Selected and New*
.... *Deadly James and Other Poems*
.... *The Force and the Reckoning*
.... *Whole Grain: Collected Poems, 1958-1989*

Ronald Fair, *Rufus* (reprint)

Naomi F. Faust, *All Beautiful Things*

489

[Faust, continued]

.... *And I Travel by Rhythms and Words*
Ray Fleming, *Diplomatic Relations*
Bill Harris, *Yardbird Suite: Side One***
Eugene Haun, *Cardinal Points and Other Poems*
Beverly V. Head, *Walking North***
Kamaldeen Ibraheem, *Roots, Flowers and Fruits*
Bruce A. Jacobs, *Speaking Through My Skin***
Lance Jeffers, *Grandsire*
.... *O Africa, Where I Baked My Bread*
Gayl Jones, *The Hermit-Woman*
...................*Song for Anninho*
.... *Xarque*
Agnes Nasmith Johnston, *Beyond the Moongate*
Nubia Kai, *Solos*
Sybil Kein, *Creole Journal: The Louisiana Poems* (reprint
                              under a new title)
...................*Delta Dancer*
Dolores Kendrick, *Now Is the Thing to Praise*
James C. Kilgore, *African Violet: Poem for a Black Woman*
Ruth Ellen Kocher, *Desdemona's Fire**
Oliver LaGrone, *Dawnfire and Other Poems*
Pinkie Gordon Lane, *I Never Scream*
Anthony A. Lee, *This Poem Means**
Monifa A. Love, *Dreaming Underground**
Naomi Long Madgett, ed., *Adam of Ifé: Black Women in Praise of
                              Black Men*
.... *Connected Islands: New and Selected
                              Poems*
.... *Exits and Entrances*

---

* Winner of the annual Naomi Long Madgett Poetry Award
** Winner of the annual Naomi Long Madgett Poetry Award
              published by Michigan State University Press

[Madgett, continued]

.....................................ed., *A Milestone Sampler: 15th Anniversary Anthology*
.... *Octavia: Guthrie and Beyond*
.... *Phantom Nightingale: Juvenilia*
.....................................*Pink Ladies in the Afternoon*
.... *Star by Star* (reprint)

Haki R. Madhubuti, *Killing Memory, Seeking Ancestors*

Herbert Woodward Martin, *The Forms of Silence*
.... *The Persistence of the Flesh*

Irma McClaurin, *Pearl's Song*

Adam David Miller, *Forever Afternoon***

E. Ethelbert Miller, *Season of Hunger/Cry of Rain*

May Miller, *Collected Poems*
.... *Dust of Uncertain Journey*
.... *Halfway to the Sun* (reprint)
....................*The Ransomed Wait*

Gunilla Norris, *Learning from the Angel*

Tanure Ojaide, *The Eagle's Vision*

Mwatabu Okantah, *Collage*

Dudley Randall, *A Litany of Friends*

Isetta Crawford Rawls, *Flashbacks*

Sarah Carolyn Reese, *Songs of Freedom*

David L. Rice, *Lock This Man Up*

Philip M. Royster, *Songs and Dances*

Satiafa (Vivian V. Gordon), *For Dark Women and Others*

Helen Earle Simcox, ed., *Dear Dark Faces: Portraits of a People*

Gary Smith, *Songs for My Fathers*

Peggy Ann Tartt, *Among Bones**

---

* Winner of the annual Naomi Long Madgett Poetry Award
** Winner of the annual Naomi Long Madgett Poetry Award
published by Michigan State University Press

Ron Welburn, *Heartland*

Jerry Wemple, *You Can See It from Here**

Paulette Childress White, *Love Poem to a Black Junkie*

..................................*The Watermelon Dress: Portrait of a Woman*

Carolyn Beard Whitlow, *Vanished**

James R. Whitley, *Immersion**

Claude Wilkinson, *Reading the Earth***

Willie Williams, *A Flower Blooming in Concrete*

College Textbook

Naomi Long Madgett, *A Student's Guide to Creative Writing* (Penway Books)

Sets of Poster-Poems

Blacksongs: Series I: Poems by Four Black Women

The Fullness of Earth (Collectors' Series. 100 copies numbered and signed by ten black poets)

Deep Rivers: A Portfolio with Teachers' Guide by Naomi Long Madgett (Poems by twenty living black poets)

Naomi Long Madgett, *Hymns Are My Prayers* (Seven poems inspired by sacred music written from the contemporary urban black perspective)

---

* Winner of the annual Naomi Long Madgett Poetry Award
** Winner of the annual Naomi Long Madgett Poetry Award published by Michigan State University Press